Slavery and Emancipation in Islamic East Africa

Examining the process of abolition on the island of Pemba off the East African coast in the late nineteenth and early twentieth centuries, this book demonstrates the links between emancipation and the redefinition of honor among all classes of people on the island. By examining the social vulnerability of ex-slaves and the former slave-owning elite caused by the Abolition Decree of 1897, this study argues that moments of resistance on Pemba reflected an effort to mitigate vulnerability rather than resist the hegemonic power of elites or the colonial state. As the meanings of the Swahili word *heshima* shifted from honor to respectability, individuals' reputations came under scrutiny, and the Islamic *kadhi* and colonial courts became an integral location for interrogating reputations in the community. This study illustrates the ways in which former slaves used piety, reputation, gossip, education, kinship, and witchcraft to negotiate the gap between emancipation and local notions of belonging.

Elisabeth McMahon is an assistant professor of history at Tulane University. Her work has appeared in the *Journal of Social History*, the *Journal of Women's History*, the *International Journal of African Historical Studies*, *Women's History Review*, and *Quaker History*. She received a PhD from Indiana University.

African Studies

The African Studies series, founded in 1968, is a prestigious series of monographs, general surveys, and textbooks on Africa covering history, political science, anthropology, economics, and ecological and environmental issues. The series seeks to publish work by senior scholars as well as the best new research.

A list of books in this series will be found at the end of this volume.

Slavery and Emancipation in Islamic East Africa

From Honor to Respectability

ELISABETH McMAHON

Tulane University

CAMBRIDGE
UNIVERSITY PRESS

CAMBRIDGE
UNIVERSITY PRESS

32 Avenue of the Americas, New York NY 10013-2473, USA

Cambridge University Press is part of the University of Cambridge.

It furthers the University's mission by disseminating knowledge in the pursuit of education, learning and research at the highest international levels of excellence.

www.cambridge.org
Information on this title: www.cambridge.org/9781107533783

First published 2013
First paperback edition 2015

A catalogue record for this publication is available from the British Library

Library of Congress Cataloguing in Publication data
McMahon, Elisabeth, 1970–
Slavery and emancipation in Islamic East Africa : from honor
to respectability / Elisabeth McMahon.
pages   cm. – (African studies)
Includes bibliographical references and index.
ISBN 978-1-107-02582-0 (hardback : alk. paper)
1. Slavery – Africa, Eastern – History.   2. Slavery – Tanzania – Pemba – History.
3. Slaves – Emancipation – Africa, Eastern – History.
4. Slaves – Emancipation – Tanzania – Pemba – History.
5. Slavery – Religious aspects – Islam.   I. Title.
HT1326.M36   2013
306.3′6209676–dc23   2012042700

ISBN 978-1-107-02582-0 Hardback
ISBN 978-1-107-53378-3 Paperback

To my grandmothers,
Cecilia Mullin McMahon and Katharine McConnell Rock,
one taught me to listen to stories, and
one taught me to write them down.

Contents

Figures

Preface

When I first began conducting research on Pemba Island for my dissertation, I was focused on the question of why Pembans responded to the revolution of 1964 so differently from people on Unguja (Zanzibar) Island. When the "anti-Arab" revolution came to the Zanzibar Islands in 1964, violence broke out on Unguja but not on Pemba. This is an old story, and a number of scholars have sought to understand the political and social dynamics of the revolution.[1] Why did it happen the way it happened? But most often scholarship focused on Zanzibar Town because that was where the revolution began. Eventually, after months, the revolution

---

[1] B. D. Bowles, "The Struggle for Independence, 1946–1963," in *Zanzibar under Colonial Rule*, edited by Abdul Sheriff and Ed Ferguson (Athens: Ohio University Press, 1991); Gary Burgess, "Youth and the Revolution: Mobility and Discipline in Zanzibar, 1950–1980" (Ph.D. dissertation, Indiana University, 2002); Thomas Burgess, *Race, Revolution, and the Struggle for Human Rights in Zanzibar* (Athens: Ohio University Press, 2010); Anthony Clayton, *The Zanzibar Revolution and Its Aftermath* (Hamden, CT: Archon Books, 1981); Jonathon Glassman, "Slower Than a Massacre: The Multiple Sources of Racial Thought in Colonial Africa," *The American Historical Review* 109, no. 3 (2004), pp. 720–54; Jonathon Glassman, "Sorting Out the Tribes: The Creation of Racial Identities in Colonial Zanzibar's Newspaper Wars," *Journal of African History* 41, no. 3 (2000), pp. 395–428; Jonathon Glassman, *War of Words, War of Stones* (Bloomington: Indiana University Press, 2011); Michael Lofchie, *Zanzibar: Background to Revolution* (Princeton, NJ: Princeton University Press, 1965); Omar Mapuri, *Zanzibar, the 1964 Revolution: Achievements and Prospects* (Dar es Salaam: TEMA Publishers, 1996); Esmond Bradley Martin, *Zanzibar: Tradition and Revolution* (London: Hamilton, 1978); Catharine M. Newbury, "Colonialism, Ethnicity, and Rural Political Protest: Rwanda and Zanzibar in Comparative Perspective," *Comparative Politics* 15, no. 3 (1983), pp. 253–80; Donald Petterson, *Revolution in Zanzibar: An American's Cold War Tale* (Boulder, CO: Westview, 2002); Abdul Sheriff and Ed Ferguson. *Zanzibar under Colonial Rule* (Athens: Ohio University Press, 1991).

snaked out across the water to Pemba Island, the second largest island in the archipelago and home to one-third of the population of the islands. The question that haunted me, as I witnessed Pembans responding to electoral conflict in 2000 (in the run-up to the 2001 elections), was why were Pembans generally so antirevolution? Pembans had a similar historical trajectory as Unguja Island, according to most scholars. Both had developed clove plantations under the auspices of Omani Arab colonization and extensively used slave labor to maintain and profit from the cloves. Both islands were colonized by the British in 1890 undergoing similar, albeit less in the case of Pemba, transformations in infrastructure such as roads, schools, courts, public health, and social welfare. My dissertation focused on the later colonial period and sought to examine how social welfare affected responses to the revolution, but I did not feel I found a satisfactory answer there. So I probed further, following the sources to the beginning of the British Protectorate and the abolition of slavery. When I followed the sources, I did not find answers in the ways I expected. I did not draw direct links between the abolition of slavery, identity formation, and the revolution. However, what I did find in looking at the sources was much bigger. Instead of seeing a case of identity formation for one particular group, I found an example of the ways in which local definitions and ideas about honor and power were transformed by the expansion of the colonial state. This transformation was not particular to Pemba Island; rather, it mirrored patterns seen across the continent.

Officials on both the islands of Unguja and Pemba handled emancipation in a similar manner, with almost equal numbers of slaves on each island seeking their emancipation from their owners between 1897 and 1909. By all accounts, at least half of Pemba's population was ex-slaves by the early twentieth century. It would make sense, then, that Pembans of slave ancestry would join in the revolution that overthrew the Arab Sultan and the administration, which was essentially put in place by the exiting British colonizers. But they did not. Since I first visited Pemba in 2000, I have been trying to understand how the history of slavery on Pemba affected the local responses to the revolution. Not so much "where did all the slaves go" in the words of Patricia Romero, but rather what were the relationships between the various populations of Pemba that allowed them to see themselves as part of the larger idea of Zanzibari identity while at the same time positioning themselves as Pemban first?[2]

---

[2] Patricia Romero, "'Where Have All the Slaves Gone?' Emancipation and Post-Emancipation in Lamu, Kenya," *Journal of African History* 27, no. 3 (1986), pp. 497–512.

The answers to the question of ex-slave identity and the passivity of Pembans at the time of the revolution have most often been framed in terms of either class or racial/ethnic issues. The arguments about class are persuasive; they argue that the disparity of wealth as found in Zanzibar Town did not exist between Arabs and Africans living on Pemba.[3] Certainly, social stratification on Pemba was limited in comparison with urban coastal populations, and many Africans actually had more wealth than Arabs during the colonial period. Additionally, scholars argued that Arabs had actively lived among and intermarried with the African populations – including ex-slaves – on Pemba in ways that did not happen on Unguja Island. The maps of ethnic enclaves made by F. B. Wilson in 1939 show that Arabs on Unguja lived almost entirely in Zanzibar Town or in small groups along the main trunk roads on the island, whereas on Pemba Arabs could be found living within a mile of most parts of the island.[4] The argument followed that people of "African" descent on Pemba did not rebel against the "Arabs" because they were related to them and saw them as neighbors and family rather than as blood-sucking former slave owners. This was certainly the image that people of Arab descent on Pemba encouraged and continued to proclaim even in 2002.[5] Contrarily, other scholars point to the census data from 1924, 1931, and 1948 that show a gradual shift in how the African population on Pemba redefined its ethnicities (and identities) to claim an indigenous identity that excluded it from having an "enslaved past."[6] Therefore, if people joined the revolution, they were displaying to all their neighbors that they had slave ancestors and were not really "local." But the problem with both of these arguments is that they suggest that African-descended Pembans were all dupes to the hegemonic Arab overlords. What about the slaves who demanded their freedom from the government by 1909? Were they and their descendants really so willing to yet again accept the domination of people descended from slave owners?

I wanted to understand how and why people on Pemba had developed an identity of "Pemban-ness." Yet the sources suggest that until the 1930s, few people on Pemba framed their existence in nationalistic terms

[3] Bowles, 1991; Ferguson and Sheriff, 1991.

[4] F. B. Wilson, *Report of the Commission Appointed to Investigate Rural Education in the Zanzibar Protectorate* (Zanzibar: Government Printer, 1939).

[5] Mzee Suliman, Konde, Pemba, October 29, 2002.

[6] Laura Fair, *Pastimes and Politics: Culture, Community, and Identity in Post-Abolition Urban Zanzibar, 1890–1945* (Athens: Ohio University Press, 2001); Helle Goldman, "A Comparative Study of Swahili in Two Rural Communities in Pemba, Zanzibar, Tanzania" (Ph.D. dissertation, New York University, 1996).

of "Pemban-ness." I had assumed by looking at the processes of emancipation that I would find the relationships between the various populations
of Pemba that allowed them to see themselves as part of a larger notion
of Pemban identity. Instead, what I found in the records was the trail of
how colonialism reshaped power and honor within a postabolition society in Africa. The patterns on Pemba were not unique to the island but
rather can be found across the continent. As colonizing powers took over
the ability to control populations and remove the capacity of slave owners, patriarchs, and local leaders to "enforce a right to respect," a radical
shift occurred across Africa.[7] I found, similarly to John Iliffe, that colonialism created a breakdown in honor culture, but the case from Pemba
demonstrates fundamentally different processes than suggested by Iliffe.
Iliffe's work focuses on the honor of "heroes and householders," people I
describe as being able to control others. Yet he argues that "respectability was the chief means by which Europeans tried to domesticate African
notions of honour, replacing their emphasis on rank and prowess with
stress on virtue and duty."[8] On Pemba, respectability was not a matter
of adopting (or even adapting) European virtues or duties because most
of the population was Muslim and did not desire to be like Europeans.
Rather, respectability was the socially vulnerable position that almost all
subjects in a colonial society encountered when confronted with their
inability to assert power over other people. Iliffe suggested that the idea
of respectability never caught on in Ethiopia because of competition with
the aristocratic elite, but after seeing the dynamics on Pemba, I would
argue that respectability never replaced honor because Ethiopia was
never colonized.[9] The Ethiopian elite never lost their ability to "enforce
their right to respect," as other Africans did in the colonial era; thus they
never became socially vulnerable in the ways found on Pemba Island and
elsewhere in Africa.

In the end, this book focuses on understanding the power vacuum
created by colonial policies such as abolition and direct control over the
local court systems, which helps to explain the ways in which political
parties in the 1950s sought to grasp power from one another in the face
of the impending colonial departure. The colonial officials held the ultimate power in the islands. Certainly Africans responded to this power,
and I argue within this book that the practice of *uchawi* ("witchcraft")

---

[7] John Iliffe, *Honour in African History* (New York: Cambridge University Press, 2004), p. 4.
[8] Iliffe, p. 246.
[9] Iliffe, pp. 258–9.

was a form of local agency. Nonetheless, since the end of colonialism was on the horizon, local groups and individuals jockeyed for the ability to demand a "right to respect" from others – knowing that colonial officials would no longer be the ultimate source of power through the courts and their policing of behavior. Thus, while I do not directly discuss the events of the revolution of 1964 in this book, the footprints of the early colonial period run across the later history in the islands.

Acknowledgments

This book is the culmination of efforts by many people, although all arguments and errors are my own. I have many debts in the United States, the United Kingdom, and most of all the Zanzibar Islands. Hajj Mohamed Hajj made my fieldwork on Pemba go smoothly and has continued to support my work over many years. To him and his family, I owe a huge debt, and I thank them dearly. I cannot describe how grateful I am for the care they have taken over me. Hajj introduced me to many people, but most important were Ridhwan Salim and Omar Ali Omar, whose efforts in helping me conduct survey research went beyond all I had hoped for. Moreover, they extended their friendship and opened their homes to me. The archivists on Pemba kindly allowed me to have access to the wonderful archives held in an old prison cell. I also extend my gratitude to all the Pembans who took the time to answer my questions about their history. On Unguja, I must thank all the staff and especially Mwalim Hamad Omar Hassan of the Zanzibar National Archives, who facilitated my research. For the extraordinary efforts of Ashura and Khadija in finding documents for me, I am most grateful.

Many thanks are owed to archivists at the Library for the Religious Society of Friends, whose persistence in finding documents related to Pemba in their vaults truly made this book possible. Lucy McCann at Rhodes House at Oxford University helpfully put together a list of Universities Mission to Central Africa (UMCA) materials related to Pemba that contained many gems. Access to materials held at the School of Oriental and African Studies Library in London and the National Archives (formerly the Public Records Office) in Kew have given me many new insights. I want to thank David Easterbrook and his staff of librarians at the Herskovits Library at Northwestern University for their help over the years. The Center for Research Libraries and the interlibrary loan departments at Indiana and Tulane Universities have been very helpful in acquiring material. A special thanks to Eric Wedig at the Tulane Library for always getting access to more materials than I could hope for.

I am very grateful to the U.S. Department of Education for awarding me a Fulbright fellowship to support my dissertation fieldwork in Unguja and Pemba while working on my PhD. I also wish to thank the History Departments at Indiana and Tulane Universities, which have funded my research since 2000, especially the Provost's office at Tulane, which awarded me several University Senate Committee on Research fellowships and a Phase II research fellowship. Last but not least, I would like to thank Jim McMahon and Lucy Kreimer for funding the research trip on which I did a significant portion of the research for this book. Without their support, this book would never have been completed. I would also like to thank several research assistants, Maura McMahon, Elizabeth Skilton, and Terre Pring, who have done work in Pemba and the United States that has been invaluable.

The support and help of my editors, Eric Crahan and Scott Parris, and their editorial team, including Kristin Purdy, the series editor Richard Robert, and the two anonymous reviewers, have been essential to this project. I cannot thank the reviewers and Richard Roberts enough for their thoughtful, clear, and eminently helpful comments on the original draft of this manuscript. Over the years, I have built up a number of debts to other scholars and staff who have given me feedback, ideas, or just support. In no particular order, I thank John Hanson, Phyllis Martin, Marion Frank-Wilson, Arlene Díaz, Alexia Bock, Laura Fair, Nathalie Arnold, Maria Grosz-Ngaté, Dana Rabin, Jean Allman, Richard Roberts, Marty Klein, Sandra Greene, Corrie Decker, Timothy Cleaveland, Nikki Brown, Beth Manley, Donna Patterson, Marie Rodet, Elke Stockreiter, Jan Georg Deutsch, Roman Loimeier, Jeremy Rich, Benjamin Lawrance, Jeffrey Ahlman, Lessie Tate, Emily Burrill, Richard Conway, Jeremy Pool, Hideaki Suzuki Cheryl Lemus, David Goodman, Nate Plageman, Kate Schroeder, Matt Carotenuto, and Hannington Ochwada.

I must single out two people in particular for their help. First is John Hanson, who has been the best advisor and friend anyone could possibly have. John will always have my fierce loyalty for his support of my academic and life choices. At every stage he has supported me and never once suggested judgment of what others may have viewed as less than ideal decisions on my part and I am deeply grateful. His unfailing sense of humor and cynical optimism always brighten my day. Corrie Decker has been a compatriot in research and discussions of teaching, and personally a great friend. She read more crappy drafts of this book than any single person, and I want to thank her for slogging through the awful drafts at the beginning. Her patience and endurance of my eccentricities are true friendship.

Since coming to Tulane, I have been blessed with wonderful colleagues. I cannot thank them all by name here, but I do wish to especially thank Jana Lipman for her brilliance on how to write a good book introduction. I also wish to thank the following colleagues for their encouragement and help: Donna Denneen, Randy Sparks, Kaya Sahin, Brian Demare, Rosanne Adderley, Rachel Devlin, Gaurav Desai, Supriya Nair, Adeline Masquelier, Dana Zartner, Thomas Adams, Karissa Haugeberg, and the faculty of the History Department and the African and African Diaspora Studies Program. I would also like to thank Lee Hampton and the staff of the Amistad Research Center, who have improved my life immeasurably.

I have been blessed with many good friends over the years. To Jamie Dewitt and Laura Campbell, I thank you for never giving up on our friendship. Thanks go to Donna Patterson and Julie and Paul O'Hara, who have listened to me blather on for more than fifteen years now. In the years since coming to New Orleans, I have had a fabulous support group of friends who welcomed me as family. I wish to thank Shelby Richardson, Anne and Denny Ogan, Laura Schrader, Alex Kriek, Kathleen George, Paul Hutchinson, Kathleen Morgan, Trent Holliday, Libby Horter, Thom Eisele, Sarah Michael, Troy Samphere, Alicia and Frank Cole, Tracy and Aaron Miscenich, Margaret Howze, Nick Spitzer, Marlene Friis, Michael Hecht, Diane and Gary Sheets, Jancy Hoeffel, Steve Singer, Mary Yetta, and Vanessa Manuel. From Audubon Park to Navarre and London, your friendships have enriched my life and wreaked havoc on my liver.

Strangely, my family members have never once asked me, "Do you really think this is a good idea?" about anything I've done. Some people in life have only two parents. I've always been so much luckier. To my parents, Mary McMahon, Jim McMahon, David Kreimer, Lucy Kreimer, Antonia Davena, Jim Raphael, and Ruth Ann Harter, thank you. You've given your love and support freely, and I am extraordinarily grateful. Not only do I have many parents, but I also have a plethora of fantastic siblings and nephews. I thank Tina, Bob, Robert, and John Dyehouse and Maura, Claire, and Dan McMahon. I could not ask for better family than you all.

Thirteen years ago I met my partner, and he's never balked once at any crazy idea I've had. He has moved four times across the country, he has gone halfway across the world, and he has given up all semblance of a normal life all so that I could do what I love. I am extremely grateful for everything that Chris Harter does – every single day. There is no day when I am not reminded of how lucky I am. Part of that reminder is that I can see our son, Wheeler McMahon, who brings us incalculable joy. His smile can light up a room, and it always lights up my heart. To my boys, you are my heart.

Glossary

Many of the definitions of words here are the definitions in the late nineteenth and early twentieth centuries. A number of definitions of words have changed in meaning since that time period.

Aibn: Shame
Askari: A policeman
Assaba: A male paternal relative such as an uncle, nephew, or cousin
Baraka: Blessings
Baraza: The benches outside of homes where men sit and gossip
Bei kataa: A fictional or conditional sale of land, often used to avoid the Islamic rule against usury
Buibui: A black covering for the head and body of women
Chuo (pl. *vyuo*): Islamic school
Dalal: A broker who sells or appraises land
Dawa: Medicine; can refer to both Western medicine and local practices such as *uchawi* or spirit possession
Dhikiri: A Sufi practice, often involving particular methods of breathing, moving, or drumming that helps practitioners get closer to God
Dhow: Large sailing boats commonly found in the Indian Ocean
Dukizi: Someone who eavesdrops on other people
Edda: The three-month period of waiting until a divorced Muslim woman can remarry
Fitna or *fitina:* Slander of a person, trouble, scandal, or intrigue

Fundi (pl. *mafundi*): A craftsman or artisan (originally referred to enslaved craftsmen); also a term used for a spirit possession leader or someone knowledgeable about *uchawi*

Hadim: A servant; commonly used by ex-slaves to denote a connection with their former owners' family or clan

Hadim wa Sirkar: Servant of the government, a slave emancipated by the colonial government

Hamali (pl. *hamali*): Porter on a dock (originally referred to enslaved porters)

Heshima: Honor, dignity, position, rank, respect, reverence, modesty and courtesy, respectability

Hunu abadu: You have no manners.

Jambia: Curved sword, often worn by men from Oman

Jinn (pl. *majini*): Spirits that can be Islamic or environmental and can be both beneficial and harmful

Kadhi (pl. *makadhi*): Judge who presides in an Islamic court

Kanga: Brightly colored clothes worn by women

Kaniki: Indigo-dyed clothes worn by men and women; often signified slave status

Kanzu: A long, shirtlike dress worn by free men

Khalifa: A leader of a Sufi religious sect

Kibarua (pl. *vibarua*): A day laborer (originally referred to enslaved day laborers)

Kijakazi (pl. *vijakazi*): A girl slave

Kikoy (pl. *vikoy*): A cloth worn as an undergarment by men

Kitwana (pl. *vitwana*): A boy slave

Kofia: A hat worn by Muslim men

Komba: A galagos, a small nocturnal animal often called a bushbaby

Kuamba: To slander

Kuheshima: A verb used to mean "to honor" someone in the nineteenth century

Kuizara: To publish things about a person to create scandal

Kunenana: To talk against one another

Kupapuriana: To pick apart one another's reputations

Kupuzika: To gossip among women

Kustahi: A verb used to mean "to respect" someone in the nineteenth century

Liwali: A governor (pl. *maliwali*, however scholars usually simply use *liwali* for both singular and plural)

Mahari: Dower

Mateka: War booty; refers to a slave brought from the interior who is "uncivilized"

Maula: Commonly used by ex-slaves to denote a connection with their former owners' family or clan

Maulidi: Celebrations of the birth of the Prophet Muhammad

Mbao: A board game

Mchawi (pl. *wachawi*): A practitioner of witchcraft, magic, or the occult

Mdunsi (pl. *wadunsi*): A person who gossips

Mganga (pl. *waganga*): The general term used for anyone who used specialized occult knowledge to help others, in either harmful or helpful practices

Mgeni (pl. *wageni*): A guest, a stranger

Mhuru (pl. *wahuru*): A free person, no longer enslaved; generally used by missionaries but not enslaved people

Mjakazi (pl. *wajakazi*): Adult female slave

Mjinga (pl. *wajinga*): A person enslaved after birth

Mkulima (pl. *wakulima*): Farm laborers

Mshenzi (pl. *washenzi*): A barbarian, someone from the interior regions of the mainland of Africa

Mtumishi (pl. *watumishi*): Servant

Mtumwa (pl. *watumwa*): Slave

Mtumwa mtumwaji: An enslaved agent

Mtumwa wa mtumwa: A slave of a slave

Mtumwa wa nyumba: A domestic slave

Mtumwa wa shamba: A farm slave

Mtumwa wa shauri: An enslaved councilor to an owner

Mtwana (pl. *watwana*): Adult male slave

Mwalimu (pl. *wali mu*): A Quranic teacher

Mwungwana (pl. *waungwana*): Nineteenth-century Swahili coastal elite

Mzalia (pl. *wazalia*): A person born into slavery

Nasab: Blood kinship

Ngoma: A dance

Ngoma ya harusi: Wedding dance

Ngoma ya kirumbizi: Stick-fighting dance performed by men

Ngoma ya msondo: Initiation ceremony

Ngoma ya pepo: Spirit possession ceremony

Nisba: Clan name

Njoli (pl. *njoli*): A term used to greet a slave of equal status among enslaved people

Nusu-bin-nusu: Dividing a land in half between the landowner and the person who does the planting work on the land

Pepo: Spirits; generally spirits that possess people

Sabab: Kinship through marriage

Shamba (pl. *mashamba*): Farm, land, plantation

Sheha (pl. *masheha*): A village-level government official

Sheria: Islamic law

Shikamoo: This means "I grasp your feet" and is now used as a greeting of respect by juniors to their elders. Originally a greeting by enslaved to freeborn people

Shule: Colonial government schools

Sifa: Reputation

Sifa mbaya: A bad reputation

Suria (pl. *masuria*): A concubine

Tarika (pl. *tarika*): A Sufi group; *tarika* literally means the "way" or "path," but it is essentially referencing a particular Sufi religious group and its practices.

Uchawi: Witchcraft, magic or the occult

Unyago: A form of female initiation

Upelelezi: Gossip

Ustaarabu: Civility and respectability based on the late-nineteenth- and twentieth-century ideals of Arabs

Utaapa: Upon your oath

Uungwana: Civility and respectability based on the pre-nineteenth-century elite ideals

Wakf: Charitable endowments dedicated to the support of local communities by providing for mosques, Quranic schools, and the care of the elderly and the poor

Wakil: A representative in the courts, similar to a lawyer

Wala: Kinship through patronage; claimed by slave owners to their slaves

Wari: Members of spirit possession groups

Watu wazee: Community elders

Zamani sana: Olden times

Slavery and Emancipation in Islamic East Africa

1

Introduction

Pemba Island is a small place. Only ten miles wide and forty miles long, it seems an unlikely place to be a crossroads of multiple continents. Yet people on the island trace their heritage to African, Arab, and Indian sailors and merchants, Baluchi mercenaries, and slaves who were drawn, whether by force or by choice, to the fecundity of the "Green Isle" – where mangrove trees reached out into the tidal creeks to greet new arrivals. The island had been the granary of the Kenyan coast in eastern Africa through the eighteenth century but gradually shifted to a cash-crop economy when the Sultan of Oman, who quickly realized the potential wealth of the Zanzibar Islands,[1] moved his capital to Unguja Island in the 1830s.[2]

[1] The Zanzibar Islands are made of two larger islands, Unguja (which is often referred to in the West as Zanzibar) and Pemba, in addition to numerous other smaller islands. I will use Zanzibar to refer to all the islands and Unguja to refer to the larger island where the capital, Zanzibar Town, is located.

[2] While the Omani sultanate claimed control over Pemba starting in 1698, a garrison was not stationed on the island until 1820. The Sultan of Oman from 1814–1856, Seyyid Said, was so impressed with Zanzibar that he moved the capital of his sultanate to the islands in the 1840s. At Seyyid Said's death, the Omani sultanate was divided between two of his sons – one became Sultan of Oman and the other Sultan of Zanzibar. For further details on the pre-twentieth-century history of the Swahili coast, see John Gray, *History of Zanzibar: From the Middle Ages to 1856* (London: Oxford University Press, 1962); Norman Bennett, *A History of the Arab State of Zanzibar* (London: Methuen, 1978); Jonathon Glassman, *Feasts and Riots: Revelry, Rebellion, and Popular Consciousness on the Swahili Coast, 1858–1888* (Portsmouth, NH: Heinemann, 1995); Bethwell Ogot and J. A. Kieran, eds., *Zamani: A Survey of East African History* (Nairobi: East African Publishing House, 1968); Randall Pouwels, *Horn and Crescent: Cultural Change and Traditional Islam on the East African Coast, 1800–1900* (Cambridge: Cambridge University Press, 1987); Abdul Sheriff, *Slaves, Spices and Ivory in Zanzibar: Integration*

By the late 1870s, the majority of the agricultural produce exported from the islands came from the second-largest island, Pemba. Oral traditions about the land and labor arrangements between the Sultan and local Africans differed between the two main islands. On Pemba, locals agreed to clear land and plant clove trees only in exchange for ownership of half the land and trees, a system known as *nusu-bin-nusu* ("half and half"), whereas on Unguja, locals planted trees but did not get ownership of any they planted. The Pemban system kept a large class of small landholders on the island of Pemba because they received half the clove trees they planted.[3] Nonetheless, by the late nineteenth century, slavery was the main form of labor on both islands. The slaves were brought from the mainland, primarily the regions of present-day Tanzania and Malawi. While the majority of slave owners were Arab, many indigenous Pembans and Indian traders also owned slaves on Pemba.[4] These slaves kept the areas around the clove trees weeded, helped to pick cloves during the harvests, and grew their own food plots in the areas around the clove trees. The social and economic systems put in place by the Omani colonization of Pemba would begin to unravel when the British declared a protectorate over the Zanzibari Islands in 1890.

In 1895, a former slave woman named Bahati successfully won her court case against an elite man, who claimed her as his slave, by demonstrating her position as a respectable member of her community.[5] While

---

of an East African Commercial Empire into the World Economy, 1770–1873 (London: James Currey, 1987).

[3] Frederick Cooper, while acknowledging the small landholding class on Pemba, suggested that plantations were still the main form of economy on Pemba. However, in his 1980 book, he noted that 70 percent of planted acreage on Pemba was in food crops, not cash crops, indicating that plantations were not the driver of the economy on Pemba. Frederick Cooper, *From Slaves to Squatters: Planation Labor and Agriculture in Zanzibar and Coastal Kenya, 1890–1925* (New Haven, CT: Yale University Press, 1980), p. 150. See also Fitzgerald's comments from 1892 that much of the land was broken up in small landholdings with few large plantations or large groups of slaves. William Walter Augustine Fitzgerald, *Travels in the Coastlands of British East Africa and the Islands of Zanzibar and Pemba: Their Agricultural Resources and General Characteristics* (London: Chapman and Hall, 1898), pp. 593–4, 597–8, 604.

[4] While the British government abolished slavery in its colonies in 1838, it still had a limited scope in the Indian Ocean because parts of India were still under company rule rather than government control. According the Abdul Sheriff, beginning with Consul Hamerton in the 1850s, several British consuls to Zanzibar tried to break the Indian community of slave owning. Sheriff questions the legality of the consuls; nonetheless, starting in the late 1850s, Indians living in Zanzibar were subject to seizure of their slaves and property and open to flogging, jail time, and deportation. Sheriff, 1987, pp. 202–8; Also see Zanzibar National Archives (ZNA) AA12/4 for a "secret" report from 1875 on Indian slaveholdings on Pemba.

[5] ZNA AC/5/2, Letter from OSB, July 27, 1896.

she did not contest that she was an ex-slave, she did argue that she had rights in her community because she was a free person who adhered to the social norms set out by elites. She used her reputation among her neighbors as evidence to gain the support of the British colonial official posted to the island. Bahati's case illustrated the ways in which marginalized members of coastal societies transformed meanings of status and reputation in the colonial courts.[6] British colonization and emancipation as a reaction to the previous Omani colonization offered enslaved people new avenues to achieve a life independent from the control of elites and slave owners, who were often one and the same.

While British enforcement of emancipation laws on Pemba created an opportunity for slaves and ex-slaves to attain new social powers, colonial officials across the continent were less than enthusiastic about enforcing abolition laws. The historical literature of Africa excoriates colonial officials for being obstructionist and obdurate antiabolitionists, as they were in Zanzibar. Missionaries in Pemba, as elsewhere in Africa, sought to force the colonial office in the metropole to hand down abolition orders. Yet, as soon as these orders were made law, colonial officials wiped their hands off slavery and simply ignored its existence. Sean Hanretta raises an important critique that some scholars discuss emancipation as an artifact of colonialism. He argues that the "triumphalist" narrative of colonial emancipation where Westerners brought "freedom," and, as such, Christianity and capitalism, to Africa reifies the perception that abolition is "alien" to African societies and thus removes the agency of Africans and Islam as sources of abolitionist ideology.[7] However, the scholarship on slavery in Africa has shown that in parts of Africa an indigenous practice of manumission existed long before colonizers imposed a discourse of abolition.[8] Manumission meant the voluntary release of enslaved people

---

[6] Margaret Strobel also noted this change. However, she found that women were the only ones who sought the help of British officials, indicating a gendered element to the use of courts in Mombasa. Strobel, *Muslim Women in Mombasa* (New Haven, CT: Yale University Press, 1979), pp. 59–60.

[7] Sean Hanretta, *Islam and Social Change in French West Africa: History of an Emancipatory Community* (Cambridge: Cambridge University Press, 2009), pp. 211–14.

[8] See, for example, Frederick Cooper, *Plantation Slavery on the East Coast of Africa* (New Haven, CT: Yale University Press, 1977), pp. 242–52; Suzanne Miers and Igor Kopytoff, *Slavery in Africa: Historical and Anthropological Perspectives* (Madison: University of Wisconsin Press, 1977), pp. 26–7; Orlando Patterson, *Slavery and Social Death* (Cambridge: Cambridge University Press, 1982), pp. 262–96; Martin Klein, *Slavery and Colonial Rule in French West Africa* (Cambridge: Cambridge University Press, 1998), pp. 12–14; Paul E. Lovejoy, "Muslim Freedmen in the Atlantic World: Images of Manumission and Self-Redemption," in *Slavery on the Frontiers of Islam*, edited by Paul E. Lovejoy (Princeton, NJ: Markus Wiener Publishers, 2004), pp. 233–62.

by their owners, whereas abolition required a state power to impose the release of slaves. Along the East African coast, state power was weak in the nineteenth century; thus abolition was virtually impossible to impose, as the British colonizers quickly discovered. Enslaved people on Pemba understood and valued the practice of manumission, which goes far in explaining the response of slaves to the British Abolition Decree.

Emancipation on Pemba did not come immediately with the announcement of the abolition decree of 1897, nor did slaves rush to receive their "freedom." A widespread exodus of slaves from the region of their enslavement to their home areas, as discussed in West Africa, does not appear to have occurred on Pemba.[9] The British began the emancipation process in 1897, when slaves, except for concubines, could apply for their freedom from colonial officials. Twelve years later, the government abolished the status of slavery; no longer could anyone legally claim a person as a slave, nor could ex-slaves claim patronage from their former owners. But what did freedom mean? Much as Patricia Romero showed for Lamu, many Pembans did not seek to leave their owners as "free" either in 1897 or in 1909.[10] Numerous individuals chose to remain living with their owners, calling themselves slaves and maintaining the patron-client systems of enslavement. These "slaves" accommodated themselves to the life offered them through the patronage of their "owners," to whom they were "mutually bound through dependency."[11]

Why were many slaves along the Swahili coast willing to remain enslaved after abolition? As found across the continent of Africa, a continuum of enslavement to freedom existed within a broad range of communities.[12] From the powerful military slaves of western Africa to the *watumwa wa mtumwa* ("slaves of a slave") of eastern Africa, enslavement and freedom had multiple meanings depending on the social structures of the community, the status of owners, and the gender, age, and skill set of the enslaved. Numerous scholars have shown that many slaves

---

[9] Richard Roberts and Martin Klein, "The Banamba Slave Exodus of 1905 and the Decline of Slavery in the Western Sudan," *Journal of African History* (1980) Vol. 21, No. 3, pp. 375–94; Klein, *Slavery and Colonial Rule*, pp. 159–77.

[10] Patricia Romero, *Lamu: History, Society, and Family in an East African Port City* (Princeton, NJ: Markus Wiener, 1997), pp. 126–32.

[11] Paraphrase of Romero, p. 129.

[12] Hanretta, 2009, pp. 212–24; Klein, 1998, pp. 178–88; Jan Georg Deutsch, *Emancipation Without Abolition in German East Africa, c. 1884–1914* (Athens: Ohio University Press, 2006), pp. 208–32; Cooper, 1980, pp. 69–120; Strobel, 1979, pp. 44–54; Wayne Dooling, *Slavery, Emancipation and Colonial Rule in South Africa.* (Athens: Ohio University Press, 2007), pp. 112–57. These are just a few examples of many.

had incredible freedom of movement and often lived away from their owners, indicating that the meaning of slavery in eastern Africa goes far beyond the chattel slavery so often conjured up in American minds.[13] Yet forms of chattel slavery existed on Pemba side by side with more mobile forms of enslavement, such as day laborers, traders, and long-distance porters who left on expeditions into the interior of eastern Africa that often took years. The ambiguities of enslavement offer an explanation for the ambivalence toward emancipation found among some groups of slaves on Pemba.

However, this does not mean that enslaved people on Pemba all embraced their enslavement either. It is impossible to identify exactly how many slaves lived on the island before emancipation because no census was done until 1910 – and even then it was limited because it did not distinguish whether the Africans counted were born on the island or elsewhere, indicative of a slave past. The 1910 census does indicate that approximately 50,000 adults living on Pemba identified or were identified by the census takers as being of African descent.[14] However, this included the indigenous WaPemba population, as well as the pre-Omani coastal elites, who were called *waungwana*.[15] Estimates for the slave population ranged from 10,000 to 60,000, with probably the best estimate given by the British Vice Consul as 40,000.[16] The numbers vary dramatically, but we do know that over 6,000 people applied on Pemba for their freedom from the government between 1897 and 1909. During this period, an additional 700 slaves were voluntarily manumitted by their

[13] Strobel, 1979, p. 30; Sheriff, 1987, pp. 149–50; Deutsch, 2006, pp. 176–8; Glassman, 1995, chaps. 2 and 3 discuss this in extensive detail.

[14] ZNA BA34/2, Report of the Native Census, 1924. The 1910 census results are included in the 1924 census for comparative purpose. There were 20,000 children in this category as well. However, because an 1890 decree declared all children of slaves born after that date were free regardless of whether their parents were enslaved, this meant that any child in 1910 was most certainly free.

[15] The pre-Omani term for "civilization" was *uungwana*. The coast elite described themselves as the civilized people and thus were known as *waungwana*; the *wa-* prefix indicates "people" in Swahili. For an excellent discussion of the transformation in terminology from *uungwana* to *ustaarabu* in the nineteenth century, see Pouwels, 1987, pp. 72–4.

[16] Dr. O'Sullivan-Beare gave an estimate in 1896 of 63,000 slaves but later noted that during the smallpox epidemic of 1898, approximately 40,000 slaves lived on the island. See *Report by Vice-Consul O'Sullivan on the Island of Pemba, 1896–7*; *Report by Vice-Consul O'Sullivan on the Island of Pemba, 1898*; Timothy Welliver, "The Clove Factor in Colonial Zanzibar 1890–1950," PhD dissertation, Northwestern University, 1990, pp. 63–4, quoting Farler from an 1899 letter to General Mathews, states that he thinks that the slave population was only 10,000 at emancipation.

owners as well.[17] This means that at least 15 percent of slaves on Pemba chose government emancipation.[18] But more than that, the differences in the responses of those who were enslaved to the emancipation order tells us that there was no one strategy for dealing with the process of emancipation.

Seemingly, the moment of emancipation should have been one of empowerment for individuals who could now choose where to live and who to work for, among other choices.[19] Yet the ambivalence of many slaves on Pemba to the abolition decree demonstrates that they saw emancipation not as empowering but as an act that could expose them to the economic vulnerabilities of life as a patronless person. Moreover, examining the weaknesses in ex-slaves' social positions illustrates the ways in which definitions of status changed over time. With emancipation, the hierarchies of society changed, and slaves' positions within communities also altered. Ex-slaves had the possibility for social mobility, but their ability to attain respectability likewise left them vulnerable in unprecedented ways because before emancipation, slaves' reputations had a limited impact economically or socially on their livelihoods. Vying for respectability exposed ex-slaves to the vagaries of community interpretations of their reputations, yet the action of being socially vulnerable created new opportunities for ex-slaves and marginalized people to expand their social capital on Pemba. Exposing themselves to the social vulnerability of respectability allowed marginalized groups to gain social capital in a way they could not when they had the security of social position in enslavement. Enslaved and marginalized groups certainly faced economic vulnerability, yet emancipation created the space for a positive element of vulnerability, the vulnerability associated with other people's interpretations of their reputations, as found in the case mentioned earlier of the ex-slave Bahati, who used her neighbors as witnesses to her respectability and positive reputation.

The experience of emancipation on Pemba is not the same as in other parts of eastern Africa. While some ex-slaves on Pemba mimicked slaves

---

[17] Cooper, 1977, cites 754 voluntary manumissions on Pemba after the abolition order and 5,468 voluntary manumissions on Unguja. Likewise, he notes that 5,930 people were emancipated by the government on Pemba, p. 244, fn. 107.

[18] In Chapter 2 I point to the potential of a number closer to 21 percent if children are included in the numbers.

[19] Emancipation was equal to vulnerability because slaves had security in their position as slaves; as free people, they lacked security of food and shelter. See Strobel, 1979, pp. 43–100.

on the mainland of Tanzania, who simply walked away from their owners and emancipated themselves with their feet, the majority did not.[20]
Frederick Cooper has argued for the Swahili coast that emancipation
did not significantly change the lives of many enslaved because essentially they went "from slaves to squatters."[21] Cooper is correct that many
ex-slaves were not able to purchase their own land and ended up arranging share-cropping relationships with former owners on Pemba, but many
others became independent land or house owners. Yet focusing on economics overlooks the very important social and cultural transformations
experienced independently of economic circumstances. Ex-slaves enjoyed
the new freedoms allowed to them in regard to dress, religious faith,
and education. Nonetheless, as the story of Bahati illustrates, ex-slaves
did not want to replicate the position of the elites but rather wanted to
coexist. Slaves on Pemba did not seek to recreate their identities; rather,
those who remained on the island accommodated themselves to the social
hierarchy of the island.[22] Even the slaves who appeared to actively resist
ex–slave owners' hegemony in economic and social aspects of Pemban
society still demonstrated their accommodation on some levels through
their continued residence on the island.

As ex-slaves sought to accommodate their lives to the new realities of
society, elites also had to face their diminished social status. Linguistic
changes in Swahili words on Pemba illustrate the shifting social dynamics
of society as terms associated with the elite, such as *heshima*, had newer
meanings grafted onto them. *Heshima* in the nineteenth century meant
"honor" and the power and fear associated with holding honor.[23] Yet,
with the emancipation of slaves, the basis for the power of slave owners
was undermined, expanding the meaning of *heshima* to the much weaker
notion of "respectability." Thus, when Bahati asserted her *heshima*, she
was not arguing that she had power but rather that she was vulnerable
to the interpretation of her reputation by her neighbors who chose to
support her case. But more important, when she won her case, it reinforced the limited power of the Arab elite, demonstrating their lost ability
to assert their honor through the control of lower-status people such as
Bahati.

---

[20] Deutsch, 2006, pp. 2–3.
[21] Cooper, 1980, pp. 4–6.
[22] For ex-slaves trying to remake their identities, see Fair, 2001, pp. 64–109.
[23] Edward Steere, *A Handbook of the Swahili Language as Spoken at Zanzibar* (Society for
Promoting Christian Knowledge, 1884), p. 286; Orlando Patterson explicated this link
in his book, *Slavery and Social Death*. See in particular chap. 3, pp. 77–101.

The history of the Swahili coast often focuses on resistance of marginalized populations against social elites. This literature includes vibrant book titles that epitomize the contested relationships of people along the coast, such as *Feasts and Riots* and *Pastimes and Politics*.[24] These books depict the Swahili coast as a place of tensions, contestation, and revelry among people of varying social statuses and ethnic identities, including Africans, Arabs, Indians, and Europeans. This book breaks from the historiography of the Swahili coast by examining an island that while not isolated from the rest of the coast, certainly never experienced the widespread resistance against elites or the colonial state as found in the urban centers of East Africa.[25] This is not a story of resistance or of collaboration, as Patricia Romero found in Lamu, but rather acculturation and accommodation among a population that was able to create networks within its communities that helped to tie individuals together even in times of great political and social flux.

Without reifying the teleology that rural communities cling to "tradition," my work shows how marginalized people, regardless of their lines of ethnic descent or income, formed a community of people who based their daily interactions with one another on an understanding of acceptable social behavior that was religiously conservative but also pragmatic. While these groups – former slaves, indigenous Pembans, migrant laborers from the mainland, and poor Arabs and Indians – worked together, lived next to each other, at times intermarried, celebrated together, and buried one another, they did not necessarily form a unified community identity. They did not imagine themselves as one group, one community, at least not yet. They had not yet identified their island and, as such, themselves as the "Cinderella" of the east coast.[26] I have suggested elsewhere that by the 1950s, Pembans began to coalesce around an identity of "Pemban-ness," but in the early years after emancipation, a notion of a distinctly "Pemban" identity had not yet developed.[27] The rural aspect

[24] Glassman, 1995; Fair, 2001.

[25] For some examples, see Glassman, 1995, pp. 146–75; Fair, 2001, chaps. 2 and 4; Justin Willis, *Mombasa, the Swahili, and the Making of the Mijikenda* (Oxford: Oxford University Press, 1993) pp. 2–5; Romero, 1997, p. 129

[26] Juma Aley titled his chapter on Pemba, "The Cinderella," suggesting that this image is an enduring one. Juma Aley, *Zanzibar in the Context* (New Delhi: Lancers Books, 1988); McMahon, 2005, pp. 30, 241, 272.

[27] WaPemba were considered an ethnic group and referred to as a particular subset of the population living on Pemba. Elisabeth McMahon, "Becoming Pemban: Identity, Social Welfare and Community During the Protectorate Period" (PhD dissertation, Indiana University, 2005).

of Pemba offered outsiders a means to lump together people on the island as old-fashioned (or without fashion in some cases), conservative, and often "stupid to an inconceivable degree."[28] Through the processes of building social networks, kinship bonds, and respectability, they sought to avoid the economic vulnerability associated with life for marginalized groups along the Swahili coast. Jonathon Glassman suggested that the consciousness of the crowd enabled lower-status groups to mobilize resistance against elites, but on Pemba, this did not happen in such an active, widespread manner.[29] Rather, resistance was individually based, through court actions, slanderous gossip, or using *uchawi* ("witchcraft") to cause misfortune, among other everyday tactics.

Contrary to much of the work on urbanized coastal communities, rural communities on Pemba had limited social stratification between the elite and ex-slaves.[30] Social hierarchy definitely existed on Pemba, but not at the level studied in places such as Pangani, Mombasa, Zanzibar Town, Bagamoyo, or Lamu.[31] Pembans with wealth often moved to other locations, such as Zanzibar Town and Mombasa, rather than remaining on the island. Ex-slaves who sought to change their social status (and even ethnic identity) also left for the more cosmopolitan Zanzibar Town or Mombasa. Because the social gap between the poor and well-off on Pemba was so small, the elite on Pemba had restricted powers to create social change, which significantly limited the desire of the vast majority to contest elite status. In many respects, both elite and marginalized populations lived an economically vulnerable existence, susceptible to the vagaries of the biannual clove crops. Fundamentally, this is a story about mediating economic and social vulnerabilities in a transitional society. Ex-slaves and other marginalized people negotiated their social vulnerability by carefully preserving their reputations, which gave them respectability and, at times, economic credit in their communities.

Ethnicity is almost always a focus of discussions of ex-slave communities along the Swahili coast as scholars show how people shifted their

---

[28] A Sultan's official told O'Sullivan-Beare that "the Zanzibar slaves are a very cunning lot; the Pemba slaves are absolute fools." The Vice Consul agreed, stating that "his description of the latter is certainly correct. The Pemba slaves, as a body, are ignorant and stupid to an almost inconceivable degree." *Report by Vice-Consul O'Sullivan on the Island of Pemba, 1896–97* (London: Harrison and Sons, 1898).

[29] Glassman, 1995, pp. 8–25.

[30] Abdul Sheriff reiterates the point in the nineteenth century that Pemba was much less socially stratified than Unguja. Sheriff, 1987, p. 129.

[31] Glassman, 1995, pp. 153–74; Strobel, 1979, pp. 29–30, 39–42; Willis, pp. 50–9; Fair, 2001, pp. 41–55; Nimtz, pp. 29–52; Romero, 1997, pp. 94–108.

identities to incorporate into local communities. This phenomenon rarely happened on Pemba because on such a small island, neighborhood networks were in place for generations, which made identity less mutable. Ex-slaves may have counted themselves in the censuses as "Swahili," "Shirazi," or "WaPemba," but that had more to do with their interpretation of themselves as "native" to the island.[32] In the probate court records, ex-slaves continued to use their mainland ethnicities into the 1940s, even while they were listed as "native" or born on the island in the census.[33] The ex-slaves recorded in the probate records were landowners, which in the literature on the coast has often been treated as a first step in a person's ability to shift his or her identity away from a mainland ethnic group.[34]

Ethnicity could be obscured in rare cases, but this was not the norm on Pemba. Ex-slaves certainly did embed themselves into local Pemban communities – the probate records also show this phenomenon – but they generally did not *assimilate* with freeborn. Most ex-slaves, especially men, did not marry into WaPemban or elite households, but they did intermarry across mainland ethnicities. Family and personal histories, especially of past enslavement, were embedded in local identities, and past enslavement would arise in conversations from the 1950s into the 1990s.[35] This indicates that few people were able to fully erase their past identities. Even when Africans of free descent tried to claim socially elite or Arab identity, they would be called out by others for trying to go above themselves.[36] While most scholarship on the Swahili coast discusses the flexibility and mutability of ethnic identity in the early twentieth century, in rural Pemba, "recreating" identity was difficult to do.[37]

[32] As well as interpretation by the census takers – see Edward Batson, *Notes on the Census of the Zanzibar Protectorate* (Zanzibar Protectorate, 1948), p. 1. Fair used the census data to argue that these shifts showed ex-slaves reclassifying themselves in urban Zanzibar Town. Fair, 2001, pp. 28–41.

[33] For examples see PNA AK1/3310 Probate Record of Hashima binti Baraka Mgindo, August 1934 and PNA AK1/46 Probate record of Baraka Mnyasa, May 1910. I will discuss this further in Chapters 4 and 6.

[34] Fair, 2001, p. 38.

[35] Bernard Freamon, "Islamic Law and Trafficking in Women and Children in the Indian Ocean World," in *Trafficking in Slavery's Wake: Law and the Experience of Women and Children in Africa,* edited by Benjamin Lawrance and Richard Roberts (Athens: Ohio University Press, 2012); Helle Valborg Goldman, "A Comparative Study of Swahili in Two Rural Communities in Pemba, Zanzibar, Tanzania," (PhD dissertation, New York University, 1996), p. 304. But, as Martin Klein discusses in detail, most people of slave ancestry were unwilling to discuss their families' past. Klein, 1998, p. 245.

[36] ZNA AI1/5: HHCZP Appeal Case No. 4 of 1920, Fatuma binti Dadi vs. Seif bin Hassan; McMahon, 2006.

[37] Fair, 2001, pp. 28–41; Glassman, 1995, chap. 4; Strobel discusses the cultural assimilation between elites and slaves, although she does not frame it as necessarily an issue of

One of the elements of acculturating into Pemban society was conversion to Islam; thus the active role the Quaker missionaries played in ex-slaves' lives on Pemba is unexpected. Most scholarship on coastal ex-slaves does not consider the role of missionaries in the day-to-day activities of ex-slaves. The works of Fred Morton and Robert Strayer are an exception because they both examined the role of missionaries in Kenya who helped slaves escape from slavery.[38] Yet seemingly most scholars of the coast equate conversion to Christianity as the mark of whether missionaries had any significant influence on the lives of slaves. Even when scholars use missionary archival materials, they do not reflect on the role of British missionaries as interlocutors for slaves in the colonial systems.[39] On Pemba, the Quakers had nearly two hundred ex-slaves living at their mission, but very few of them actually converted to Christianity. Most residents of Banani, the Friends' mission plantation, continued to practice Islam, yet the Friends played an active role in helping people across the community, from elite Indian women to the ex-slave workers on Banani. This study offers new insights into the ways in which missionaries profoundly impacted the lives of ex-slaves, who still remained deeply connected to the Islamic mores of the local communities.

SLAVERY ON THE EAST AFRICAN COAST

The language for forms of enslavement along the Swahili coast specifically detailed the age at enslavement, gender, and often occupation of the enslaved.[40] With so much attention paid to this terminology, it is easy to forget that both free and enslaved people used these terms to locate the enslaved on a continuum of enslavement, much like the social hierarchy of the free. The most common term for slave during the nineteenth and early twentieth centuries along the coast was *mtumwa* (pl. *watumwa*).

---

identity; Strobel, 1979, pp. 8–21; Willis, pp. 5–6. It makes sense that people who wanted to reinvent themselves went to the urban centers of Zanzibar Town and Mombasa to do so, which may help to explain why identity was seemingly so flexible in those locations.

[38] Robert Strayer, *The Making of Mission Communities in East Africa: Anglicans and Africans in Colonial Kenya, 1875–1935* (London: Heinemann, 1978); Fred Morton, *Children of Ham: Freed Slaves and Fugitive Slaves on the Kenya Coast, 1873 to 1907* (Boulder, CO: Westview Press, 1990).

[39] See, for example, Alpers, 1983; Cooper, 1977, 1980; Glassman, 1995.

[40] Morton, p. 2; Abdulaziz Y. Lodhi, *The Institution of Slavery in Zanzibar and Pemba* (Uppsala: Scandinavian Institute of African Studies, 1973), pp. 5–8; Mtoro bin Mwinyi Bakari, *The Customs of the Swahili People: The Desturi za Waswahili of Mtoro bin Mwinyi Bakari and Other Swahili Persons*, edited and translated by J. W. T. Allen (Berkeley: University of California Press, 1981) pp. 169–77.

However, specific terms identified when a person was enslaved, whether later in life (*mjinga*, pl. *wajinga*) or at birth (*mzalia*, pl. *wazalia*). Being categorized as *mzalia* placed one much higher on the hierarchal framework of enslavement because it meant that the person was born on the coast and, as such, into "civilized" society. Someone who was *mzalia* was likely to have been raised as Muslim and know the social mores of coastal society. As someone born inland, a *mjinga* was considered a "barbarian" or *mshenzi* (pl. *washenzi*) and, as such, was perceived as a person of lower social status by freeborn and *wazalia*. Some slaves held important positions within the households of their owners. For instance, a *mtumwa mtumwaji* was an agent and a *mtumwa wa shauri* was a councilor to the slaveholder. These were positions of power and respect relative to other positions of slavery.[41]

Terminology that identified both age and gender was also used for slaves. A *mtwana* was an adult male slave, whereas a *kitwana* was a boy slave. A *mjakazi* was an adult female slave, and a *kijakazi* was a girl slave. However, females could also be *suria* (pl. *masuria*), or concubines. A *suria* was ideally treated as a "little wife" in the household and held a position of respect, according to most descriptions.[42] The children of *masuria* were free and had equal rights to inheritance with their freeborn siblings. However, in coastal Kenya, the daughters of *masuria* could be made into *masuria* themselves in a way that freeborn girls could not.[43] However, a *suria* who did not bear children for her owner or whose children died young would often be demoted in the household and married off to another slave.[44] Women could also refuse to become *masuria* to their owners, although, as I will show in Chapter 6, refusal had potentially negative consequences. *Suria* is both a gendered and an occupational identity.

Most of the occupational terminology for enslavement was not gendered. For instance, *watumwa wa nyumba* were domestic slaves of either gender. *Vibarua* (s. *kibarua*), the day laborers who were hired out by mostly Indians and Europeans who could not own slaves, were both men and women. *Vibarua* carried water and hauled buckets of coral stone and other building materials regardless of their sex, although it

---

[41] Lodhi, pp. 5–6.

[42] Lodhi, pp. 13–14; Strobel, 1979, pp. 49–51; Romero, 1997, pp. 123–4.

[43] Morton, p. 2

[44] See Case AI1/44 HHSCZ Civil Appeal No. 15 of 1934, Bahati binti Serenge vs. Mohamed bin Musa bin Burhan Shirazi; see also Sarah Mirza and Margaret Strobel, eds. and trans., *Three Swahili Women* (Bloomington: Indiana University Press, 1989), p. 32.

appears that on Pemba many of the *vibarua* were women.[45] The temporary nature of *vibarua*'s work is exemplified in their name, which means "letter." However, the *hamali*, who were porters, and the *mafundi* (s. *fundi*), who were skilled artisans or carpenters, were generally men. The farm laborers, known as *watumwa wa shamba*, were often both men and women, although it appears that women also predominated in this area of enslavement on Pemba.

Within the social world of slaves there existed a hierarchy based on gender, occupation, and the process of enslavement. Slaves of equal social status referred to each other as *njoli*.[46] Thus *vibarua* would describe each other as *njoli*, but a *kibarua* would not call a *mtumwa ya nyumba* a *njoli* because their positions were not socially equal. *Vibarua* usually lived in urban centers independent of their owners. They paid a daily or monthly wage to their owners, wherein *mtumwa ya nyumba* mostly lived in rural areas doing hard agricultural labor under the oversight of owners or overseers. This distinction based on occupation helps to explain why the enslaved girl, Mzuri Kwao, discussed in Chapter 2, reacted so viscerally to her sale. As I will show, Mzuri Kwao became a *mtumwa ya mtumwa*, a slave of a slave. This is a term that is rarely discussed in the literature on enslavement along the coast.[47] Yet it comes up several times in the documentation of slavery on Pemba.[48] Being the slave of a slave meant that the slaveholders had little benefit to offer slaves in terms of social status or even security. If slaveholders were enslaved themselves, they could not guarantee where their own slaves could live, whether they would be resold, and who would inherit them at the death of their owner, among other problems. However, the ownership of slaves by other slaves indicates the ability of slaves to own property even before the British Abolition Decree.

---

[45] Henry Stanley Newman, *Banani: The Transition from Slavery to Freedom in Zanzibar and Pemba* (New York: Negro Universities Press, 1969, reprint of 1898 ed.), p. 36; July 5 1899, Vice-Consul Pemba, Letter AC5/3, ZNA.

[46] Lodhi, p. 7.

[47] Prestholdt discussed the concept of slaves owning slaves as a means to remake their status in the society. Jeremy Prestholdt, *Domesticating the World: African Consumerism and the Genealogies of Globalization* (Berkeley: University of California Press, 2008), pp. 134–40. Abdul Sheriff mentions this in passing for mid–nineteenth century Zanzibar Town. Sheriff, 1987, p. 149. Klein notes in passing that is was a common system in West Africa; rather than slaves buying their emancipation, they bought their own slaves because it gave them more security in old age. Klein, 1998, p. 13.

[48] Story of Mzuri Kwao discussed in Chapter 2; also see Friends Industrial Mission (hereafter FIM) TEMP MSS 419/1–7, Theodore Burtt, Notebook, 1899; Africa No. 7 (1896). *Correspondence Respecting Slavery in the Zanzibar Dominions.* 1896, Inclosure no. 3, Mr. A. Hardinge to the Earl of Kimberley, April 27, 1895.

As the preceding discussion shows, the terminology of enslavement along the coast was complex. Fred Morton argued that freeborn saw slaves as "nonassimilable" and that "slavery was a brand transmitted as a birthmark. It was ... not quickly cleansed."[49] This argument fits with a nineteenth-century proverb that states, "A keen sense of honour is not a characteristic of the slave class."[50] Other aphorisms directly linked slave status to a lack of Islamic beliefs by saying that "a slave is ... an enemy of God and the Prophet."[51] These proverbs point to the image of enslaved people as non-Muslim barbarians, although many slaves converted to Islam after living along the coast, and *wazalia* were born into the Islamic faith. The distinction that Morton is making is not one of slave/non-slave but rather of coastal/noncoastal, for people of the coast saw the people of the interior ethnic groups as *washenzi* ("barbarians"). The "birthmark of slavery" was not necessarily a taint of enslavement but of being from the interior. As Elke Stockreiter argues, "Religion was the dividing line between owner and slave between civilized and uncivilized, and thus ideologically separated the Muslim coast from the non-Muslim interior."[52] Yet, as much as this idea was espoused by the elites, the reality was that even some slaves from the interior were Muslim, such as many Nyamwezi. Enslaved people embraced Islamic practice not simply because they wanted to be like their owners but also because they found personal value in their beliefs.[53] While slaveholders certainly tried to use the hegemonic ideology of Islam to assert a paternalistic power over their slaves, slaves were not devoid of real religious faith, and their conversion was not simply a sign of respect for their owners.[54] Within this discourse is the implication that slavery may have been a continuum, but it was a set path that one could not erase.

---

[49] Morton, pp. xv, 2.

[50] Rev. W. E. Taylor, *African Aphorisms; or Saws from Swahili-land* (London: Society for Promoting Christian Knowledge, 1891), no. 281, p. 64.

[51] Taylor, 1891, no. 351, p. 78.

[52] Elke Stockreiter, "Tying and Untying the Knot: Kadhi's Courts and the Negotiation of Social Status in Zanzibar Town, 1900–1963" (PhD dissertation, SOAS, University of London, 2007), p. 266

[53] Louise Rolingher argued that a significant lacuna in the literature on Islam on the East African coast is that "few seriously consider the slaves to be 'agents' or even significant in either the spread or construction of Islam in East Africa." Rolingher, "Constructing Islam and Swahili Identity: Historiography and Theory," *MIT Electronic Journal of Middle East Studies*, Special Issue: Islam and Arabs in East Africa: A Fusion of Identities, Networks and Encounters, Fall 2005, p. 14.

[54] For a discussion of paternalism on the East African coast, see Cooper, 1977, pp. 153–6, 194–5; for my discussion of religious faith, see Chapter 4.

FROM HONOR TO RESPECTABILITY

Historically, having *heshima* was highly prized by all freeborn individuals in the Zanzibar Islands. In the twentieth century, *heshima* has been glossed as "respectability," but according to Edward Steere, an avid scholar of the Swahili language in the nineteenth century, as late as the 1880s the term *heshima* had no other meaning than "honor." In his 1884 dictionary, he states that *kuheshima* meant "to honor" someone, whereas having respect for someone was *kustahi*. The term "respectability" did not exist in Steere's dictionary of the Swahili language.[55] The word *heshima* shifted substantially in meaning between the nineteenth and twentieth centuries in response to the social transformation brought on by emancipation. Similar to Randall Pouwel's exploration of how the concept of civility along the Swahili coast shifted from *uungwana* to *ustaarabu* in response to the rise of Arab political hegemony, I show that the term *heshima* changed in meaning from "honor" to "respectability" in association with the events of British colonization in the early twentieth century.[56] This is not to say that the original meaning of *heshima* was entirely lost in the twentieth century, but it was dramatically curtailed because of the lessened power of elites to claim patronage based on the control of people.

Even in 1939, *heshima* was still defined as "honour, dignity, position, rank, ... respect, reverence, modesty and courtesy."[57] William Harold Ingrams, a colonial official in the Zanzibar Islands from 1919–1927, explained (in reference to Arabs):

Nothing ... is more important to the Arab than good manners and *heshima* ... *Heshima* is a very comprehensive and expressive word, which means not only respect, but the maintenance of that position to which respect is due.... I shall have further to say on the politeness and hospitality of the Arab when I speak of the same thing among the natives, for it is impossible entirely to dissociate the two.[58]

Ingrams further explains that for "natives," "it is a great insult to say to anyone *hunu abadu* (You have no manners); in fact this often leads to blows and litigation."[59] In both these definitions, honor is still a critical

[55] Steere, 1884.
[56] Pouwels, 1987, pp. 72–4.
[57] Frederick Johnson, *A Standard Swahili-English Dictionary* (Nairobi: Oxford University Press, 1939), p. 132.
[58] William Harold Ingrams, *Zanzibar: Its History and Its People* (London: H.F. & G. Witherby, 1931), pp. 206–7.
[59] Ingrams, 1931, p. 266.

element, but a number of other factors that illustrate respectability slowly became equally descriptive of the term. Exploring the significance of honor demonstrates that its meaning effectively changed from a person who had a "right to respect" because of his or her power to someone who sought respectability, a term that implies a social vulnerability to the actions and perceptions of others. Due to its association with hegemonic structures of power, honor was more difficult to lose than respectability. In turn, respectability had the potential to dismantle the very structures of power that in the nineteenth century predetermined honor.

John Iliffe's significant overview of honor in Africa takes its definition of honor from the work of Frank Stewart, who argued that "honor was a right." Iliffe furthers this statement to claim honor as "a right to respect."[60] While both men try to define honor in its simplest form, as a right or right to respect, neither can fully stop at that definition because of the multifaceted uses of the term "honor." Both scholars then draw out the ideas of vertical and horizontal honor. "Horizontal honor" is a right to respect from a social equal, whereas "vertical honor" is "the right to special respect enjoyed by those who are superior, whether by virtue of their abilities, their rank, their services to the community, their sex, their kin relationship, their office or anything else."[61] Vertical honor is the honor received by owners from their slaves, whereas horizontal honor is that which neighbors of equal standing would show toward each other. Iliffe specifies that honor is both subjective and objective – moving beyond the vertical and horizontal aspects to explore the way individual honor is negotiated. He suggests that the subjective understanding of honor is the respect "individuals believe they are entitled to," and the objective aspect is if "others treat them with respect and ... if the individuals can if necessary enforce respect."[62] This notion of force in connection with honor is a key element in a slaveholding society because the honor accorded to slave owners was often in relationship with the power they held over others, be they slaves or lower-status freeborn members of the community.

According to the objective aspect, honor is not in the control of the individual. Individuals can do their best to maintain their honor, but they

---

[60] John Iliffe, *Honour in African History* (New York: Cambridge University Press, 2004), p. 4; although Frank Stewart states that "personal honor was originally described ... as a right to respect." Frank Henderson Stewart, *Honor* (Chicago: The University of Chicago Press, 1994), p. 54.

[61] Stewart, p. 59.

[62] Iliffe, p. 4.

cannot control the world around them, their birth, nor their luck in life. William Ian Miller argues that in Europe and Latin America, the idea of honor was "more than a set of rules for governing behavior. It was your very being. For in an honor-based culture there was no self-respect independent of the respect of others ... unless it was confirmed publicly."[63] This implies that honor was not simply a right to respect but rather a set of characteristics and social conventions governing behavior that would earn an individual the respect of other people. In essence, Miller argues that in slave-owning societies, being a slave owner was a characteristic of honor, and being a slave was not. Scholarship shows that slaves may have striven for honor, but by definition they could never fully attain honor itself.[64]

The term *heshima* translated as "public honor," but this was an honor borne from power. Honor implicated power; a respected person was (and in most cases still is) someone with power or authority. The ability to instill subterranean channels of fear within a community allowed a person to have honor because people understood the potential harm that person could cause them.[65] The "right to respect" on Pemba was not given lightly but had to be earned and proven. Arab lineage played into a person's *heshima* on Pemba because most of the early Arab settlers to the island were powerful. They gained control over the island through force, they had shown their power, and as slaveholders, this power continued to lie under the surface of society throughout the nineteenth century. Likewise, the fear of those who controlled spirits and practiced the occult gave them respect and *heshima* in their communities. Practitioners of the occult, called *wachawi* (s. *mchawi*), were so honored on Pemba that they were not hunted and ostracized, as found in other parts of the

---

[63] William Ian Miller, *Humiliation and Other Essays on Honor, Social Discomfort, and Violence* (Ithaca, NY: Cornell University Press, 1993), p. 116.

[64] See Sandra Lauderdale Graham, "Honor Among Slaves," in *The Faces of Honor: Sex, Shame, and Violence in Colonial Latin America*, edited by Lyman L. Johnson and Sonya Lipsett-Rivera (Albuquerque: University of New Mexico Press, 1998), pp. 201–228; see also Martin Klein's discussion of Iliffe's description of military honor because most of the soldiers Iliffe accorded honor were slaves. Martin A. Klein, Review of Iliffe, John, *Honour in African History*. H-SAfrica, H-Net Reviews, April 2006. Available at: www.h-net.org/reviews/showrev.php?id=11644.

[65] Newbury pointed out that in nineteenth-century Zanzibar, *heshima* was "derived from a large number of dependents ... a value, perhaps more important to the Arab elite than the maximization of profits." A person with many dependents had the power to control others. M. Catherine Newbury, "Colonialism, Ethnicity, and Rural Political Protest: Rwanda and Zanzibar in Comparative Perspective," *Comparative Politics* 15, no. 3 (1983), p. 261.

continent.[66] "Being frightening, then, was a prerequisite to being treated with respect (*heshima*)."[67] They held power in their communities, which, in turn, accorded them *heshima*.[68]

Honor could not simply be "a right" because implicitly this means that all individuals are born with this right, yet obviously some people were not born with the "right to respect." Anyone who was not freeborn would not have this right, nor would anyone enslaved later in their lives. Enslavement stripped people of their rights, and ostensibly honor was one of the rights of which they were stripped. If "honor is a right," it would appear that when slaves were emancipated, they would be entitled to the right of honor again. However, because they were "outsiders" to the communities in which they had been enslaved, they had to prove themselves through their behavior to earn respect and honor from their neighbors. Even people manumitted by their owners often went through a transitory stage before they could be accepted by the wider community as a member.[69] In slave societies, honor was often received at the expense of others in the community; thus, at emancipation, *heshima*, a hegemonic system of honor in the nineteenth century, transformed into a network of relationships defined by respectability in the twentieth century.

Honor is often discussed as normatively male, and any honor held by women was simply a response to the honor held by male family members.[70] In most discussions of honor in Mediterranean cultures, both European and Arab, blood is a critical element in understanding the transmission of honor and transgressions against it.[71] The idea of blood ranges from the "purity" of lineage to the sexual implications of blood and virginity. "In Arabic, *'ird* (honor, good repute, dignity) ... can only be lost or redeemed

---

[66] Nathalie Arnold, "Wazee Wakijua Mambo! Elders Used to Know Things!: Occult Powers and Revolutionary History in Pemba, Zanzibar" (PhD dissertation, Indiana University, 2003). This is one of Arnold's core theses in her dissertation.

[67] Arnold, p. 254.

[68] Other scholars agree with this interpretation of honor – that respect *and* fear were evinced by those with honor. For examples, see Cooper, 1977, pp. 154–5; Phyllis Martin, *Leisure and Society in Colonial Brazzaville* (Cambridge: Cambridge University Press, 1995), p. 74.

[69] Miers and Kopytoff, pp. 26–7; Klein, 1998, pp. 12–14.

[70] Stewart, *Honor*, p. 107.

[71] Nancy Shields Kollmann, *By Honor Bound: State and Society in Early Modern Russia* (Ithaca, NY: Cornell University Press, 1999), p. 3; Beth Baron, *Egypt as a Woman: Nationalism, Gender, and Politics* (Berkeley: University of California Press, 2005); Lila Abu-Lughod, *Veiled Sentiments: Honor and Poetry in a Bedouin Society* (Berkeley: University of California Press, 1986); Stewart, *Honor*; Sarah Chambers, *From Subjects to Citizens: Honor, Gender, and Politics in Arequipa, Peru, 1780–1854* (University Park: Pennsylvania State University Press, 1999).

and is mostly connected with a woman's body, ... honor in the Arab world was a collective affair."[72] "The entire family's honor – and in this context, 'family' means those related by blood through the male line – resided in the conduct of its women."[73] Similarly, Latin American honor was based on the chastity and purity of the female members, although families were often more pragmatic about concerns over purity and worked to cover up any "faults" on the part of women.[74] Regardless, a discussion of "blood" was a significant element of Mediterranean honor and explains the development of duels and honor killings as means to "cleanse the blood" of the dishonored. In contrast to this focus on blood and honor, in Zanzibar, honor was connected to power. While purity and chastity were certainly an ideal for elite women, no culture of blood retribution existed.[75] However, property-owning women, especially slave owners, on Pemba were not jural minors and held their own claim to honor. In the postemancipation period, men on Pemba certainly tried to demonstrate their honor through the control of women's bodies, especially concubines, yet they were not always successful in doing so, as I will discuss further in Chapter 6. As Pemban society moved from a framework of honor to one of respectability, women exerted further control over their individual reputations.

The transition caused by the emancipation of slaves created a time of great confusion over who had the right to respect. Debates abounded among colonial officials about the status of slaves who sought their freedom from the government versus those who remained enslaved.[76] Colonial officials regularly argued that slaves who sought their freedom from the government were socially restricted by those who remained enslaved or who were manumitted by their owners. However, as increasing numbers of slaves sought their emancipation through the government, the social constraints based on whether or by whom a person was

---

[72] Miller, *Humiliation*, p. 119; Faramerz Dabhoiwala argues that if a woman had unquestionable chastity, her honor was based on the same social and economic criteria used for male honor. Faramerz Dabhoiwala, "The Construction of Honour, Reputation and Status in Late Seventeenth and Early Eighteen Century England." *Royal Historical Society Transactions* 6, no. 6 (1996), p. 208.

[73] Baron, *Egypt as Woman*, p. 41.

[74] Ann Twinam, *Public Lives, Private Secrets: Gender, Honor, Sexuality, and Illegitimacy in Colonial Spanish America* (Palo Alto, CA: Stanford University Press, 1999); Baron, *Egypt as a Woman*.

[75] The knife fights over honor were often between or caused by Manga Arabs who were recent migrants from Oman and thus still acculturated to Arab understandings of honor.

[76] FO2/284, Despatches to and from the Consul General Zanzibar, 1900.

emancipated began to break down, especially as ex-slaves continued to live among those who remained enslaved, even within the same household.[77] The ways enslaved people reacted to the abolition order of 1897 illuminates the social dynamics of the power invested in honor on Pemba. On Zanzibar and in many cases on Pemba, the *wazalia* (people born into slavery) were less likely to seek their emancipation, although they were also more likely to be manumitted by their owners, especially on Unguja.[78] For these ex-slaves, many still accepted the hegemonic ideal of slavery and the assumption that the power inherent in slave ownership explicitly connoted honor or *heshima*.[79]

Confusion over who could hold honor was not limited among slaves but also between classes. As Sarah Chambers noted for Latin America, "By using conduct as well as status as the standard among their peers, plebeians rejected the elite's exclusive claim to honor. Nevertheless, they abided by a code that recognized and respected hierarchy, particularly important in a society where members of different classes frequently intermingled."[80] As seen with the terminology of slavery, even within the enslaved classes, some people were accorded respect in ways others were not, mirroring the freeborn hierarchies. Assuming that honor was a right to respect and one of the fundamental ways slaves were kept in check, then the attempt to emancipate oneself in the courts was a direct challenge to an owner's right to respect. Slaves who stayed with their owners offered those owners honor as patrons, which confirmed their status in the community as honorable individuals. The fear of losing honor in the community drove some owners to take extreme measures to keep their slaves, even when offered compensation by the government or when slaves were difficult to control or keep. This was seen especially in the case of concubines, because control over women became the last venue for elites to exert their power. Thus the very definition of *heshima*, which denoted "power" in the nineteenth century, began to shift as slaves had the ability to circumvent the power of their owners.

Ex-slaves quickly sought to attain the accoutrements of *heshima*, but the clothing and other paraphernalia of slave owners did not come with the power implied in the earlier definition of *heshima*. As Laura Fair notes

---

[77] FIM, *Annual Report for 1914*; FIM PZ(F)/3, Committee of Missionaries, 1916–32.

[78] Cooper, 1977, p. 244, fn. 107. 5,468 voluntary manumissions on Unguja.

[79] This helps to explain why so many ex-slaves wanted to buy slaves of their own because they understood the power of ownership to give *heshima*.

[80] Chambers, pp. 161–2.

in her discussion of clothing in postabolition Unguja, one way in which former slaves sought to display their new respectability was by dressing with *heshima*.[81] But this was a different kind of *heshima*: Wearing shoes no longer meant the ability to control others. Wearing the *buibui* (head and body covering) of elite women did not allow ex-slave women to control the labor of others for their benefit. Fair and other scholars do not interrogate the shifting meaning of *heshima* itself because they are focused on its twentieth-century definition, but it clearly evolved with abolition. What ex-slaves hoped to gain from changing their clothing was *heshima*, or honor, but what they ended up with was respectability. While ex-slaves and elite used the terminology of *heshima* to denote their goal of attaining honor, the responses of others indicated that respectability is what they achieved.

As elites sought to shore up their position in the community without the power of force over ex-slaves, they emphasized the value of wealth, lineage, and piety. These three elements came to dominate the expressions of *heshima* by both the elite and the lower classes. A critical factor in these values was that they were more malleable than older markers of *heshima*. Although they tried to control these new factors of *heshima*, people could not dictate their economic status, whom their children chose to marry, and whether or not the community viewed them as pious. All of these were elements people could *try* to control, which is the crux of the changing meaning of *heshima*. In the past, *heshima* was commanded through power; now it was sought through patronage and behavior – on both ends of the social spectrum. No longer did *heshima* represent power and the ability to control others because the meaning had shifted to encompass trying to gain symbolic capital, an "accumulation of prestige and power" that allowed people to "gain and exercise authority."[82] Thus, when Fair's informants discussed their excitement about "dressing with *heshima*," the very meaning of what they were trying to attain had changed.

Heshima was used by ex-slaves and local elites as a method of social acculturation. Ex-slaves used the new markers of *heshima* as a means

---

[81] Fair, 2001, pp. 67–95. For examples of ex-slaves attempting to behave in ways to attain *heshima*, see also Robert N. Lyne, *Zanzibar in Contemporary Times: A Short History of the Southern East in the Nineteenth Century* (New York: Negro Universities Press, 1969), p. 221; first published 1905 by Hurst and Slackett.

[82] David Robinson, *Paths of Accommodation: Muslim Societies and French Colonial Authorities in Senegal and Mauritania, 1880–1920* (Athens: Ohio University Press, 2000), pp. 5–6.

to show their respectability to the free community, a means of showing they "belonged." Orlando Patterson famously made the point that to be enslaved, a person could not "belong" within the community and that through several generations of enslavement, a person could eventually "belong."[83] In Western societies, "freedom means autonomy," but "in most African societies 'freedom' lay not in a withdrawal into a meaningless and dangerous autonomy but in 'belonging.'"[84] Yet belonging to a community could be as oppressive as slavery. By using *heshima* to "belong," ex-slaves were constantly vulnerable to rejection of their respectability and tarnishing of their reputations.[85] Communities on Pemba used *heshima* as a control mechanism by idealizing the notion of *heshima* as a model for good citizenship, a model similar to that described by Bill Bravman in reference to mainland communities.[86] Community leaders used *heshima* as a hegemonic concept that helped to maintain the social hierarchy in the postemancipation era, when Pemban society was in a state of flux. To maintain the social hierarchy, notions of social credibility had to be imposed to differentiate the classes. As both Randall Pouwels and Jonathon Glassman note, marginalized people worked to gain status, whether through the accumulation of wealth, the manipulation of their lineage, or public displays of piety; *heshima* was a means for coastal elite to impose their notions of social norms on the lower classes. Ex-slaves did not erase their enslaved pasts, but they did find ways to negotiate a place for themselves within the wider Pemban society.

An important caveat to the transformation of *heshima* during the postemancipation era is that it did not happen all at once, nor did the older meaning of *heshima* as honor wholly disappear. Many people remained living "as slaves" into the 1920s, continuing to offer their owners *heshima* as honor. As I demonstrate in Chapter 5, occult practices continued to offer individuals the ability to hold power over others through fear and, as such, allowed older meanings to break through. While change occurred over time in the meanings, individuals often believed that they were due honor when what they received was respectability throughout the spectrum of Pemban society. Thus a powerful witchdoctor who was

---

[83] Patterson, 1982, chaps. 1 and 10.

[84] Miers and Kopytoff, p. 17.

[85] Frederick Cooper, Thomas C. Holt, and Rebecca Scott, *Beyond Slavery: Explorations of Race, Labor, and Citizenship in Postemancipation Societies* (Chapel Hill: University of North Carolina Press, 2000), p. 5.

[86] Bill Bravman, *Making Ethnic Ways: Communities and Their Transformations in Taita, Kenya, 1800–1950* (Portsmouth, NH: Heinemann, 1998), p. 5.

a former slave could receive *heshima* as honor, whereas members of a previously illustrious Arab family fallen on hard times might only receive *heshima* as respectability because they could no longer command their dependents to act in particular ways. Transformations in power dynamics and definitions of *heshima* did not occur in a linear fashion but rather intermittently over time.

The public reputation of ex-slaves within their communities displayed their social acceptance within Pemban society. The Swahili word for reputation (*sifa*) implies a positive attribute, unless prefaced with a negative adjective. It refers to common knowledge within the society. But this does not explain how someone creates and gets a reputation. Obviously, individuals' parentage defined their reputation in childhood until they could act for themselves and, as such, build a reputation in the community. A reputation was gendered and developed within a social milieu, but what was reputable among the elite was often out of reach of lower-status people. Likewise, what was reputable for men would be inappropriate for women because Pemban society functioned with separate spheres for men and women in their leisure time. Much like *heshima*, a reputation was a public good, created and destroyed in the public realm by other people through their conversations. In a community, "gossip ... is part of the very blood and tissue of that life."[87] Gossip served as a historical record of communication and values in a community, and thus it helped to create a person's reputation within the community and demonstrate the ways in which communities constructed their value systems and disciplined members into accepting those value systems.[88]

Gossip about people and their reputations happened throughout the island, from the female space of the courtyards to the male space of the *baraza*. Gossip could certainly affect individuals' reputations in their neighborhoods, but gossip was treated as an illegitimate source of information.[89] As I discuss in Chapter 4, coastal societies frowned on gossiping while continuing to participate in it. However, the courts acted as a particularly significant public space to debate the reputations of individuals in a way that legitimated the discussion of reputation as something

[87] Max Gluckman, "Gossip and Scandal," *Current Anthropology* 4, no. 3 (June 1963), p. 308.
[88] Luise White, *Speaking with Vampires* (Berkeley: University of California Press, 2000), p. 64; White states that gossip helped to discipline community members, p. 58.
[89] See Marc J. Swartz' work for a modern discussion of *aibu* ("shame") and the role gossip played in causing *aibu* among Mombasan communities. Marc J. Swartz, "Shame, Culture, and Status Among the Swahili of Mombasa," *Ethos* 16, no. 1 (March 1988), pp. 24–7.

higher than gossip. Because of the prestige of the judges, the analysis of reputations that occurred during court cases put the discussions of reputation from the courts into the realm of communal knowledge rather than gossip.

GOING TO THE COURTS

British officials quickly involved themselves in the court system on the islands because this was the perfect location for "civilizing" Zanzibari society. In the decades leading up to the declaration of the Zanzibar Protectorate, British officials from India to the Caribbean all argued that through the use of colonial power and justice, especially in the colonial courts, subjects would be "civilized,"[90] first by teaching communities how to resolve disputes civilly rather than through public violence and second by defining the state as the controlling party over judicial violence. By moving the resolution of disputes into the colonial purview, officials co-opted the local elite doubly by moving disputes out of individuals' hands and controlling the Islamic judges as employees of the state. Thus not only did elite potentially lose their slaves (if the slaves chose to seek their freedom), but they also lost their ability to physically defend their honor through public fights. Similar to the British shift in the courts in Zanzibar, Nancy Shields Kollmann demonstrated how the tsarist government of Muscovy co-opted elite power in early modern Russia by offering a legal structure for the defense of honor.[91] By taking this role, the government moved extrajudicial violence over honor into government-controlled courts. Similarly, the colonial government of Zanzibar slowly created a court system controlled by it that mediated local conflicts and criminalized extrajudicial violence as "assault" or "murder" regardless of the cause. Through the new courts and the policing of violence, colonial officials usurped the power of elites and reshaped the meaning of *heshima* from honor to respectability. Not only did slave owners lose their ability to control people through fear, but they also lost their ability to control the outcome of disputes through violence. Moreover, nonelite people such as former slaves could bring cases against former slave owners into the courts – and win!

[90] James Patterson Smith, "Empire and Social Reform: British Liberals and the 'Civilizing Mission' in the Sugar Colonies, 1868–1874," *Albion: A Quarterly Journal Concerned with British Studies* 27, no. 2 (1995), pp. 270–1.
[91] Kollmann, *By Honor Bound*, pp. 2–26.

Previous to colonial interference, the courts on Pemba primarily consisted of the two *liwali* ("governors") for the regions of the island (located in the towns of Wete and Chake Chake), who acted as surrogates for the Sultan. The *liwali* heard all criminal cases and often settled civil disputes.[92] The position of *liwali* was a political post given by the Sultan to his supporters and did not require knowledge of Islamic law. If a case required knowledge of Islamic law, litigants took the case to one of several *makadhi* (s. *kadhi*, "judge") scattered across the island. These men were viewed locally as educated in *fiqh* ("Islamic jurisprudence"), although local customary beliefs crept into their interpretations. Most disputes were settled through the use of these courts or intimidation and outright violence toward property or person. Into this system the British injected organization and money. The British designated three *makadhi* for the island of Pemba and then paid them a regular salary. This was to both remove the taking of bribes to settle disputes but also to regularize and "civilize" the Islamic courts. The colonial office learned a lesson 30 years before in the Morant Bay insurrection that "deficient and corrupt justice threatened control and could be costly" to the state; consequently, officials sought to remove any suggestion of impartiality from the colonial courts.[93] From the first consular court on the island in 1895 to the consolidation of the dual court system (Islamic *kadhi* and British magistrates) in the 1920s, British officials sought to direct and refine the ways in which people on Pemba handled disputes. By criminalizing public violence, officials forced people of all levels of society to accept their suzerainty over the process of disputes. This change also shaped the behaviors that were deemed to show *heshima* as the debates over what *heshima* meant moved into the courts.

In the early years of the changing system, lower-status litigants, such as ex-slaves, who had difficulty getting their cases heard by *makadhi* used missionaries and government officials as interlocutors. Over time, this became unnecessary as the colonial-employed *makadhi* began accepting cases from ex-slaves and women. As colonial officials sought to regularize the *kadhi* courts, they inserted district commissioners (and later magistrates) into the judicial process, creating what became known as the dual system of courts. While litigants in civil cases could choose which

---

[92] It should be noted though that Sultanate and Protectorate officials defined criminal behavior differently. Thus physically defending one's honor was acceptable to Sultanate officials but was a crime of assault to Protectorate officials.

[93] James Patterson Smith, "Empire and Social Reform," p. 267.

courts to bring their cases to, colonial officials hoped to move away from the *kadhi* courts altogether, except for cases of family law. However, litigants often sought out the *kadhi* courts, especially on Pemba, because they privileged oral over written evidence. Most disputes over property involved moneylenders who benefited from the colonial emphasis on written sources. Yet the majority of the Pemban population was functionally illiterate, including many elites, and thus they preferred a system of dispute resolution based on oral evidence and the value of individual reputations.

The colonial courts quickly became a location in which reputations were publicly debated and analyzed. The open-air nature of the courts made the discussions of reputation even more public because anyone near the court could add their views. Consequently, reputation and, as such, a person's *heshima* were pronounced on publicly. The shaming, or potential shaming, that occurred through these disputes in the court helped to modify the behavior of people at all levels of society. The use of the courts as a vetting site for individuals' reputations created a disciplinary mechanism. As Foucault noted, "the perfection of power should tend to render its actual exercise unnecessary."[94] As more people on Pemba accepted the hegemony of *heshima* meaning respectability, the less colonial officials had to monitor behavior or work toward "civilizing" people. The courts were a central site of this engagement with respectability because they were a public forum for the discussion of the reputation and *heshima* of litigants. Thus former slaves used litigation in the courts to build their *heshima* and achieve a new status in Pemban communities, whereas former slave owners sought to keep their reputations as patrons and important people by using the courts rather than public violence.

SOURCES

This is primarily a history of people who negotiated the transition from enslavement to emancipation on Pemba. However, the language that people used during this transition varied so dramatically that using local terms, as suggested by Suzanne Miers, is an impossible task in this work. As discussed in more depth in Chapter 2, different terms were used for

---

[94] Michel Foucault, *Discipline and Punish: The Births of the Prison*, trans. by Alan Sheridan (New York: Vintage Books, 1979), pp. 192–202. For a further discussion of disciplinary mechanisms, see Timothy Mitchell, *Colonising Egypt* (Berkeley: University of California Press, 1991), chaps. 3, 4, and 5.

people manumitted by their owners and those who were emancipated by the government. Ex-slaves associated with Christian missions were often called different terms than the previous two groups. Owners used a variety of words to describe their former slaves, whereas the government attempted to classify ex-slaves by their forms of labor. All these terms overlapped at different points in individuals' lives, and it is nearly impossible to pinpoint for the majority of ex-slaves how they referred to themselves. Therefore, I have chosen to use the term "ex-slave" to describe former slaves regardless of the method of their emancipation. It is unfortunate that using the term "ex-slave" reifies their position; however, it is important for this study to distinguish ex-slaves from other marginalized populations on the island. In the twentieth century, ex-slaves lived among mainlanders who came to pick cloves on the island and did not leave, such as many Nyamwezi, as well as the indigenous WaPemba, WaTumbatu, and some WaHadimu. These are the indigenous people of the three largest islands among the Zanzibar Islands. Few WaHadimu lived on Pemba because most lived on Unguja. However, a large population of WaTumbatu resided in southern Pemba. Some WaPemba were well off and had a higher social status; nonetheless, the majority of WaPemba were also marginalized in the social hierarchy of Pemba. Identity was (and still is) a complex issue in the islands, and I prefer to distinguish different groups from one another in the historical record. Nonetheless, at times it is appropriate to collectively refer to people living on Pemba regardless of ethnicity or social status, at which point I use the term "Pemban."

The rich documentation of life on Pemba Island in the late nineteenth and early twentieth centuries illustrates the everyday lived experience of slaveholding elites, slaves, and ex-slaves as they negotiated their relationships with one another. The one group most excluded from these sources and hardest to tease out is the freeborn Africans living on the island before the arrival of the Omani colonizers in the early nineteenth century. The indigenous elite, generally referred to on the Swahili coast as *waungwana* (s. *mwungwana*), and the WaPemba rarely appear in the government and missionary records that make up the majority of the sources for this study. Thus I reference freeborn individuals when I have sources for their relationships, but otherwise I am generally examining the lives of members of the slaveholding and enslaved populations and their descendents. This is an important caveat to this study because it is not a complete history of early twentieth century Pemba, but it does address the lives, disputes, and problems of the majority of the population.

The government documents, which are the largest set of documents used for this study, ranged considerably from the letters and reports of the Vice Consul to the island's probate and civil appeals court cases, all of which are housed in the Zanzibar National Archives branches on Unguja and Pemba Islands. Many other government documents are also included, such as the Slavery Commissioners' letters and reports, as well as documents from the Consul General and, later, the British Resident of the island, most of which are housed in the Parliamentary Papers. A number of documents remain in the foreign office and colonial office papers in the National Archives in the United Kingdom as well. These documents span from the mid–nineteenth century for those found in the Parliamentary Papers to the 1950s for the court records from Pemba. The most intensive period of time covered starts in 1895, when the first Vice Consul was assigned to Pemba, through the 1930s, with the court records and annual reports from the islands. It was during this period that colonial officials slowly consolidated their control over the government structures on Pemba.

The documents of the Vice Consul, Dr. O'Sullivan-Beare, are a wealth of material because he regularly wrote letters to the Consul General concerning issues of slavery, cases of runaway slaves, wrongly enslaved people, and disputes between owners and slaves. After emancipation, he continued to report on its progress on the island, going into detail about many individual cases. His reports were further supplemented by those of the Slavery Commissioner, John P. Farler, who was forced to write voluminous reports for the Consul General and later British Resident because of his ongoing feuds with the Friends missionaries on the island. These reports give specific details on how the courts systems worked and, more important, how people used the courts and felt about them. One of the most valuable aspects of these documents is that they introduce the changing meaning of *heshima*. It is clear from the way people on Pemba brought their cases to the courts that both elite and marginalized people continued to work with the premise that *heshima* meant a "right to respect" or honor, but a look at the day-to-day employment of the concept in the court records reveals the transformation in its meaning. It becomes abundantly clear that even though the elite still believed they held *heshima* in the older meaning, they did not. Elites understood *heshima* to mean "respectability" only for ex-slaves, but the way in which elites were treated and coped with emancipation shows that the new meaning clearly affected them. All members of the community were subject to the social vulnerability of reputation embedded in this new articulation of *heshima*.[95]

Yet the Vice Consul and Slavery Commissioner reports were always filtered through the lens of a European. We know from missionary records that colonial officials encountered *uchawi* ("the occult"), and yet official documentation rarely speaks of these encounters.[96] Clearly, many aspects of colonial interactions with people on Pemba did not make it into the official record. Early cases with O'Sullivan-Beare were also filtered through translators, although his Swahili became very effective within the first year. Officials such as John Farler, who had been in the region for decades and likely spoke Swahili fluently, were well versed in the complex local language of slavery and the social distinctions it indicated. Unlike German colonial officials on the mainland, as Jan Georg Deutsch has argued, British officials in Zanzibar were quite aware of the "social nuances between free and unfree."[97] Interestingly enough, it was the missionaries, most of whom were active abolitionists, who refused to distinguish among slaves or ex-slaves but rather saw the relationships in dichotomous terms because acknowledging distinctions among these groups would complicate the abolitionist message.

Several missionary groups existed on Pemba, two of which left behind significant collections of material. The Universities Mission to Central Africa (UMCA) was started in 1857 in response to David Livingstone's call to end the slave trade and slavery in East and Central Africa. The UMCA started stations on the mainland (1860) and in Zanzibar (1864) several decades before it started a mission on Pemba in 1897, just months before the emancipation order was made. While UMCA records are not extensive, the letters, newsletters, and pamphlets still available are remarkably rich for examining the relationships and personalities of officials and missionaries on Pemba, as well as the practice of *uchawi*

---

[95] Megan Vaughan argues that for elites in the Mascarene Islands, "reputation, and the mutual recognition that lay behind it, was an extremely fragile commodity in what was in some senses (and despite its avowed rigidities) a highly mobile society." Megan Vaughan, *Creating the Creole Island: Slavery in Eighteenth-Century Mauritius* (Durham, NC: Duke University Press, 2005), p. 181.

[96] UMCA files at Rhodes House, Oxford; one file, ZNA AB31/20, Witchcraft in Pemba, in the Zanzibar Archives contains a wealth of government reports on *uchawi* in Pemba, but otherwise, mention of *uchawi* was rare in colonial reports from Zanzibar. More information is available for the mainland; see PRO CO691/126/10, Death penalty, murder and witchcraft, 1932; PRO CO847/13/11, Laws relating to witchcraft, 1938. These files include some discussion with Zanzibari officials.

[97] Deutsch, 2006, p. 7.

among ex-slaves. The Friends (Quaker) missionaries, on the other hand, left a veritable treasure trove of documents detailing their disputes with John Farler in his position as Slavery Commissioner, the daily lives of laborers and boarding school students, and life histories of ex-slaves, in addition to other sources. The Friends held monthly meetings beginning in 1897, when they opened their mission, that detailed the concerns of the missionaries, their interactions with laborers on their plantation, any converts, the salaries of their employees, the feasts they held, the progress of building up a plantation and a mission, and especially their activism in trying to end the legal status of slavery on the island. These meeting minute books were kept until the missionaries were forced to leave the island in 1964. Several of the missionaries remained on the island for more than thirty years, bringing an incredible level of consistency in their reports, including in-depth knowledge of their laborers and their lives. Moreover, they kept what they called the "sacred book" of all slaves who sought help from them in getting their emancipation. This book contains approximately one thousand names of slaves seeking emancipation, as well as the names of the owners, any kinship relations among the slaves, their ethnicities, and various other occasional notes.

Theodore Burtt, one of the first Friends missionaries, who stayed from 1897 to 1932, also kept his personal letters that give details of individual slaves' complaints. Burtt interviewed twenty-six slaves during his time in Pemba, writing down their life histories in a notebook. These histories were clearly answering specific questions: How were they enslaved? Did they like their owners? Why did they leave? Who did they leave with? Did they have any children during their lifetimes? and How many times had they married? None of the answers were formulaic, and Burtt took the time to write down such details as whether or not they "loved" their spouses or how a child or spouse died from *uchawi*. While these histories are relatively short, they are incredibly rich in the depth of how slaves and ex-slaves constructed their relationships with one another as well as with their owners.

Another significant file from the Friends was the diary of the Boys Home, which was a boarding school that was nominally for "orphan" boys, although that term was applied very loosely. In fact, few of the boys were orphans because the diary records the missionaries' efforts to get permission for the boys to stay at the school from their parents. These records document the efforts of slave owners who continued to exert control over slaves and their children, as well as the refusal of slaves – even when remaining enslaved – to place their children in a similar position to themselves. The generational differences within slave families leap from the pages of the diary, as children refused to obey anyone – the missionaries, their parents, or the owners of their parents. The behavior of the boys, and their parents' refusal of slaveholders' demands that parents remove the children from the school, demonstrates the loss of power by the elites to control their dependents and claim a "right to respect." Additionally, the diary explains how children developed friendships with one another that sustained them as they grew up. It also tells (or rather complains!) about the nocturnal pursuits of the boys and their leisure activities. The tapestry of ex-slaves' lives, especially the interactions between enslaved and slaveholder, is created through the warp of government documents and the weft of the Friends and UMCA documents.

Much as Kristin Mann notes for Nigeria, the UMCA missionaries did not challenge the colonial state or its policies.[98] Because they supported the status quo of slavery on Pemba, the documents reflect this perspective in many cases. The UMCA missionaries later became a thorn in the side of the government because of their insistence that the government regulate *uchawi*. In opposition to the UMCA, the Friends missionaries were immediately antagonistic to the colonial state and the Sultan's officials on the island because of their opposition to slavery. It was after the full abolition of slavery in 1909 that the Friends became less militant in their response to colonial officials. Missionary documents generally have biases, just as any other form of document, that must be read against in order to draw useful information. Since Pemba was primarily Muslim, people who associated with the Christian missionaries showed their lower status in local society. Yet, at the same time, the missionaries on Pemba were spectacularly ineffective at converting ex-slaves. Until the 1930s, with the influx of mainland laborers to the island, the Friends had no more than a handful of confirmed converts at any given time. The Friends missionaries generally interacted with ex-slaves, not those who remained enslaved. Except for the diary of the Boys Home, when they had to deal with enslaved parents and their owners, the silence on those who remained enslaved is deafening in their documents. The premise of the Friends mission was that slaves *must want* freedom, and it contradicted their mission that the majority of slaves did not seek freedom from the government. Therefore, Friends documents focus on, and perhaps exaggerate, the desires of slaves to remove themselves from their owners.

[98] Kristin Mann, *Slavery and the Birth of an African City: Lagos, 1760–1900* (Bloomington: Indiana University Press, 2007), p. 19.

The missionary documents continue into the 1930s, but court records inform the post-1910 period of this study. The work of Richard Roberts in *Litigants and Households* offers a wonderful model for writing a history of emancipation and communities from court records. Yet Richard Roberts had an incredible wealth of court cases – many thousands – that enabled him to show statistical significance in ways that few scholars of Africa can duplicate.[99] Similarly to Kristin Mann, in her recent work on slavery in Lagos, I have far fewer cases than Roberts. However, as Mann explained, what these cases lack in statistical significance they have in depth and richness of detail.[100] The cases I use include a full dossier, with notes on each meeting for the case, all the summons, Arabic documents produced during the case, and transcriptions of witness testimony in English – although not in Kiswahili. The most precious aspect of these records is the voices of Pembans recorded by scribes because they offer rich insights into the lives and thinking of people on Pemba.

In the appeals court records, the witness testimony and the questions posed by the *wakil* ("lawyers") and *kadhi*, as well as the answers, appear to be verbatim in many cases. However, there remains the methodologic issue for understanding the "theater" of the court and how litigants and witnesses constructed their testimony.[101] Pemban litigants performed respectability in the courts in an effort to secure their reputations and preferred outcomes.[102] Yet, from the records, there is no way to know what other people in and around the court may have added to the proceedings or how the *kadhi* responded to any interruptions in the hearings. For example, when one slave woman went to ask for her freedom in 1902,

---

[99] In their pivotal volume on the history of law in Africa, Richard Roberts and Kristin Mann noted that "none of the participants thought there was much to be gained from quantitative study of court cases. Records of individual cases are often complex texts, requiring close analysis to extract their meaning. The true significance of cases can rarely be reduced to a set of quantifiable variables." Kristin Mann and Richard Roberts, eds., *Law in Colonial Africa* (Portsmouth, NH: Heinemann, 1991), p. 47.

[100] Mann, 2007, pp. 19–21.

[101] Peterson, Derek, "Morality Plays: Marriage, Church Courts, and Colonial Agency in Central Tanganyika, ca. 1876–1928," *American Historical Review* 111, no. 4 (2006), pp. 983–1010.

[102] For a discussion of performing respectability, see Susan Hirsch, *Pronouncing and Persevering: Gender and the Discourses of Disputing in an African Islamic Court* (Chicago: The University of Chicago Press, 1998) pp. 28–9; Ariela Gross, "Litigating Whiteness: Trials of Racial Determination in the Nineteenth-Century South," *Yale Law Journal* 108 (1998). It is hard to tell if litigants used the linguistic pragmatics as suggested by Hirsch for Mombasa; however, the use of *wakil* by women on Pemba in order to maintain respectability indicates an awareness of how to manipulate aspects of the courts and the *kadhi*.

the missionary who attended the court with her said that the women endured "much abuse" during the hearing and eventually gave up her request for freedom.[103] This hints that court cases could be vehemently contested and difficult for the participants, none of which is recorded in the archival documents. Additionally, the courts were not private venues but rather open-air locations that could allow a myriad of interruptions not only from people in the courts but also from those passing by the courts.

As with any set of court records, the ones on Pemba are useful as "illustrations of social processes."[104] Yet, in considering these social processes, the question of who wins the case often is secondary to the wealth of information regarding the case and its participants that is presented in the court documents. Elke Stockreiter argues, however, that the winners are important because it shows that *makadhi* increasingly relied on ethnicity as a way to give preeminence to the elite social classes in the Zanzibar courts.[105] Yet on Pemba those who could convince the judges that they were "respectable" and worthy were more likely to win, regardless of ethnicity. The ineffectiveness of the colonial state in guaranteeing the execution of court orders suggests that Pembans were more interested in the publicity for their cases that going to the courts brought them.[106] The most interesting information that emerges from the documents is how individuals related to one another in antagonistic circumstances. I examine how intervention on the part of British interlocutors – whether colonial officials or missionaries – shaped the court systems themselves and how that affected those who participated in the courts. I explore why individuals felt the need to call on the British to intervene on their behalf. While the court records cannot be studied in a vacuum, the depth of the cases illustrates their value as a source of social processes on Pemba.

---

[103] FIM, PZ(F)/3, Register of Slaves, Banani, 1897–1909; "The Story of Msichoke," *The Friend* (British), October 3, 1902, pp. 644–6.

[104] Marcia Wright, "Justice, Women, and the Social Order in Abercorn, Northeastern Rhodesia, 1897–1903," in *African Women and the Law*, edited by Margaret Jean Hay (Boston: Boston University African Studies Center, 1982), p. 36.

[105] Stockreiter, p. 19.

[106] This is not to say that people absolutely did not want to win; certainly they did so. However, winning did not necessarily mean a resolution to the case because many of the appeals cases show several attempts to appeal the case back and forth between litigants. Also, sometimes when a litigant won his or her case, the opposing litigant refused to let anyone enter the property to take possession, and the courts were ineffective in completing these transactions.

The probate records range from 1910, when the British regularized the taxation and records concerning inheritance cases, to 1954. Although the earlier years of the records were more detailed than the later years, and the kinds of information changed between the various years, all give valuable insights into the relationships between individuals and families, as well as an emphasis on economic information that illustrates the negotiation and use of reputation in ordinary peoples' lives. For the most part, the probate records listed the names, ethnicity, and death dates of individuals along with the size of their estate, a listing of all immovable property (including animals), heirs, and debts and credits owed by and to the estate. In some cases, a full listing of household contents was provided, but this was rare. In the years after 1935, the age of the deceased was included in the dossier. This was a crucial element that was missing from the earlier cases because it was unclear how old a person was when he or she died. In the earlier records, the deceased's age could be estimated if he or she had children because the ages of children were generally included. However, many people in the probate records had no children. The cases also included wills, if they existed, and whether there was any contestation over who was eligible as an heir.

By correlating the death totals for Pemba listed in the annual reports of the Protectorate with the number of probate cases listed per year, it appears that approximately 10 percent of cases went to probate. It is unlikely that this is representative of the entire property-owning population on Pemba. Most people who knew they were dying began to transfer property to their heirs before their deaths. Also, the *masheha* (s. *sheha* – "village-level government official"), who were responsible for reporting deaths and any property left behind had a limited ability to ensure that people honestly reported property at the death of their relatives. It is apparent from the number of childless people in the probate records that it was common practice to pass on land to children before death to avoid the probate taxes, which could be as high as 15 percent.[107] Very few people in the probate records were very wealthy, indicating that either wealthy families chose not to reside on Pemba or that they handed over property before death in an effort to outwit the colonial state. Clearly, the records cannot illuminate all forms of familial relationships; however,

---

[107] In PNA AI1/4 HHCZP Appeal Case No. 2 of 1920, the plaintiff admitted that he lied when the *sheha* asked him about the property at the death of his mother. This indicates that people did try to avoid the probate courts. On occasion in the probate records a family would send in the money to pay off the debts of an estate but refuse to send in the costs of the probate court, much to the magistrate's annoyance.

they still offer a wealth of information that helps to flesh out aspects of the civil appeals cases, and as such, they provide a glimpse into life in colonial Pemba.

The probate records are particularly useful for looking at a variety of issues: how people identified themselves ethnically and whether they had previously been enslaved, the terms of credit and debt on the island and how people framed their discussions of credit and debt, the myriad forms of kinship among people, how reputation played out within communities and when people accepted individuals' reputations, and the role of oaths, among others. In cases of inheritance, the discourse of witnesses and judges can be measured against the outcomes of cases in order to determine the boundaries and ambiguities of kinship. The probate records not only reveal points of conflict in societies, but they can also highlight the ability of some families to resolve conflicts easily, with little contestation. The records show, for example, how some people who owed debts to the deceased willingly appearing in court to testify to those debts. The sum of the probate documents illustrates the diversity of experiences in ex-slaves' lives.

In addition to missionary and court records, other colonial documents for the post-1910 period, housed in the Zanzibar National Archives and the National Archives in the United Kingdom, have informed this study. These include the Annual Reports of the Zanzibar Protectorate; several files on education, landownership, census data, and conflict among communities; and a substantial file on *uchawi*. The file on *uchawi* is particularly insightful for examining its prevalence on Pemba, as well as the identity of its participants. While the file reflects a mostly standard colonial interpretation that condemned *uchawi*, surprisingly, most officials and missionaries who lived on Pemba for several years had some belief in the efficacy of *uchawi*. Several memoirs and ethnographies written by colonial officials provide a balanced perception of *uchawi*, although most were horrified at the elements of "cannibalism" practiced by *wachawi*.[108] These books, such as J. E. E. Craster's 1913 account of his year living on Pemba while he mapped the island and Harold Ingrams' 1931 ethnography of the islands, are a wealth of information on *uchawi*, Sufi groups, slave perceptions, and many other details of daily life. Dictionaries from the 1870s through the 1930s; collections of proverbs, poems, and other

---

[108] As I will discuss in detail in Chapter 5, to become a full *mchawi*, an individual had to kill a family member, and not a distant member, but one whom he or she loved very much, usually a child or a sibling. The dead relative would then be "eaten" at a feast with all the other *wachawi*, thus implicating all *wachawi* in the death of the one individual.

aphorisms; newspaper articles; published law reports; and more recent unpublished anthropological dissertations all help to fill in the gaps of court and missionary records.

I conducted oral interviews with elders on Pemba in 2002 and 2004 and use those data, where relevant, in this book. Yet, as Jonathon Glassman argued for Zanzibar, oral sources are "understandings of the past, not records of them."[109] Using oral sources for discussions of slavery is extremely difficult and laden with "understandings" based on present-ist concerns. Scholars who work on slavery in Africa have pointed out that generally people with slave ancestry do not wish to talk about their pasts. Thus I never directly asked anyone that question. In oral interviews conducted by me and Hajj Mohamed Hajj, we asked about names, ages, ethnicity, ethnicity of both parents, occupations, and parents' occupations. Many of the questions I asked were related to education, hardship, *heshima*, and civility (*ustaarabu*), as well as the leisure activities of themselves and their parents. These interviews give insights into what people on Pemba valued in their educations and what level of education they obtained – both in Quranic schools called *vyuo* (s. *chuo*) and government schools called *shule*. They also allowed me to see how individuals and families built networks around religious and leisure activities, which were often one and the same. By examining hardship, I gained insights into the debt cultures on the island and the ways in which families worked together to mitigate the economic vulnerability inherent in a monocrop cash economy. These interviews provide invaluable insights into how Pembans view themselves and their communities.

The time period I focus on here has several layers. The core of this book is focused on the period between 1895 and 1928 because that was the period shaped most directly by the abolition of slavery and the insti-tution of the dual court system of *kadhi* and magistrate courts. However, many of my documents radiate beyond these years, especially into the period of World War II. I include material from later sources because it reflects the solidification of patterns begun in this earlier period. In reading the historical documents that remain about the lives of people on Pemba, I emphasized the collection of stories first. I wanted to find the voices of Pembans – when they showed outrage and sadness, when they were gleeful, and when they expressed happiness and satisfaction. As I have read through and thought about these stories, I have sought to examine what these experiences meant to individuals and what they

---

[109] Glassman, 2011, p. xi

represented about social norms more broadly across Pemban society. As I show in Chapter 5, by offering an alternative interpretation of events in the Zanzibar Islands, as Pembans who believed in *uchawi* might view them, I believe that historians cannot read historical documents just for events but also for the meanings people attached to them.[110] In many respects this is why I worked to supplement the documents with changing definitions of terms, proverbs, and poetry – because those sources offer insights into how people viewed their society and its significance to them. Thus, on the one hand, I use no single methodological approach to the documents for this study, but on the other, a driving force throughout the book is the examination, as much as possible, of what everyday events meant in the lives of individuals, especially those marginalized in Pemban society.

CHAPTER OUTLINES

Reputation and talk are fundamental elements in the first three chapters of this book. No one definitive reputation existed for any individual, but a variety of reputations based on the talk of their neighbors, family, government officials, and others. These interpretations of reputation could have varying implications on the position of the individual talked about and how that person was positioned in relationship to others in his or her community. Chapter 2 uses the story of an enslaved woman named Mzuri Kwao to expose how talk affected the perceptions of colonial officials and the changes brought by British-controlled courts. This case also illustrates the problems in defining the status of slaves and slavery, even in the preemancipation era, because of the multiplicities of meanings of these terms on Pemba. In the end, the case sets out the lines of economic and social vulnerability that affected slaves and especially women, who worked within the patriarchal framework of slavery in order to mitigate their vulnerability in their communities. In many respects, Chapter 2 is an ethnography of the years around emancipation on Pemba. It sets up a basis for understanding how life did and did not change after the abolition order of 1897.

---

[110] As Marcia Wright so famously said in her book, *Strategies of Slave Women*, a certain amount of inference from the historical sources must be done – as long as it is clearly understood this is what the author is doing. Thus, in one section of Chapter 5, I am clearly offering what I believe would be a local interpretation of events from my reading of the documents. See Wright, 1993, p. ix.

Chapter 3 examines the arc of the court systems of Pemba, from the precolonial era when most slaves had difficulty bringing cases to court to the crystallization of the colonial court systems in 1910. Yet, even as the British sought to regularize the courts into a "dual jurisdiction" between British magistrates and the Sultan's *makadhi*, a crucial aspect of the courts remained – talk. This included the talk of witnesses, the oral agreements made between litigants, and the taking of oaths to bring a resolution to the cases. Through this discussion of talk, the reputations of community members are analyzed within the courts, as well as their rights to *heshima* and what that meant to individuals.

The discussion of *heshima* continues and is expanded on in Chapter 4, as I explore the foundations of the term and its shift in meaning over time. I examine the variety of ways in which marginalized members of the community worked to build *heshima* for themselves by manipulating the talk of their neighbors to their benefit. Marginalized people sought to build respectability through their appearance, education, and piety. All these actions furthered peoples' participation in communities of practice that allowed them to build social networks beyond that of their families. The talk of neighbors built and destroyed peoples' reputations, which affected their ability to access the credit necessary for survival in an agricultural society where income was generated during harvests.

Examining the "landscapes of power" that were reshaped by the introduction of colonialism and other influences allows insight into how marginalized communities affected power relations. Richard Roberts argues that the transformation from the precolonial to the colonial era was an uneven series of power shifts among African actors, as well as the colonial state. These shifts required actors to have intentionality about their actions.[111] As Roberts notes, colonial power was not hegemonic; Pembans shifted from using the visible landscape of slavery to the invisible landscape of the spirit world to engender the respect and fear associated with power and honor in the precolonial era. Chapter 5 explores the ways in which the colonial court systems redrew the lines of dispute resolution on the island while simultaneously transforming the landscape of power to a colonial framework. Yet, as the colonial state strengthened its visible control through the courts, Pembans expanded another landscape of power in the invisible world, the world of *uchawi*. Through the fear created by their knowledge of *uchawi*, some people living on Pemba were able to achieve the *heshima* of an earlier era. However, while *uchawi* offered a

[111] Roberts, 2005.

landscape of power to some, it offered increasing vulnerability to many others. Because of the requirement that to become *mchawi*, a person had to kill a close relative, *uchawi* had the potential to destabilize kinship ties on the island.

Life was hard for people on Pemba, as the preceding chapters illustrate. Misfortune and vulnerability were always around the corner, especially for marginalized populations on the island. This is not to suggest that ex-slaves and other marginalized groups accepted their positions in society; they most certainly tried to alleviate their weakness socially and economically, but this was not easy to do. For most ex-slaves, building up ties of kinship with others was the most effective means they could use to moderate the value of talk in harming them. Through an exploration of the different forms of kinship, blood and marital ties, connections linked through enslavement, and the networked family (fictive) ties, I illuminate in Chapter 6 the numerous ways ex-slaves found to create families for themselves. I also seek to expand beyond the often discussed links between ex-owners and ex-slaves to examine why and when slaves and ex-slaves refused to create familial links with their former owners. I demonstrate that even when slaves did not leave their owners after emancipation, this had little to do with the benevolence of their owners and everything to do with mitigating the vulnerability of having been ripped from their families of birth through the processes of enslavement.

Were those who were enslaved on Pemba truly as "ignorant and stupid to an almost inconceivable degree," as Dr. O'Sullivan-Beare, the Vice Consul of Pemba, so derogatorily suggested in his report for 1896?[112] Unlikely. Their voices, opinions, ideas, and creativity come out of the many stories found in the archives. Rather, what that comment implied is that government officials could not understand why anyone would willingly live in a location where life was difficult to maintain and work was constant. The colonial obsession with ex-slaves desiring to move to Zanzibar Town reflected, on some levels, a reality – but also their own views on Pemba and a desire to be away from this "great green grave."[113] Ex-slaves have so often been represented as foreigners to the island, brought by force, yet by remaining on the island they demonstrated their deep sense of belonging to the place and the community. This sense of belonging is illustrated in

[112] *Report by Vice-Consul O'Sullivan on the Island of Pemba, 1896–97* (London: Harrison and Sons, 1898).

[113] For an in-depth discussion of colonial perceptions of Pemba and the isolation they felt living on the island, see McMahon, "Becoming Pemban," chap. 4. For the description of Pemba as a "great green grave," see Burton, 1872, vol. II, p. 7.

the words of an ex-slave who was asked in 1912 if he would return to the mainland now that he was free. He responded, "Return to those pagans? No way. Besides I have my house here, and a small piece of land, and my son is a rich man, a silversmith in the town and he works hard."[114] These were the elements of life that the ex-slave sought, the ability to express his religious faith, landownership, reputation, and family, which all indicated his accommodation to postemancipation life on the island.

---

[114] John Evelyn Edmund Craster, *Pemba: The Spice Island of Zanzibar* (London: T.F. Unwin, 1913), p. 95.

2

Mzuri Kwao and Slavery in East Africa

One of the earliest cases brought before Dr. Daniel O'Sullivan-Beare, the new Vice Consul on Pemba Island, involved an enslaved Manyema girl.[1] Mzuri Kwao dramatically arrived on Dr. O'Sullivan-Beare's doorstep in May 1895, seeking his protection from her owner, who was trying to sell her. The details of her case, the intricacies of the relationships among the individuals involved, and eventual outcome demonstrate the ways in which Pemban society was transformed by both individual agency and changes brought by new policies of British governance during the late nineteenth and early twentieth centuries. Such watershed British policies as the emancipation of slaves hung over the actions and lives of individuals on Pemba regardless of class and gender. Yet it was the response to those policies by people living on Pemba that ultimately restructured society. Manumission of slaves itself was not radical; it was what government-sponsored emancipation signified about people's reputations and positions in the community. Government-sponsored emancipation allowed any slave to impugn the *heshima* of his or her owner by demonstrating that the owner no longer had the ability to control him or her. As newly emancipated people began competing for economic resources to which they previously had limited access, they further shifted social relations on the island. Both free and enslaved people struggled to alternately upset and reinforce the status quo, which profoundly affected the

[1] ZNA AC9/2, Letter Vice Consul Pemba May 12, 1895. The Manyema are an ethnic group found in present-day Tanzania. Before 1900, the Vice Consul's name was always listed as Dr. O'Sullivan, but after 1900, it became O'Sullivan-Beare. I use the full appellation throughout for continuity sake.

everyday lived experience of class, gender, and status.[2] The diversity of
social statuses among both free and enslaved in the 1890s created a plethora of definitions, meanings, and terminology as individuals and groups
vied over their place in the hierarchy of Pemba. As illustrated by the story
of Mzuri Kwao, it was the women and ex-slaves of Pemba Island who
traversed especially unstable ground in this postemancipation world, one
in which they were expected to be attached to a supervising male, be it a
brother, father, owner, or husband.[3]

When Dr. O'Sullivan-Beare learned about Mzuri's case, he took
immediate action, not because he was moved by Mzuri's story of capture and sale, but because her most recent owner, Nasoro Mega, was
a British subject. Nasoro was a well-off Muslim Indian merchant living in Chake Chake, the economic capital of Pemba Island at the time.
Because Nasoro was a British subject, O'Sullivan-Beare viewed the case
as an important one to pursue because ownership of slaves was illegal for
the Indian population.[4] However, the intricate web of relationships that
O'Sullivan-Beare uncovered while investigating Nasoro surprised the
Vice Consul. From the women who participated in the sale of Mzuri to
Nasoro's extended familial relationships, O'Sullivan-Beare's account of
Mzuri's story demonstrates the variable positions of slaves on the island.
The role of a female slave who brokered the deal to sell Mzuri, as well as
Mzuri's new position as an *mtumwa ya mtumwa* ("a slave of a slave"),
demonstrates the malleability of the status of slaves on the island.

The case of Mzuri Kwao represents the dual possibilities for women in
the early period of the British Protectorate. In many respects, her case is
an anomaly – a slave woman who seeks help from the British Vice Consul
because she is being sold. Most slave women did not seek legal redress in
the way Mzuri did, although the Vice Consul records certainly show that
some did. Nonetheless, her case details the lives of multiple female slaves

---

[2] Elizabeth Dore speaks of the interconnectedness of gender, ethnicity, and class in individuals' lives so that the three elements can rarely be examined successfully in solitude to
one another. Elizabeth Dore, *Myths of Modernity: Peonage and Patriarchy in Nicaragua*
(Durham, NC: Duke University Press, 2006), pp. 1–13.

[3] Wright argued, "[I]n all societies a woman remained in legal terms a perpetual dependent.
Without a husband, uncle, brother, or father to represent her, she lacked access to the
judicial process." Wright, 1993, p. 25; Strobel argues that along the Swahili coast women
were expected to be subordinated to men at all times. Strobel, 1979, pp. 54–8.

[4] As discussed in Chapter 1, footnote 4, Indians were not allowed to own slaves in the
Zanzibar Protectorate. For further details, see Sheriff, 1987, pp. 202–8. However, colonial
officials suspected Indians on Pemba of ignoring these laws, and Dr. O'Sullivan-Beare was
instructed to pay special attention to Indians owning or purchasing slaves. See Africa No.
7 (1896) *Correspondence Respecting Slavery in the Zanzibar Dominions*. Enclosure no.
2, Mr. A. Hardinge to the Earl of Kimberley, April 22, 1896.

with varying levels of status within their community, of which only Mzuri chose to go to the colonial courts for help. Mzuri's seeking of assistance from the British Vice Consul was because she was being sold, an action that was illegal by 1895. Although the other women involved in the case were not being sold, one, Mami Rehani, was being asked to do something illegal by her owner and could herself have gone to the Vice Consul to complain, but she did not. The contrasting actions of Mami Rehani and Mzuri Kwao demonstrate the very different ways that the enslaved population reacted to colonial policies regarding slavery and abolition.

Mzuri's story provides an entry point into the examination of the ways in which slavery, status, reputation, and identity worked on Pemba in the pre-Protectorate era, as well as the ways in which women, both slave and free, would begin challenging the status quo. The relationships exposed in this story also set the stage for exploring the mutability of status (and in some cases identity) along the entire Swahili coast. For example, Mzuri's resistance to being sold had perhaps as much to do with her distress at learning that she would be a *mtumwa ya mtumwa*, a very low status, rather than a concubine, whose status would be closely linked to that of her owner. While it is impossible to definitively know Mzuri's motivations, she set in motion a process that would become familiar to people living on Pemba, wherein those who were refused a hearing in the Islamic *kadhi* courts sought the help of the British officials and missionaries living on the island – a process that became more common on the Swahili coast as European colonizers settled in the region.[5]

THE SLAVE TRADE ON THE EAST AFRICAN COAST

The first Sultan of Zanzibar encouraged the planting of clove and coconut trees in Unguja and Pemba during the early nineteenth century. He and his allies, as well as many other free people living in the islands, began devoting plots of land ranging from small *mashamba* ("farms" or "land," s. *shamba*) to large plantations for the cultivation of these profitable tree crops. This agricultural change, away from food crops such as rice, dramatically transformed the physical, economic, and human landscapes of the islands.[6] Increasing numbers of slaves were imported to work on the

---

[5] Strobel, 1979, pp. 58–63; Romero, 1997, pp. 110–13.
[6] Before clove cultivation began, Pemba was known as the "breadbasket" of the Swahili coast, particularly Mombasa. See Catherine Coquery-Vidrovitch, *The History of African Cities South of the Sahara: From the Origins to Colonization* (Princeton, NJ: Princeton University Press, 2005), p. 201; see also Jan Knappert, "Pemba," *Annales Aequatoria* 13 (1992), p. 43.

land – weeding, picking, drying, and stemming the cloves and coconuts.[7]
By the 1870s and 1880s, following abolition of the slave trade from the
coast in 1873, thousands of slaves were smuggled to various destinations
in the Indian Ocean region. Pemba, which became the major producer of
cloves in the region following the destruction of many of the clove trees
on Zanzibar by a hurricane in 1872, was the destination for many slaves.
With the increase in slave traders along the coast and the illegality of the
slave trade, kidnapping became a commonplace event, resulting in the
enslavement of many people who previously were not at risk, and many
of the slaves living on Pemba were brought there after being abducted
from their owners along the coast.[8]

Kidnapping was a common form of enslavement, as well as reenslavement, in both the interior and coastal regions of nineteenth-century eastern
Africa.[9] From as far north as Lamu to the interior districts and the southern coastal region, opportunistic capture of slaves was a common means
of enslavement during the late nineteenth century.[10] As Patricia Romero
noted, the British official stationed in Lamu in 1884–5 complained regularly about the "slave stealers, of whom there are plenty in the area."[11]
In 1895, the Vice Consul on Pemba complained about a disreputable
Arab who "was a notorious bad character and stealer of slaves."[12] Katrin
Bromber stated that in German-controlled territories it was not uncommon for "the capture and sale of already freed slave women."[13] While she
argues that this was "clearly different from the accepted norm," I would

---

[7] The labor-intensive harvesting of cloves required abundant labor for brief periods of time
    and served to fuel the ongoing trade in slaves even after the abolition of the slave trade
    between the mainland and the islands.

[8] Elisabeth McMahon, "Trafficking and Re-enslavement: Social Vulnerability of Women
    and Children in Nineteenth Century East Africa," in *Trafficking in Slavery's Wake: Law
    and the Experience of Women and Children in Africa*, edited by Benjamin Lawrance and
    Richard Roberts (Athens: Ohio University Press, 2012).

[9] Both Jan Georg Deutsch and Michael Tuck suggest that small-scale opportunistic kid-
    nappings were the most common kind of violent capture of slaves in East Africa during
    the nineteenth century. Jan Georg Deutsch, "Notes on the Rise of Slavery and Social
    Change in Unyamwezi," in *Slavery in the Great Lakes Region of East Africa*, edited by
    Henri Médard and Shane Doyle (Athens: Ohio University Press, 2007), p. 88. Michael
    Tuck, "Women's Experiences of Enslavement," in the same volume, pp. 176–7.

[10] See Deutsch and Tuck citations above. Also Romero, 1997, pp. 55–9; Katrin Bromber,
    "Mjakazi, Mpambe, Mjoli, Suria: Female Slaves in Swahili Sources," in *Women and
    Slavery: Africa, the Indian Ocean World, and the Medieval North Atlantic*, Vol. 1, edited
    by Gwyn Campbell, Suzanne Miers, and Joseph C. Miller, pp. 118–19.

[11] Romero, 1997, p. 59.

[12] ZNA AC5/1, Letter July 31, 1895.

[13] Bromber, pp. 118–19.

counter that it may not have been "accepted," but it certainly happened with regularity. Justin Willis argued that around Mombasa, kidnapping occurred as early as the 1840s but that it increased by the end of the century.[14] As late as 1920, according to a colonial official, people living on Tumbatu Island fled on his arrival because "in the old days slave raiders used suddenly to descend on the island and kidnap any women and children they found."[15]

Harold Ingrams' statement reinforces the notion that women and children were especially vulnerable to kidnapping.[16] Even the (in)famous narrative of Olaudah Equiano began with a child's abduction.[17] However, while kidnapping narratives often focus on children, adults were also regularly kidnapped along the East African coast during the nineteenth century.[18] Just as children and women kidnapped from beaches and homes were taken aboard ships, men hired as porters for those boats often found themselves subsequently tied up and then sold elsewhere with the rest of the "cargo."[19] The issue of kidnapping is significant for understanding the social and physical vulnerability, especially of women and children, in a slave-owning society. Even freeborn people had to protect themselves from the predations of known slave traders. These kidnapped slaves illuminate the irony of describing the slave trade as "ended" in 1873. As long as slaves were needed to expand the clove economy on Pemba and control over the trade was limited, the slave trade continued, which meant that the status of marginalized populations, whether freeborn or enslaved, was increasingly vulnerable as the nineteenth century came to a close.

[14] Willis, p. 74.

[15] William Harold Ingrams, *Arabia and the Isles* (London: Kegan Paul International, 1998), p. 29.

[16] Paul Lovejoy, *Transformations in Slavery*, 2nd ed. (Cambridge: Cambridge University Press, 2000), pp. 3–4; Patrick Manning, *Slavery and African Life: Occidental, Oriental, and African Slave Trades* (Cambridge: Cambridge University Press, 1990), pp. 88–9.

[17] For the debate over Olaudah Equiano, see Vincent Carretta, *Equiano, the African: Biography of a Self Made Man* (Athens: University of Georgia Press, 2005); Paul E. Lovejoy, "Autobiography and Memory: Gustavus Vassa, Alias Olaudah Equiano, the Africa," *Slavery & Abolition* 27, no. 3 (2006), pp. 317–47; Vincent Carretta, "Response to Paul Lovejoy's 'Autobiography and Memory: Gustavus Vassa, Alias Olaudah Equiano, the African," *Slavery & Abolition* 28, no. 1 (2007), pp. 115–19; Paul E. Lovejoy, "Issues of Motivation – Vassa/Equiano and Carretta's Critique of the Evidence," *Slavery & Abolition* 28, no. 1 (2007), pp. 121–5.

[18] Michael Tuck showed that 36 percent of the women whose biographies he studied in Buganda had been kidnapped into slavery. Tuck, p. 176.

[19] For an example of men kidnapped, see ZNA AC2/24, Vice Consul letter February 17, 1897.

During the nineteenth century, Europeans increasingly played a role in coastal East Africa. The British, especially, used economic pressure to slowly extract concessions concerning the slave trade between eastern Africa and Arabia from the reigning Zanzibari sultans.[20] Even if the sultans had wanted to help end the slave trade (which they did not), their control over the coast was too limited to enforce any decrees they made; implementation was left to the British. Enforcement of treaties made between the British and the Zanzibari sultans between the 1820s and 1870s were handled by the British Consul in Zanzibar; thus, during periods when the Consul was less inclined to impose the treaties, the slave trade thrived in the Sultanate.[21] For example, the appointment of Consul Christopher Rigby from 1858 to 1862 introduced the Sultanate to what implementation of the antislave trade treaties would look like. During Rigby's tenure, numerous ships were captured, and the slaves were sent to Mauritius as "free" labor. In addition, Rigby forced Indians, as British subjects, to emancipate their slaves. He personally signed letters of freedom for approximately 6,000 slaves; however, when Rigby left, Indians began purchasing slaves again, and the trade flourished.[22]

After the death of the reigning Sultan, Seyyid Majid, in 1870, the British played "kingmaker" in order to put his brother, Barghash, on the throne in Zanzibar. Implicit in British support was the understanding that Barghash would help them end the slave trade. Although Barghash resisted these efforts, in 1873, he gave in to economic pressure and signed a treaty to end the slave trade, though not slavery.[23] While slaves could no longer be exported from the mainland, nor could they be transported from one port to another within the Sultanate, domestic slavery itself was not abolished. Slave owners were still allowed to take their own slaves with them when they traveled, and this was often used as a ruse to move small numbers of slaves between regions.[24] Even with this treaty, the slave trade continued, albeit in a lesser fashion, and slaves were regularly smuggled

---

[20] Moses D. E. Nwulia, *Britain and Slavery in East Africa* (Washington, DC: Three Continents Press, 1975), p. 46; McMahon, 2005, pp. 14–18.

[21] John Gray, *History of Zanzibar: From the Middle Ages to 1856* (Oxford: Oxford University Press, 1962); Norman Bennett, *A History of the Arab State of Zanzibar* (London: Methuen, 1978).

[22] R.W. Beachey, *The Slave Trade of Eastern Africa* (London: Rex Collings, 1976), p. 56.

[23] In 1872, a hurricane hit Unguja Island devastating the clove industry on the island. However, it did not affect the clove trees of Pemba, and it was from this date forward that Pemba became the main clove producer in the islands.

[24] Fitzgerald, p. 610.

into the islands of Unguja and Pemba.[25] Starting in the 1870s, the channel between the islands and the mainland was blockaded by British cruisers in search of *dhows* ("boats") smuggling slaves.[26] Because of the blockade, the price of slaves jumped tremendously during clove booms, which, in turn, increased the cost associated with picking cloves. A provision of the 1873 treaty prohibited the Sultan from receiving a tariff on each slave sold, which limited his economic power and put the Sultanate further in "debt" to the British. This set up a cycle in which clove producers became increasingly indebted to moneylenders for assistance in purchasing slaves, which mirrored the Sultan's increasing dependence on British power to maintain his political position.[27]

Just seventeen years after abolition of the slave trade and with the "agreement" of a newly appointed Sultan of Zanzibar, the British government declared a Protectorate over the Sultan's territories. In August of that year, the British also had the Sultan put forth a decree declaring that the "exchange, sale or purchase of slaves – domestic or otherwise is prohibited."[28] While slavery as an institution was allowed to continue, several policies were put into place by the 1890 decree that would force its decline. First, the decree ruled that slaves could only be inherited by the children of the deceased. This meant that other relatives could not inherit slaves, nor could slaves be sold as part of the estate. Another critical element of the decree was the granting of legal rights to slaves. For the first time, slaves could sue their owners for ill-treatment and initiate other cases in court. This access to the courts was a major change; despite injunctions in the Quran that slaves should be able to use the courts, slaves had been denied this option in Zanzibar.[29] A number of other rules

---

[25] The slave trade switched to moving slaves along the coastal mainland, taking much longer and probably killing far more people. Slaves were now marched from Kilwa as far north as Somalia and then sent on *dhows* into Arabia. Coastal plantations on the mainland also boomed; see Glassman, 1995, pp. 105–6.

[26] Captain Colomb, *Slave-Catching in the Indian Ocean: A Record of Naval Experiences* (New York: Longmans, Green, 1873); George Lydiard Sulivan, *Dhow Chasing in Zanzibar Waters and on the Eastern Coast of Africa: Narrative of Five Years' Experiences in the Suppression of the Slave Trade* (London: Dawsons of Pall Mall, 1873).

[27] While the Sultanate was hereditary, so many possible heirs existed that competition from other contenders for the throne was a constant worry. The first Sultan of Zanzibar himself became the Sultan of Oman by killing his uncle, who had been ruling before him, setting the precedent of the most powerful heir being the ruler.

[28] Quoted in "Abolition of Slavery in Zanzibar," *The British Friend*, September 1, 1890, pp. 215–16.

[29] Elke Stockreiter notes that slaves were able to bring cases in the *kadhi* courts after the 1897 abolition order. Stockreiter, p. 18.

came out of the decree, such as the granting to slaves of the ability to purchase their freedom and the statute that all children born to slaves after 1890 were automatically free. The changes the decree brought to the legal rights of slaves had, by default, significant implications for the rights of owners as well. As such, elite Arab and European businessmen protested the decree, and within a year, it was virtually ignored as a legal document.[30] Thus, when the new Vice Consul arrived on Pemba Island in 1895 and began enforcing the laws of the 1890 decree, many of the slave-owning public were baffled and angered by his intrusions into their "affairs."[31]

The trade in smuggled slaves was of particular importance in the history of Pemba. With the closing of the slave market in Zanzibar Town in 1873, Pemba became a major destination for imported slaves. It has been estimated that Pemba received as many as 1,000 slaves per month in 1875.[32] The British navy regularly patrolled the waters around Pemba, and later skirmishes between naval vessels and slave-carrying *dhows* often occurred in Pemban waters. Because of this shift, Pemba became internationally known through Western newspapers as a place of slavery and resistance to the British treaties.[33] This notoriety attracted the interest of the British Friends Anti-Slavery Committee to start a mission on the island. The Friends put a spotlight on Pemba by writing letters to the editor of the *Times* newspaper of London condemning the British Protectorate government for ignoring conditions of the slave trade and

[30] Bennett, pp. 166–7.

[31] See ZNA AC9/2; in a letter from September 10, 1896, the Vice Consul complained about Moosa bin Salem beni Harusi, who continuously tried to incite violence against the British officials because of their rulings on slaves. Also see letters in ZNA AC9/2, November 24, 1896, and February 18, 1897, for examples of residents of Pemba who were "baffled" by the laws regarding the sale of slaves and stated that they had no idea selling or buying slaves was illegal. Both were described by the Vice Consul as living in rural "out of touch" areas. In 1898, Emily Keys noted that the Friends missionaries had again riled up the Arab elite "who were threatening to shoot all newcomers to the island" (meaning Europeans). UMCA E2, Emily Key "Notes from Pemba," January 16, 1898.

[32] See "Geography and Travels," *American Naturalist* 12, no. 11 (1877), p. 763; Nwulia, 1975, p. 140.

[33] The *Times* of London articles that mention Pemba include "The Story of the Fatal Encounter, Near Pemba," January 4, 1882; "The Pemba Slave Trade," October 25, 1888; "The Zanzibar and Pemba Slaves," February 22, 1895; "Slavery in Zanzibar and Pemba," October 15, 1895; and "Slavery in Zanzibar and Pemba," April 16, 1900. The *New York Times* usually followed with articles from the London newspapers. See also Alfred Bellville, "Journey to the Universities' Mission Station of Magila, on the Borders of the Usambara Country," *Proceedings of the Royal Geographical Society of London* 20, no. 1 (1878), pp. 74–8. The story of the death of Colonel Brownrigg was part of the infamy of Pemba and the slave traders there. See also Lyne, pp. 107–26.

slavery on the island.[34] Once the Friends missionaries settled on Pemba in 1897, British officials were kept on their toes by the constant barrage of accusations from Theodore Burtt and Herbert Armitage of the Friends mission about the working of the antislave trade and antislavery treaties.[35]

Even with "direct" control over the islands and coastal region after declaration of the Protectorate in 1890, British officials hesitated to declare a full emancipation of the slaves. Concern over where the slaves would go and whether they would continue working after emancipation delayed any action on the part of Protectorate administrators.[36] The lessons of emancipation in India and Egypt remained in the minds of administrators, who regularly complained to the home office that if they emancipated the slaves, it would wreck the islands' economy.[37] However, pressure at home, fueled by Quaker missionaries living on Pemba, forced the hand of local officials and the Sultan, who decreed the "abolition of the status of slavery" in 1897.[38]

---

[34] For letters to the editor of the *London Times* by Friends, see Horace Waller, October 25, 1888, p. 13; February 22, 1895, p. 3; Francis William Fox, October 22, 1895, p. 10; Charles Allen, August 23, 1895, p. 8; June 26, 1896, p. 12; April 2, 1897, p. 7; April 12, 1897, p. 10; October 8, 1897, p. 9; December 21, 1897, p. 10; December 31, 1897, p. 4; July 26, 1898, p. 12; Theodore Burtt, November 30, 1897, p. 8; Donald MacKenzie, April 16, 1897, p. 4; March 7, 1898, p. 9; July 29, 1898, p. 15; December 5, 1898, p. 6; Travers Buxton, November 17, 1899, p. 12.

[35] For examples, see ZNA AC9/2, May 12, 1898; ZNA AC8/5, April 28, 1903; *London Times*, October 8, 1897, and November 30, 1898. As I will discuss in later chapters, the Friends missionaries were particularly loathed by the European officials. For example, in Lyne's 1905 book on Zanzibar, he gives six full pages to the UMCA and French Catholic missions and only one sentence to the Friends. Lyne, pp. 210–16.

[36] For more information about British concerns, see Welliver, pp. 60–120; Fair, 2001, p. 14; Cooper, 1980, chap. 2.

[37] See Africa No. 6 (1895), *Correspondence Respecting Slavery in Zanzibar* (London: Harrison and Sons, 1895). Includes letters from Rennell Rodd, Consul General at Zanzibar, December 31, 1893, arguing that abolition was not feasible at the time – citing Sir John Kirk's memorandum of 1884 stating that "slavery ... is essential to prosperity in Pemba." Also see letter from the Earl of Kimberly to Mr. Hardinge (newly appointed Consul General to Zanzibar), November 27, 1894, citing abolition from India and Egypt. Hardinge's reply of February 26, 1895, goes on to say that it is not advisable to abolish slavery at that time but that they should continue to focus on ending the slave trade so that slavery can "die out."

[38] See letter from Charles Allen, *Daily News*, May 9, 1893. Government response to Allen's letter: Africa No. 6 (1893), *Paper Respecting the Traffic in Slaves in Zanzibar* (London: Harrison and Sons, 1893). For an ongoing discussion of the advisability of emancipation, see letters enclosed in Africa No. 6 (1895), *Correspondence Respecting Slavery in Zanzibar* (London: Harrison and Sons, 1895) and Africa No. 7 (1896), *Correspondence Respecting Slavery in the Zanzibar Dominions* (London: Harrison and Sons, 1896).

Officials in Zanzibar purposely wrote the abolition order as a means to appease abolitionist parliamentarians at home and yet keep slaves working on the plantations of their owners.[39] The Consul General in 1895, Arthur Hardinge, stated that he was willing to allow rules that would appease people in London but would have little appreciable "benefit to the slaves, but would prove of advantage to Zanzibar if it helped to put off, if only for a time, any general measure of abolition."[40] In actuality, the order of 1897 neither abolished slavery nor affected the status of slaves. There were a number of caveats to the decree that limited slaves' access to freedom. Not only were slaves required to inform their owners they wanted to be freed, but their owner's permission was needed in order for slaves to travel to one of the regionally based Slavery Commissioners to apply for freedom. The Slavery Commissioners would hear the request and then decide if the slave would receive a freedom paper. Of course, this entirely depended on whether the slave found the Slavery Commissioner available, which was an ongoing problem because the islands had only one commissioner each.[41] Since the Protectorate government gave subsidies to the owners for the loss of their slaves, the commissioners did what they could to discourage slaves from seeking their emancipation.[42] Furthermore, concubines were exempted from the emancipation decree. The colonial government decided to treat concubines as wives, and thus they could not seek emancipation except in cases of cruelty. Even in such cases, the women had to leave their children with the owner. Divorce was common for wives but impossible for concubines, so their status

Nwulia argued forcefully that the Friends' pressure on the government is what caused officials to declare the abolition of slavery. See Nwulia, 1975.

[39] Arthur Hardinge complained, "[I]n view of the strong demand now being made in England for early abolition," he would have to come up with some measure that would not bring "ruin" to the Arabs but appease the antislavery groups. See Africa No. 7 (1896), *Correspondence Respecting Slavery in the Zanzibar Dominions* (London: Harrison and Sons, 1896). Hardinge to Earl of Kimberly, April 29, 1895.

[40] Africa No. 7 (1896), *Correspondence Respecting Slavery in the Zanzibar Dominions* (London: Harrison and Sons, 1896). Hardinge to Earl of Kimberly, April 29, 1895.

[41] FIM PZ(F)/3, Meeting minute book for 1898–1902; Africa No.4 (1901), *Correspondence Respecting Slavery and the Slave Trade in East Africa and the Islands of Zanzibar and Pemba.*

[42] Mr. Farler framed his desire to have slaves make agreements with their owners (rather than outright freedom) as a worry that slaves would be deserted in their old age. However, it had more to do with concerns over paying compensation to owners. Nonetheless, the records abound with complaints from officials that some owners manumitted slaves who were sick, disabled, or old; thus discouraging emancipation did not protect slaves. See Africa No. 6 (1895), *Correspondence Respecting Slavery in Zanzibar* (London: Harrison and Sons, 1896). Letters from Arthur Hardinge.

within the community was very different. Even though the children of both groups had equal right to inheritance by law, that right was not always applied in reality. All slaves, including concubines, received their independence in 1907 on the mainland and in 1909 in the island dominions of the Sultan. However, even then, many people continued to live as "slaves" because many formerly enslaved individuals continued to live on their former owners' lands and claim the patronage of their owners in exchange for their labor.[43] However, this was a relationship that could be broken by either side at any point after 1909 without legal recourse, which could leave elderly slaves in a particularly vulnerable position.[44]

Colonial officials and missionaries often reported affection between some owners and slaves, which they used to explain why only 15 percent of slaves sought emancipation once it was available.[45] According to Romero, in Lamu, some owners and slaves colluded for the owners to collect compensation for releasing their slaves, but then the slaves stayed with the owners.[46] This suggests that a bond between the two remained. Cooper argues that slaves "had to weigh the opportunities they would have" by leaving and that it was simply an economic decision on their part.[47] However, the life histories of slaves from the Banani mission outside Chake Chake indicate that it was not simply economics. The example of Fundi Kamna illustrates the possibility of a close bond between an owner and a slave.[48] Fundi Kamna was born to slave parents but stolen away from Zanzibar when he was about twelve. He was sold to his owner on Pemba, who took him into the household and made sure that Fundi Kamna learned a trade. When Fundi Kamna reached adulthood, his owner freed him voluntarily. Fundi Kamna continued to visit his owner as he aged and eventually paid for his owner's funeral. Seemingly, the relationship between the two was more of surrogate father to a forcibly orphaned boy than an owner/slave relationship. This example helps to explain why some slaves did not leave their owners. Many of the slaves who ended up at the Banani mission stated that they had good owners

---

[43] Mirza and Strobel, pp. 20–1; Romero, 1997, chap. 8.

[44] PNA AI1/44 HHSCZ, Civil Appeal No. 15 of 1934; even before 1909, older slaves had difficulties; see FIM PZ(F)/3, Meeting minute book for 1903–1915; see also reports for June 1904, January 1905, February 1906, and February 1907 for examples.

[45] Commissioner Farler to Sir Lloyd Mathews, January 26, 1900, in *British and Foreign State Papers*, p. 926.

[46] Patricia Romero, "Where Have All the Slaves Gone?: Emancipation and Post-Emancipation in Lamu, Kenya," *Journal of African History* 27, no. 3 (1986), p. 500.

[47] Cooper, 1980, p. 75.

[48] FIM TEMP MSS 419/1–7, Theodore Burtt, Notebook, 1899, Fundi Kamna.

but when the owners died and the children of their owners were not good, the slaves left. Thus a relationship that was beneficial to slaves was worth maintaining for some of them, yet the economics of vulnerability likely did factor into their decisions if no bond of affection or loyalty existed. If slaves no longer received benefits from their owners, such as clothing, support, and the right to earn their own income several days a week, these could all culminate in a reason to leave. While it may have been described as the owner being "bad," ex-slaves may have meant that it was no longer economically viable to remain enslaved. In the case of Mzuri Kwao, she told her story to Dr. O'Sullivan-Beare after she no longer valued her connection to an owner. Mzuri had stayed with her owner on the mainland for many years before she was sold by him. When her first owner sold her, Mzuri learned of the vulnerability of slaves to the whim of their owners and saw freedom as valuable to her.

Mzuri's story, as told to O'Sullivan-Beare, included a travelogue of her movements across modern-day Tanzania and a cast of characters in Pemba that demonstrates the interconnected lives of the men and women of various ethnic and social positions. Mzuri recounted her time spent with a network of people who dealt in the slave trade across the mainland and especially in the islands. Her path into slavery and to Pemba illustrates the typical routes of the slave caravans on the mainland in the late nineteenth century and the mechanics of the illegal slave trade in the 1890s. She was born on the mainland of the African continent to Manyema parents and was captured around 1890 by a slave caravan reputedly owned by the slave trader Tippu Tip.[49] After enslavement, Mzuri initially lived in Bagamoyo along the East African coast across from Pemba Island but soon moved with her owner to Ujiji in the interior lakes region 750 miles away from the coast. After about four years, she and her owner went to Kilwa on the southern Tanganyika coast – another trip of at least 750 miles – where he sold her to Hamadi bin Shorte. It is likely that Mzuri had been captured as a child and had reached puberty, precipitating her sale at Kilwa in the hopes of earning a higher price for her as a concubine. Hamadi bin Shorte, a notorious slave dealer on the coast and, being from the Comoros Islands, a French subject, took Mzuri to Zanzibar.[50] He smuggled Mzuri into Zanzibar Town, a feat that was

---

[49] Tippu Tip was one of the most famous slave traders on the East African coast in the nineteenth century. See Leda Farrant, *Tippu Tip and the East African Slave Trade* (New York: St. Martin's Press, 1975).

[50] The Comoros Islands are located between Madagascar and the East African mainland. The Comoros are considered part of the Swahili world but were colonized by the French

easy to do with one slave at time.[51] Mzuri did not remain in Zanzibar Town long, only about three months, during which time she lived with Hamadi's sisters, before Hamadi took her to Pemba to sell.

Mzuri's travels were not uncommon for slaves during the nineteenth century and illustrate the caravan routes and links between communities on the coast and those of the interior of eastern and central Africa.[52] Pemba was an end point for many slaves coming from the African interior, but certainly not for all slaves transported to the island. Histories recorded by Friends missionaries from a number of slaves living on their mission show the commonness of Mzuri's paths. For example, one woman named Chaosiku, who was born on the mainland in the 1850s, was transported back and forth between the coast and interior throughout her life.[53] After being kidnapped as a small child, she was transported to and sold in Zanzibar, where she lived for approximately ten years. She was then resold and sent to a location on the mainland, the name of which she could not remember. She remained on the mainland for at least sixteen years until her owner decided to sell her teenage son around 1895. Chaosiku asked to be sold instead of her son and was illegally bought by a Mpemba man, with whom she went to Pemba.[54]

Likewise, another woman named Zafarani was stolen from her home by people she described as WaNyao after she had reached puberty. She was taken to Kilwa and then embarked for Zanzibar, where she remained

instead of the British, which set up divisions between the region in the late nineteenth and early twentieth centuries. During the 1890s, many Zanzibaris claimed a Comorian identity because the French were more lenient about slave dealing and the British could not seize ships flying a French flag. One case from the Vice Consul records in Pemba suggests that individuals would claim to be Comorian but did not actually have Comorian ancestry, pointing to both the ways in which "identities" were claimed and the inability of the early colonial officials to pinpoint the meanings of particular identities. See ZNA AC5/4, Letter from Vice Consul O'Sullivan-Beare, October 25, 1899.

[51] Fitzgerald, p. 610: "[M]y interpreter Masud afterwards told me that slaves had been brought over on [the government steamer] ... the women being dressed in bright clothes by the Arabs, and passed off as their concubines." This would also help to explain why more women were enslaved in the 1890s because they were less likely to raise questions.

[52] Stephen J. Rockel, *Carriers of Culture: Labor on the Road in Nineteenth-Century East Africa* (Portsmouth, NH: Heinemann, 2006), p. xvii; Wright, 1993, pp. 4–7; Edward Alpers, "Story of Swema," in *Women and Slavery in Africa*, edited by Claire Robertson and Martin Klein (Madison: University of Wisconsin Press, 1983), pp. 189–98; Edward Alpers, *Ivory and Slaves in East Central Africa: Changing Pattern of International Trade in East Central Africa to the Later Nineteenth Century* (Berkeley: University of California Press, 1975).

[53] FIM TEMP MSS 419/1–7, Theodore Burtt, Notebook, 1899.

[54] FIM PZ(F)/3, Meeting minute book for 1898–1902.

for five months. She was then taken back to the mainland to Tanga, where she lived for many years. Eventually, her owners both died from small-pox, and their son pawned her to an Indian merchant. However, soon after being pawned, she was kidnapped by Shihiri Arabs and brought to Pemba, where she was purchased by a Mpemba man.[55] Zafarani died in 1930, indicating that she came to Pemba sometime after 1890, when the sale of slaves was illegal.[56] Numerous other accounts of the movements of enslaved men and women recorded by Friends missionaries tell the story of the multiplicity of slave routes from the interior to the coast.[57] While the stories of all these slaves ended in Pemba, their travelogues make it clear that many other slaves were sent on to work in Mauritius, Reunion, Madagascar, Oman, and Arabia or even back to the mainland, among other destinations.[58]

Mzuri's story also demonstrates the communication among slaves and their understanding of the new British laws. Mzuri went to O'Sullivan-Beare complaining that her owner was trying to *sell* her, which implies that she knew this was illegal. Other examples from the islands indicate that some slaves understood the laws concerning slavery and the sale and movement of slaves. Another woman named Mia went to O'Sullivan-Beare for help one year after Mzuri. Mia had been a freed slave who was kidnapped one night by her landlord and given to a man named Masood, who lived in an isolated district of Pemba.[59] When Mia took her case to O'Sullivan-Beare, she categorized her kidnapping and transfer to Masood as a *sale* of a slave, not as a kidnapping. Confronted with language describing the selling of a slave, O'Sullivan-Beare was forced to get involved in the case because the sale of slaves was illegal by that time. Mia's movement in the wider community before her abduction

[55] FIM TEMP MSS 419/1–7, Theodore Burtt, Notebook, 1899.

[56] It is unclear how old Zafarani was when she died; however, she was an adult at the time she was brought to Pemba, which means that she was at least twenty years old, if not more. Given that she died in 1930, if she had been twenty years old in 1890, she would have died at age sixty, a very old age for a woman on Pemba.

[57] I have found twenty-five such histories thus far in the FIM archives and have other records of slave "histories" from the Vice Consul records held in the Zanzibar National Archives.

[58] For a discussion of trade in the wider Indian Ocean, see several excellent articles in the book, *The Structure of Slavery in Indian Ocean, Africa and Asia*, edited by Gwyn Campbell (London: Routledge, 2004). Especially useful chapters are Gwyn Campbell, "Slavery and Other Forms of Unfree Labour in the Indian Ocean World," pp. vii–xxxii; and Richard B. Allen, "The Mascarene Slave-Trade and Labour Migration in the Indian Ocean During the Eighteenth and Nineteenth Centuries," pp. 33–50.

[59] AC9/2, ZNA, Vice Consul Pemba, letter, July 5, 1896.

offered her an opportunity to learn more about the new Vice Consul and his politics, as well as the 1873 decree against slave trading. Mia and Mzuri were not the only slaves who showed agency in their dealings with slave traders, owners, and the British colonial state. An earlier case from 1885 of a slave woman who did not want to be transferred by her owner to Pemba from Zanzibar again illustrates slaves' understanding of the 1873 decree. In that case, the slave woman told a friend who worked for the British Navy that she was being taken "against her will" to Pemba and on what day and boat she was leaving. After the boat got under way, the British Navy stopped it and liberated the female slave.[60] While many rural slaves did not know the details of decrees made by the Sultan, those who were able to move freely in their communities and urbanized areas such as Chake Chake and Zanzibar Town understood how to use the language of the law to protect their interests and freedom.[61] In the slave histories written by the Friends, most of the slaves sought their freedom when they heard from other slaves about the emancipation decree, suggesting that information initially acquired in urban areas flowed through the informal networks of slaves from village to village.[62]

The trade in slaves to Pemba was an essential aspect of society on the island in the nineteenth century; thus abolition of the trade and emancipation of slaves fundamentally changed Pemba society, even if the majority of slaves remained tied to their former owners. No longer were owners assured of the labor of their slaves, but slaves were also no longer guaranteed a home in their old age either. More than anything, the changes represented by the British orders increased the vulnerability of all people living on the island. However, Mzuri's story also points out the particular vulnerability of women, who were more likely to be kidnapped into slavery and had a harder time escaping it. The female actors in Mzuri's story demonstrate the difficulty women had in creating an identity of their own outside the space of a man.

---

[60] This manipulation of the system may not have been uncommon. In *Records from Correspondence with British Representatives and Agents Abroad and Reports from Naval Officers and the Treasury Relative to the Slave Trade, 1885* (London: Harrison and Sons, 1886), no. 101.

[61] FIM TEMP MSS 419/1–7, Theodore Burtt, Notebook, 1899. See examples of Mama Chogo and Mziwao, who did not seek emancipation until 1912 on Pemba because they did not learn about the emancipation order until then.

[62] Slaves were able to learn information from each other easily because of the twice-yearly clove harvests on Pemba, where laborers, including slaves, moved around, frequently working on different properties.

SLAVERY AND EMANCIPATION

As discussed in the Introduction, the number of slaves on the islands is unknown. However, I use the estimated number of 40,000 for Pemba based on Dr. O'Sullivan-Beare's 1899 estimate.[63] Adding to the confusion on the numbers is the instability of the free population who could be kidnapped into slavery as well.[64] Collectively, almost 12,000 slaves applied for freedom papers on Unguja and Pemba between 1897 and 1909, yet scholars agree that the majority of slaves did not apply for freedom.[65] While Theodore Burtt of the Friends may have claimed in 1898 that there were five women for every man on the island, the reality was less imbalanced.[66] Nonetheless, the number of female slaves seeking emancipation ranged anywhere from 55 to 63 percent per year.[67] This suggests that women were the majority of slaves, yet it could also indicate the particular difficulties women had in escaping slavery. While some men certainly stayed enslaved when their wives left, it was more often the other way around.[68] Contrary to suggestions made by colonial officials that enslaved women were mostly barren, of the ninety-four familial units who sought emancipation through the Friends in 1898 and 1899, 43 percent had children as part of the family.[69] This shows that enslaved women did have children; whether those children survived to adulthood is a different matter. It may be that slaves with small children were more likely to seek the help of Friends, and that is the reason so many children are documented in the Friends register. One of the other important distinctions to make is

---

[63] Welliver, pp. 63–90; Africa No. 4 (1901), *Correspondence Respecting Slavery and the Slave Trade in East Africa and the Islands of Zanzibar and Pemba*, Enclosure no. 4, Report for year, Pemba, by O'Sullivan-Beare.

[64] Africa No. 7 (1896), *Correspondence Respecting Slavery in the Zanzibar Dominions.*

[65] Cooper, 1980, p. 73; Welliver, pp. 68–70.

[66] Africa No. 6 (1898), *Correspondence Respecting the Abolition of the Legal Status of Slavery in Zanzibar and Pemba*, Enclosure no. 1 in No. 16, Letters from Mr. T. Burtt, FIM Pemba, September 4, 1897.

[67] FIM PZ(F)/3, Register of slaves, Banani, 1897–1909; ZNA AC5/5; 55 percent of slaves applying for freedom in 1899 were women; in 1901, it was 63 percent. In 1904, it was 56 percent.

[68] FIM TEMP MSS 419/1–7, Theodore Burtt, Notebook, 1899.

[69] For a discussion of birth rates, see Africa No. 4 (1909), *Dispatch from His Majesty's Agent and Consul General at Zanzibar Furnishing a Report on the Administration, Finance, and General Condition of the Zanzibar Protectorate*; Africa No. 4 (1901), *Correspondence Respecting Slavery and the Slave Trade in East Africa and the Islands of Zanzibar and Pemba*, p. 5; statistics drawn from FIM PZ(F)/3, Register of slaves, Banani, 1897–1909; Welliver states that anecdotal evidence suggests that slaves were not reproducing, p. 77.

that according to the 1910 census, children accounted for 28.5 percent of the population on Pemba. Children were not "freed" by the government because they were considered born free under the 1890 law. A total of 6,725 slaves sought their emancipation via the government on Pemba, but they likely brought almost 2,000 children with them into freedom; thus the percent of slaves "freed" by the government may be closer to 21 percent of the enslaved population.

What happened to those slaves who remained in bondage? Many just walked away from their owners' plantations and did not bother to get freedom papers.[70] Especially for men, this was an option because they could potentially hire themselves onto a boat leaving for the mainland as a sailor or as a porter for a caravan leaving for the hinterland. However, it was much more difficult for women to move freely off the island because boat manifests were checked by colonial officials, who questioned all women leaving. Adult women were ideally married and under the control of their spouses, so it was expected that any woman trying to travel would have to have the permission of a man, either her owner or her husband. A single woman traveling was highly suspect by colonial officials, who feared that unattached women were all "prostitutes."[71] Even though legally ex-slave women were jural majors once they received their emancipation, British officials had their own interpretation of what was acceptable for women, and one of those was not traveling alone. Thus the options for slaves, especially those who walked away from their owners, were highly gendered.

Escape was more difficult for women, as noted earlier, but another reason why many slaves did not leave their owners initially can be found in the rates of reenslavement. Consistently found in the stories of slaves are tales of obtaining their freedom only to be reenslaved at a later date through capture. In one case a slave tells of running away from a good owner because he did not want to be enslaved only to be recaptured into slavery and sold to a very bad owner.[72] As long as the status of slavery was legal in the vicinity of the islands, reenslavement was always a

---

[70] Cooper, 1980, p. 74; Welliver gives a number of other reasons as well, pp. 81–90. Very interestingly, Welliver quotes a court case where a WaPemba slave owner stated that although his slave continued to squat on his land, the slave refused to work for the owner, p. 69.

[71] Africa No. 4 (1901), *Correspondence Respecting Slavery and the Slave Trade in East Africa and the Islands of Zanzibar and Pemba.*

[72] FIM TEMP MSS 419/1–7, Theodore Burtt, Notebook, 1899. This is one reason that Welliver does not offer in his extensive list of reasons why slaves did not seek freedom.

possibility. Cooper argued that selling slaves once they had been brought into Zanzibar was "frowned upon."[73] Yet it happened all the time. Many slaves who went to the Vice Consul and Friends told stories of being resold several times in their lifetimes, including being kidnapped away from one owner and sold to another.[74] Mzuri's story illustrates this point because she was brought to Pemba and sold to one owner but was in the process of being resold. Emancipation might mean freedom, but freedom offered no security to individuals. At least if they were slaves, their owners would protest if they were kidnapped away, but as free people, they had very little recourse to help, reiterating the vulnerability of life for freeborn, as well as enslaved.

The comparison of efforts on the part of women and men to incorporate themselves into a community at emancipation is generally framed by the limitations faced by women in moving outside familial networks. Marcia Wright argues that because men were not an "integral part of domestic productive units," they could more easily move around.[75] She suggests that women, on the other hand, could and likely *had* to incorporate themselves into households in order to survive. As Wright notes, "[I]n times of extreme crisis, men raised capital by disposing of low-status women."[76] This suggests a level of powerlessness on the part of women in their relationships and could explain why so few slaves on Pemba sought emancipation. If the majority of slaves were women, and women were "exposed to the raw fact of negotiability" in their status, then for many women little benefit existed to being emancipated.[77] Clearly, Mzuri felt that it was worthwhile to seek her freedom, as did other women; however, slave accounts from the Friends Mission indicate that many female slaves remained with their owners until the owner's death unless they had a husband willing to run away with them.[78] This suggests that for the majority of enslaved women, they sought a network of support, whether through men or mission societies, when confronted with "freedom."

For all the people who sought their freedom, emancipation required a new terminology of status to coexist with the existing language of enslavement. The British, slaveholders, and former slaves all had to find

---

[73] Cooper, 1977, pp. 213–14.
[74] McMahon, 2012.
[75] Wright, 1993, p. 42.
[76] Wright, 1993, p. 43.
[77] Wright, 1993, p. 43.
[78] FIM TEMP MSS 419/1–7, Theodore Burtt, Notebook, 1899; see stories of Salama, Mama Chogo, Tafarani, Faida, Mama Juma, Bahati, and Sanura as case examples.

new ways to distinguish those who had received their freedom from those who had not, as well as distinguish between the different "forms" of emancipation. Previous to the government-imposed emancipation, when individuals received their freedom from their owners, they could adopt any of several appellations. People might continue to call themselves *wazalia* or in many cases sign their name ending with *hadim* ("servant of") or *maula* and the clan name of their former owner. These practices continued into the postemancipation era.[79] Some ex-slaves who were emancipated by the government then styled themselves as *hadim ya Sirkar*, or "servants of the government."[80] Nonetheless, some former slaves refused to accept this terminology because they were no longer working for their former owners; thus the slaveholding class came up with new terms. On Pemba, these differed from the more urban locations. As Dr. O'Sullivan-Beare described in 1899:

The Arabs experienced some difficulty at first in finding a suitable appellation for the freed slaves who entered into contracts, or otherwise took service with them; but they seem to have decided, ultimately, amongst themselves upon what strikes one as being a very odd term for that purpose. They elected, apparently, to speak of those freed slaves as "servants," for which expression there are, of course, corresponding words in Arabic and in ki-Swahili; but hearing us Europeans habitually address our house servants by the term "boy" – which is universally employed throughout the East in that connection – the Arabs evidently inferred that such must be the generic and proper term for a servant of any kind, and so they adopted it. Thus one now hears them constantly employ it to designate any freed slave in their service, whether the individual in question be male or female, while for the plural number they make use of the ki-Swahili prefix and, still ignoring any distinction of gender, speak of *waboy*![81]

Thus slaveholders on Pemba began to call their employees who were former slaves *boy* or *waboy*. On Zanzibar, they were generally referred to by slaveholders as *watu wangu* ("my people").[82] Illustrating the significance of the court system as an arbiter of social change, British officials working for the Sultan's government used the courts to enforce a language change by classifying all former slaves who worked on *mashamba*

[79] See, for example, *Zanzibar Gazette*, January 12, 1914, "Notice of the probate of Oman bin Ibrahim H. Mauli." The H. stands for *hadim*. Also, *Zanzibar Gazette*, October 9, 1911, "The *wakf* notice of Zahor Hadim Safer Juma. FIM TEMP MSS 419/1–7, Theodore Burtt, Notebook, 1899, story of Bahati.
[80] For example, see PNA AK1/198, Ferezi hadim Sirkari, September 16, 1912.
[81] Report by Vice Consul O'Sullivan on the Island of Pemba, 1899 (London, 1900).
[82] *Papers by Command*, Vol. 48 (parliamentary papers), no. 11, Enclosure no. 1, Sir Lloyd Mathews to Sir C. Eliot, Zanzibar, January 31, 1901.

as *wakulima* ("farm workers") and all other former slaves working for others as *watumishi* ("servants").[83]

Yet all this terminology of enslavement and emancipation describes how others situated the slaves and former slaves and does not help us to understand how these groups described themselves, especially after emancipation. While some former slaves took on the terminology of a "free person" (*mhuru*, pl. *wahuru*) early on, this is not a term found in the colonial documentation but rather in missionary dictionaries of the time. Officials noted the distinctions made among slaves and ex-slaves in their terminology for one another. Arthur Hardinge, the Consul General in Zanzibar, remarked that "there is, I believe, a good deal of difference made among slaves themselves between those of their own class who have been freed by their owners, in accordance with the Mahommedan law, and those freed by the government in defiance of it. The latter, who are known as *mateka*, are regarded by freemen and slaves alike as inferior socially."[84] *Mateka* means "war booty"; thus it implies an uncivilized person, a raw slave who did not know the difference between respectable forms of emancipation. However, Zanzibar was Hardinge's reference point. A 1902 report from Pemba noted that while initially there was a prejudice against *hadim wa sirka* ("government-emancipated slaves"), by 1902, there were too many to fully exact a social hierarchy based on this terminology, and while those individuals freed by their owners still viewed themselves as socially superior, they did not ostracize ex-slaves freed by the government.[85] Jeremy Prestholdt claims that slaves in Zanzibar remade themselves as *waungwana*, a term that denoted "gentility, freeborn status, and urbaneness." The association of the term with urban living may explain why it does not show up in the record for slaves and ex-slaves on Pemba.[86]

The probate records housed in the archives on Pemba indicate that some former slaves, especially those who were not born into slavery, began using their ethnic identity as a way to categorize themselves rather than

---

[83] *Papers by Command*, Vol. 48 (parliamentary papers), no. 11, Enclosure no. 1, Sir Lloyd Mathews to Sir C. Eliot, Zanzibar, January 31, 1901.

[84] FO2/284, Despatches to and from the Consul General Zanzibar, 1900.

[85] Africa No. 6 (1902), *Correspondence Respecting Slavery and the Slave Trade in East Africa and the Islands of Zanzibar and Pemba*, p. 22; also see the Friends comments that ex-slaves were not stigmatized as suggested by colonial officials., although the Friends certainly were biased in that respect. FIM, Annual Report for 1912. J. T. Last argued that slaves found "honour" in belonging to particular houses. Africa No. 14 (1904), *Correspondence Respecting Slavery in the Islands of Zanzibar and Pemba*.

[86] Prestholdt, pp. 140–1.

rely on a term borne out of the institution of enslavement. For example, in 1910, Baraka Mnyasa did not signify in his will that he was a former slave, and it was only in the testimony of a man who had been held by the same slaveholder that Baraka's slave past comes into the record. Instead, he went by his ethnic identity, Nyassa.[87] This shift to mainland identities was noticeable in the Friends' slave register as well. Through 1901, most slaves seeking their freedom only gave their names, but after 1902, the register began recording the mainland ethnicity of the slaves, as well as names.[88] As the census records of 1924 indicate, many former slaves began calling themselves Swahili. A ten-year sample (1913–23) of the probate and *wakf* notices from the *Zanzibar Gazette* corroborate this shift because many of the people classified as Waswahili had names indicating their former slave status.[89] Historically, the term "Swahili" has had a very different meaning between the coastal communities of Mombasa, Bagamoyo, and Lamu and the islands of Zanzibar and Pemba, where it quickly became associated with "free slave" in the twentieth century.[90] People who described themselves on Pemba in the nineteenth century as Swahili had often specified their identity by the twentieth century with a clan name to distance themselves from people of slave descent.[91] Yet, as

[87] PNA AK1/46; PNA AK1/3316, Probate record of Msabah bin Songoro, March 1935, is another probate case from 1935 where it is not clear that the deceased was a former slave. He was Mgindo, and his executors identified themselves as Zaramo, Mnyasa, and Shirazi – all of which could suggest a variety of scenarios. The one point it does indicate is that many individuals with "outsider" identities allied themselves with other "outsiders" because normally Mgindo, Zaramo, and Mnyasa, all mainland ethnic groups, would not be socializing with each other. However, it is far more likely that these three men had been enslaved to one owner and built a connection with one another. The deceased's lack of children, even though he was married, also indicated his slave identity.

[88] FIM PZ(F)/3, Register of slaves, Banani, 1897–1909. It is unclear whether this shift was something the slaves insisted on or a noticeable change in the way missionaries recorded the names. Either way, it shows a consciousness among people living on Pemba of an ethnic identity as significant to the attachment of individual's names.

[89] See, for example, *Zanzibar Gazette*, October 13, 1913, March 23, 1914, April 19, 1915, May 3, 1915, December 10, 1917, and September 7, 1923. As Frederick Cooper argued, many former slaves had identifiable first names such as Juma, Mabruk, Baraka, essentially non-Muslim names that indicated their slave heritage. However, names cannot always indicate slave identity because the most famous and powerful Arab in the Wete region during the late nineteenth century was Mohammed bin Juma.

[90] Laura Fair discusses the census records of 1924, 1931, and 1948 as illustrating the way former slaves shifted their ethnic identities and moved into "mainstream" Zanzibar society. Fair, 2001, pp. 28–41.

[91] PNA No Accession Number: Kadhi's Court, Wete, Civil Case No. 253 of 1945, Hamida binti Athman vs. Abdulla bin Omar and Athman bin Omar. I photographed this case in 2002, but it was no longer in the archives when I returned in 2006 thus it does not have a proper accession number.

the case of Baraka Mnyasa shows, not all freed slaves defined themselves as Swahili either. This was the terminology of use in the probate records, where Hashima binti Baraka Mgindo was described as "a Swahili and one of H. H.'s subjects."[92] Hashima's ethnic identifier was Mgindo, showing that she was originally from the mainland. Her will indicates that she was a former slave, and as such, the colonial probate court defined her as "Swahili," even though her mainland ethnic identity was known. Because she was formerly enslaved, the British defined her as "Swahili" in 1934; thus it is unclear how many ex-slaves actually self-identified as Swahili. Nonetheless, ex-slaves began identifying themselves in the same way as free people through an ethnic affiliation rather than a term signifying an occupation or position in the household of a slaveholder.

When ex-slaves used a specific ethnic identity, even one from the mainland, it demonstrated that they aimed to assert the *heshima* of a freeborn person. A *mzalia*, to whom slave owners generally accorded a higher status than those enslaved after their births, was not born free and technically had no ethnic identity of his or her own, leaving the individual perpetually "enslaved." *Wazalia* were more likely to use *hadim* or *maula* and the clan name of their owner; nonetheless, the clan appellation was not their own. Numerous cases show that ex-slaves used the terminology of *maula* or *hadim*, indicating that they were manumitted by their owners.[93] However, claiming to be *hadim* also implied a continued relationship with their owner, something that many ex-slaves were unwilling to do. But was it a strategic effort on the part of ex-slaves to use a mainland ethnic identity or were they forced to by neighbors, peers, and the elite, who never let them "forget" their mainland ethnic affiliations?[94] The use of mainland ethnicities was a way for former slaves to distance themselves from their enslavement and as such their owners. The case of Baraka Mnyasa is particularly insightful for showing how a former slave claimed a genuine position in the community as a devout Muslim through his pious actions while rejecting the relationship of slavery that in many ways legitimated his "Muslim-ness." Definitions of enslavement

[92] PNA AK1/3310; for other examples, see PNA AK1993, Probate record of Waziri bin Khamis el-Murimi, November 1925; PNA AK1/2773, Probate record of Alley bin Usi Mtumbatu, June 1928; and PNA AK1/4209, Probate record of Deluu binti Simba Mhiyao, November 1941.

[93] See, for example, *Zanzibar Gazette*, January 12, 1914, "Notice of the Probate of Oman bin Ibrahim H. Mauli; also see *Zanzibar Gazette*, October 9, 1911, "The *wakf* Notice of Zahor hadim Safer Juma. Newman, p. 33; PNA AI1/19.

[94] As Fair shows, Siti binti Saad, the famous taarab singer who was also an ex-slave, was never allowed to forget her past. This suggests that for some ex-slaves, trying to "remake" themselves was a futile effort, and they knew it. Fair, 2001, pp. 169–224.

such as raw slave versus *mzalia* implied that slave owners were the cause of slaves' conversion to Islam; thus enslavement became a means of legitimating a person's conversion to Islam in the eyes of slave owners. This allowed the slave-owning elite a measure of social hegemony by continuing to place themselves above ex-slaves. The adoption of mainland ethnic identities offered some ex-slaves on Pemba a way to reject their subjective position in the community. Their rejection of their owners' power by seeking emancipation through the government was the first symbolic move they made to reject the power of slaveholders.

The use of mainland ethnicities is an interesting case on Pemba because most scholarship focuses on the use of terms such as *waungwana* or "Swahili" to "remake" or "reidentify" ex-slaves living in Zanzibar.[95] As Laura Fair argues, the term "Swahili" came to signify ex-slaves living in urban Zanzibar. By looking at the census records, the changing terminology, and how people "reidentified" themselves in the early twentieth century, she argues that we can see the mutability of identity.[96] Fair states that people did not completely abandon earlier ethnicities; rather, they learned to manipulate the identities of the colonial state. However, the records on Pemba indicate that it was the state that created categories and placed people in them rather than people placing themselves in those categories. When looking at how people living on Pemba identified themselves in the probate and civil court records and among the Friends mission records, few self-identified as Swahili. Even the 1910 census, which stated that there were over 70,000 "Swahili" living on Pemba, grouped people who otherwise perceived and reported their identities as WaPemba, WaTumbatu, Kilinidini, Mnyasa, and Mgindo, among others. When asked in court to identify themselves, people rarely used the term "Swahili" – even ex-slaves. As illustrated in the Bonus Scheme records of the 1920s, over eighty-five different "ethnic" identities were self-reported to colonial officials.[97] This suggests that those jumps in identity as offered in the census records of 1924, 1931, and 1948 were as much about the colonial interpretation of African identities than a reality on the ground.[98]

---

[95] Prestholdt, pp. 138–42; Fair, 2001, pp. 28–33. Even I suggested this argument in my dissertation; McMahon, 2005, chap. 2.

[96] Fair, 2001, pp. 28–33.

[97] McMahon, 2005, p. 58; see also ZNA AP29/5–8, Clove bonus registers. The Bonus Scheme records listed every clove tree owner in the islands. These records listed the person's name, ethnicity, and number of clove trees owned.

[98] Records from the 1948 census show, as Fair notes, that census takers were instructed to identify people in particular ways ethnically based on their answers to questions. We have no evidence of this kind for the earlier censuses, but given the British officials' changing interpretations of identities during that time, this would not be surprising. Batson, Notes on census.

Historians of Zanzibar generally focus on slaves' efforts to "remake" their identities, assuming that only through remaking their identities did former slaves achieve agency in their lives and acceptance as residents in the islands. However, on Pemba, some ex-slaves rejected coastal identities while still maintaining the practices of devout Muslims, showing that a coastal identity alone did not define a person as a civilized Muslim.[99]

VULNERABILITY

The position of women in Pemban society was obviously one of contrasts – some women relied on men and others did not, some were vulnerable and others were not. The sources for examining women's lives often highlight the vulnerability of women, and yet Mzuri's case indicates a woman who sought solutions to her vulnerability through the colonial state. Other sources indicate that women could be mercenary at times and left ex-slave men in dire straits.[100] A young woman such as Mzuri had a variety of options: She could do the work of a day laborer carrying loads (*kibarua*), she could be a prostitute, she could arrange to marry a man who offered to maintain her, among other options, but it was a risky existence. Female *vibarua* often did not get paid enough to support themselves and had to live collectively or within a family. Prostitutes had to rely on male customers and harassment from the state. Married women hoped their husbands always maintained them, but the sad reality for poorer women was that this rarely happened. The Friends commented in 1898 that "the great difficulty regarding native women is for the most part in their exceedingly dependent position. They are usually dependent on their owners for the means of subsistence, and it requires unusual force of character and boldness for them to strike out a new course of their own."[101] Older women in some cases found it easier (and perhaps safer) to remove themselves from village life in order to live outside the notice of "men or ghosts."[102] Rather than showing independence,

---

[99] In many respects, this buttresses Glassman's arguments about later issues of identity in Zanzibar concerning elite Arab efforts to rigidly define Arab versus African. See Glassman, 2004, 2005.

[100] FIM TEMP MSS 419/1–7, Theodore Burtt, Notebook, 1899, Songoro Makonde.

[101] Newman, pp. 109–20. Of course, they were conflating all "natives" to mean slave or ex-slave women.

[102] Craster cites an old widow who lived near a British grave site who said that she had no fear because "neither men nor ghosts take any notice of a withered old woman like me." Craster, pp. 70–1. Given that we cannot know the Swahili word she used for "ghosts" it is likely she meant spirits. Likewise, in UMCA A1 (XIV) no. 54, "The Two Thieves of

in many aspects, Mzuri's life history emphasized women's dependence on men in coastal society. As concubines, wives, sisters, mothers, daughters, or slaves, women relied on the men in their lives for economic support.[103] But this reliance was a two-way street, as Mzuri's owner Hamadi relied on a network of women for his illegal activities, and in turn, he supported them with the profits of his slave trading and the protection of his reputation.

During her stay on Zanzibar, Mzuri lived under the watchful eye of two of Hamadi's sisters, and after three months with the sisters, Hamadi took Mzuri to Pemba to sell her. On Pemba, Hamadi had one of his female slaves on the island, Mami Rehani, find a buyer for Mzuri. Mami was Hamadi's slave-trading agent, although she was still his slave and, therefore, his dependent. Mami told Hamadi that she knew of a recently married woman who wanted a slave, and she soon sought out the husband in order to negotiate a price. It took some organization, but eventually in 1894 Mami facilitated contact between Hamadi and Nasoro Mega, the husband of the newly married woman, to conclude the sale. Four witnesses were brought to certify the sale – three free men and one slave man. The sale illustrates that even though the men knew that the proceedings were illegal according to the 1890 decree, Hamadi and Nasoro were businessmen and knew that any unwitnessed transaction could have later repercussions. They were both careful to have the money counted out and exchanged in front of the four witnesses. The account of the transaction shows three aspects of life on Pemba in 1894: People did what they wanted regardless of British laws and did not expect to face repercussions for breaking the laws; it was a society based on oral contracts and negotiations; and lastly, some slaves held a higher status in the community because normally slave witnesses only counted as half of a witness due to stipulations as such in the Quran, suggesting that this slave was particularly trusted and held a higher status in the community.

When Nasoro married his African wife, Sanura, he legitimated the marriage by paying a dowry to Binti Asmane, an Arab woman who "treated

Pemba," by Leslie Matolo, a translation from Swahili, n.d., the mother lives in a shed in the middle of nowhere by herself where she "likes to stay here by herself, away from people and their noise."

[103] See Richard L. Roberts, "Women, Household Instability, and the End of Slavery in Banamba and Gumbu, French Soudan, 1905–1912," in *Women and Slavery: Africa, the Indian Ocean World, and the Medieval North Atlantic*, edited by Gwyn Campbell, Suzanne Miers, and Joseph C. Miller (Athens: Ohio University Press, 2007).

the girl as if she were her own daughter."[104] But Sanura never left her "mother's" house, and so Nasoro continued to support Binti Asmane as well as his wife.[105] He gave Binti Asmane money regularly because she was poor, and although he bought Mzuri for his new wife, she was an asset to the entire household. The fact that Sanura did not (or perhaps could not) leave the house makes it clear that although Binti Asmane thought of her as her "daughter," Sanura was a slave, just like Mzuri. However, Nasoro's payment of a dowry and continued financial support of Binti Asmane implies that he considered Binti Asmane an in-law despite being his wife's owner and of no blood relation to her. Furthermore, Nasoro did not purchase Sanura from her owner; he *married* her and must therefore have done so for love or desire rather than economic investment. There was one final twist to the story: Binti Asmane was, reputedly, "a half caste who was a former slave herself." To sum up, Binti Asmane, a former slave, bought a slave girl Sanura, who, in turn, received a slave of her own (Mzuri Kwao) on marriage to Nasoro. Mzuri was therefore a gift for the household of Binti Asmane, a household in which all three women had been or were still enslaved but now related to each other and to Nasoro through new kinship ties. This case illustrates the axiom provided by British officials when explaining slavery in the islands to abolitionists in the metropole: Slaves did not long for freedom, but for ownership of other slaves and integration into existing social networks.[106] The web of "kinship" that O'Sullivan-Beare uncovered in Mzuri Kwao's case sheds light on the complex ways in which freeborn, *hadim*, and slaves defined their relationships with one another. As Chapter 6 demonstrates, it was not uncommon for one household to contain ex-slaves, current slaves, and freeborn members.

Dr. O'Sullivan-Beare initially accepted at face value Binti Asmane's assertion that she was an Arab woman when he questioned her about

---

[104] I use the term "dowry" here because Nasoro paid the money to Binti Asmane, not to Sanura. As the bride, Sanura should have received the dower, but because she was a slave, her owner received the payment, making it a dowry.

[105] The name of Nasoro's African wife was never given in the record. I use the name Sanura as a place marker to make the story clearer for the reader.

[106] *Report by Vice Consul O'Sullivan on the Island of Pemba 1896–1897*. O'Sullivan-Beare tells the story of a slave girl who came to him to complain of cruelty from her mistress. The mistress had flogged her badly (the mistress was an Arab woman). He sent her to the Wali, who then consulted back with O'Sullivan-Beare about what to do. The girl was freed and the mistress was fined because she could not be imprisoned. The girl was given the fine money (40 rupees). "On my asking her what she proposed to do with such a sum, she naively told me that she hoped to be able to purchase therewith a young slave for herself."

Mzuri. It was later, on further inquiry, that Dr. O'Sullivan-Beare learned that Binti Asmane was a "half-caste" of possible slave ancestry. Regardless of whether she had a slave ancestry, the accusation by her neighbors affected her reputation, her level of *heshima* in the community, and the way government officials responded to her. As demonstrated in Chapters 3 and 4, in a society based on oral contracts such as Pemba, reputation and respectability were valuable currencies. Consistently, reputation was used in the courts as a marker of "credit." The emancipation decree of 1897 required compensation to be paid to owners, but the Slavery Commissioner would not pay out until a person of impeccable reputation vouched for the slave owner. This required slave owners to have good enough reputations that others would risk their own *heshima* for them. The fact that Binti Asmane's status was in question and that her neighbors willingly impugned her *heshima* through their testimony to the Vice Consul had economic as well as social consequences, suggesting that her identity was questioned because of her poverty rather than any evidence otherwise.

Although most slaves purchased their freedom before they could or would be able to buy a slave for their own use, some slaves along the coast did own other slaves.[107] Generally, the slaves who were owned by other slaves were women because women subordinated to an owner themselves then had difficulty exerting control over their male slaves. Also, women's jobs were the least desirable; therefore, owning a slave was one way for wealthier slaves (and concubines in some cases) to demonstrate that they were above such duties themselves. Pamela Scully's work in the Western Cape of South Africa suggests that male slaves in a highly patriarchal society often dominated the women in their lives in an effort to compensate for their own constrained social positions.[108] In Zanzibar, the ability to subjugate dependent women served as a relative marker of status for both women and men.

Mzuri's case illustrates the very active role that women of varying statuses played in the illegal slave trade. Often the slave trade is discussed by scholars as a "male domain" in terms of the capturing, transporting, and selling of slaves.[109] Hamadi fit that model with his purchase of

[107] FIM TEMP MSS 419/1–7, Theodore Burtt, Notebook, 1899; Africa No. 6 (1895), *Correspondence Respecting Slavery in Zanzibar*, p. 41.

[108] Pamela Scully, *Liberating the Family? Gender and British Slave Emancipation in the Rural Western Cape, South Africa, 1823–1853* (Portsmouth, NH: Heinemann, 1997), pp. 167–75.

[109] An exception to this rule is the female slave traders of West Africa. For example, see George Brooks, "A Nhara of the Guinea-Bissau Region: Mae Aurelia Correia," in

Mzuri and her transport from Kilwa to Zanzibar and then to Pemba. However, women played an important role in his network, too. His sisters, not Hamadi himself, harbored Mzuri. It is likely that the sisters were "training" Mzuri in an effort to make her more salable. It was then Mami Rehani, not a man, who found a buyer for her owner. This tells us that women were active participants in the trade, regardless of their dependent positions vis-à-vis the men in their lives. Mzuri's story demonstrates the vulnerability of women during this period, a vulnerability that never goes away, and yet her story shows that women did have agency in finding ways to take care of themselves, although it was often through an alliance with a brother, husband, or slave owner.

The complicated nature of slavery, identity, status, gender, and reputation in the early years of the British Protectorate of Zanzibar is illuminated through Mzuri's story. Slavery was endemic in Pemban society and could be oppressive in ways that made Mzuri seek her emancipation. Yet slaves often had many freedoms, as shown with Mami Rehani and Sanura, Nasoro's wife. Mami Rehani lived independent of her owner Hamadi, but he could rely on her to help him in his business, even though it was illegal. Sanura was able to marry an elite free man, who paid *mahari* ("dower") for her. Slaves could be included in or excluded from the families to which they were connected. John Farler reported that many slaves expressed contentment with their workload and felt real affection for the family for whom they worked.[110] When Friends missionaries asked former slaves about their owners, the vast majority said that they had good owners, and, if not, then they found ways to leave.[111] Yet others, especially those who worked in the fields, did not want to remain with their owners and sought their freedom at any cost, as confirmed by the nearly 12,000 slaves who received their emancipation from the government. The complexity of the relationships between slaves and owners further expanded after the abolition of slavery in 1897.

Women and Slavery in Africa, edited by Clarie C. Robertson and Martin A. Klein (Madison: University of Wisconsin Press, 1983).

[110] Commissioner Farler to Sir Lloyd Mathews, January 26, 1900, in *British and Foreign State Papers*, p. 926.

[111] FIM TEMP MSS 419/1–7, Theodore Burtt, Notebook, 1899. Slaves responded that they left if their good owner died and they were inherited by children who were not good owners. Also, some had good owners and then were kidnapped away and taken to bad owners. The Friends were not disposed to owners, and their records show a certain surprise that many of the slaves were happy with their owners.

CONCLUSION

Pemba is often presented as a rural, "backward" island off the beaten path of history in the region and lacking in the cosmopolitan character of the cities of Zanzibar Town, Mombasa, and other locations.[112] Robert Lyne noted in 1905 that "the Waswahili from Zanzibar laugh at the Wapemba, they call them foolish."[113] Even Arabs living on Pemba were perceived to be "wilder" and more dangerous than Arabs living elsewhere.[114] Yet the story of Mzuri defies this characterization of Pemba because the people with whom she interacted included Africans, Arabs, Indians, Comorians, and British – individuals from throughout the Indian Ocean world. Her story shows the deep links between Pemba and the rest of the Indian Ocean communities during the 1890s. Pemba was far from removed but rather was a central transit point for people, ideas, and agricultural produce. However, Pemba lacked both the concentrations of population and the wealth found in the coastal cities that allowed for cosmopolitan ideas to take hold.

Mzuri's story also shows that women were expected to assume the consequences for men's misbehavior on Pemba. Consistently in the colonial records from 1895 to the 1940s, men expected their female slaves and relatives to endure male misuse of their property, desertion from husbands, and even forced marriage as early as the ages of nine or ten. The records do show moments when women contested this control, such as when Mzuri sought her freedom two years before the emancipation decree was passed. However, the documents often hint at the times when women accepted the behavior of their male relatives and owners, such as when Binti Asmane tried to "protect" Nasoro in the British court by claiming Mzuri as her slave rather than his because she was not a British subject and therefore could legally own slaves (if they had been purchased before 1890). Nonetheless, in the postemancipation period, women began to shift the gender norms and expectations that had existed on Pemba previously. Female slaves refused to become concubines but accepted their position as enslaved. Sisters who had previously allowed their brothers

---

[112] Although in recent scholarship this has more to do with Pemba being closed off from outsiders for a generation during the revolutionary era. Anthony Clayton and Linda Giles were two of the only Westerners to visit Pemba for a twenty-year period. Little work was done on the island until the 1990s, and even then, the number of researchers is considerably fewer than on Unguja.

[113] Lyne, p. 241.

[114] McMahon, 2005, p. 153.

to pawn their land eventually refused to accept such practices and went to court to save their property. Women still remained dependent on men in many cases, but increasing numbers of women in the twentieth century used the court system to assert what they viewed as "their rights," and the courts were no longer the domain of men.[115]

[115] Elke Stockreiter argues similarly that women increasingly used and won in the courts at the turn of the century. Stockreiter points out that this contradicts Laura Fair's statements about the inability of women to effectively use the courts. However, both Stockreiter and I are looking at local women challenging men within their communities, and Fair was analyzing several cases where elite women were challenging the colonial state. Stockreiter, pp. 133–4; Fair, 2001, pp. 125–9.

3

Reputation and Disputing in the Courts

During the colonial period, British officials introduced a new emphasis on the courts as one of the main locations in which the colonial state could both exercise its authority over the colonized and try to shape cultural behaviors and expectations.[1] In June of 1917, when Mtwana bin Feruzi brought an unusual case to the magistrates' court, Magistrate J. E. R. Stephens was unsure of how to handle the case and wrote to the attorney general for reassurance that he had taken the correct path. Mtwana accused his sister and uncle of being *wachawi* ("witchdoctors," s. *mchawi*; *uchawi*, "witchcraft"). Stephens was stumped as to how to proceed because the government did not have a witchcraft ordinance, so he could not charge the two with practicing witchcraft, as found elsewhere on the continent. He also complained that Mtwana did not offer "a tittle of evidence" of a crime. Mtwana simply explained in the court that he would see his sister in his dreams and then he would wake up and find a *komba* ("bushbaby") in his room eating his bananas. Mtwana was convinced that his sister had turned herself into the *komba* and that she was coming into his room to lure him to a *wachawi* feast in which he would be the meal. Instead of being shocked by these accusations, the British court official dismissed them as being the "hallucinations of a disordered brain." Rather than handle the case as a criminal procedure, Stephens used local cultural principles by forcing the uncle and sister to take an Islamic oath that they were not *wachawi* and would not practice *uchawi*. While the historical records show cases where individuals

[1] See similar argument in Kollmann, pp. 5–17.

71

complained to officials about their fears of relatives' practicing *uchawi*, Mtwana is one of the few who brought a complaint into the courts.[2] It appears that Mtwana's point of bringing his accusation into a public forum was because he understood the courts as a location for debating the reputation of members of the community.

The conversations Stephens conducted in the court during Mtwana's case indicate the ways in which the court systems, both of the British magistrate and the Islamic *kadhi* courts, were a site to debate the reputation of individuals within the Pemban communities. In deciding what to do about the case, Stephens began asking other people in the court – his clerk and *askari* ("police officer"), as well as litigants and witnesses waiting to have their cases heard – what they thought of *uchawi* and whether they believed in it. This discussion of belief in *uchawi* demonstrates how community values were publicly debated within the courts. Some people in the court denied believing in *uchawi*, but others openly admitted their beliefs. One person in the court claimed Mtwana's uncle was a wizard based on "his eyes." Nathalie Arnold argues that the eyes and the metaphor of "seeing" what others could not see were viewed as standard descriptions of *wachawi*; thus the uncle's eyes were examined by people in the court and pronounced on. Stephens does not record how the uncle and sister responded to this dissection of their appearance and reputation as the community debated whether or not they were *wachawi*, but it is unlikely that they mutely sat in the court. On that June day, the court became a theater where Pembans debated the practices of *uchawi*, along with the reputations of two people. Having a reputation as *wachawi* could give people power and authority in their communities, but admitting to the reputation was not something most people wished to do, especially in such a public forum, because it also implied that the people purposely caused others harm.

Courts along the Swahili coast have acted as arbiters of reputation for a long time. Although most of the scholarship focuses on *kadhi* courts as institutions of "family law," even these cases demonstrate the debates over reputation and respectability in the courts.[3] In many parts

---

[2] Missionaries and others brought complaints to officials, but this is the only case in which I can find a record concerning *uchawi* accusations going to court.

[3] Hirsch, 1998, *passim*; Erin Stiles, "A *Kadhi* and His Court: Marriage, Divorce, and Zanzibar's Islamic Legal Tradition" (Ph.D. dissertation, Washington University, 2002), *passim*. Anthropological works on *kadhi* courts do not discuss in detail the ideas of reputation and respectability, yet the concepts are implicated in the ways judges make their

of the Islamic world in the nineteenth and early twentieth centuries, colonizers introduced new court systems that sidelined *sheria* ("Islamic") courts to deal with "family law."[4] Colonial officials slowly moved the limits of what cases a *kadhi* ("Islamic judge," pl. *makadhi*) could hear. In the Zanzibar Islands, first they removed serious criminal cases, then all criminal cases, and eventually civil cases with a dispute involving over 500 rupees. Each shift moved the *kadhi* courts closer and closer to "family law" until by the 1930s, most cases being heard were about divorce and small disputes. Yet, even in the space of familial disputes, in order to make an oath, a person's reputation was examined.[5] Susan Hirsch's work in Mombasa shows how women used language to present themselves to the *makadhi* as persevering wives and, as such, having a reputation of respectability. While the cases Hirsch discusses were not heard in a public forum, the outcomes were public because either a couple was divorced by the *kadhi* or not. People in the community knew who won the case, but they did not have input into the judges' decisions on cases, which is very different from the early colonial period on Pemba. Even when a new courthouse was built in Chake Chake in the 1950s, the court room was still open for members of the community to participate.

A few differences existed between the colonial court systems on Pemba Island and Unguja Island. In the early years, Unguja did not have *liwali* ("governors"), whereas Pemba did. Difference in the size of the courts was significant between the two islands. On Pemba, for each judge, there was one clerk who also acted as an interpreter and one *askari* to help the judge. However, on Unguja, for each judge, there were five clerks and interpreters and four *askari*s.[6] Unguja also had more judges than Pemba, which encouraged "court shopping" in the early period. Anne Bang and Elke Stockreiter argue that in the pre-1908 period, litigants would consider the different judges and how they might interpret the case

rulings. Elke Stockreiter does not discuss the reputation of litigants but rather colonial officials' concerns with the reputation of the courts and judges. Stockreiter, pp. 76–80.

[4] Iris Agmon, *Family and Court: Legal Culture and Modernity in Late Ottoman Palestine* (Syracuse, NY: Syracuse University Press, 2006), pp. 6–7; Stockreiter argues vehemently that *makadhi* defended their control over "family law" rather than the colonial state relegating family law to them; Stockreiter, pp. 37–44; Dominique Sarr and Richard Roberts, "The Jurisdiction of Muslim Tribunals in Colonial Senegal, 1857–1932," in *Law in Colonial Africa*, pp. 131–45.

[5] Agmon, p. 86.

[6] PRO FO2/188, Despatches to and from the Consul General Zanzibar, 1899.

and then take their case to the judge they thought would be best.[7] It also appears that courts on Unguja, which were held in enclosed buildings, were less public than on Pemba.[8] Especially in the transitional emancipation period, missionaries were important interlocutors in the district courts on Pemba, but it is unclear if missionaries on Unguja participated at all in the courts.[9]

Missionaries, particularly the Quakers (Friends), offered new forms of patronage to ex-slaves on Pemba, especially in the courts. The role of the Friends delineates an important point about court cases on Pemba, one raised by Richard Roberts in his work on Mali. As he notes, in all the court cases he examined, the cases were about getting "definitive judgments rather than reconciliation."[10] For ex-slaves who brought cases to court, they wanted a final judgment in their favor. Before bringing a case to the *kadhi* or district courts, a person generally exhausted all means of reconciliation, such as councils of the *watu wazee* ("elders") or the *masheha* pictured in Figure 3.1 ("village-level government officials"). Unevenness in status and reputation between disputing parties could affect how reconciliation efforts were carried out; thus a lower-status person may have felt that he or she did not receive a fair outcome and sought to bring his or her case to court. Ex-slaves who had left their owners were also hampered by any ill-will held by ex-owners, who may or may not have been the other disputants in the case. Patronage was still an element in Pemban society that helped to get cases to court before 1910, and the Friends missionaries were important interlocutors for some litigants, especially ex-slaves.

---

[7] Anne Bang, "Cosmopolitanism Colonised? Three Cases from Zanzibar, 1890–1920," in *Struggling with History: Islam and Cosmopolitanism in the Western Indian Ocean*, edited by Edward Simpson and Kai Kresse (New York: Columbia University Press, 2008), pp. 178–9; However, Stockreiter argues that the ability to "court shop" was removed by a 1904 decree stating that litigants had to go to the judge of the district in which they resided to handle their disputes; Stockreiter, p. 57; Richard Roberts calls this "venue shopping" and argues this was not an effort about securing "the best judgment ... but to underscore their strategic evaluation of different legal outcomes available at different courts"; Roberts, 2005, p. 232.

[8] Stockreiter, p. 37.

[9] Little work has been done on missionaries in Zanzibar, and studies that involve courts do not mention missionaries at all. Julia Allen gives a brief overview of the work of the UMCA with ex-slaves in Zanzibar, but it does not mention courts or individual Africans. See Julia Allen, "Slavery, Colonialism and the Pursuit of Community Life: Anglican Mission Education in Zanzibar and Northern Rhodesia 1864–1940," *History of Education* 37, no. 2 (March 2008), pp. 207–26.

[10] Roberts, 2005, p. 323.

FIGURE 3.1. The *Sheha* of Vitongoji and his retainers. (Reprinted from J. E. E. Craster, *Pemba: The Spice Island of Zanzibar.* London: T.F. Unwin, 1913.)

In the end, though, the colonial courts changed, and the missionaries no longer acted as intermediaries for ex-slaves. After 1910, the colonial courts, including the *kadhi* courts, became systematized as a site to contest power and reputation.[11] Nancy Shields Kollmann argued that "litigation

[11] Iris Agmon argues against using the term "qadi-justice" or in Swahili terms "*kadhi* courts" because it alludes to an Orientalist discourse of the *kadhi* as a singular judge who does not base his decisions wholly on *sheria* but rather on his own discretion. I continue to use the term "*kadhi* courts" in an effort to distinguish between *makadhi, liwali,*

over honor can be the last step in an escalating tension between parties that can then be settled by the cathartic experience of public exposure."[12] As the case of Mtwana demonstrated, reputations were constructed and deconstructed in the courts in very important ways. The hermeneutics of reputation allowed even a lowly *askari* the opportunity to pronounce on the reputation of others and have his opinion heard, even if it was among a cacophony of other voices. While Mtwana's case was unique for its focus in the records of court cases on Pemba, it represents the mechanisms in place for changing reputations. Moreover, it demonstrates how Pembans used the courts in an effort to shift the relations of power within communities, neighborhoods, and families.

COURTS ON PEMBA

When Dr. O'Sullivan-Beare was assigned to be the Vice Consul on Pemba in 1895, he found a court system that was inconsistent in its handling of disputes. Across the island, a series of *makadhi* settled disputes. However, the qualifications to be a *kadhi* on Pemba were not standardized, and often the most learned Arab in the area constituted himself "a *kadhi*." Dr. O'Sullivan-Beare found that most people agreed that one man, Rashid bin Mohamed el-Mosli, was the most learned in the *sheria* on the island; thus his *kadhi* court acted as a court of appeal for all the other *kadhi* courts on the island.[13] Another set of courts was held by the two *liwali* ("governors") on the island. The two principal towns, Chake Chake and Wete, each had a *liwali* appointed by the Sultan to oversee justice on the island. For the most part, the *makadhi* constituted a civil court, and the *liwali* were criminal courts, although both sets of judges could adjudicate in criminal or civil cases. However, the *liwali* and *makadhi* could refuse to either hear or decide on a case because these positions were not fully supported by the government.[14] They were poorly remunerated and generally only offered their occupants prestige and a certain amount of power in the community.

and magistrates, who all used an amalgam of British, *sheria*, and local customary laws. See Agmon, pp. 68–9.

[12] Kollmann, p. 28.

[13] Africa No. 7 (1896), *Correspondence Respecting Slavery in the Zanzibar Dominions* (London: Harrison and Sons, 1896), Inclosure No. 17, Report of Mr. O'Sullivan upon the Island of Pemba.

[14] Donald Mackenzie, "A Report on Slavery and the Slave-Trade in Zanzibar, Pemba, and the Mainland of the British Protectorates of East Africa," in *The Anti-Slavery Reporter* (London: British and Foreign Anti-Slavery Society), Issue 2, June 1, 1895, p. 72.

The 1890 decree enacted by the Sultan that finalized the demise of the slave trade and stated that no one could be enslaved after 1890 included a provision that slaves could now sue their owners in a court of law. However, in most cases, the *liwali* were not willing to hear the cases of slaves. On occasion they did, but until the British Vice Consul began sitting on the court with the *liwali* and *makadhi*, rarely were the cases of lower-status people brought into the courts.[15] However, even with the presence of the Vice Consul, he could only be in one court at any given time, which meant that *liwali* and *makadhi* who were not being observed could still refuse cases. This is why slaves and lower-status people on Pemba began flocking to the Vice Consul's door for help with their disputes and problems. The Vice Consul would listen to "their various complaints, ... take careful note of their grievances and then refer them to one of the [li]Walis."[16] This put the *liwali* on notice that they had to respond to the problems slaves brought to the courts. O'Sullivan-Beare reported that the *liwali* always checked in with him about the cases he sent to them, acknowledging the Vice Consul's position in the hierarchy of the island. Technically, O'Sullivan-Beare's jurisdiction did not cover the subjects of the Sultan; rather, his consular court was supposed to focus on cases involving British subjects. The vast majority of British subjects on the island were Indians who worked as moneylenders and shopkeepers. Nonetheless, O'Sullivan-Beare involved himself in cases that included slaves (subjects of the Sultan) if the Abolition Decree of 1890 was being violated. In general, the cases brought before O'Sullivan-Beare involved Indians collecting debts owed to them by Arab and African subjects of the Sultan. The Vice Consul's work also entailed registering deeds, contracts, and other documents involving British subjects. While the consular court eventually would end, the registering of documents continued to be a duty of the Vice Consul position until it was abolished in 1908.[17]

With the promulgation of the abolition order of 1897, the Sultan not only abolished the right of ownership over slaves, but he also instituted significant changes to the court systems in the islands.[18] At the local level,

---

[15] ZNA AC7/26, Vice Consul Pemba, Court Register. In the register, the Vice Consul sent notes to the *liwali* of Chake Chake asking him to hear cases brought by slaves and women. He also had to continuously ask the *liwali* to "follow the rule of this court" and "not to delay to execute decree." See entries for 1898.

[16] *Report by Vice Consul O'Sullivan on the Island of Pemba, 1896–1897.*

[17] ZNA AC9/7, Vice Consul Pemba, letters.

[18] For details on the restructured courts, see PRO FO107/111, Jurisdiction in Pemba, 1897–1901.

the *liwali* and *kadhi* courts were combined and retitled "district courts." In the district courts, the *liwali* would rule on criminal cases and the *kadhi* on civil matters, but they were to consult with each other on tough cases. The *kadhi* could hold a petty court to examine civil cases that involved amounts less than 100 rupees without the attendance of the *liwali*. In the district courts, civil cases could not entail more than 500 rupees and criminal cases could not involve more than six months of imprisonment. Cases above these criteria were sent to the "Court for Zanzibar and Pemba," which had jurisdiction over both islands. Two *makadhi* and a British official (who did not have voting rights in the case) sat in judgment in this court. All appeals from the district courts were also heard in the Court for Zanzibar and Pemba. Appeals from this court were heard in the Supreme Court for Zanzibar and Pemba, which was held by the Sultan or the First Minister, depending on who was available and who the litigation involved.

Within a month of the abolition order, the Sultan also opened two subordinate courts, one on each island, that were overseen by Slavery Commissioners. The Slavery Commissioners were officials of the Sultan's government but were of British descent. These men were responsible for handling the cases of slaves who applied for their freedom. The Sultan was forced to open this court on Pemba because of the *liwali*'s reluctance to respond to the Abolition Decree, although the *liwali* claimed that it was slaves' refusal to come to them. When the 1890 Abolition Decree was instituted, the Sultan's officials on Pemba ignored its provisions until forced by the arrival of the Vice Consul in 1895 to recognize some of the rules. The *liwali* of Chake Chake, Suleiman bin Mbaruk, in particular responded to the 1897 Abolition Decree in a similar manner.[19] He had been *liwali* of Chake Chake since 1893 and had worked for the Sultan before that for four years, so his tenure with the Sultan's government predated British colonization. The First Minister of the Sultan's government had to reprimand Suleiman bin Mbaruk, who responded that his court was open to slaves, but they refused to come to his court.[20] The

[19] Africa No. 6 (1898), *Correspondence Respecting the Abolition of the Legal Status of Slavery in Zanzibar and Pemba*, Inclosure No. 2 in No. 11, Rev. J. P. Farler to Sir L. Mathews, Pemba, August 2, 1897.

[20] The First Minister was a British citizen who was an advisor and stand-in for the Sultan in the Sultan's government. Technically, the loyalty of the First Minister was to the Sultan, not the "protecting power," although in reality he was expected to push the British agenda. The first First Minister was General Mathews, who had been in charge of the Sultan's armed forced before the Protectorate had been declared. General Mathews was admired for striking a balance between the wishes of the Sultans and the needs of the

British Consul thought it likely that "in Pemba, [the *liwali* courts] ... have existed for a long time past, and have, under the old system when the legal status of slavery was recognized, enforced the rights of owners, and punished idle and mutinous slaves, so that the latter are a good deal more shy of them than is the case" in Unguja.[21] Once the subordinate court was opened on Pemba, slaves began coming for their freedom.

The Slavery Commissioner always held court with either a *liwali* or a *kadhi* so that slave owners could not complain that they did not have Arab representation in the court when their slaves applied for freedom. On Pemba, the Slavery Commissioner was John P. Farler, a former Anglican missionary with the Universities Mission to Central Africa (UMCA). While his work with an abolitionist missionary organization suggests that he would have been a foil to slave owners, Farler was not. Slaves did not always have an easy time getting a hearing with the Slavery Commissioner, whose paycheck it was well known came from the Sultan and not the British government. Ironically, Farler, who twenty years earlier had defended an enslaved man with his life, later described slaves on Pemba as, "these niggers ... they are a degraded hopeless lot and sooner they all die off the better!"[22] Farler's comments are a reminder that British citizens working for the Sultan were not as sympathetic to the plight of slaves as the metropole British government's antislavery rhetoric would suggest.

The consular court that had been run by the Vice Consul of Pemba was turned into the "Court of Delegated Jurisdiction." This court was essentially a British-run court for all cases that did not involve "subjects" of the Sultan as plaintiffs. The British defined subjects of the Sultan as anyone of Arab or African ancestry, the one exception being Comorians, because the Comoros were under French "protection." Almost all the Indian population was deemed British subjects because of British colonization in

British colonizing power. His replacements after his death were never as effective, and the position was soon replaced with a British Resident.

[21] Africa No. 6 (1898), *Correspondence Respecting the Abolition of the Legal Status of Slavery in Zanzibar and Pemba*, No. 13, Sir A. Hardinge to the Marquess of Salisbury, Zanzibar, September 8, 1897.

[22] "Rescue of a Fugitive Slave Recaptured by Arab Traders by a Missionary," *The Anti-Slavery Reporter*, Issue 12 (London, 1877), November 1, front page; Rhodes House, Bodleian Library, University of Oxford, UMCA Files A1 (XIII), 252, Hines to Travers, Wete, 23 February 1905. The bishop often stayed with Farler; thus he did not have an antagonistic relationship with Farler the way the Quaker missionaries did. However, by the time of writing this letter, Bishop Hines commented that he was increasingly uncomfortable with Farler, whom he described as a drunk. Farler died two years later in June 1907.

India; thus, if they had legal disputes, they were forced to use the British consular courts. This is an important distinction because the majority of the moneylenders and shopkeepers in the islands were from the Indian population, and most debt disputes were between Indians and subjects of the Sultan, which shuffled those cases into the new British Court of Delegated Jurisdiction.

The Court of Delegated Jurisdiction was subsumed into the district courts in 1908.[23] Up to 1905, the Vice Consul acted as the judge in this court, and then, between 1905 and 1908, the collector and assistant collectors in Wete, Chake Chake, and Mkoani acted as ad hoc judges in the Court of Delegated Jurisdiction. The collector was in charge of collecting taxes and fees in the islands. Keeping track of imports, exports, and control over the ports of the island were also under his purview. For many years, the assistant collector in Wete was the only European official in that area of Pemba, and he often chafed at official intervention in his duties.[24] In 1906, the colonial officials in Zanzibar decided that the government needed to be restructured. This transition in government also allowed the British to exert more direct control over the Sultan's government. When the government was restructured, it comprised a resident who supervised three new sections. One of the new sections was led by an attorney general, who took charge of oversight on all court systems from probate, civil, and criminal jurisdictions. It was the new attorney general who analyzed the court systems and proposed changes in the courts over the next few years. In 1909, the proposed changes were accepted into law and coincided with the 1909 Abolition Decree. The 1909 Abolition Decree finally terminated the status of slavery for the entire Protectorate, including for concubines, who had been exempted from the 1897 Abolition Decree. In a move that solidified the image of Britain as a colonizing power rather than a "protecting" power, as British representatives had stated for the first two decades of the Zanzibar Protectorate, the Court of Delegated Jurisdiction became a magistrate's court. The courts were now also differentiated by the terminology of His Highness's (HH) courts and Her British Majesty's (HBM) courts, making clear the distinction between "native" and "colonial" courts.

---

[23] ZNA AC8/8, Letter from Vice Consul to Consul, 1905; Stockreiter, p. 55.
[24] PRO FO881/10268X, Annual reports for 1909 and 1910; Africa No. 4 (1909), *Despatchs from His Majesty's Agent and Consul-General at Zanzibar Furnishing a Report on the Administration, Finance, and General Condition of the Zanzibar Protectorate* (London: Harrison & Sons, 1909).

In addition to holding his own court, the magistrate was expected to sit with local judges in the *kadhi* courts. In the previous system, the appeals courts were run by *makadhi* with a nonvoting British member, but now these courts were run by British judges with a nonvoting *kadhi* in attendance. Moreover, "natives" could now bring their cases to the magistrate's court for a hearing. No longer were they required to be in a dispute with a British subject to bring their case in front of British officials. The new magistrate, who arrived in 1910, stated in his annual report that he wished the people on Pemba would stop using the *kadhi* courts altogether.[25] Officials hoped that with the magistrate sitting in the *kadhi* courts, it would cut down on issues of corruption by the *makadhi* and encourage Pembans to bring their disputes directly to the magistrate's court. The assistant collector of Wete reported that the magistrate's presence in the *kadhi* court was "regarded by the people as a sign that they will now be able to get their cases finished without the endless delays that were formerly put in the way of final settlement."[26] This concern was very real for ex-slaves especially, who at times had difficulty in getting *makadhi* to pronounce a final judgment on their cases.[27]

After the 1909 Abolition Decree, a Slavery Commissioner was no longer needed. The position, which had essentially been ceremonial since around 1904 when the number of slaves seeking emancipation dwindled to the barest of trickles, was now ended. The magistrate was the new face of slave rights by using the courts to strike down any claims of slave ownership or rights of owners over the people who remained as "their slaves" even past abolition. The magistrate also took over almost all but the lowest-level criminal cases.[28] This change increasingly limited the power and prestige of the *liwali* and the *makadhi* as arbiters of law. Yet many people on Pemba insisted on bringing their cases to the *makadhi* as a means to circumvent British interpretations of law. In one case, a man told the *kadhi* that he brought his case to the *kadhi* court

[25] PRO FO881/10268X, Annual reports for 1909 and 1910.

[26] PRO FO881/10268X, Annual reports for 1909 and 1910.

[27] ZNA AC8/9, Letter from FIM (Herbert Armitage), July 16, 1906. In this case, the estate of a man was contested by his nephews, who declared that his wife, who was an ex-slave, should not inherit. Even when she brought witnesses of rank to testify for her, the *kadhi* simply refused to rule on the case. ZNA AC8/7, Letter Vice Consul Pemba, February 9, 1904.

[28] The *liwali* were replaced with British District Commissioners within five years of when the Protectorate switched from being under the Foreign Office to the Colonial Office in 1914. L. W. Hollingsworth, *Zanzibar under the Foreign Office 1890–1913* (London 1953), *passim.*

because it would be decided based on *sheria* law, which limited the value of slaves as witnesses. The man claimed that the *kadhi* had to rule against his opponent because she only had "slave" witnesses, even though slavery had been abolished ten years before he brought his case.[29] The continued and expanding use of the *kadhi* courts on Pemba indicates a form of communal resistance to the introduction of British courts on the island. Going to the *kadhi* court offered a person *heshima* because it showed their religious faith and value of *sheria* over colonial justice.

With the removal of the Slavery Commissioners from the subordinate courts, the courts were reconstituted in 1910 with the newly created assistant collectors as the judges. These low-level courts were meant to hear trivial civil and criminal cases in order to free up the magistrates' case loads, expand the services of British-run courts, and undermine the use of *kadhi* courts. However, the assistant collectors were not trained in the law and had little idea of how evidence should be assessed or law administered.[30] At times, assistant collectors had to be removed from oversight of courts because they were making a mess of the courts and creating more appeals work for the magistrate.[31] Harold Ingrams' description of his first case hearing as an assistant collector in 1919 is instructive of how inconsistent and arbitrary these courts could be and explains why so many Pembans – even ex-slaves – went to the *makadhi* in the 1910s and 1920s. Ingrams recalls:

The very first case I tried was one of criminal trespass and assault. I was not entirely clear as to what this meant, but the meaning grew on me as the case proceeded. The first witness told the story of how the accused claimed that his next door neighbour's *shamba* or plantation was his. This did not sound very serious but then it transpired that when the neighbour declined to admit the claim, the accused went into his plantation and tore up three young coco-nut plants. By this time I was beginning to wonder what sort of sentence I ought to pass. Perhaps a fine of ten rupees or a week or so. It seemed that the owner of the *shamba* had been very forbearing about this, and other witnesses said the accused had, after

---

[29] PNA AI1/4, His Highness's Court for Zanzibar and Pemba (hereafter His Highness's Court ZP), Appeal Case No. 2 of 1920, Juma bin Ahmed Swahili vs. Mwana Kombo binti Said Nabahani.

[30] Sir T. S. Tomlinson and G. K. Knight-Bruce, *Law Reports Containing Cases Determined by the High Court for Zanzibar and on Appeal There from by the Court of Appeal for Eastern Africa and by the Privy Council*, Vol. III, 1923–1927 (London: Waterlow and Sons, 1928), pp. 55–7. The appeals judge complained about the common legal errors made by the justices in the subordinate courts on Pemba.

[31] FO 881/10268X, Annual reports for 1909 and 1910, Annual Report 1909, p. 14. The magistrate was forced to give work to *makadhi* over the incompetent assistant collectors.

an interval, torn up a lot more coco-nuts. The option dropped out of my calcula-
tions; it must be at least a month, I thought. Then I heard that the owner had lain
in wait for our trespasser and got really angry with him when he came to pull up
more coco-nuts. The accused had knocked him down. The penalty now rose in a
steep curve, as the mathematicians say. I thought of three months and waited to
hear what the accused had to say in his defence. He said nothing in his defence;
in my mind he was making things much worse by glorying in his pulling up of
promising coco-nuts. "It is my *shamba*," he said. "Why shouldn't I pull them up?"
When the case was over I quickly wrote my judgment. I did not want to show
hesitancy as I had an idea that I had to show unfaltering decision. I gave him six
months. I thought the court looked rather taken aback at this.[32]

Ingrams' inexperience and lack of knowledge about Pemban society, even
his complete lack of Swahili language skills at the time of his appointment, came together to illustrate the way British "justice" was meted out
in the lower courts.

Throughout their colonial possessions in Africa, the British brought
criminal legal systems in line with their own laws, but they let the civil
law remain mostly intact. The magistrate's court was a definite effort to
move people away from *sheria* law and into British civil law codes. The
years of 1909 and 1910 also saw a slew of new decrees from the government creating new taxes, fines, and regulations covering everything
from owning a canoe to holding a wedding. Twenty-six decrees were
promulgated in 1909 alone, and some Pemban officials and Pembans
themselves found the array of new rules frustrating. As the collector of
Pemba noted, the multiple decrees were mostly "unenforceable and ineffective." Furthermore, locals had begun to complain that when there was
"less 'law' in the country," things could be handled more easily and people obeyed the law better. "A command from the Collector or Assistant
Collector was sufficient for all practical purposes."[33] A key point of these
changes that was quite purposeful on the part of colonial officials is that
no longer was the island being run by "personalities."[34]

---

[32] Ingrams, 1942, p. 14.

[33] FO 881/10268X, Annual reports for 1909 and 1910, Assistant collector of Weti report,
p. 178.

[34] Africa No. 4 (1909), *Despatchs from His Majesty's Agent and Consul-General at
Zanzibar Furnishing a Report on the Administration, Finance, and General Condition
of the Zanzibar Protectorate* (London: Harrison & Sons, 1909). In this report, Consul
Cave raised several key points about the colonial staff. First, that because of the isolation of Pemba, many officials there treated their districts as their own "personal fief-
dom" and "resented" supervision by anyone else. Second, that while the government
said it wanted officials to be knowledgeable about the communities, it wanted a balance
between knowledge and loyalty. Third, in 1906, the government changed the pension

No one magistrate was assigned to Pemba, as in the past with other colonial officials. For instance, Dr. O'Sullivan-Beare was the only Vice Consul of Pemba. Others had replaced him temporarily, while keeping up their own jobs on the island, when he went on leave, but for the entire thirteen-year period of the Vice Consulate on the island, only one man held the title of Vice Consul. On the other hand, when the new magistracy was introduced to Pemba, the Zanzibar officials purposely created a policy of changing the magistrates every three to four months on the island. In the first year of the magistracy in 1910, three different men were assigned at different times to Pemba. The head magistrate on Zanzibar stated this policy was imposed because "Firstly, that at present the quarters there are bad, and that, together with the climate makes it advisable that the Magistrates, for the sake of health, should not remain there longer than possible; and secondly, which perhaps ought to have come first, a frequent change *will prevent the Magistrate from falling into a groove*, and make him equally conversant with the work and people of Zanzibar as well as of Pemba."[35] The head magistrate did not want officials to develop affiliations among the people of the island, as was clearly the case among the officials who lived on Pemba before 1910.

JUDGES AND INTERLOCUTORS IN THE COURTS

Numerous people were active participants in the court system, from the various local judges such as the *masheha*, *makadhi*, and *liwali* to the British Vice Consul, magistrates, collectors, district commissioners, and their various assistants. Additionally, numerous other locals participated in the economy of the courts as clerks, translators, *wakil*, and brokers. Each of these people could aid individuals as their cases moved through the courts or they could be a stumbling block. The broker who forgot to turn in the estimate on a *shamba* could and did hold up cases for months.[36] Witnesses were also a critical element in the courts; although they were not paid by the courts, they could delay cases by not showing up. *Wakil* were not the only people who acted as advocates for litigants,

---

scheme of the Zanzibar positions in order to attract "a better class" of colonial officials, which opens questions about the officials hired before 1906.

[35] PRO FO 881/10268X, Annual reports for 1909 and 1910, p. 14 (emphasis added).

[36] In case PNA AK1/3310, a broker was reprimanded by the judge for taking over four months to complete an evaluation of a property and was threatened with a five rupee fine.

the Friends missionaries on the island were active in helping individuals in the courts, especially ex-slaves. When a person brought a case to court, whether in His Highness's (HH) or Her British Majesty's (HBM) courts, they interacted with a host of personalities who had their own interpretation of the case and how it should end.

In the nineteenth century, the *liwali* of Wete and Chake Chake were the two most powerful judges on the island. Even into the early twentieth century, they still had a significant say in the criminal and, at times, civil courts. The *liwali* often came from powerful Arab families who could command the respect and obedience of their neighbors through their lineage connections and *heshima*.[37] The *liwali* often socialized with young, single male British officers sent to the island who felt isolated on Pemba. The *liwali* of Wete during the first sixteen years of the Protectorate, Khamis bin Salem el-Hosni, regularly welcomed colonial officials and even offered a place in his home for them to stay because no hotel was available on the island.[38] Khamis was replaced around 1907 by Said bin Isa el-Ismaili, another generous man who sought to keep the peace between British policies and the Arab population of the northern portion of the island.[39] Because Chake Chake was the principal town for colonial officials on Pemba, the Arabs living in the northern part of the island, including the town of Wete, were used to ruling themselves and resented too much outside control.

For over thirty years of the early Protectorate, one man was the *liwali* of Chake Chake. Suleiman bin Mbaruk el-Mauli started working in the Sultan's government in 1889, the year before the Protectorate was declared, and by 1893, he was made the *liwali* in Chake Chake. He garnered the respect of a wide range of colonial officials but the ire of the Friends missionaries.[40] Suleiman, whose father had been the *liwali* before him, had considerable experience in government and saw many

---

[37] These men were also substantial land and slave holders.

[38] For information on Khamis bin Salem el-Hosni, see, W. W. A. Fitzgerald, pp. 587–9; PRO FO107/111, Jurisdiction in Pemba 1897–1901; PNA AI1/19, His Highness's Court ZP, Civil Case District Court at Weti No. 673 of 1919, Hasina binti Nasibu vs. Abed bin Said el Mayyahi of Jambaji.

[39] See PRO FO881/9209, Distress in Pemba 1906; Ingrams, 1942, p. 15.

[40] For commentary on Suleiman from colonial officials, see letters from Arthur Hardinge, Consul to Zanzibar in Africa No. 6 (1898), *Correspondence Respecting the Abolition of the Legal Status of Slavery in Zanzibar and Pemba*; PRO FO107/111, Jurisdiction in Pemba 1897–1901; PRO FO881/9209, Distress in Pemba 1906; PRO FO 881/10268X, Annual reports for 1909 and 1910; and Ingrams' loving reminisces about Suleiman in *Arabia and the Isles*, 1942, pp. 29–33.

officials and policies come and go over time.[41] While he willingly upheld British-imposed policies, he often waited until prodded to do so. Thus Arthur Hardinge, the British Consul to Zanzibar, had to remind Suleiman when the Abolition Decree of 1897 was made that it had to be enforced and not ignored. With gentle prodding, Suleiman acquiesced, but not before Theodore Burtt of the Friends Mission created a public scandal by publishing in English newspapers accusations against Suleiman that he was corrupt and allowed the sale of slaves and even the castration of a male slave.[42] Suleiman was careful not to treat the Friends as they treated him, but he did demand the right to face his accuser. Theodore refused to attend a hearing called by Consul Hardinge, who dropped all charges against Suleiman and made a point of chastising Burtt as having "made a serious charge against the [li]wali ... his character is at stake."[43] Suleiman continued to be a favorite of British officials who enjoyed his lavish hospitality, his wise advice, and his good sense of humor. Suleiman was a man British officials trusted, and they trusted that they controlled him, which explains his longevity in the position of *liwali*.

The *makadhi* were also central figures in the court system and members of elite society on Pemba. While the *liwali* were often chosen because of the political prestige of their families, the *makadhi* were chosen based on their education and knowledge of *sheria*. Sultan bin Mohamed was the principal *kadhi* of the Wete district during the 1890s until he was fired from the post around 1910. While no one ever publicly accused Sultan of being corrupt, he moved slowly on the cases he found problematic.[44] Given that he was a *kadhi* during a time of great change in Pemban society, it is not surprising that he exhibited many of the same tactics of the *liwali* who only imposed policies when forced to by British officials.[45] Mohamed bin Khamis el-Busaidi, who became the *kadhi* of

---

[41] ZNA AC9/2, Mia and Lasi, July 5, 1896. Mia mentions that the *liwali* of Chake Chake in 1896 was the son of the *liwali* in 1883.

[42] Africa No. 6 (1898), *Correspondence Respecting the Abolition of the Legal Status of Slavery in Zanzibar and Pemba*, pp. 29–30.

[43] FIM PZ(F)/3, Meeting minute book for 1898–1902, Letter from Arthur Hardinge to Theodore Burtt, January 1, 1898. Zanzibaris do not have "last" names; thus at times it seems that I use last names in an unequal way between British and Zanzibari officials. This is a function of naming systems and not a demonstration of unequal relations between the two groups.

[44] No proof was ever given of Sultan being corrupt, but the district officer of Wete in 1909 stated that he believed Sultan was corrupt even if he had no proof. PRO FO 881/10268X, Annual reports for 1909 and 1910, p. 13.

[45] O'Sullivan-Beare reminded Suleiman bin Said to execute the orders of his court on numerous occasions. ZNA AC7/26, Consular Court Register.

Wete soon after Sultan, was a strong presence in the Wete courts and shaped the use of evidence in the courts, much to the consternation of British magistrates.[46] Mohamed remained a *kadhi* through the 1920s, pointedly ignoring the oaths and evidence decrees of the late 1910s. The *kadhi* of Chake Chake in the early twentieth century, Garib bin Ali el-Ofi, was accused of corruption in 1915.[47] The charges against him were eventually dropped, but only when he agreed to resign from his post. The interference of colonial officials in the *kadhi* courts and the removal of *makadhi* reinforced the shift in power dynamics and means of showing *heshima* among the Arab elite. The removal of *makadhi* such as Sultan bin Mohamed and Garib bin Ali by British officials publicly reinforced to people living on Pemba that elite Arabs no longer had the power they had in the nineteenth century.

In addition to the number of assistant or subordinate *makadhi*, the judges were assisted in their courts by numerous clerks and interpreters. Documents brought to the courts were usually in either Gujarati, Ajami (Swahili written in Arabic characters), or Arabic. Rarely were documents in Swahili in Roman script and even less often in English. Thus colonial officials had to hire a number of translators. O'Sullivan-Beare's only salary complaint was related to the cost of hiring so many translators and interpreters for the consulate court.[48] Interpreters were so important in the courts that Her British Majesty's (HBM) Court on Pemba was brought to a standstill for several months in 1919 until a new translator was hired.[49] These men were usually Indians or Arabs born in the islands who appreciated the regular wages offered by a colonial job. The clerks had powerful positions in the courts, especially the magistrate courts,

---

[46] For examples of Mohamed's resistance against colonial rules about evidence and oaths, see cases: PNA AI1/2, His Highness's Court ZP, Appeal Case No. 11 of 1918, Khalid bin Marenge Shirazi vs. Mohamed bin Juma el Rassadi; AI1/4: His Highness's Court ZP, Appeal Case No. 2 of 1920, Juma bin Ahmed Swahili vs. Mwana Kombo binti Said Nabahani; AI1/5, His Highness's Court ZP, Appeal Case No. 4 of 1920, Fatuma binti Dadi vs. Seif bin Hassan; AI1/6, His Highness's Court ZP, Appeal Case No. 5 of 1920, Idi bin Haji vs. Ahamed bin Khalfan; AI1/7, His Highness's Court ZP, Appeal Case No. 5 of 1920, Mame Saifu, Mwana Asha and Salima binti Ahmed bin Juma el-Swahili vs. Ismail bin Fakih and Mvitanga Swahili.

[47] PNA AI1/7, His Highness's Court ZP, Appeal Case No. 5 of 1920; for his dismissal, see Zanzibar Protectorate, *Administrative Reports for the Year 1915* (Zanzibar: Zanzibar Government Printer, 1916).

[48] ZNA AC9/2, Vice Consul Pemba Letters.

[49] Zanzibar Protectorate, *Administrative Reports for the Year 1919* (Zanzibar: Zanzibar Government Printer, 1920); again in Zanzibar Protectorate, *Administrative Reports for the Year 1921* (Zanzibar: Zanzibar Government Printer, 1922).

because they often kept the court going, receiving payments and sending summonses while the magistrate or *kadhi* was working in another part of the district. In 1918, several clerks were fired in Chake Chake in both His Highness's and Her British Majesty's Courts for misappropriating funds.[50] Moreover, clerks could be the focus of jealousy, envy, and frustration on the part of litigants, who found them to be "petty tyrants" at times.[51] Nonetheless, for clerks with patience who earned the trust of the colonial officials, they could become subordinate judges themselves. By 1920, an Indian man, Framji Robadiva, was acting magistrate on Pemba, helping to solve the problem of the constant shortage of suitable British magistrates.[52]

The *wakil* and *dalal* ("brokers") were another key group in the courts. The *wakil* represented clients in the courts and often in business transactions for women in purdah. While not all litigants hired *wakil*, most did at the appeals level, especially women. *Wakil* had to be accepted by the courts in order to practice in Zanzibar.[53] Most *wakil* self-identified as Indian and Arab, the groups that had the most access to an education; however, self-identified African men also acted as *wakil*.[54] *Wakil* were

---

[50] Zanzibar Protectorate, *Administrative Reports for the Year 1918* (Zanzibar: Zanzibar Government Printer, 1919).

[51] Her British Majesty's Court, Zanzibar, Criminal Case No. 790 of 1910, Dayabhai Jivanlal Multani vs. Chaturbhooj Jagjivan, posted in the *Zanzibar Gazette*, January 3, 1911.

[52] See cases PNA AI1/2, His Highness's Court ZP, Appeal Case No. 11 of 1918; PNA AI1/4, His Highness's Court ZP, Appeal Case No. 2 of 1920; PNA AI1/5, His Highness's Court ZP, Appeal Case No. 4 of 1920.

[53] Joseph Schacht, "Notes on Islam in East Africa," *Studia Islamica*, no. 23 (1965), pp. 91–136. "There were *wakil*s (advocates) in Zanzibar, who were admitted to practice before the *makadhi* courts only; not all enjoyed an equally high reputation. (A prominent *wakil* on Pemba Island was also called *muhami*, and this was locally interpreted as meaning "protector of the *sheria*.") These *wakil*s also attested documents, unless the *kadhi* did it himself." Schacht, p. 118.

[54] In the case PNA AI1/19, His Highness's Court SC, Civil Case District Court at Weti No. 673 of 1919, the female Indian moneylender had a Shirazi man as her *wakil*. Other *wakil* working on Pemba in the 1920s were Mr. Ahmed Ayyab, Mr. Pereira, Mohamed bin Sultan el-Mughairi, Hamadi bin Ali bin Mjaka Shirazi, Mohamed bin Habib, and Ghulam Ali. No patterns are noticeable on the ethnicity of *wakil* in their hiring. See cases PNA AI1/12, His Highness's Court ZP, Appeal Case No. 10 of 1920, Kombo bin Makurizo of Chanjani vs. Hilal bin Amur; PNA AI1/19, His Highness's Court SSC, Civil Case District Court at Weti No. 673 of 1919; AI1/20, Her British Majesty's Court, District Registry of High Court for Pemba, Civil Case No. 16 of 1926, Abdulhussein Mussaji vs. Mohamed bin Muhijaji bin Mzee el-Bajuni; AI1/21, High Court for Zanzibar, Civil Case No. 189 of 1920, Khamis bin Hathar freed slave of Ebrahim bin Msondo vs. Labuda bin Suroor freed slave of Bani Riany, Juma binti Abood (ex-wife of Labuda), Makame bin Labuda, Mwana Mkoo binti Labuda.

particularly useful to their clients because they understood the different court systems and could suggest an appropriate location for the particular litigation. They also could help with appeals and in knowing on what grounds appeals could be made. One clever *wakil* noticed in 1919 that the district officer in the subordinate court marked the wrong court on the judgment, allowing the *wakil* to appeal for his client and win.[55] Mistakes by inexperienced colonial officials happened on occasion, and a savvy *wakil* could take advantage of this for his client.

The experience and knowledge of colonial officials working in the courts ranged dramatically. The first British men living permanently on Pemba were John P. Farler, who was the government agent, and Herbert Lister, who was the overseer of the Sultan's plantations on Pemba, both of whom arrived on the island in 1894. Both Lister and Farler were employees of the Sultan's government rather than officials of the "protecting power," as Britain was called in the 1890s. The first British government official assigned to Pemba was Daniel O'Sullivan-Beare, who became the Vice Consul in 1895. Farler and Lister had both come out to East Africa as missionaries with the Universities Mission to Central Africa (UMCA) and worked on the mainland, as well as in Zanzibar, before coming to Pemba.[56] O'Sullivan-Beare was a newly assigned official in the colonies and initially relied heavily on Farler and Lister, as well as the *liwali* of Chake Chake, Suleiman bin Mbaruk. At first, all three British men were in the awkward position of not officially being judges in local courts but receiving appeals from African women and men, especially slaves, for help.

O'Sullivan-Beare was in charge of the consular court, which he viewed as a "considerable portion" of his work.[57] Africans went to him seeking help with complaints that they were either afraid to or unable to get assistance for from the *liwali* or *makadhi*. O'Sullivan-Beare made a point of not interfering in the local courts, but he regularly communicated with the *liwali* and *kadhi* of Chake Chake.[58] Suleiman bin Mbaruk would respond to whatever O'Sullivan-Beare thought was a good resolution to the case. Suleiman always did whatever was suggested by the Vice Consul, but no more. The *liwali* did not consult O'Sullivan-Beare on

---

[55] Ingrams, 1942, p. 15.

[56] The movement from being a missionary to a colonial official was not unheard of and happened with several of the Friends missionaries as well; for example, Mr. Roylance and H. W. Sellars moved over.

[57] ZNA AC9/2, Letter from O'Sullivan-Beare to Hardinge, January 10, 1896.

[58] ZNA AC7/26, Vice Consul Pemba, Court Register.

other cases, indicating his reluctance to incorporate the Vice Consul into the local court system. Between 1895 and the time of the 1897 Abolition Decree, O'Sullivan-Beare became a regular visitor to the courts, checking in on the cases of people who flowed to his door for help.[59] Slaves quickly understood that having a colonial official interested in their case usually helped them. This is especially the case of enslaved people, who were the primary petitioners to O'Sullivan-Beare. Contrary to what Margaret Strobel found in Mombasa, the gender of petitioners on Pemba was split fairly evenly between men and women.[60] The Vice Consul was careful to sort through the stories of slaves to get at the dispute in question and whether he viewed it as legitimate and worthy of investigation.

The year of 1897 brought two significant changes to the courts and removed O'Sullivan-Beare from the position of direct interlocutor for slaves. First, 1897 was when the Friends missionaries opened their mission with locations in Chake Chake and a large plantation about four miles down the creek from Chake Chake called "Banani." The primary missionary among the Friends was Theodore Burtt, who remained working in Pemba for thirty-five years.[61] The Friends missionaries, whose mission was focused on ending slavery and the slave trade, became vocal advocates for slaves regardless of the "validity" of the complaint. The second change came about from the Abolition Decree. While the *liwali* were originally supposed to handle the application of slaves for freedom, it quickly became apparent that this system would not work. Ostensibly, the problem was not with the *liwali*'s unwillingness to fulfill the decree by freeing slaves but rather Suleiman bin Mbaruk's constant barrage of questions about how to handle each case to colonial officials. Within months, Farler was asked to take on the job of Slavery Commissioner to manage the complaints of slaves against their owners and their requests for freedom. When Farler took on this job, O'Sullivan-Beare simply directed all slaves to take their cases to Farler.

---

[59] Newman, p. 84; the Vice Consul files in the Zanzibar National Archives contain many letters from O'Sullivan-Beare indicating his participation in court cases. For examples, see files ZNA AC2/24, AC5/1–5, AC8/5–9, and AC9/2.

[60] Margaret Strobel found that women were the primary petitioners to the British officials in Mombasa; Strobel, 1979, pp. 59–62; see ZNA AC9/2, Letters from O'Sullivan-Beare concerning cases brought to him by enslaved people. Examples: August 21, 1896, December 22, 1896, May 1, 1896, February 17, 1897, June 27, 1896, July 2, 1896, July 10, 1896, July 27, 1896, August 25, 1896, May 4, 1895, November 24, 1896, and February 18, 1897.

[61] FIM P2/F, Committee of Missionaries, 1933–1949. Burtt arrived in 1897 and retired in 1932. He died in England in 1944.

As noted earlier, though, Farler was not an advocate for slaves in the way O'Sullivan-Beare had been; thus the Friends missionaries stepped into the void left by the Vice Consul. Theodore Burtt arrived in 1897 and was soon joined by Herbert Armitage and his sister, Cecelia. A year later, Burtt's wife, Jessie, and her sister, Emily Hutchinson, arrived as well.[62] The Friends had been tasked by the British and Foreign Anti-Slavery Society to work on Pemba to end the illegal slave trade and work toward the abolition of slavery on the island. The Friends stepped onto Pemba with an antagonistic attitude toward colonial officials whom they believed to be dragging their feet over abolition.[63] Even after the Abolition Decree was declared, the Friends immediately made their displeasure about aspects of the decree publicly known.[64] Burtt argued in the aftermath of the Abolition Decree, "[U]nless slaves are cruelly treated, or well backed up by some Englishman, there seems now to be small chance of their freedom."[65] The Friends protested the refusal to free concubines and the requirements of ex-slaves to have a place to live and work in order to be emancipated. The Friends were active correspondents with people in London who regularly wrote to the London *Times* and other newspapers in addition to protesting to parliamentary leaders.[66] As discussed before, when Burtt accused Suleiman bin Mbaruk of corruption, his constant communications home were a substantial barb to the colonial government. In particular, Burtt and Farler had a venomous relationship and mostly communicated through letters because Farler refused to be in Burtt's presence.[67]

---

[62] FIM PZ(F)/3, Meeting minute book for 1898–1902.
[63] PRO FO107/108, Mr. R. G. Edib's Charges Against the Zanzibar Slavery Administration, 1899.
[64] *The Times*, London, Editorial by Theodore Burtt, November 30, 1897, p. 8.
[65] Africa No. 6 (1898), *Correspondence Respecting the Abolition of the Legal Status of Slavery in Zanzibar and Pemba*, Inclosure No. 1 in No. 16, letters from Mr. T. Burtt, FIM, Pemba, September 4, 1897.
[66] For letters to the editor of the London *Times* by Friends, see: Charles Allen, October 8, 1897, p. 9; December 21, 1897, p. 10; December 31, 1897, p. 4; July 26, 1898, p. 12; Theodore Burtt, November 30, 1897, p. 8; Donald MacKenzie, April 16, 1897, p. 4; March 7, 1898, p. 9; July 29, 1898, p. 15; December 5, 1898, p. 6; Travers Buxton, November 17, 1899, p. 12.
[67] UMCA A1 (XIV) No. 51, Herbert Armitage to Rev. Duncan Travers, Pemba 16 March 1903; UMCA A1 (XIII), No. 214, Hines to Travers, Pemba 19 May 1904; UMCA A1 (XIII), No. 216, Hines to Travers, Pemba 30 May 1904; when one of the Friends missionaries died in 1900, the only nonmission people to attend were Mr. Lister and "one or two lesser government officials." Report of January 1900 in FIM PZ(F)/3, Meeting minute book for 1898–1902. This shows how disliked the Friends were on Pemba because in most instances funerals were large occasions where all leaders in the community came to pay their respects.

Theodore Burtt was a particularly strident person with a faith in his calling to missionary service that was especially strong. Even when his wife, Jessie, had to permanently move back to England in 1907, Burtt continued to live on Pemba and only returned to England and his family every three years when on furlough until his retirement in 1932. His sister-in-law, Emily Hutchinson, became so attached to Pemba that when she retired from missionary work, she continued to live on the island.[68] The initial interactions of Burtt with locals proved to slaves that he would advocate fully for them, including going to court with women who were claimed as concubines but swore they were not.[69] The presence of Burtt on the island offered slaves a sustained support that was no longer available to them elsewhere. While the UMCA and Catholic missions started at the same time on the island, they did not advocate for slaves in the same manner as the Friends.[70] Suleiman bin Mbaruk cynically noted that the Friends had a large plantation but needed labor to work it; thus they advocated for slaves in order to get laborers.[71] While Burtt and other Friends were deeply insulted by such insinuations, Suleiman's comments illustrate the way local landowners viewed the Friends. Suleiman, Farler, and Consul Basil Cave got their revenge on the Friends at Farler's death. Farler owned an adjoining *shamba* to the Friends, and Suleiman purchased it before the Friends learned of the sale. The Friends tried to claim the right of preemption to buy the land, but the *liwali*, Suleiman, ruled

---

[68] Emily Hutchinson died on Pemba in 1947. While she left no letters behind that might explain her choice to remain on Pemba, she came to Pemba at such a young age that she had few other ideas of a home when she retired from the mission (she lived on Pemba for almost fifty years, so she likely was not more than twenty when she came to Pemba in 1899). Also, a comment made in a letter by H. E. Sellars, a FIM missionary who was forced to quit the mission in 1909, accused Emily of carrying on an affair with Dr. DeSouza, the Goan doctor in charge of the hospital at Chake Chake. FIM TEMP MSS 419, Private letters of Theodore Burtt, November 8, 1909, from Theodore Burtt to E. W. Brooks.

[69] Africa No. 6 (1902), *Correspondence Respecting Slavery and the Slave Trade in East Africa and the Islands of Zanzibar and Pemba* (London: Harrison & Sons, 1903), pp. 18–27; "The Story of Msichoke," *The Friend* (British), October 3, 1902, pp. 644–6; "Letter from Armitage Detailing Further Developments in Case of Msichoke," *The Friend* (British), November 7, 1902, p. 738; "The Story of Msichoke," *The Friend* (British), November 14, 1902, p. 747.

[70] Moses Nwulia, "The Role of Missionaries in the Emancipation of Slaves in Zanzibar," *Journal of Negro History* 60, no. 2 (1975), pp. 268–87. Nwulia argues that the vociferousness of the Friends' efforts to end slavery on Pemba is what forced officials to issue the 1897 Abolition Order.

[71] Africa No. 6 (1898), *Correspondence Respecting the Abolition of the Legal Status of Slavery in Zanzibar and Pemba*, pp. 33, 75.

against them. When they tried to argue to other colonial officials their right to purchase the land, they were informed that everything had been above board and that Suleiman was their new neighbor.[72]

One of the key points when looking at the early Protectorate years on Pemba was the consistency of staff. John Farler, who acted as government agent and then Slavery Commissioner until 1905, moved up to the position of collector of Pemba until his death in June 1907. Herbert Lister was in charge of the government plantations between 1894 and 1905. He then replaced Farler as Slavery Commissioner until Farler' death in 1907, when Lister became the collector of Pemba, a position he served in until his retirement at the end of 1908.[73] Dr. O'Sullivan-Beare remained on the island from 1895 to 1905, when the Vice Consulate position was closed down. O'Sullivan-Beare was reassigned to the Consulate of Rio de Janeiro, where he remained for decades. It is noticeable that the core group of colonial officials on Pemba – Lister, Farler, and O'Sullivan-Beare – all left or died between 1905 and 1908, and the new laws and legal system were implemented between 1906 and 1910. A central tenet of the new magistrate system designed in 1909 was that colonial officials quickly rotated in and out of Pemba. Zanzibar officials did not want anyone with significant power on the island entrenched in their positions and the community as Lister, Farler, and O'Sullivan-Beare had been. Colonial officials could do little about the missionaries on the island, but even then it was only Theodore Burtt and Emily Hutchinson among the Friends who showed a proclivity for prolonged residence on the island. After the 1909 Abolition Decree ordering the end of slavery, the Friends remained to care for the emancipated slaves, but they no longer had reason to put political pressure on the colonial government. The transition in the courts and the abolition of slavery on the islands swept in a new system of government that viewed all subjects and litigants as equal in the courts but left a limited desire to create continuity among colonial officials on Pemba.[74]

---

[72] A comprehensive correspondence between the Friends, the *liwali*, the chief justice for Zanzibar, Mr. Lascari, and the British Resident, Basil Cave, can be found in FIM PZ(F)/3, Meeting minute book for 1903–1915.

[73] PRO CO 618/52/9, Deportation of H. Lister from USA to UK.

[74] Court officials in Pemba between 1910 and 1930 included (but are not limited to) Mr. Sills, Captain McRoberts, Mr. Haythorne Reed, Harold Ingrams, Mr. Shaw, Mr. Sheldon, ... ptain Shelwell-White, William Addis, and Charles A. Gordon. See ... iess's Court ZP, Appeal Case No. 11 of 1918; PNA AI1/7, His ... ppeal Case No. 5 of 1920; PNA AI1/12, His Highness's Court ZP, ... 1920; Ingrams, 1931, 1942.

EVIDENCE AND OATHS

Evidence accepted by the rules of *sheria* was primarily oral, either through confession, oaths, or oral testimony of witnesses. Written evidence could be entered into court proceedings, but the written evidence could only be used to support oral testimony and could not be accepted without two witnesses orally testifying to the information incorporated in the written evidence.[75] In civil proceedings, two male, free, Muslim witnesses who were not related to any of the litigants and were morally and religiously upstanding were required by the rule of evidence to prove a point.[76] The witnesses had to be able to bear witness to events and not simply provide hearsay. Two female or slave witnesses counted as one male witness. However, by the 1910s, witnesses were generally treated as equal regardless of gender or status. Witnesses were screened (*tazkiya*) as to their eligibility and their "habits of truthfulness and falsehood."[77] While in conservative courts the piety of a witness could be considered in declaring them *ta'dil* ("competent to provide evidence in the court"), it appears that this was not the case in Zanzibari courts.[78] In His Highness's (HH) courts on Pemba, the primary forms of evidence were witness testimony and oaths.

The oath in Islamic and Western jurisprudence holds a very different purpose. In HBM courts, the oath was "precautionary" and taken as a condition to testifying in the court. However, in HH courts, the oath was used to remove the burden of proof from litigants. In Pemba, taking the oath was proof itself. If litigants refused to take an oath, it may or may not have counted against them, but in general, a refusal did not bode well for the outcome of their cases. In the Islamic courts, it was assumed that a person making the oath was a Muslim, a believer in the faith; otherwise, the oath had no value. Within the understanding that the oath taker was Muslim was also that the person was honorable and deserving to take the oath. In the later nineteenth century, the phrase *utaapa* ("upon your oath") was common enough for missionaries to include it in a list of "useful and idiomatic phrases."[79] Making an oath was a common practice, reliant on a person being of good reputation in the community.

---

[75] Wael B. Hallaq, *Shari'a: Theory, Practice, Transformations* (Cambridge: Cambridge University Press, 2009), pp. 342–53; Ghislaine Lydon, *On Trans-Saharan Trails: Islamic Law, Trade networks, and Cross-Cultural Exchange in Nineteenth-Century Western Africa* (Cambridge: Cambridge University Press, 2009), pp. 287–90.

[76] Hallaq, pp. 342–53.

[77] J. N. D. Anderson, *Islamic Law in Africa* (London: Cass, 1970), p. 378.

[78] Anderson, 1970, pp. 357, 376.

[79] Steere, 1884, p. 452, n. 174.

The meaning of an oath comes out of a pre-Christian idea of the self-curse – that unless individuals were truthful in their word, something terrible would happen to them.[80] According to Helen Silving, a self-curse was originally associated with societies whose cosmologic framework was based on magic. Slowly, the self-curse shifted from a connection with magic to one with religion, especially monotheistic religions; thus the curse was no longer something one brought on oneself but rather God brought on the untruthful individual. The oath emerged as a means to show both a belief in a particular religion and afterlife and as recognition that individuals relinquished control over their afterlife if they were unfaithful in their word. In an honor-based society, a person's word and oath before God became a critical feature of daily life because people had no other way to ensure the validity of business and legal transactions. Moreover, in parts of Europe, lying under oath had the implication of social exclusion if a person was proven to have done so.[81] Oaths have been accepted historically in many courts as a form of evidence, not only among Islamic courts but also in Christianized European courts.[82]

However, on Pemba, the distinction between magical and religious worlds was not as clear-cut as Silving proposes. Oaths were a feature of everyday life for people who believed in both Islam and *uchawi* ("magic, occult, witchcraft"), which was a sizable portion of Pemban society irrespective of ethnicity, gender, or social class. Oaths were used in the *kadhi* courts, but they were also used in *uchawi* on the island. A *mchawi* ("witchdoctor," for lack of a better translation) made an oath not to reveal the secrets of *uchawi* and sealed that oath with the death of a relative.[83] In nineteenth-century Mombasa, the word for charms and oaths was the same, showing that people along the coast associated oaths with *uchawi*.[84] Individuals certainly feared the wrath of God in

---

[80] Helen Silving, "The Oath: I," *Yale Law Journal* 68, no. 7 (1959), pp. 1329–90.

[81] F. R. P. Akehurst, "Good Name, Reputation, and Notoriety in French Customary Law," in *Fama: The Politics of Talk and Reputation in Medieval Europe*, edited by Thelma Fenster and Daniel Lord Smail (Ithaca, NY: Cornell University Press, 2003), p. 91.

[82] Madeline H. Caviness and Charles G. Nelson, "Silent Witnesses, Absent Women, and the Law Courts in Medieval Germany," in *Fama: The Politics of Talk and Reputation in Medieval Europe*, edited by Thelma Fenster and Daniel Lord Smail (Ithaca, NY: Cornell University Press, 2003).

[83] Whether the "death" was metaphorical or real is not wholly clear. *Uchawi* on Pemba is discussed in detail in Chapter 5.

[84] Steere, 1884, p. 303: *kiapo* is defined as either an oath or an ordeal; Johann Ludwig Krapf, *A Dictionary of the Suahili Language*, edited by Robert Needham Cust (1882), p. 378: *kiapo* is defined as either a charm or an oath; Arthur Cornwallis Madan, *English-Swahili*

the afterlife, but they also had immediate fears of the everyday effects of *uchawi* in their communities, and thus the value of these oaths. Therefore, the experience of taking an oath in court, while strongly linked to a belief in God, was mapped onto the fear associated with the daily experience of *uchawi* in individuals' lives. Thus oaths had very real, as well as religious, meanings for people and shows why people would refuse to take an oath in court, even when it meant losing their case.

In 1917, the Evidence Decree was introduced into Zanzibari courts, which directly contradicted many aspects of *sheria*. This decree stated that "witnesses had to be heard without being screened or questioned about their religion."[85] However, in an appeals case from 1934, a witness was excluded because he "had no religion." J. N. D. Anderson, a scholar of Islamic law in Africa, noted in the 1950s that *makadhi* still did not allow non-Muslims to be witnesses in cases involving only Muslims.[86] The Evidence Decree also stated that if a witness had an interest in the case, he or she could not act as a witness. This was flagrantly disregarded in some cases.[87] Most radically, the Evidence Decree declared that no litigants could be made to take an oath and that written evidence should be privileged over oral testimony.[88] Consistently in the cases heard before Sheikh Mohamed bin Khamis, the Wete *kadhi* in the 1910s and 1920s, he refused to obey the rules of the Evidence Decree and rarely accepted written evidence as useful.[89] Oaths were a central form of evidence according to *sheria*, and *makadhi* refused to limit their use as required by the Evidence Decree.

    Dictionary (1902), p. 259, still lists *kiapo* as an oath, but he also put *laana*, which means a "curse," under the definition of *kiapo*, indicating the linkage between oaths and curses.

[85] Stiles, 2002, p. 68.

[86] PNA AI1/77, His Highness's Court ZP, in the court of Kathi Sheikh Said bin Nasor, Civil Case No. 189 of 1934, Asha binti Seif bin Hamed el-Ismailia, represented by Ahmed bin Kheri (*Wakil*), vs. Abdulla bin Salim el-Ismaili; Anderson, 1970, p. 69.

[87] Hallaq, p. 349; PNA (no Accession number), *Kadhi*'s Court, Wete, Civil Case No. 253 of 1945; PNA AI1/58, Khamisa binti Mwallim and Hija binti Mwallim vs. Administrator General Agent of the Estate of Mohamed bin Khamis Deceased, Fatuma binti Abdulrehman, Amour bin Abdulrehman, by Guardian Khalfan bin Khamis, Her Britannic Majesty's Court for Zanzibar (hereafter Her British Majesty's Court), District Registry of High Court held at Weti, No. 10 of 1931.

[88] Scholars of Islamic courts argue that in the nineteenth century oral evidence was critical in Islamic courts, and judges would not accept written evidence in its place. Agmon, 2006, p. 88; Lydon, 2009, pp. 287–90.

[89] For examples, see cases such as PNA AI1/2. His Highness's Court ZP, Appeal Case No. 11 of 1918; PNA AI1/4, His Highness's Court ZP, Appeal Case No. 2 of 1920; PNA AI1/5, His Highness's Court ZP, Appeal Case No. 4 of 1920; PNA AI1/7, His Highness's Court ZP, Appeal Case No. 5 of 1920.

Oaths were a critical element within the Pemban courts, and many decisions were based on the willingness of one litigant to take an oath over another. Even when the *kadhi* decided a case based on witness testimony, if the losing litigant threatened to appeal, the *kadhi* suggested the winner take an oath to satisfy the loser. *Makadhi* also showed their distrust of individuals when they did not allow them to take an oath. Alternatively, the taking of an oath could give a litigant some status in the eyes of the *kadhi* if he felt the oath was taken in good faith. An example of this is found in the case of Khamis bin Hathar versus Labuda bin Suroor.[90] Khamis was suing Labuda for possession of a cow that Labuda had sold to Khamis. The problem in the case was not really between these two men but between Labuda and his ex-wife. Labuda's ex-wife, Mwanajuma, went to Khamis' house and took the cow, claiming it as her own. Khamis sued Labuda for either the return of his money or the return of the cow. The *kadhi* asked Labuda to swear an oath that the cow belonged to him and was his to sell. Labuda willingly took the oath, and his ex-wife did not initially come to the court to protest this action. The *kadhi* then placed claim against Mwanajuma for falsely taking the cow. When Mwanajuma came to court, she brought a written deed of sale of the cow. The *kadhi* had to decide if Labuda had lied under oath. Before the *kadhi* made a judgment, he told Mwanajuma to get a *wakil* to represent her in the court. She refused to do so, arguing that the cow was hers, she had written proof, and she did not see why the *kadhi* was questioning her. She clearly did not want to take on the added expense of paying for a *wakil*, especially when she had documentary proof of her ownership of the cow. Her attitude toward the *kadhi* and the procedures of the courts undoubtedly made the *kadhi* question her demeanor, her respectability, and her evidence. Despite written evidence showing that Mwanajuma bought the cow from her ex-husband, the *kadhi* ruled against her and for Labuda. Labuda's willingness to take the oath and his demeanor worked in his favor in the eyes of the *kadhi* because he offered the only evidence viewed as valid according to *sheria*. Mwanajuma appealed the case in front of a British magistrate, who, based on the written evidence, quickly declared that the cow belonged to Mwanajuma and overturned the *kadhi*'s decision.[91]

[90] PNA AI1/21, Khamis bin Hathar Freed Slave of Ebrahim bin *Msondo* vs. Labuda bin Suroor Freed Slave of Bani Riany, Juma binti Abood (ex-wife of Labuda), Makame bin Labuda, Mwana Mkoo binti Labuda; His Highness's Court, No. 189 of 1920. This is the original case and PNA AI1/14, His Highness's Court ZP, Appeal Case No. 13 of 1920, is the appeal to this case.

[91] PNA AI1/14, Mwajuma binti Abud of Mkanjuni vs. Khamis bin Nadhar, His Highness's Court ZP, Appeal Case No. 13 of 1920.

The case of Labuda and Mwanajuma illustrates the conflicting methods of British colonial and Islamic law and evidentiary usage. For the
British, the only evidence that could be truly trusted was written evidence that had been properly registered with the colonial court system.
However, most written documentation on Pemba had not been registered
through the colonial courts – even by 1917 when the Evidence Decree
was issued, twenty-seven years after the British colonized the territory.
Moreover, written evidence was often tampered with or limited in value
because of the multiple languages used on the island and the illiteracy
of much of the population. As seen with lawsuits dealing with *bei kataa*
("fictional sales") cases, often the borrowers did not fully understand
the written contract they were making. British evidentiary usage privileged educated elites over the majority of the population. This is a key
contradiction of the colonial and Islamic courts. In the early years of
emancipation, ex-slaves and many women viewed the British as advocates and preferred to have their cases heard by British judges. However,
over time, as the colonial judges became less connected to and less knowledgeable of the local communities and the people in them, they no longer
were advocates for ex-slaves and women. Once the British courts began
privileging written, registered evidence, which was often costly to pro-
cure and not always comprehensible to undereducated people, a shift
occurred of wanting cases to be heard in the *kadhi* courts. Contrary to
the stated desires of the magistrate in 1910, the number of cases brought
to the *kadhi* courts in the 1910s and 1920s only increased.[92] Such an
increase demonstrates the continuing emphasis and acceptance of oral
evidence by *makadhi* in their courts. For *makadhi*, reputation in the community still had significant meaning in the courts.

In addition to the Evidence Decree that privileged written evidence,
colonial officials also promulgated the Oaths Decree, which stated that
individuals no longer had to swear an oath to give evidence in HBM
courts.[93] As colonial officials tried to assert their own procedures, they
declared that litigants and witnesses only had to swear to tell the truth;

[92] Statistics from *Administrative Reports of the Zanzibar Protectorate from 1908–1910*
and *1915–1931* show that the number of cases on Pemba and Zanzibar in the British and
Sultan's courts increased, whereas on Zanzibar the number of cases going to the Sultan's
court decreased by the late 1920s. *Administrative Reports for the Years 1915–1931*
(Zanzibar, 1915–1931); PRO FO881//10268X, Annual Report for Zanzibar, 1909 and
1910 (these reports included information from the year 1908 as comparative to 1909).

[93] J. H. Vaughan, *The Dual Jurisdiction in Zanzibar* (Zanzibar: Government Printer,
1935).

they no longer had to take specific Islamic oaths. As officials attempted to place Western notions of the oath into the Pemban courts, they encountered problems because swearing to tell the truth was not an oath, it was not a testament to a person's beliefs, it was not viewed locally as binding on them, and it was nothing that would make or break an individual's reputation. HBM judges began complaining in the 1920s that litigants regularly perjured themselves in court because they did not view swearing as binding. By 1935, the Oaths Decree was abolished, and the use of oaths was reinstated in the colonial courts.[94] The purpose of the oaths was more than simply as evidence but also as a statement of litigants' and witnesses' reputations.[95]

DISPUTES IN THE COURTS

Disputes in the courts covered numerous topics from personal problems between husbands and wives to conflict between strangers over rights to land. Most disputes were decided by the community elders and settled immediately. However, some disputes could not be settled to the satisfaction of the litigants, leading to distrust and questioning of reputations. For instance, in the 1890s, a WaPemba woman buried her money and had her best friend witness the location. Later, the woman went looking for her money and could not find it. She accused her friend in the *liwali*'s court of stealing the money. The friend denied the accusation, but both women lived with the cloud of this argument until their deaths.[96] Records of these kinds of daily conflicts between friends, relatives, and neighbors are few and far between. Instead, the colonial court records focus primarily on disputes over property, which privileges the history of hard-fought property disputes over the daily quarrels over money, love affairs, chores, and other mundane details of life. The emphasis on property disputes is very telling about the shifts occurring in Pemban society in the postemancipation period; nonetheless, it is just one aspect of the daily disagreements that individuals in a community had at one time or another.

---

[94] "Oaths (Amendment), A Decree to Amend the Oaths Decree," *Zanzibar Gazette,* December 21, 1935.

[95] This was recognized by colonial officials, who noted that "an unexplained refusal to take an oath in the Mosque by a Moslem litigant may be regarded as a part of his demeanour, and thus properly weigh with the Court in estimating his credibility." Hugh Kingdon, *The Conflict of Laws in Zanzibar* (Zanzibar: Government Printer, 1940), p. 45.

[96] FIM PZ(F)/3, Diary of the Boys Home, May 7, 1902. The money was eventually found by the Friends missionaries but not before both women had died.

In 1969, Lloyd Fallers argued that every society has its "trouble spots" that show up in the litigation among members of the community.[97] The trouble spots represent the place where members contest the interpretation of social and cultural norms and expectations in their society. Richard Roberts later argued that focusing on the trouble spots in legal discourse allows scholars to see a road map of changes within a society and understand the conflicts underlying those moments of flux.[98] It is difficult to know, given the limited number of cases remaining in the appeals court files, if property disputes indicate one of these trouble spots where nonelite people on the island were challenging the hegemonic norms of property ownership held by the slave-owning elite. Faller's trouble spots complicate something seemingly as simply as a boundary dispute into an issue of shifting definitions of what was moral or right in the society. The widespread emphasis on land disputes on Pemba indicates that individuals viewed access to and control over land as a moral right.[99] When examining the specific elements of cases, patterns emerge that show how fallow lands were quickly being claimed by elites, WaPemba, and ex-slaves within very different spheres of understanding. WaPemba claimed land through an interpretation of being "first owners" of the island, Arab elites claimed land through the right of conquest, and ex-slaves claimed land through the understanding of cultivation as ownership. These three conflicting views of how landownership was declared indicate the inconsistencies in the legal and moral views of Pemban society during this tumultuous period.

Another aspect of the property disputes that emerges from court transcripts is that often a third party was involved within the dispute. While the court case was framed within the language of plaintiff and defendant, often the defendant had purchased the property through another person. The third party either was a moneylender who took possession of the land from a defaulted mortgage or a relative or neighbor who had claimed the property and then sold it to the defendant. While this indicates a problem with title deeds and proof of ownership, it again points to shifts occurring in the communal assumptions about defining ownership. It also illuminates the gendered elements of landownership and

---

[97] Lloyd Fallers, *Law Without Precedent: Legal Ideas in Action in the Courts of Colonial Busoga* (Chicago: The University of Chicago Press, 1969), pp. 84–100.

[98] Roberts, 2005, pp. 1–32.

[99] Besides the appeals cases, anecdotal evidence such as the 1923 murder case over land and Ingrams' story mentioned earlier of land disputes shows that property issues were very important on Pemba. *Annual Report for the Zanzibar Islands*, 1923; Ingrams, 1942.

representation because male relatives assumed control over their female relatives' property and male neighbors tried to usurp their female neighbors' property.[100] Lastly, this pattern of third-party involvement points to the changing interpretations of evidence and value in witnesses, changes that the colonial courts required of the local Islamic courts.

Disputes between moneylenders and their debtors were the most common cases in HBM courts because two-thirds of moneylenders on Pemba were Indian and had to take their cases to the British courts.[101] Contributing to the commonality of these cases was the fact that debt on land was a function of the economic structure on the island. Even in the nineteenth century, before the end of slavery, clove growers borrowed money during the two periods between the clove harvests. They used their land as security for these debts, and most had mortgaged their land to Indian moneylenders.[102] Because Indians had not been able to legally own slaves since the 1860s on the islands, many Indian moneylenders

---

[100] For an example of a brother taking over his sister's property, see ZNA AC5/2, Letter, July 27, 1896; for an example of a male neighbor encroaching on his female neighbor's property, see PNA AI1/58, His Highness's Court ZP, Civil Case No. 8 of 1933; Elke Stockreiter argues that women became active participants in the courts by the beginning of the twentieth century in defending their rights; Stockreiter, pp. 133–4; ZNA AC7/26 August 1898, involves a woman trying to get a male buyer to pay her for the land he purchased, indicating that women could have difficulty representing themselves in business transactions.

[101] FO 881/10268X, Annual reports for 1909 and 1910; *Zanzibar Gazette* listings of license applications for moneylenders in the three districts of Pemba from 1914–1918 indicate that two-thirds of moneylenders were Indian, whereas the other third were Arabs, with only a few Africans acting as moneylenders.

[102] The clove market was open to the boom/bust cycles that occurred with other natural products. Clove harvests were generally larger every three years, but there was no certainty about good years because extra rain could spoil a large crop at the last minute, after the cloves had been picked but not dried. Also, the world price for cloves fluctuated dramatically depending on multiple variables. So one year with a huge crop could bring a low per-pound price and hold the same total price value as a small crop that had a high per-pound price. However, the costs of picking the larger crop were higher; thus that year could be a loss, even when the crop was large. Additionally, in the later 1880s and into the 1890s, the bottom fell out of the clove market. This coincided with British efforts to cut off the supply of slave labor to the islands, forcing landowners to either use wage labor, which was difficult to find, or to pick fewer of the cloves on the trees. Each year that went badly made it harder for landowners to pay down their debts from the previous season. When the Abolition Decree of 1897 required that owners pay wage labor, their financial needs before the harvest became even greater, and their debt increased. It is likely that many wealthy landowners existed on Pemba before 1880, but by 1910, few large-scale landowners were left. The Clove Bonus Registers of the 1920s indicated few large-scale properties remaining on Pemba. ZNA AP29/5–8, Clove Bonus Registers.

allowed their Arab and African debtors to remain living on the land and simply pay the interest on their mortgages. Once emancipation came, many moneylenders began calling in their debts and selling the land. As one of the main moneylenders in Chake Chake told the Vice Consul in 1897, "[H]e had squeezed the Arabs dry."[103] He felt he had gotten all the value he could in terms of interest, and now he was ready to sell the mortgaged land he controlled because its value had dropped so precipitously.

Conditional or fictional sales of land, known as *bei kataa*, complicated land disputes on Pemba because Muslim moneylenders used them to avoid the Islamic proscription against usury.[104] According to the 1935 report by Last and Bartlett, using *bei kataa* allowed a moneylender to "practise usury with impunity, and without the publicity which may be undesirable for professional or religious reasons."[105] Usury is forbidden to Muslims; this means that they should not profit from another person's ill-fortune. This partially explains why many of the moneylenders were Indians, yet the vast majority of moneylenders on Pemba were Muslim, regardless of ethnicity. Thus moneylenders resorted to *bei kataa* to legalistically avoid breaking the rules of their religion. For example, in a *bei kataa*, a person might "sell" his or her land to a moneylender for 100 rupees – even though the land was worth 150 rupees – with the condition that the original owner had the first right to repurchase the property when the moneylender put it up for sale after a specified period of time. The borrower would then continue to live on the land and pay "rent," which was really interest on the loan, to the moneylender. Most borrowers saw this as a straight mortgage and expected the moneylenders to hold onto the land until the debtors could repay the purchase price. However, the *bei kataa* were registered as outright sales in the courts, and usually the "conditions" of the sale were either oral or, if written, contained in a separate document. Most people who made these agreements made them in good faith with the intention of repaying the debt. However, life intervened, and they delayed repayment, and usually moneylenders gave people an extra year or even longer to repay. Colonial officials suggested that

<hr />

[103] *Report by Vice Consul O'Sullivan on the island of Pemba,1896–1897*, p. 9.

[104] The terminology of *bei kataa* comes from the J. S. Last and Bartlett report of 1933, but in ZNA AI1/2, His Highness's Court ZP, Appeal Case No. 11 of 1918, the term *ikala* was used. The Arabic term for a conditional sale is *bei khiar*. Last and Barlett argued that many moneylenders used the *bei kataa* in order to avoid paying for government licenses; J. S. Last and C. A. Bartlett, *Report on the Indebtedness of the Agricultural Classes, 1933* (Zanzibar: Government Printer, 1934).

[105] Last and Bartlett, p. 6.

elite Arabs, especially in Zanzibar, had no intention of repaying debts, but as the court cases attest, poorer individuals had to repay their debts eventually.[106] Nonetheless, in due course, the moneylenders would sell the property to a new owner, who would then attempt to evict the original owner. The original owner was often confused or frustrated when he or she brought the moneylender to court, claiming it was a mortgage, not an outright sale.[107] Since the conditions of the agreement were often oral, the *kadhi* and magistrates were left trying to decide if the sale was indeed conditional and, if so, what the conditions were. While the *kadhi* understood the reasoning behind *bei kataa*, the British magistrates found conditional sales impractical and wasteful. One of the differences between *makadhi* and magistrates in these disputes was that *makadhi* could make litigants swear an oath about the oral aspects of the contracts. This was generally an effective measure, as seen in a case where the Arab moneylender had insisted the sale was outright and not conditional, but when faced with taking an oath, he admitted that it was conditional.[108] While magistrates in the British legal system could demand litigants to swear oaths, as seen with the case of Mtwana at the beginning of this chapter, magistrates generally resisted using this tactic for property disputes.

Not only was ownership of property an issue, but litigation of property disputes also arose from a lack of clear boundary lines in title deeds. The Consul General complained in 1908 that "the boundaries … are as a rule entirely undefined, and the surveyor has frequently to depend upon the evidence of some of the older inhabitants who are guided, not by any ordinary landmarks, but by the reputed ownership of each individual tree."[109] The "reputed ownership" meant that disagreements were often contests between two people and their witnesses, leaving judgment to rest on whomever was believable and, as such, could prove their respectability.

---

[106] Africa No. 4 (1909), *Despatchs from His Majesty's Agent and Consul-General at Zanzibar Furnishing a Report on the Administration, Finance, and General Condition of the Zanzibar Protectorate.*

[107] For examples, see cases PNA AI1/2, His Highness's Court ZP, Appeal Case No. 11 of 1918; AI1/78, His Highness's Court CZ, the District Registry of the High Court, Appeal No. 10 of 1934, Mariam binti Khamis bin Bakari el-Mafazi vs. Hamadi bin Shame; AI1/90, His Highness's Court CZ, the Resident Magistrate's Court Pemba, Civil Case No. 136 of 1952, Athman bin Bakari vs. Salim bin Rashid el-Husni; (no accession number) His Highness's Court CZ, the District Registry of High Court Pemba, Appeal No. 6 of 1946, Jokha binti Abdulla el-Maskria vs. Mbaruk bin Abeid el-Mahrusi.

[108] PNA AI1/2, His Highness's Court ZP, Appeal Case No. 11 of 1918.

[109] Africa No. 4 (1909), *Despatchs from His Majesty's Agent and Consul-General at Zanzibar Furnishing a Report on the Administration, Finance, and General Condition of the Zanzibar Protectorate*, p. 12.

Officials lamented that until the survey of Pemba was completed (which happened in 1912), no real title deeds could be given for property regardless of efforts to do so. Because so few properties had title deeds, as they were handed down by family members and never went through the court systems, land could remain unregistered even into the 1940s, thirty years after the British consolidated the colonial bureaucracy on Pemba. Thus limited knowledge of boundaries and few title deeds created a chaotic system of lending in which borrowers would sometimes mortgage the same piece of property to multiple moneylenders.[110] Savvy moneylenders had to know who owned what property and if it was mortgaged to anyone else, which explains why one moneylender could tell a man trying to mortgage his sister's property that she knew that it did not belong to him and that his reputation concerning land deals was shaky at best.[111]

Moneylenders tended to win their cases because they understood the systems of the courts and how to protect their interests. The British accepted the premise of charging interest on money lent, although they thought the rates of interest charged in the islands were usurious, thus HBM courts were a place of protection for the rights of moneylenders. Worried colonial officials brought in a number of consultants to study the "problem of indebtedness" of landowners in the islands.[112] The difference between indebtedness on Pemba and Zanzibar was a matter of scale. On Zanzibar, large landowners had huge debts, wherein on Pemba, many individuals had small debts. In examining *bei kataa* written in Pemba between 1913 and 1914, the amount borrowed by Arabs averaged 137 rupees, among WaPemba and Shirazi it was 74 rupees, and ex-slaves averaged loans of 55 rupees.[113] These debts correspond to the sizes of plots of land owned by individuals. In the bonus scheme records of the 1920s, in the three areas that made up the Chake Chake district, 56.4 percent of

---

[110] Africa No. 4 (1909), *Despatchs from His Majesty's Agent and Consul-General at Zanzibar Furnishing a Report on the Administration, Finance, and General Condition of the Zanzibar Protectorate*. However, I suspect this was more of a problem in Zanzibar than on Pemba because moneylenders tended to be in less competition with each other on Pemba.

[111] PNA AI1/19, His Highness's Court SC, Civil Case District Court at Weti, No. 683 of 1919.

[112] Last and Bartlett, 1934; Vincent H. Kirkham, *Zanzibar Protectorate: Memorandum on the Functions of a Department of Agriculture with Special Reference to Zanzibar*. (Zanzibar: Government Printer, 1931); Ernest M. Dowson, *A Note on Agricultural Indebtedness in the Zanzibar Protectorate* (Zanzibar: Government Printer, 1936); for secondary literature discussing the indebtedness crisis, see Cooper, 1980, pp. 139–44; Welliver, 1990, pp. 279–97.

[113] ZNA AM13/1, General deeds from Pemba 1893–1929; ZNA AM14/1, General deeds from Pemba 1893–1929.

owners owned fewer than fifty trees, a small plot.[114] Ninety-two percent of landowners in the district had fewer than 200 trees on their land. Arabs still dominated ownership of clove tree land, with 40 percent of owners in the district being Arab, even though they only made up approximately 17 percent of the population. Arabs were the primary owners of the few larger plots of land, whereas most Africans, who made up almost 36 percent of landowners, owned plots of fifty trees or less. Yet the probate records also show that many Africans owned land that was not planted with clove trees. Nonclove land was exempt from inclusion in the bonus schemes, which have been the main tool scholars have used to calculate the percentages of landownership on the islands.[115] All these forms of land were mortgaged at various times.

Boundary disputes were not found just in mortgaged properties but were common among neighbors as well. When the Friends missionaries bought the plantation of Banani, they gathered all thirty of their neighboring landowners and walked the boundary of the land together to clarify the boundary lines. As the Friends recalled, even when they were pretty certain about a boundary, they erred on the side of giving in to their neighbors. The Friends then carefully marked the boundaries in an effort to avoid future disputes.[116] Ingrams' recollection of his first case, related earlier, also tells of a long-simmering boundary dispute between neighbors that remained unsettled even after Ingrams sentenced one neighbor to prison. Disputes over the edges of a property tended to be resolved by *masheha* or in the lower-level subordinate courts, if not by force. The property cases that usually ended up being appealed in the *kadhi* courts were cases where the ownership of an entire piece of property was in question, although disagreements over boundaries and neighbors encroaching on property did go through the appeals process on occasion.[117]

---

[114] This information is based on a collation of data from the three registers for the three Chake Chake districts. ZNA AP29/5–8, Clove Bonus Registers.

[115] Coconut trees were as commonly held as clove trees. However, rice land and "barren" lands were also commonly owned by Africans. See as examples PNA AK1/50, Zubeda binti Yakuti, May 26, 1910; PNA AK1/52, Barki bin Faki, May 21, 1910; PNA AK1/57, Hadia binti Uledi, July 5, 1910; PNA AK1/61, Khamis Alawi Mpemba, July 24, 1910; PNA AK1/80, Bakari Fakih Bakari, November 14, 1910; PNA AK1/206, Fundi Haji bin Sharbo, August 25, 1912; PNA AK1/321, Hamadi wadi Nasibu, June 11, 1913; PNA AK1/565, Kingwaba wadi Salmini, June 3, 1917; PNA AK1/1643, Rehandi bin Amani, December 10, 1925.

[116] Newman, pp. 171–3.

[117] PNA AI1/58, His Highness's Court SCZ, Civil Case No. 8 of 1933; PNA (no accession number), *Kadhi*'s Court at Chake Chake, Case No. 263 of 1945, Said bin Suleiman

In the late nineteenth century and into the twentieth century, squatting on land was a problem, as Frederick Cooper suggested.[118] However, it was not only former slaves claiming land but also Arabs claiming lands in areas with large WaPemba populations. Arabs claimed this property as having been taken through the conquest of their ancestors, and local Africans actively resisted this interpretation of events and ownership.[119] Much of this land was not necessarily good clove land; thus it had not previously interested Arab elites. Because of the indebtedness crisis, many elites lost their land to moneylenders and were looking for "vacant" land. These lands were assumed by WaPemba as lands that they could let lay fallow and were owned communally. Nonetheless, these cases began showing up in the courts after emancipation, in addition to the cases of ex-slave squatters. Most of the cases that went to the appeals court over property disputes were from one person selling or trying to cultivate the land that another person viewed as his or her own. The dispute could be based on problems with conditional sales, ex-slaves squatting on the land of their former owners, and seemingly vacant land – especially if it was owned by minors or relatives disputing over the right to property.[120] On occasion, two completely different unrelated people of freeborn status claimed the same piece of land. From many of these disputes, it is apparent that many pieces of property on Pemba did not have obvious owners, and if they were not cultivated and maintained on a yearly basis, people without land moved onto the land and eventually sued in the courts to claim and receive documentation of ownership.[121] What comes out most

Bajuni vs. Omar bin Juma Swahili; PNA AI1/89, His Highness's Court SCZ in the Resident Magistrates Court, Chake Chake, Civil Case No. 135 of 1952, Salim bin Ahmed bin Juma al-Mazrui vs. Muhenne bin Ahmed bin Juma Mazrui.

[118] Cooper, 1980, pp. 125–72.

[119] Newman, pp. 82–5; PRO FO 881/10268X, Annual reports for 1909 and 1910; annual report from the assistant collector of Wete noted that the Arabs were moving onto WaPemba lands.

[120] Only two appeals cases involved ex-slaves who appear to have been squatting on the land of their former owners. This suggests that either most ex-slaves did not see themselves as having a right to the land or they could not afford to take cases to the courts. In both cases involving ex-slaves, they were the defendants, not the plaintiffs, in the cases; thus they were forced into the courts. See cases PNA AI1/34, Her British Majesty's Court SCZ FCS Court, Chake Chake, Civil Case No. 986 of 1928, Fatuma binti Ali bin Sababu vs. Hamadi Kheri and Juma Kheri; PNA AI1/44, His Highnesses Court SCZ, Civil Appeal No. 15 of 1934, Bahati binti Serenge vs. Mohamed bin Musa bin Burhan Shirazi.

[121] "Pemba," *The Friend* 5 (September 1902), pp. 578–88. "The working population are drifting, cultivating vacant plots of land indiscriminately, and both Arabs and natives are allowing a large area of country to lie uncultivated."

clearly in the appeals cases is the desperation of some litigants. In most cases, one litigant was in a much more precarious position than the other, which influenced his or her ability to win the case.

PUBLICIZING REPUTATION

Located within a few feet of nearby buildings, the *kadhi* courts before the 1920s were two-story structures without walls (Figure 3.2). The first floor, barely high enough for a person to stand up in, had space for the waiting litigants, whereas the court was conducted on the upper level. The top floor was open on all sides with a railing made from mangrove poles and a thatched roof. The *kadhi* sat on a chair, and the litigants, witnesses, and court clerks sat on the floor on mats or stood against the balustrades. The voices of angry litigants who loudly accused others carried across the paths to neighboring homes and businesses, thus creating a public spectacle of the cases. Most litigants had already publicly stated their cases in front of the local *masheha* but had found their dispute resolutions unsatisfactory. Once cases came to the *kadhi* and magistrates courts, they had already been aired publicly for months or even years. Participants in the courts came to court in order to win their cases, but winning in court was not necessarily about getting control over money or property – winning was about publicly showing that others with authority such as the *makadhi* agreed with a position, that the litigants were "right," and as such gaining them *heshima*.

From remaining images and descriptions of the courts, it appears that the courts were gendered as a male space. Women came to the courts as litigants and witnesses, but they often sought to have male representation in the courts in order to demonstrate their respectability. Women were not required to use *wakil* to speak for them because women were jural majors, yet on several occasions a *kadhi* requested that a woman get a *wakil* to represent her. The *makadhi* were elite men who also had to maintain their *heshima*, and speaking to unrelated women was not appropriate for them. This explains why the *makadhi* asked women to have a male representative in the courts. Even though women were not the primary occupants of the courts, they were still active in the court space and could take away information about the proceedings of the courts to discuss with other women in their villages. The gendered dynamic of the courts allowed participants to demonstrate their *heshima* and build their reputations, or in some cases their behavior caused them to lose *heshima*.

FIGURE 3.2. The *kadhi* courthouse in Chake Chake. (Reprinted from J. E. E. Craster, *Pemba: The Spice Island of Zanzibar*. London: T.F. Unwin, 1913.)

When Ali bin Abdallah and his sons were arrested and tried in court in the 1890s (which I will discuss further in Chapter 5), the court made public what most people only said in private by questioning the *heshima* of the family for behaving beyond what was respectable for a slave owner, even one antagonized by runaway slaves.[122] During the time when the family had the power to coerce the legal system through the *liwali* of the area, they were treated with *heshima*, but out of fear, not respect. However, once Ali and his son were sent to prison, their dishonorable

[122] See the work of Ann Twinam for a discussion of how knowledge about families that was "known publicly" if kept "private" could maintain the honor of the family. For instance, if a girl got pregnant out of wedlock, she would be sent away for a year and have the baby elsewhere and then return. Most people understood implicitly the reason the girl left – so it was "publicly known," yet it remained "private" at the same time. Ann Twinam, *Public Lives, Private Secrets: Gender, Honor, Sexuality, and Illegitimacy in Colonial Spanish America* (Palo Alto, CA: Stanford University Press, 1999), pp. 59–88.

reputation was publicly confirmed. Ali bin Abdallah el-Hinawi's descendants continued to have a questionable reputation as cantankerous and difficult people in the community who were always ready to start an argument with others, as I will discuss in Chapter 5.[123] Ali's family still had *heshima* because they remained wealthy and had an elite heritage, but their reputations were questionable enough that other families refused marriage offers from them.[124] Another case from the late nineteenth century suggests that the poor reputation of certain families became increasingly publicized in their communities. The Vice Consul sent a message to the head judge in Zanzibar that "Sheikh Suleiman bin Said [the *liwali*] informed me that the members of the Addi family have always given him trouble whenever they were called upon to settle their debts."[125] The *liwali* was not complaining simply about the two sons who refused to pay the debts of their dead father; he condemned the entire family as having a poor reputation and limited *heshima*. The *kadhi* courts were similar to the *liwali* courts as a public venue to critique individuals' *heshima*.

Similar to the expanding definition of *heshima*, medieval European societies used the word *fama* to represent the reputation, common knowledge, and "talk" of individuals.[126] In medieval European courts, investigators interrogated a person's *fama* through witnesses. Reputation was a vital aspect of evidence in these courts, pointing to similar parallels to that found in the courts of Pemba. Both court systems accepted written and oral evidence and allowed the use of oaths as a form of evidence.[127] Although judges on Pemba did not always specifically ask witnesses about individuals' reputations, a person's ability to bring respectable witnesses to court helped to cement his or her reputation. Additionally, in the probate courts, local *kadhi* vetted the reputations of witnesses and claimants through oaths and testimony of witnesses whose reputations were known to the judges. Individuals could demonstrate *heshima* through their behavior, clothing, and speech, among other elements, but respectability was ultimately conferred by others. Exploring European concepts of *fama* and the notion that individuals had "multiple *fama*" opens new ways to consider *heshima* in Zanzibari courts. As scholars of medieval

[123] ZNA AB70/3, Disturbance created by Manga Arabs at Wete, Pemba.
[124] ZNA AB70/3, Disturbance created by Manga Arabs at Wete, Pemba.
[125] ZNA AC9/2, Pemba Vice Consul to Judge Cracknall, Letter, September 30, 1898.
[126] Thelma Fenster and Daniel Lord Smail, "Introduction," in *Fama: The Politics of Talk and Reputation in Medieval Europe*, edited by Thelma Fenster and Daniel Lord Smail (Ithaca, NY: Cornell University Press, 2003), *passim*.
[127] Caviness and Nelson, 2003, pp. 60–3, 71–2.

Europe point out, because different circles of people interpreted or witnessed events differently, a person could have different *fama* or reputations among various members of the community. This suggests that people along the Swahili coast could likewise have "multiple *heshima*"; thus, in the courts, litigants negotiated the reputations of each other and their witnesses.[128]

Kadhi viewed their treatment of appellants as a public dialogue about the *heshima* of the litigants by regularly pronouncing on litigants' respectability. In medieval Europe, infamy was a legal category that prevented a person whose reputation was questioned from testifying in a court.[129] Likewise on Pemba a person with a bad reputation (*sifa/heshima mbaya*) would pervert the process of justice. Such a person could not be a witness in court, and as demonstrated in Chapter 4, the inability to be a witness could mean being disinherited or unable to claim debts from the courts. The Pemban courts did not have an official category of infamy; nonetheless, judges indicated their unwillingness to accept testimony from some individuals and questioned their reputations. In 1919, a *kadhi* became so disgusted with a litigant, Idi bin Haji el Bori, that the *kadhi* called him a liar in the court and dismissed the case based on Idi's reputation.[130] The *kadhi* noted that in a previous case involving Idi's sister and the sale of a cow, Idi lied under oath, which was proven by evidence later provided in the court. His lie under oath was viewed by the judge as a pernicious action and permanently marked Idi as unworthy of a hearing and lacking *heshima* and any right to pursue cases in the courts. In a later court case, a *kadhi* complained about a litigant, "This defendant has formed a habit of this type in all the cases. He is evasive and stubborn, both in his statements and replies to the court."[131] *Makadhi* knew many of the litigants outside the courts and would at times bring their own opinions of cases into the courts. In this particular case, the *kadhi* noted that the litigant was obstructionist "in all cases" of disputes with others.[132] *Kadhi* rebukes

---

[128] Chris Wickham, "*Fama* and the Law in Twelfth-Century Tuscany," in *Fama: The Politics of Talk and Reputation in Medieval Europe*, edited by Thelma Fenster and Daniel Lord Smail (Ithaca, NY: Cornell University Press, 2003).

[129] Jeffrey Bowman, "Infamy and Proof in Medieval Spain," in *Fama: The Politics of Talk and Reputation in Medieval Europe*, edited by Thelma Fenster and Daniel Lord Smail (Ithaca, NY: Cornell University Press, 2003), pp. 95–6.

[130] PNA AI1/6, His Highness's Court ZP, Appeal Case No. 5 of 1920, Idi bin Haji vs. Ahamed bin Khalfan.

[131] PNA AI1/77, His Highness's Court SCZ, Civil Case No. 189 of 1934.

[132] Sir T. S. Tomlinson and G. K. Knight-Bruce, *Law Reports Containing Cases Determined by the High Court for Zanzibar and on Appeal Therefrom by the Court of Appeal*

to litigants were a very direct and public questioning of individual litigants' behavior, reputation, and morals. Thus, even though infamy was not a legal practice in the Pemban courts, clearly, reputation was used by judges to remove a litigant or witness from the court.

Courts served as sites to debate individual's reputations and their *heshima*, allowing family and neighbors the opportunity to publicly reproach questionable behavior. In 1918, Fatma binti Dadi proved to a court full of men and the *kadhi* that her cousin, Seif bin Hassan, was fully justified in being angry with her. Fatma brought Seif to court to deny that he was her cousin or had a right to inherit from her sister's estate.[133] Other women had brought male "relatives" to court before and won, so her choice to bring him to court was not unusual, but Fatma's behavior in the court and her inability to get witnesses to testify for her reified Seif's presentation of her as lacking *heshima*. Even though Fatma was the one who brought the case against Seif, he immediately turned the tables on her in the court, bringing in numerous witnesses who all questioned her claims of Arab descent, her respectability for leaving her husband, and her rejection of Seif as a cousin, even though he had acted as a dutiful guardian by arranging her marriage for her.[134] Fatma lost the most credibility by being unable to get a single witness to come to court on her behalf. Her lack of witnesses was particularly significant because she simply needed two people to testify that they knew her father and that he was not related to Seif. Seif's witnesses testified to the public conversations they and others had had about Fatma's reputation in the community. One witness reported that another man told him that she was not from the Arab clan from which she claimed descent. This gossip, accepted as evidence by the court, illustrated that gossip was used in the courts. By the end of the case, the *kadhi* decreed that she was "unjustified in bringing this action" and that her behavior lacked respectability. However, it is unlikely that this court case changed Fatma's reputation, which was already questionable given that a British magistrate had already ruled that Seif was her cousin a year before. What the court case did was give Seif a public acknowledgment that he was right and remove any imputations

---

for *Eastern Africa and by the Privy Council*, Vol. III, 1923–7 (London: Waterlow and Sons, 1928). In one case, the British appeals court judge complained about the presiding *kadhi*, who "imported knowledge" into the case.

[133] PNA AI1/5; Seif inherited as an *assaba*, a paternal male relative.

[134] Stockreiter argues that women on Zanzibar offered their status as married women as a sign of their respectability. Likewise, Pamela Scully shows this to be the case in nineteenth-century South Africa. Thus Seif's questioning of Fatma's status as a divorced woman demonstrates his perception of her as lacking respectability.

made by Fatma that he was the one lacking *heshima*. The case of Fatma and Seif demonstrates how judges used the courts to publicly declare a person had a bad reputation.

The public environment of the *kadhi* and magistrate courts acted as a newspaper for the nonliterate members of Pemban society. Just as elites and the government used the *Zanzibar Gazette* as a method to communicate information about individuals' creditworthiness, such as posting bankruptcy listings and *wakf* notices, the courts were a community-sanctioned and public method of finalizing interpretations of individuals' reputations and *heshima*. Discussions of reputations occurred outside the courts because people gossiped – and even sang songs in the cases of public and elite figures – about the events and people involved in disputes. Neighbors and relatives obviously took sides in these disputes. Imputations against people's reputations occurred all the time through accusations of witchcraft, theft, usury, adultery, drinking alcohol, gambling, gossiping, thriftlessness, idleness, or laziness, among others. How people responded to the accusations depended on their positions in the community and whether they felt the accusations were harming their ability to conduct their daily affairs. By taking cases to court, individuals hoped to bring the debates over their behavior and reputation to a public forum that would give them a final decision because, as Steere noted in 1875, "[I]t was a secret, but it oozed out."[135] Very little remained hidden in a society where talk was so important in people's lives.[136]

CONCLUSION

The first fifteen years after the British became a presence on the island in 1895 were a critical time that changed the way people looked at the courts. Elites had to accept that slaves, ex-slaves, WaPemba, and others had an equal right of access to the courts. No longer was the outcome of a case determined by the power of an individual to muster physical support for his or her cause. However, rather than creating systemic change, the transformation of the courts was often associated with the personalities of the individual officials. Slaves could take cases to the courts, but unless they had a British interlocutor in their cases, they may or may not

---

[135] Steere, 1884, p. 452, n. 174.
[136] Fenster and Smail argue for using the terminology of "talk" rather than "gossip" because it removes the moralizing and pejorative implications of gossip while encompassing all aspects of oral language and communication; Fenster and Smail, 2003, p. 10.

have been heard by the *liwali* and *makadhi*. However, the institutionalization of the courts around 1910 was supposed to bring consistency in the deployment of colonial law. Corrupt and inefficient *makadhi* were fired, and no longer were courts to be run on personality but rather the law. Of course, there was still room for problems, as shown with the assistant collectors' inability to consistently apply the law. In the long run, though, the colonial courts lost their position as the champion of the downtrodden, the poor, the ex-slaves, and women because they moved to emphasize the use of written documentation for evidence, which was rarely available for marginalized members of society.

In many respects the institutionalization of the courts turned the *kadhi* courts into the ideal location for women and ex-slaves to take their disputes with the elite. The *makadhi* certainly resisted efforts by colonial officials to change the *sheria* rules of evidence. However, they accepted some changes, such as giving women and slaves equal weight as witnesses, while rejecting others, as seen in the prohibition of using oaths as evidence. The refusal to end the use of oaths made the *kadhi* courts into an arbiter of reputation in the community. A person's willingness or ability to get written documentation showed their education, but nothing was proven in the courts in terms of reputation and *heshima*. The orality of the *kadhi* courts merged with the expectations of local communities that individuals staked their reputation on their word, and individuals' word was only as good as their reputations. Courts were one of the places where a person's word and reputation were publicly confirmed on Pemba.

4

Reputation, *Heshima*, and Community

In 1912, just a few years after the complete abolition of slavery along the Swahili coast, J. E. E. Craster, a colonial surveyor, was discussing emancipation with a former slave. As mentioned at the end of Chapter 1, Craster asked the man if he intended to go back to his home area and was surprised to receive the answer, "Return to those pagans? No way. Besides I have my house here, and a small piece of land, and my son is a rich man, a silversmith in the town, and he works hard."[1] This man's response to Craster encompassed many of the changes that occurred on Pemba during the transition from a slaveholding to a free society and raises a number of questions concerning former slaves' view of Islam and investment in respectability. His response also illustrates the ways in which definitions of *heshima* shifted in the postemancipation era. First, the man articulated his identity as a good, pious Muslim who would not consider living among pagans. Second, he pointed to the role of kinship networks for successful survival, explaining that he would not leave because he had family in the area. Third, his son was wealthy – emphasizing the role wealth had in giving someone *heshima*. The man himself had a "small piece of land" that gave him economic independence as well. Fourth, he explained that working hard was no longer a sign of subservience, as it was before abolition. By working hard, his son had amassed wealth and, as such, a position in his community. The ex-slave implicated to Craster that he had a good reputation by claiming an identity as a good Muslim with links to wealthy family members.

[1] Craster, p. 95.

The introduction of British officials into Pemba was a major turning point in the way *heshima* was deployed at the turn of the century. Prior to the declaration of the British Protectorate in 1890, *heshima* was intrinsically linked to lineage, because an individual's power and respectability was based on his or her ability to muster up support if engaged in a dispute. Lineage support was not guaranteed for those of elite birth, though, because even elite Arabs who behaved badly could be severed from lineages and denied recognition of respectability from community members.[2] Slowly, as the British became the "enforcers" in dispute resolution with their increasing control over the Islamic court system, lineage became less significant for *heshima*. Within twenty years of the declaration of the Protectorate, wealth and its display became far more important in qualifying a person's *heshima* than lineage. This shift allowed lower-status people, such as former slaves, who were economically successful to build *heshima* and, as such, move up the social ladder locally. While wealth offered a key point of entry to social success, it was what people did with their wealth that gave them respectability. *Heshima* could only be gained through displaying an understanding of the tenets of Islam. Individuals had to show their knowledge of Islamic principles through their dress, behavior, and piety. Moreover, they had to build reputations as honest, creditworthy neighbors in order to survive the lean periods between clove harvests. This shift is also seen in the changing definition of *heshima*. In the nineteenth century, *heshima* was associated with honor, as discussed in Chapter 1, but by the twentieth century as ex-slaves claimed rights to *heshima*, it took on the meaning of respectability. Implicit in this change was that ex-slaves could never have honor, but they could be respectable.

In a number of slaveholding societies, owners gained prestige by dressing their slaves elaborately. Robert Ross has shown in seventeenth- and eighteenth-century Cape Town that the government had to create laws to curb the excessive display by slave-owning men and women who would dress their slaves in elaborate clothing in order to demonstrate the owners' honor.[3] Tamara Walker highlights a similar trend in eighteenth-century

---

[2] ZNA AC5/1, Letter Vice Consul Pemba, July 31, 1895. In this letter, an Arab with a bad reputation was arrested after stealing the slaves of an Arab with a good reputation. And all the "respectable residents" of the town were happy with the arrest.

[3] Ross argues that this was because women would fight over status symbols and the government was trying to prevent men going bankrupt. Although I would interpret these laws as men trying to control women who were viewed as exerting an influence beyond "their place." Robert Ross, *Status and Respectability in the Cape Colony* (Cambridge: Cambridge University Press, 1999), pp. 11–13.

Peru.[4] Jeremy Prestholdt calls the dressing up of slaves "symbolic subjection" and argues that slaves became symbols first of their owners and later of the European "redeemers," both of whom treated the enslaved as blank slates on which they could project their desires and identities.[5] Likewise he argues that emancipated ex-slaves attempted to remake themselves through clothing, naming, and their identification as *waungwana* ("freeborn"). However, this incisive analysis of the larger patterns similarly loses sight of the slaves' continuing humanity. Even at enslavement and after, no one was a blank slate, no matter how much they were treated as a "symbol." Walker points to the way access to nice clothing allowed slaves to articulate respectability for themselves, thus reversing their subjection. While slaves had more leeway to articulate their interests and desires once manumitted, many slaves refused to accept submission to others even during their enslavement. The story of Hamida, a slave of Binti Abdulrahim, makes this case in point. Hamida endured the affections, including sexual intercourse, of Binti Abdulrahim's brother Masoud because she accepted this as part of being a slave (and likely also being a woman).[6] However, when Masoud attempted to make her his concubine, making her a symbol of his fantasies by essentially treating her as a blank slate, she refused. She went to the *liwali* and complained; she refused to be made a concubine. Thus, while I agree that enslavers and redeemers attempted to treat slaves as blank slates, even before emancipation, slaves actively rejected "symbolic subjection" by others. Emancipation simply accelerated and expanded the processes of "remaking themselves."

This chapter explores the ways ex-slaves worked to reorder definitions of *heshima* to privilege wealth and communal reputation over lineage. Differing greatly from Zanzibar Town, ex-slaves on Pemba used the British-controlled courts to expand the role of reputation in local perceptions of individuals' *heshima*. Fair argues that emancipation gave ex-slaves in Zanzibar Town more opportunity to critique the wealthy and question their *heshima,* but urban court "decisions ... [rarely] coincided with local conceptions of justice."[7] The urban courts ruled to make urban

---

[4] Tamara Walker, "He Outfitted His Family in Notable Decency': Slavery, Honour and Dress in Eighteenth-Century Lima, Peru," *Slavery and Abolition* 30, no. 2 (September 2009), pp. 383–403.

[5] Prestholdt, chap. 5.

[6] Africa No. 6, *Correspondence Respecting the Abolition of the Legal Status of Slavery in Zanzibar and Pemba,* No. 21, Sir A. Hardinge to the Marquess of Salisbury, Zanzibar, January 3, 1898.

[7] Fair, 2001, p. 195.

ex-slaves pay land rent on *wakf* land that had been donated decades previously for the poor. The density of well-born, wealthy, and powerful Arabs and Indians in Zanzibar Town allowed them to dominate the courts in ways that were not feasible to the much poorer and highly indebted elite of Pemba. Elite and poor alike on Pemba needed credit during the nonharvest months in order to make ends meet; daily survival required a good reputation. Moreover, definitions of labor changed dramatically as elites began working at government jobs where they were no longer in positions of absolute authority. A person's reputation became a powerful component of *heshima* on Pemba, where individuals and families had to publicly demonstrate their *heshima* rather than be born with it.

REPUTATION

In the nineteenth century, reputation meant a person of character, someone who had *sifa*. *Sifa* connoted praise or commendation of character; it still means "good reputation" in Swahili.[8] However, the word *heshima*, as it shifted away from connoting "honor" to indicating "respectability," also came to mean "reputation" in the twentieth century.[9] A person with a good reputation had *heshima*. When *heshima* meant simply honor, the person's reputation was not linked to *heshima* per se. For instance, Ali bin Abdallah had *heshima* through his lineage and connections to the Sultan, but he also had a reputation for being overbearing and brutal.[10] While his reputation was not positive, it did not affect his access to power and *heshima*. However, as *heshima* shifted to mean "respectability," reputation became integral to the meaning and value of *heshima*. The vulnerability inherent in respectability was directly linked to the question of one's reputation.

Just as the terminology of *heshima* changed, the language of reputation, gossip, and slander changed as well. In the nineteenth century, reputation had few words to describe it – *sifa*, *nemsi* in Mombasa, and eventually, *heshima* by 1902. However, the language for affecting or destroying a person's reputation was varied. *Nenana* was to "talk against one another," as *kupapuriana* meant to "pick apart one another's reputations." *Puzika* meant "to gossip among women." An *mdunsi* was

---

[8] Steere, 1884; Krapf, 1882; Madan, 1902; Johnson, 1939.

[9] In neither Steere (1884) nor Krapf (1882) is *heshima* defined as "reputation." However, in Madan (1902), reputation can be translated as either *sifa* or *heshima*.

[10] Africa No. 7, *Correspondence Respecting Slavery in the Zanzibar Dominions* (1896), p. 42.

someone who "asks many questions about family matters and spreads about immediately what he heard privately." Many proverbs and poems of the late nineteenth and early twentieth centuries warned people against idle gossip about others.[11] *Izara* was "to publish things about a person to create scandal." *Fitina* meant "to sow discord," and "to slander" was *kuamba*. A *dukizi* eavesdropped on other people. *Mzuzi* (*msusi*), *mwongo* (*mwong, mrongo*), *mjanja, mnafiki,* and a *mukari* were all synonyms for a "liar." *Kudanganika* meant "to prove someone to be a liar," especially in court. All these words illustrate the ways in which a person's reputation could be affected by the speech and actions of others, by their *upelelezi* ("gossip"). Even the word for gossip showed intriguing change over time. By 1902, the Madan dictionary translated gossip as *mazumgumzo* ("conversation"). No longer did a distinction between gossip and conversation exist.[12] Parallel in time to the impact gossip could have on a person's reputation, gossip became the norm of conversation. It became conversation itself, suggesting the everyday nature of gossip in people's lives and how they found ways to negotiate their reputations through the treacherous waters of scandal and rumor on the island.

Most disputes never made it to the courts, and those which did more often focused on property rather than reputation. Yet these disputes existed beyond the elite. For example, Mwajuma, an ex-slave living on the Friends' plantation with her husband, Daniel, became suspicious of Sanura Mama Sudi and accused her of adultery with Daniel.[13] Sanura, who was also married, denied the allegations, but the missionaries nevertheless kicked her off the *shamba*. This dispute had very real consequences for both Sanura's reputation and her livelihood. Sanura's husband believed her and moved off of Banani plantation with her. Eventually, Sanura was welcomed back by the Friends, years later after they began to question Mwajuma's reputation. The case of Sanura shows how even disputes that never reached the courts had potentially damaging effects. It is also evident from such cases that gossip was a key aspect of reputation on the island. Harold Ingrams, in his 1931 ethnography of the Zanzibar Islands, emphasized the importance of gossip as a part of daily life. Whether it was gossip in the morning as women began their

---

[11] Abdulaziz, pp. 203, 225; Jan Knappert, *An Anthology of Swahili Love Poetry* (Berkeley: University of California Press, 1972), p. 17; Goldman recites a Pemban proverb: "Better a witch than a slanderer"; Goldman, pp. 375–6.

[12] Luise White notes a similar phenomenon among the Bemba; White, 2000, chap. 2; definitions of words come from Steere (1884), Krapf (1882), and Madan (1902).

[13] FIM TEMP MSS 419/1–7, Theodore Burtt, Notebook, 1899, Sanura Mama Sudi.

household chores or stopping at the coffee shop in the afternoon for men, gossip about neighbors, officials, and others was the main entertainment in rural communities.[14]

When a person's reputation was tarnished with gossip, rumors, or scandal, he or she had to respond in order to repair his or her reputation. However, as Laura Gowing pointed out, sometimes fighting to reestablish reputation would not restore it because the public fight itself could affect the reputation in question.[15] This was especially true for elite women, for whom passivity was often more effective, whereas lower-status women were less afraid to actively defend their reputations in court.[16] Chris Wickham shows that confrontation was not always the most effective means to restore reputation for men either.[17] For example, generosity could allow people to acknowledge a person as worthy of repute, even when his or her previous behavior was questionable. Jonathon Glassman argues that "in societies in which the hegemony of the state and the marketplace were weak or uneven, such discursive struggles had substantial consequences: a man ridiculed for stinginess would lose public prestige, personal dependents, and power."[18] He argues that a "politics of reputation" forced patricians in Pangani to support feasts, *ngoma* ("dances"), and *maulidi* ("celebrations of the birth of the Prophet Muhammad") of which they did not approve in order to appear generous and gain clients. Monetary support of these events transformed marginalized people into clients, transforming the power of slave owners in the nineteenth century into the *heshima* of patricians in the twentieth century. The politics of

---

[14] Ingrams, 1931, pp. 250–3; *kupuzika* means "to gossip" or "to talk with the women"; Krapf 1882; Fair, 2001, pp.182–4, 188–9; Africa No. 6, *Correspondence Respecting Slavery and the Slave Trade in East Africa and the Islands of Zanzibar and Pemba* (1902), p. 15. Reverend Farler recommended putting women in solitary confinement in prisons so that they could not gossip.

[15] Laura Gowing, "Women, Status and the Popular Culture of Dishonour," *Transactions of the Royal Historical Society*, Sixth Series, 6 (1996), p. 226.

[16] For historical examples of women in the courts in Mombasa, see Strobel, 1979, pp. 54–8; for modern examples in Mombasa, see Hirsch, *passim.* Hirsch argues that women of all classes sought to defend their reputations through their use of language in the courts. However, Strobel notes that upper-class women were often less likely to go to the courts to protect themselves because of the taint on the reputation suggested by court action.

[17] Wickham, 2003, pp. 3–24.

[18] Glassman, 1995, p. 22; Glassman notes that Frederick G. Bailey coined the phrase "politics of reputation." Bailey argued that whether looking at reputation in a small village or large city, the mechanisms of reputation remain the same – a reputation "is not a quality that [a person] possesses, but rather the opinions which other people have about him"; F. G. Bailey, "Gifts and Poison," in *Gifts and Poison: The Politics of Reputation*, edited by F. G. Bailey (Oxford: Basil Blackwell, 1971), p. 2.

reputation represents the demise of the authority of elites in the face of colonial usurpation of the power to make and uphold law.

On Pemba, efforts by both elite and nonelite to gain reputations as generous, as people with *heshima*, centered on providing elaborate feasts during *ngoma*, weddings, and funerals. In 1907, the acting Vice Consul, Herbert Lister, informed officials on Zanzibar that Arabs on Pemba were facing extreme debt, which meant that they could not bring in labor to pick the clove crop.[19] When Zanzibar officials investigated, they complained that only four of the twenty-eight elite men were justifiably facing hardship. All the others had expenses they "incurred for extravagant personal expenditure, the cost of funeral and marriage feasts."[20] These men were clearly trying to buy into the politics of reputation and maintain their *heshima* in the community through lavish spending.[21] One of the biggest complaints by elites on Pemba about the Friends missionaries was their inadvertent use of networks of patronage to gain converts.[22] No longer could many of the elite offer clients land, clothing, and feasts in the manner that the Friends began to do. Even the Friends used the politics of reputation to build a following for themselves among the poor.

The politics of reputation was a hollow exercise, though. It attempted to recreate the power hierarchies of the precolonial meaning of *heshima*, but it could not do so fully. The power offered by the politics of reputation was ephemeral because it was not based on the more permanent power associated with slaveholding and lineage. Clients' loyalty could be temporary, as suggested by Glassman, and allegiances could rapidly change (e.g., if a person was viewed as less generous), in ways that did not happen with slaves and kin.[23] On Pemba, in the early years after emancipation, the elite tried to use the politics of reputation to reestablish their position in society. This effort worked for the first two decades because

---

[19] PRO FO881/9209, Distress in Pemba, 1907, letters between Mr. Lister and Mr. Cave; also see ZNA AB31/20, Collector report from Mkoani, 1910, that discussed in detail the competitiveness of these groups and the significance of elite sponsorship.

[20] PRO FO881/9209, Distress in Pemba, 1906, Inclosure No. 5, Report by Messrs. Akers and Lyne on the Reputed Acute Distress in Pemba.

[21] Megan Vaughan argues that the position of elites on the Mascarene Islands was "fluid" and thus caused them "anxiety" about their positions in society, which was why "they were continually engaging in disputes over honor and reputation"; Vaughan, p. 182. However, elites on Pemba appear less to be arguing over their reputations among each other as their reputations as patrons among nonelites.

[22] Africa No. 6, *Correspondence Respecting Slavery and the Slave Trade in East Africa and the Islands of Zanzibar and Pemba* (1902), p. 3.

[23] Glassman, 1995, pp. 22–5.

the colonial state on Pemba held an "uneven state power." However, by 1910, colonial power had asserted itself on Pemba in such a way that limited the value of the politics of reputation. The state positioned the *liwali*, *makadhi*, and other government officials in power, and it was only the colonial state that could remove these people from their positions.

Similar to the politics of reputation, Sara Berry suggests a patronage politics in networks of support, which could be based on kinship, neighborhoods, ethnicity, or membership in communities of practice.[24] On Pemba, similar groups acted as venues through which individuals could show their generosity and gain recognition and *heshima*. Stinginess could be a real problem for people whom others envied or who were perceived to have more than their share. People "picked apart" the reputations of misers.[25] One Indian clerk on Pemba found this out the hard way, when another Indian man began attacking his reputation in a newspaper.[26] The clerk was accused of corruption and public drunkenness. His reputation and behavior became the talk of the town. The publisher of the newspaper reported on stories and complaints about the clerk that he gathered from others. The clerk's British supervisors were apprised of the affair, which led to an investigation of the clerk's work habits and whether he was in fact corrupt. In the end, it appears that the clerk was slow to handle cases for individuals who then accused him of corruption because they believed he was trying to help the opposition in their cases. The clerk sued his accuser for defamation of character and turned the tables on the publisher. The two men publicly "picked apart each other's reputations" (*kupupakiana*). The clerk eventually won because his colonial supervisors sided with him in the case and closed down the publisher's newspaper. The publisher was branded by the state as a "difficult" and "troublesome" fellow who was simply out to sell papers through sensationalistic reportage about respectable members of the community. Through the actions of colonial officials, the state helped to define the reputation of figures associated with it.

As seen earlier, slander and gossip could bring a person's reputation into the public sphere as a subject of discussion for people far beyond

---

[24] Sara Berry, *No Condition Is Permanent: The Social Dynamics of Agrarian Change in Sub-Saharan Africa* (Madison: University of Wisconsin Press, 1993), pp. 160–3.

[25] Steere (1884) and Krapf (1882) define *pupakiana ku* in the nineteenth century as "to pick apart one another's reputations or characters." By 1902, Madan simply describes it as "bickering."

[26] "HBM Court, Zanzibar, Criminal Case No. 790 of 1910," *Zanzibar Gazette*, January 3, 1911.

firsthand knowledge of the people and incidents being discussed. Laura Fair's work on the taarab singer Siti binti Saad argues that even though songs transmitted gossip about public figures, it rarely affected their positions of power, and even when their own behavior brought them down, marginalized people had little influence on this process.[27] However, on Pemba, two *makadhi*, one in 1910 and one in 1915, were removed from their jobs, ostensibly for corruption, although both were encouraged by colonial officials to resign in order to protect their reputations.[28] Public figures on Pemba seemingly had less power than in Unguja because marginalized people on Pemba could affect their reputations and government positions. It was still the colonial state that removed the men from power; there was no direct link between the marginalized members of the community and the fall from grace of these men. However, gossiping about corrupt officials could slowly affect a person's reputation – if colonial officials paid attention to the gossip. Reputation could affect a person's social or communal status, but it did not always have an immediate effect on the standing of people connected to the government.[29]

LEISURE AND LABOR

Both before and after emancipation, leisure was a critical element in demonstrating *heshima*. Because slaves had no right to their own leisure, by definition, leisure was associated with the status of freeborn. Yet slaves longed to express their rights to leisure. Jeremy Prestholdt shows that many slaves sought to purchase their own slave so that they could attain space for leisure.[30] Likewise in Peru, for many slaves, the greatest value of freedom was the right to leisure and to dispense largess among peers.[31] Tamara Walker shows how enslaved people attempted to emulate the freeborn by taking on the accoutrements of freedom, such as clothing, participating in leisure activities, and giving gifts to their friends. Walker's work connected thefts by slaves not for survival but to achieve honor within their own social class. Within different class groups, the

[27] Fair, 2001, pp. 193–8.
[28] For the case of the *kadhi* fired in 1910, see PRO FO 881/10268X, Annual report 1910, and for the case from 1915, see *Administrative Reports for the Year 1915*.
[29] See Fair's discussion of corrupt officials on Zanzibar who people sang about but eventually were undone by their corruption coming to the notice of colonial officials; Fair, 2001, pp. 193–5.
[30] Prestholdt, pp.117–46.
[31] Walker, 2009, pp. 383–403.

measurement of status was expressed through their ability to participate in leisure activities.

During the 1880s and 1890s on Pemba, slaves who continued to live near their owners could only hope to attain the *heshima* of their servile status. However, similarly to Walker's cases in Peru, some slaves engaged in "free" activities on Pemba. When a young man was accused of stealing money from his owner in 1903, he denied the theft charge, even though his fellow slaves claimed that he had given them each 4 pice.[32] The young man swore the pice were from his clove-picking wages, but the other slaves pointed out that it was not clove season when they received the money. The young man was trying to assert an identity as a free man through his largess as a means to build alliances with and gain respect from the other slaves who, according to their testimony, did not appear to hold him in high regard.[33] What is important in this example is that slaves understood particular behaviors as assisting them to attain the *heshima* of free individuals, even when it did not work for them.

Leisure activities ranged broadly from the daily time spent sitting on the *baraza* ("benches on the front of buildings") gossiping with neighbors to participation in *ngoma* ("dances"). For most men, some time was spent gossiping, playing cards, or playing *mbao* (a board game using seeds). Sometimes gambling was part of the games of cards and *mbao.*[34] Cockfighting was popular among men by the 1910s in the villages, although it was illegal.[35] Pemba was also famous for its bullfights, which people of all statuses attended as either observers or participants. The various locations for watching the bullfights indicated the amount the person paid to attend, whether on raised benches for the elite, in the fenced area for lower-status women, or out in the open on the ground.[36] Singers could be hired for an evening of entertainment, singing ribald songs or reciting the coastal style of religious poetry, depending on the interest of the purchaser, who was generally male.[37] *Ngoma* (dances) were held

---

[32] A pice was equivalent to 1/64 of an Indian rupee, the main form of currency on Pemba at the turn of the century.

[33] The other slaves did not seem to like this slave and dismissed many of the claims of the slave, who tried to accuse his owner of killing another, younger slave in an effort to redirect the investigation into his thefts. The other slaves had left their owner when they testified, indicating that it was not loyalty to the owner on their part that made them testify against the young man.

[34] Ingrams, 1931, pp. 223–4; Craster, p. 148.

[35] Craster, p. 229.

[36] Ingrams, 1931, pp. 419–20.

[37] Craster, p. 216.

throughout the Swahili coast region, and the term is a generic one. Many different forms of *ngoma* existed in the nineteenth and twentieth centuries, from the *ngoma ya harusi* that occurred with weddings, the *ngoma ya pepo* of spirit possession, or the *ngoma ya msondo* of girls' initiation. Competitive *ngoma* groups abounded along the Swahili coast and acted as one of the most common communities of practice for men and women. Many scholars have shown the significance of competitive dance groups for building social cohesion and elevating social status among the lowest members of coastal society.[38] *Ngoma* on Pemba were common outside the clove harvest seasons and could be heard occurring most nights in the outlying districts.[39] *Ngoma ya kirumbizi* ("stick-fighting dances"), *ngoma ya msondo* ("initiations"), and weddings were all popular among Pembans.[40] The *ngoma* ranged widely in their purposes, but many were sex-segregated competitive dances between two groups who sought to increase their social prestige through their performances.[41] Being able to participate in all these forms of leisure cost money both in specie and in the time spent participating, indicating that people were free and had the right to leisure. Leisure time continued to be an indicator of and means to build *heshima* in the community, even after emancipation. However, more people could take part in leisure activities, and in some cases, the activities themselves changed to reflect the new status of participants.

Yet, just as leisure changed after emancipation, labor and the status attached to labor also changed. Proverbs gathered by Mervyn Beech in the 1910s give insight into the ideas about labor, *heshima*, and shifts

---

[38] Terrence O. Ranger, *Dance and Society in Eastern Africa, 1890–1970: The Beni Ngoma* (Berkeley: University of California Press, 1975); Strobel, 1979, pp. 156–81; Marjorie Ann Franken, "Anyone Can Dance: A Survey and Analysis of Swahili *Ngoma*, Past and Present" (Ph.D. dissertation, University of California, Riverside, 1986); Laura Fair, "Identity, Difference, and Dance: Female Initiation in Zanzibar, 1890 to 1930," in *Mashindano!: Competitive Music Performance in East Africa*, edited by Frank Gunderson and Gregory Barz, p. 157; Kelly Askew, "Female Circles and Male Lines: Gender Dynamics Along the Swahili Coast," *Africa Today* 46, nos. 3–4 (1999), pp. 67–102; Glassman, 1995, pp. 158–9; Rebecca Gearhart, "*Ngoma* Memories: How Ritual Music and Dance Shaped the Northern Kenya Coast," *African Studies Review* 48, no. 3 (2005), pp. 21–47.

[39] Craster claimed to hear the *dhikr* almost every night and other *ngoma* regularly while camping outside the towns; Craster, pp. 173, 263–4, 307–8, 310–311.

[40] Halima Rashid, Pandani, December 2004; Asha Hamad, Bopwe, December 2004; Baba Mohamed, Mtambile, December 2004; Muhammed Khamisi, Mtambile, November 2004.

[41] Craster complained in 1912 that "cattle [on Pemba] all belong to dining clubs." He was referring to the members of competitive dance organizations, who kept cattle for their feasts during competitions; Craster, p. 185.

in social hierarchy on Pemba during this period.[42] Beech's collection of proverbs is limited in that it contains the knowledge of only a few men. However, it gives a rare glimpse into the language used on Pemba concerning respectability. The social privilege of Beech's informants helps to construct both the cultural ideals perpetuated by the upper class and their fears about social disintegration in the postabolition period. These proverbs suggest the ideals conveyed by the elite of Pemban society to their lower-status neighbors on how people *should* behave to build *heshima*: People should care for one another, work hard, and know their place. An undercurrent in the proverbs indicates the difficulty of dealing with "strangers," known in Swahili as *wageni* (s. *mgeni*), who did not "fit" and might disrupt local social mores.[43] Both the ideals and the concerns about *wageni* point to an elite struggling with new social constructions where they could no longer control who moved up the social ladder.

The proverbs show the communal ideals of Pemban society, where people were encouraged to help one another through their labor. They suggest that individuals could not exist without the help of others, reinforcing both the need for former slaves to integrate into local society and the need for elites to treat ex-slaves with respect.[44] To gain access to fertile land, former slaves often had to work within the connections they already had in the community – their former owners. Their former owners needed their help because during the clove harvest all hands were needed to get the cloves off the trees before they rotted. The Pemban proverbs reminded people that "a solitary tree builds not," and it was best for everyone, not just the elite or ex-slaves, to build a strong communal identity.[45]

---

[42] Mervyn W. H. Beech, *Aids to the Study of Ki-Swahili: Four Studies Compiled and Annotated* (London: K. Paul, Trench, Trubner, 1918); Beech collected these proverbs while working in Mombasa. However, one of his informants was from Pemba, and Beech was careful to distinguish which aphorisms came from Pemba and were in the Pemban dialect of Kiswahili.

[43] In general, Pembans (and people on the Swahili coast) called outsiders *wageni* (s. *mgeni*), or "guests." However, people without *heshima*, and especially slaves from the mainland, were *washenzi* (s. *mshenzi*), or "barbarians." Thus a person could graciously be called *mgeni* while people actually viewed that person as *mshenzi*.

[44] Trevor Getz also argues that former slaves and owners were often dependent on one another in the postemancipation period in colonial Senegal. Trevor Getz, *Slavery and Reform in West Africa: Toward Emancipation in Nineteenth-Century Senegal and the Gold Coast* (Athens: Ohio University Press, 2004), pp. 129–33; Romero makes a similar argument suggesting that some island communities in Africa had particular issues based on limited access to land.

[45] Beech, p. 118, *mti pweke haujengi*.

While building a strong community was important, how community members should behave was also displayed in the aphorisms collected by Beech. The ideal ways people should live were embedded in the proverbs: being humble, not gossiping, being respectful of others even if they are of a lower social status, and being gracious of spirit. John Middleton noted that "by behaving with courtesy, sensitivity, and goodness toward someone else, a person both acquires *heshima* and bestows it on the person addressed."[46] Thus the proverb "to respectfully answer is no sign of servitude" underscores the idea that all members of society could display *heshima* and that showing respect toward others did not simply connote slave ancestry or lower status.[47] In fact, O'Sullivan-Beare reported to his pleasure in 1899 that the ex-slave population had taken to greeting people they met in the roadways. Not only did they greet people, but they used the Arabic greetings rather than "abasing" themselves with the term *shikamoo*, meaning "I grasp your feet" in Swahili.[48] Yet the proverb could certainly be seen as a rebuke to former slaves who had adopted practices of free people, such as their greetings. The elite men reciting the proverbs to Beech clearly expected ex-slaves to maintain their respect for former owners and to continue to labor in similar ways to the preabolition era.

Discussion of work habits constituted a large number of Beech's collection of proverbs.[49] These sayings point to the contradictory nature of how elite Pembans defined leisure in contrast to "laziness" rather than labor. Shaaban bin Muhamad, one of Beech's Pemban informants, explained that proverbs about the value of work were said to "lazy people," showing that earning *heshima* from neighbors did not come easily. They also implied that "lazy" people inherently have less *heshima* than hard workers. Yet in the preabolition era, leisure was associated with wealth and, by default, *heshima*; the elite proved their *heshima* by *not* working. Phyllis Martin's definition of leisure as "more than play, for it is juxtaposed with work and it can involve both non-obligated

---

[46] John Middleton, *The World of the Swahili* (New Haven, CT: Yale University Press, 1992), p. 194.

[47] Beech, p. 123, *lebeka si utumwa*. Interestingly, the proverb *kiburi si maungwana* ("Pride is not the sign of a gentleman") reinforces the older terminology of *uungwana* versus *ustaarabu*, suggesting that the ideal of "Arabness" had not yet become hegemonic on Pemba by the turn of the century.

[48] Report by Vice Consul O'Sullivan on the Island of Pemba, 1899.

[49] Beech's book was designed to teach colonial administrators about coastal culture and language. His focus on "work" belies his own conscious or subconscious effort to teach other officials how to spur on the workers because an 1891 book of aphorisms had comparatively few proverbs about work.

activities ... and activities that involve fulfilling social obligations, such as membership of an association or visiting relatives" shows that leisure was more than simply not working.[50] Laura Fair also noted that in Zanzibar Town, leisure time spent talking in the *baraza* was "an essential element of community membership."[51] Consequently, the way people spent their nonworking time was critical to their development of *heshima*. If they participated in community obligations, their leisure was a marker of respectability rather than laziness, regardless of their economic or social status. However, it is important to keep in mind that most leisure activities had some economic cost, whether it was time spent not working or actual contributions of money or food; thus participation in leisure was a sign of financial health and freedom.

Often in postemancipation East African coastal societies, few people trusted strangers (*wageni*) unless they needed their labor. The majority of former slaves living in small island communities often remained working, in some form, for former slave owners because the alternatives were limited.[52] On Pemba, there was not a large-scale exodus of former slaves at emancipation, although census records show that the number of people claiming to be former slaves diminished radically. The Pemban aphorisms collected by Beech highlight the concerns people had about trusting outsiders. For the preemancipation period, Pouwels argues that "the overriding predicament faced by these [coastal] societies, then was that of having to absorb strangers, Africans and Asians alike, into their midst, and to indigenize them in order to avoid potentially destabilizing changes."[53] This suggests that being an outsider could be difficult for the individual, as well as the community trying to absorb the stranger. How and for whom a person labored in a community were important factors in their acceptance.

Most ex-slaves chose not to labor for their former owners if they could help it, unless they had a good relationship before emancipation. Many ex-slaves tried to shift the benefit of their labor from helping someone else to helping themselves. By 1899, O'Sullivan-Beare reported, "[F]reed

[50] Martin, 1995, p. 7.

[51] Laura Fair, "Kickin' It: Leisure, Politics, and Football in Colonial Zanzibar, 1900s–1950s," *Africa* 67, no. 2 (1997), p. 236.

[52] Getz, pp. 79–80, 125–31; Suzanne Miers, "Slavery to Freedom in Sub-Saharan Africa: Expectations and Reality," in *After Slavery*, edited by Howard Temperley (London: Frank Cass, 2000), p. 255.

[53] Randall Lee Pouwels, "Eastern Africa and the Indian Ocean to 1800: Reviewing Relations in Historical Perspective," *International Journal of African Historical Studies* 35, nos. 2–3 (2002), p. 411.

slaves have managed to save up sufficient money wherewith to purchase for themselves small holdings."[54] The Friends missionaries also reported making loans to ex-slaves so that they could purchase land for themselves.[55] These examples demonstrate how Pembans sought to harness their labor for their benefit and, as such, control their labor and their leisure. Other former slaves transformed their reputations and positions in the community into government jobs as *sheha* and assistant *sheha*.[56] This allowed them a form of labor that did not require physically heavy work but rather handling disputes within the community and reporting information to the colonial officials. These positions became especially valuable as new definitions of labor and means of accessing wealth forced elites into also working for the colonial government. However, *masheha* walked a fine line in the community because they represented the colonial state, whose policies were not always appreciated by rural communities.[57]

Indebtedness of large landowners to moneylenders on Pemba was endemic by the 1890s. The emancipation of slaves was blamed by both slaveholders and colonial officials for the decreasing viability of large plantations. However, evidence suggests that the problem started long before emancipation.[58] Moreover, the world market price for cloves decreased tremendously in the middle to late 1890s, even though the clove crops increased. Regardless of why, many elite could no longer afford to maintain their lifestyles and had little wealth with which they could keep up the leisure necessary to maintain *heshima*.[59] Colonial officials longed

---

[54] Report by Vice Consul O'Sullivan on the Island of Pemba, 1899.

[55] FIM, Annual report for 1912, p. 6.

[56] Many of the *masheha* were of mainland origin, indicating their ex-slave status. For instance, Khamis bin Musa Zaramo was a *sheha*, as reported in probate cases PNA AK1/3310 and PNA AK1/3316. In the WaPemba areas, they had their own *masheha*, but among the ex-slave communities, which were the majority of Pembans, the *masheha* were of ex-slave descent. Ingrams mentions a man named Fundi Yakuti as the *sheha* of the ex-slaves until his death in the 1920s; Ingrams, 1931, p. 222.

[57] As discussed elsewhere, the *masheha* could be very unpopular when they reported the deaths of their constituents because that brought the government into the process of distributing the estate and forced heirs to pay unwanted taxes.

[58] See the 1840s comments of John Leigh about Arabs being bad businessmen, and Colomb's comments about Arabs being indebted to Indians in 1870s. James S. Kirkman, "The Zanzibar Diary of John Studdy Leigh, Part I, *International Journal of African Historical Studies* 13, no. 2 (1980), pp. 281–312; Colomb, pp. 378–9.

[59] This is borne out in the probate records, where some Arabs owned many personal possessions but very little land. See examples PNA AK1/55, Ali bin Mohamed Bashmak, June 5, 1909; PNA AK1/63, Said bin Hamed bin Ali Lemki, August 21, 1909; PNA AK1/68, Mohamed bin Abdullah Mendiri, August 1910; PNA AK1/4195, Mmanga binti Khamis el-Husunia, 1945.

for the Arab elite to "develop habits of energy" in managing their lands, but because so many had lost all of their land, they turned to government service as a means of earning an income. "Arabs of good family" began to "compete keenly for those situations under government which are open to them, but the acceptance of which, formerly, would have entailed upon them loss of that '*heshima*' to which Arabs attach so much importance."[60] Publicly working in a job, for someone else – namely the government – was now acceptable among the elite and did not cause them to lose all *heshima*. Previously, laboring under the direction of a supervisor (as all non–British government employees had) was an automatic signifier of lacking *heshima*. However, individuals' reputations could suffer if their behavior as government officials was perceived as corrupt.[61]

Leisure and labor did not entirely switch values in Pemban society after emancipation, but they both changed significantly. Leisure was now open to people of all classes and had developed new meanings for those individuals. Previous to emancipation, when a slave participated in a competitive *ngoma*, he or she did so at the behest of his or her owner, to bring him or her *heshima*. Dancing in *ngoma* was "work" – something that lower-status people performed for the benefit of their owners. After emancipation, though, the value of that work shifted to the individual. Thus, when a person took part in a *ngoma*, the *heshima* he or she earned through his or her actions went to that person, not to his or her owner.[62] Definitions of acceptable labor also shifted as former slaveholders began taking on roles within the government under the management of British officials while ex-slaves purchased land and worked for themselves.

DISPLAYING *HESHIMA*

The postemancipation period offered former slaves the opportunity to access *heshima* in ways previously inaccessible to them; however, they had to have the economic wherewithal to display it. Former slaves could now display *heshima* in a variety of ways, including wearing the clothing of the elite and consuming luxury goods. However, for many ex-slaves, building *heshima* meant creating their own choices of what was

---

[60] Report by Vice Consul O'Sullivan on the Island of Pemba, 1899.

[61] "HBM Court, Zanzibar, Criminal Case No. 790 of 1910," *Zanzibar Gazette*, January 3, 1911; *makadhi* who had to step down in 1909 and 1910 because of corruption charges are discussed in Chapter 3; Fair, 2001, pp. 189–94.

[62] Although it certainly still benefited the patron of the dance group; see Fair, 2000; Strobel, 1979, pp. 156–81.

respectable. For example, women who came to the islands enslaved and wearing ornaments made out of bone in their ears did not always adopt the coastal preference for ornaments made out of silver and gold. Some chose to wear rolls of colored paper and a brass stud in their noses.[63] Some male ex-slaves chose to engage with global fashions, adopting and mixing Western and coastal clothing styles, as noted by others across the Swahili region during this time.[64] On Pemba, some ex-slaves certainly participated in the domestication of global fashions, but the vast majority did not. In many respects, slaves wanted clothes that were sewn, which, regardless of where they came from and what culture they represented, is what made them have *heshima*. Clothing that was simply wrapped around the body was by definition less desirable. The dominant paradigm of *heshima* on Pemba focused on the adoption of coastal appearance and religious beliefs and practices, likely because Pemba was not urbanized. Maintaining the respect of neighbors was important in rural communities, and appearance could have a profound role in how people judged another person's *heshima*.

Quranic education, Islamic piety, and etiquette were also important indicators of *heshima*. As Randall Pouwels noted in Mombasa, building wealth allowed for shifts in "modes of behavior, etiquette, family alliances, the house in which one lived, attention to religious duties, devotion to learning and even genealogy."[65] Yet most ex-slaves did not have enough wealth or time in the immediate aftermath of their emancipation to build stone houses or become Quranic scholars. The newly emancipated often demonstrated their *heshima* to former owners and other neighbors in more immediate ways, such as through clothing and participating in Friday prayers, leaving *wakf* property for the support of mosques and other religious practices. In the long term, former slaves often made sure that their children had the opportunity to attend schools, especially Quranic schools, as a means to build *heshima* for the family, in addition to purchasing land and trying to arrange advantageous marriages.

Clothing was the easiest and most accessible way to signify to others a new social status and respectability. Photographs from 1900 and the 1920s show this shift in physical appearance of women and men as they began dressing with *heshima* by covering their heads and bodies

[63] Craster, p. 40.
[64] Ingrams, 1931, pp. 221–2; Prestholdt, chap. 4; Fair, 2001, chap. 2.
[65] Pouwels, 1987, p. 78.

more thoroughly.[66] Slaves did not have the right to wear shoes or cover their heads, both of which were markers of pious Muslims. Thus these were two of the earliest innovations at emancipation.[67] In 1899, the Vice Consul on Pemba noted the "little vanities" of freed slave men who always wore the *kofia*, or cap, and *kanzu*, the long shirt-dress of freeborn men.[68] For slave men, who generally were only given a cloth to wrap around their waist, the *kanzu* and *kofia* indicated to others in the community their newly acquired status. More than that, it identified them as understanding the value of such clothing for their new position in the community as free citizens and religious devotees. By wearing the clothing of good Muslims, freed men illustrated their ability to acquire *heshima*. Women, likewise, began to wear head coverings and other accoutrements of status. Clothing was one of the few items that held value but was easily transportable; thus it was very important for all classes of people as a status marker. Laura Fair and Margaret Strobel have discussed the changes in women's dress during the postemancipation period. Both scholars argue that former slave women began adopting the more conservative clothing of the elite and other aspects of *purdah* after emancipation.[69] Because most former slave women on Pemba worked as manual laborers and most were still very poor, *kaniki* cloth, which was associated with slavery, was still worn during work hours. But during leisure time, women began wearing brightly colored cotton cloths known as *kanga*. In 1904, a huge clove boom increased imports to the island of Pemba, 56 percent of which were *kanga*.[70] Craster noted in 1912 that elite women were "nominally secluded" and could be seen "walking about unveiled" around their houses a "great deal" during the daytime.[71] By the 1920s, however, elite women were wearing the black silk *buibui* that covered their heads and bodies, with a veil across their faces.[72] And in the early

---

[66] See images in PRO CO1069/170, Photos of the Clove Industry in Pemba, 1900, in comparison with images from Ingrams, 1931, pp. 256, 316.

[67] Laura Fair, "Dressing Up: Clothing, Class and Gender in Post-Abolition Zanzibar," *Journal of African History* 39, no. 1 (1998), pp. 67–8.

[68] Report by Vice Consul O'Sullivan on the Island of Pemba, 1899.

[69] Fair, 2001, pp. 85–6; Strobel, 1979, pp. 73–6. Likewise, Barbara Cooper discusses a similar phenomenon in Niger, whereby lower-status women and their families sought to live in purdah and wear veils as a means to assert a freeborn status; Barbara Cooper, *Marriage in Maradi: Gender and Culture in a Hausa Society in Niger, 1900–1989* (Portsmouth, NH: Heinemann, 1997), pp. 9, 25–8, 135–6.

[70] Foreign Office No. 3375, Annual series, Report on the trade of Pemba for the Year 1904.

[71] Craster, p. 209.

[72] Ingrams, 1942, pp. 33–4.

1940s, some ex-slave women owned *buibui*, even in Pemba.[73] As Fair noted, "[W]omen equated the adoption of the *buibui* with their families' growing respectability, adherence to Islam, sense of belonging within the island community and wealth."[74]

As an important status signifier, clothing was a commodity that was highly valued and thus often stolen. In a parable about two thieves on Pemba, one steals the lizard-skin shoes of two wealthy Arabs when they go into the mosque to pray.[75] The thief knows that these shoes are very valuable, but he also recognizes that he cannot easily explain why someone of his lowly status would possess shoes such as these. He begins by telling people who question him that he is a traveling shoemaker. Clearly, the thief's clothing did not match the shoes, but he hoped to sell them for a lot of money, which he could then use to buy nicer clothes for himself, a legitimate demonstration of *heshima*. Theft of clothing happened frequently among the boys of the Friends mission school.[76] The boys were almost exclusively the children of slaves, and many of their parents remained enslaved while the boys sought the benefits of living in the mission orphanage. All boys who came to the mission, most of whom arrived around the ages of ten to twelve, received new sets of clothes on joining the mission, with the missionaries inadvertently replicating the rituals of enslavement by giving their converts new clothes.[77] The boys themselves could also purchase new items of clothing with the wages they earned from both daily work on the mission and seasonal labor during the clove harvests. These purchased garments were the envy of the other boys because the mission clothing was quite plain and did not necessarily reflect local images of social status given that they were in two pieces. On numerous occasions, therefore, boys stole clothing from other boys or from their neighbors on the mission station.[78]

---

[73] PNA AK1/4197, Muweza binti Khamis Mhiyao, April 1941. Notably, the *buibui* this woman left was considered old and worn out, suggesting that she had owned it for quite a number of years.

[74] Fair, 2001, pp. 86–7.

[75] UMCA, A1 (XIV) No. 54, "The Two Thieves of Pemba" by Leslie Matolo, a translation from Swahili, n.d.

[76] FIM PZ(F)/3, Diary of Boys Home, June 6, 1904.

[77] Taylor, 1891, No. 313, "Give the Strange Slave a New Clothe That He May Forget His Home"; FIM PZ(F)/3, Diary of Boys Home. See Prestholdt's arguments about symbolic subjection; Prestholdt, chap. 5; boys returned their clothes when they left the mission. See FIM PZ(F)/3, Diary of Boys Home, August 14, 1901, and February 1, 1905.

[78] FIM PZ(F)/3, Diary of Boys Home; see entries for March 1903, June 16, 1905, June 25, 1904, and July 6, 1904, for examples.

Clothing was also a means for enticing the labor and loyalty of individuals. The missions on Pemba were not above using clothing as a means to solidify the loyalty of people residing at the mission. They did so not only through the gift of clothes to boys living in the orphanage, who had to return the clothing if they left the mission school, but also through annual presents to workers on the station. At Christmas each year the missionaries gave out fabric and clothing to their employees, saving the best pieces for their most dutiful and hardworking employees.[79] Much to the missionaries' consternation, owners could also give their slaves clothing in an effort to win back their labor to their *mashamba,* as the Friends found out when one boy left the orphanage to return to his owner when the owner bought him a new set of clothes.[80] This occurrence also has implications for the *heshima* of the owner. When his slave became a part of the Christian mission, the boy wearing mission clothes was physically rebuking his owner for not doing his duty as a good Muslim to convert his slave to Islam. By wearing a mission outfit, the slave boy was, in effect, "shaming" his owner. The owner's gift of clothing was a sign of his efforts to regain *heshima* in the eyes of his subordinate and the community at large. Regardless of why the boy switched clothes, his interest in stylish clothes shows the very real desires and concerns of ex-slaves to dress with *heshima,* regardless of whose "symbol" they were. When the owner of this slave boy dressed him in fine clothes, he was seeking the boy's return and also certainly articulating his own respectability through the use of his slave's body as an extension of his own.[81] However, for the slave boy, the new clothing made him the envy of his compatriots from the boys' school on the mission. His new clothing denoted his status as a valued person in his owner's household, creating a reciprocal *heshima* between slave and owner.

Clothing was also a key means for outsiders to a community to signify their freeborn status and to try to gain social acceptance among the local population. Clothing and personal possessions were one of the few ways to quickly denote the status of someone traveling far from home. For instance, when Mohamed Hemed Sawafi died in 1910 while visiting Pemba, he had no land on the island – his family was in Oman – yet his clothing indicated that he was a man of some status, although not wealthy. He was traveling with seven *vikoy* (a cloth used as an

[79] FIM PZ(F)/3, Monthly minute book, 1898–1902; see reports for January 7, 1899, and January 8, 1900.
[80] FIM PZ(F)/3, Diary of boys home; see entry for February 23, 1904.
[81] Walker, 2009, p. 391.

undergarment; s. *kikoy*), a *kanzu*, a vest, and the requisite *jambia* of a man from Oman.[82] His other effects were simple: one cooking pot, one bed sheet, and one knife, which indicated that he was not living on the island. Thus, having clothing was important for his introduction to the community. He also had several small wooden boxes, which were prized by people on Pemba as a valuable commodity.[83] The listing of Mohamed's possessions is unusual and likely due to the fact that he had no relatives on the island who would have inherited his clothing before the case came to the probate court. Mohamed's possessions give us a glimpse at the significance of clothing for travelers, who had to establish their *heshima*. Generally, in the case of people from the island, the probate records did not itemize household effects. When they did, most items were either related to the running of the household – cooking pots, knives, etc. – or related to the business of the individual.

In addition to clothing, other personal possessions could also be markers of *heshima* as items of display that represented extraneous wealth or the ability to host others and, as such, show the person as a generous neighbor. Over the years after emancipation, ex-slaves began to own more possessions.[84] This represented the collection of material goods within a family over time and signified a person's status as free. Possessions alone, though, did not represent wealth, as seen through the probates of Arabs who died leaving many possessions but little unmortgaged land and thus a very small inheritance for their heirs.[85]

The theft of clothing, though, indicates the transience of the respectability clothing offered to the individual because of how easily it could be stolen. If a person's respectability was based solely on his or her clothing and the clothing was stolen, would the person's respectability also be taken away from him or her? This is one of the issues with making the argument that ex-slaves could use clothing alone as a means to demonstrate their *heshima* to the wider community. Clothing could display a

---

[82] A *jambia* is a curved knife in a scabbard. This was the most valuable thing that Mohamed had on his person. It was valued at 11 shillings – the value of a locally built mud house; PNA AK1/71, Mohamed Hemed Sawafi, May 1910.

[83] FIM, Annual Report for 1912 discusses the orders for boxes that their workshop had from people of all classes on Pemba. Wooden boxes, especially large ones, were often the most valuable household items listed in probate records.

[84] See PNA AK1/77, Fundi Feruzi bin Mkelef, October 1910; PNA AK1/2165, Juma Khamis Mgindo, November 1926; PNA AK1/3683, Tofilli wadi Zaid, June 1938; and PNA AK1/4197, April 1941, as examples of the increasing numbers of material possessions over time.

[85] Compare the estates of PNA AK1/2773 and PNA AK1/3097.

person's understanding of what *heshima* meant, but for many ex-slaves, landownership and displaying an understanding of religious practice gave far more *heshima* than clothes.

HESHIMA AND ISLAM

Islam dominated coastal people's lives, regardless of their social status. Islamic practice required that slaveholders converted their slaves as a statement of their own piety. While for some enslaved this conversion may have been titular, many slaves clearly took the new religion to heart. As slaves gained their emancipation, they had to embrace Islamic practices in order to successfully integrate with their neighbors. Ex-slaves found a number of ways beyond clothing to demonstrate their religious beliefs to their communities. The writing of wills, sending their children to Quranic schools, and participation in a Sufi *tarika* (pl. *tarika*; this literally means the "way" or "path," but it is essentially referencing a particular group and their practices) all allowed ex-slaves a means to achieve reputations as good Muslims and, as such, publicly demonstrate their *heshima*.

In 1893, Mabruk wadi Sunizani did a fairly unusual thing for a Pemban of the time, he wrote a will.[86] In a primarily oral culture such as existed in precolonial Pemba, written documentation of the wishes of individuals after death was rare, regardless of social class. Mabruk was all the more atypical because he was a slave. His will and the wills of several other former slaves suggest the ways in which religious affiliation and piety were avenues to respectability for lower-status individuals.[87] While most of the wills made a point of requesting someone to read the Quran over the grave, the wills of slaves often listed other religious practices that would publicly show their dedication to their faith. The wills of former slaves show their apprehensions about their place in Pemban society and whether they would be truly treated as Muslims and receive all the usual funeral arrangements. Moreover, writing a will was a public proclamation of one's religious beliefs and debts to one's neighbors, who were aware of the contents of the will because of the requirement for at least two

[86] Ingrams, 1931, p. 36; PNA AK1/58, Mabruk Wadi Sunizani, July 1910. Only 14 percent of people in the probate records surveyed had wills.

[87] PNA AK1/46m, May 1910; AK1/58, July 1910; AK1/76, Kichipele Mrashi, October 1910; AK1/3310, August 1934; death notice of Malim Ibrahim bin Omar, *Zanzibar Gazette,* January 12, 1914; death notice of Khamis bin Hamadi Swahili, *Zanzibar Gazette,* October 13, 1913.

witnesses to the will.[88] The vast majority of wills in the probate records on Pemba were from either former slaves or elite men and women who were born elsewhere from the island and had extensive family networks in East Africa or Oman. This indicates that one reason people wrote wills was because they perceived themselves to be outsiders to the community and wanted to make sure that their religious wishes were fulfilled.[89] The wills of former slaves illustrate the significance of Islamic duty to the will's authors. As Ann McDougall has noted, by adopting the Islamic faith, slaves were "reducing their marginality vis-à-vis the fully Muslim … society into which they were integrating."[90] The wills also show the agency of ex-slaves who may not have had full confidence in their last wishes being fulfilled otherwise.[91]

Mabruk wadi Sunizani wrote his will on February 4, 1893, but he did not die until July 1910. Sunizani's will is not clear if he was still a slave when he wrote it or if his owner had manumitted him by that date because slavery was still legal in 1893.[92] In his will, Sunizani left money for the washing of his body, the digging of his grave, and other expenses. He also asked that 50 rupees, over one-sixth of his estate, be used to send someone to Mecca in his place. He also stipulated that the Quran be read over his grave and that all mourners "should say '*loa-hi-la-haits-allah*' seventy thousand times" in his name.[93] All the funeral expenses were allotted to one-third of his estate, a sizable portion. Sunizani could not

---

[88] Elizabeth Colson offered insight into Tongan society and why they refused to adapt to wills. Among the reasons were fear of witchcraft against the heir and the difficulty of mediating the responsibilities associated with bride wealth. Her research emphasizes that for mainland Africans who were enslaved on Pemba, writing a will to demonstrate their faith in Islam and defining their relatives illustrates their significant break with the beliefs of their indigenous communities; Elizabeth Colson, "Possible Repercussions of the Right to Make Wills upon the Plateau Tonga of Northern Rhodesia," *Journal of African Administration* 2, no. 1 (1950), pp. 24–35.

[89] Technically, all Ibadhi adherents were supposed to write wills when they were in their teens, but few Muslims on Pemba were Ibadhi – even among the Arabs, many of whom had converted to the Sunni sect.

[90] E. Ann McDougall, "A Sense of Self: The Life of Fatma Barka," *Canadian Journal of African Studies* 32, no. 2 (1998), p. 300.

[91] Tomlinson and Knight-Bruce, 1928. These law records show a case from January 28, 1925, from Chake Chake in which the *kadhi* allowed Raschid bin Abdulla to inherit from his "slave," Suwedi bin Hamadi, because there were no other heirs. Normally, Suwedi's estate would go to the *beit-el-mal* in support of the poor and mosques on the island.

[92] Although given the legal proscription of slaves passing on property at death, because technically they could not own property as slaves, it is likely that Mabruk had been manumitted when he wrote his will.

[93] PNA AK1/58, July 1910.

have been sure that his will would be upheld because he wrote it before
the emancipation order, which helps to explain why he left one-third of
his estate to his former owner.[94] While Sunizani's will replicates the for-
mat of wills written by elites, his will undermines the power of slave
owners to define slaves as not fully Muslim. Slaves, even after conversion, were not expected to make the pilgrimage to Mecca; indeed, they
had to receive permission from their owners to do so. Thus, by leaving
money for someone else to go to Mecca in his place, Sunizani effectively
subverted his owner's control over him as a Muslim.[95]

In October 1906, Kichipele Mrashi bin Amur, another former slave,
wrote a will that requested the usual procedures of Islamic funerals.[96]
Contrary to Sunizani, Mrashi did not ask that anyone go to Mecca in her
place, but she did leave 120 rupees to pay for the Quran to be read for
three days after her death. Thus she declared her faith and the need for
elaborate rituals to publicly show it. Mrashi, who had purchased a slave
after receiving her own freedom, manumitted her only slave at the same
time she wrote her will, giving her slave a plot of land with seven clove
and five coconut trees. For this act of kindness, Mrashi hoped to attain
baraka ("blessings") after death. Another former slave, Baraka Mnyasa
wrote his will and died within the same year.[97] His will followed the usual
proscriptions for an Islamic funeral; however, he paid for someone to fast
for one month after his death. Each of these former slaves sought public
recognition of their status as respectable Muslim citizens of their communities through their wills. While each asked for a different practice,
all were to be done publicly, and all used a substantial portion of their
estates to subsidize proper Islamic funeral arrangements. In replicating
customary funeral practices of elite Arabs, they attempted to display their
piety and their *heshima*, even in their deaths.

Whether their wishes would be upheld or not was obviously a worry
for some ex-slaves, and they had good reason to be concerned. Once the
funeral occurred, division of the estate would begin. The rules of division
are incredibly detailed and based on three forms of relationship: blood
(*nasab*), marriage (*sabab*), and patronage (*al-wila* or *wala*). All blood
relatives would be considered for the purposes of inheritance, but not all

---

[94] Cooper, 1977, p. 236, notes that "those slaves who did accumulate some property could
not be sure of passing it on to the children, since the property of a deceased slave passed
to his master."

[95] Cooper, 1977, p. 215

[96] PNA AK1/76, October 1910.

[97] PNA AK1/46, May 1910.

relatives through marriage would receive part of the estate. Slaves married to free people were not counted in Zanzibar as having a valid marriage for the purposes of inheritance.[98] The last category of relationship, *wala*, was very important for former slaves. When an owner manumitted his or her slave, it created a bond between them that was "similar to *nasab*" ("blood"). While this did not allow former slaves to claim an inheritance from their former owners, it did entitle former owners and their agnate heirs to any remaining portion of the estates of former slaves.[99] However, in some cases, *wala* was used to keep ex-slaves from devolving property onto their heirs. In some rural parts of the Swahili coast, Islamic judges still upheld *wala* into the 1920s, allowing an owner to inherit all his or her former slaves' land.[100] The argumentation given for these cases was that the slaves were not freed by their owners but by decree of the government; therefore, according to Islamic law, they were still slaves and must follow the legal precedents that technically any property "owned" by a slave belonged to the owner. This remained a problem for ex-slaves well after emancipation.[101] Some ex-slaves tried to avoid this problem by having powerful executors for their wills. Khamis bin Hamadi Swahili had an Indian and an Arab as his executors in order to ensure that his ex-owner could not claim the estate.[102] Wills were one means to subvert slaveholders' claims to property; declaring property as *wakf* was another that had the additional benefit of publicly demonstrating religiosity and *heshima*.

Beyond personal possessions and wills, respect could be garnered and displayed through Islamic knowledge and piety. For example, Ali bin

---

[98] Elisabeth McMahon, "'A Solitary Tree Builds Not': *Heshima*, Community and Shifting Identity in Post-Emancipation Pemba Island," *International Journal of African Historical Studies* 39, no. 2 (August 2006), pp. 197–219.

[99] Laleh Bakhtiar, *Encyclopedia of Islamic Law: A Compendium of the Major Schools* (Chicago: The University of Chicago Press, 1996), p. 289; For Zanzibar specific cases, see Anderson, 1970, p. 378.

[100] Anderson, 1970, p. 118; see also the case of Raschid bin Abdulla and Another vs. Administrator General, originally heard in 1924 in the Kathi [Kadhi] court at Chake Chake, appeal heard January 28, 1925, found in Tomlinson and Knight-Bruce, 1928, p. 32.

[101] ZNA AC8/7, Letter from the Friends' Industrial Mission Pemba to the Vice Consul of Pemba, January 19, 1904.

[102] See probate listing for Khamis bin Hamadi Swahili, *Zanzibar Gazette*, October 13, 1913. This follows a pattern illustrated by Vincent Brown in Jamaica, where slaves would have elite whites as executors of their wills in order to prevent owners from usurping the property; Vincent Brown, *The Reapers Garden: Death and Power in the World of Atlantic Slavery* (Cambridge, MA: Harvard University Press, 2008), pp. 117, 124–5.

Sababu, a slave who was manumitted by his owner in the 1890s, built a mosque on his land as a representation of his piety.[103] Ali's actions were not unusual along the coast because Frederick Cooper and Margaret Strobel also noted ex-slaves who built mosques to show their piety.[104] John Craster noted the rural minarets and mosques dotting the countryside of Pemba (Figure 4.1). Many former slaves declared property as *wakf* to benefit mosques, the poor, and their own relatives. *Wakf* endowments were generally made of land that was dedicated to the support of local communities by providing for mosques, Quranic schools, and the care of the elderly and the poor, among other things, through the rent received from the land. Donations to charity or *wakf* dedications were a fundamental way for Muslims to express their piety and gain symbolic capital.[105] Much like the ex-slaves who wrote wills in order to make sure that their wishes were upheld at their deaths, *wakf* were another public means of controlling their estates and showing their knowledge and practice of Islam.[106] It was common for elite to leave *wakf* property for their ex-slaves. Therefore, it was ironic when ex-slaves left *wakf* property for the benefit of their former owners.[107] Some former owners may have encouraged their ex-slaves to declare property *wakf,* but it is just as likely that ex-slaves of particular owners found *wakf* to be a more effective means than wills for keeping avaricious owners from appropriating their estates. For example, two ex-slaves of Safor bin Juma left their property as *wakf* for the benefit of their descendants in order to keep their

---

[103] PNA AI1/34, HBM CZ, Civil Case No. 986 of 1928; *Wakf* of Hamis bin Abdalla hadim Koomba for the benefit of mosque built by him at Ngamba, *Zanzibar Gazette,* May 10, 1915.

[104] Cooper, 1977, p. 250; Mirza and Strobel, pp. 37–8.

[105] Anne K. Bang, *Sufis and Scholars of the Sea: Family Networks in East Africa, 1860–1925* (London: RoutledgeCurzon 2003); Timur Kuran, "The Provision of Public Goods under Islamic Law: Origins, Impact, and Limitations of the Waqf System," *Law and Society Review* 35, no. 4 (2001), pp. 841–98; Robinson, pp. 5–6.

[106] *Wakf* notice of Zahor hadim Safer Juma for benefit of the mosque and his descendants, *Zanzibar Gazette,* October 9, 1911; *Wakf* notice of Hamis bin Abdalla hadim Koomba for the benefit of mosque built by him at Ngamba, *Zanzibar Gazette,* May 10, 1915; *Wakf* notice of Johari khadim Safor bin Juma for the benefit of descendants and the poor, *Zanzibar Gazette,* November 5, 1917; PNA AK1/3315, Bahati binti Muya Manyema, November 1935.

[107] For elites leaving *wakf* for their servants, see *Wakf* notice of Ali Mahene bin Hamed for benefit of his hadims, *Zanzibar Gazette,* October 9, 1911; *Wakf* notice of Moosa bin Daud for benefit of Bibi Mwana, Kombo bin Rashid, and Rohea binti Abdul Rahman, *Zanzibar Gazette,* April 19, 1915; for ex-slaves leaving property, see *Wakf* notice of Bwana Mpate bin Alibakar for benefit of descendants of Mwana Halima binti Ali bin Amur As-Subhia, *Zanzibar Gazette,* July 11, 1911.

FIGURE 4.1. Rural minaret on Pemba. (Reprinted from J. E. E. Craster, *Pemba: The Spice Island of Zanzibar*. London: T.F. Unwin, 1913.)

ex-owner from claiming the property during their lifetimes and after their deaths.[108]

While some slaves were educated in the Quran by their owners, this was rare. However, with the process of emancipation, more and more

---

[108] *Wakf* notice of Zahor hadim Safer Juma for benefit of the mosque and his descendants, *Zanzibar Gazette*, October 9, 1911; *Wakf* notice of Johari khadim Safor bin Juma for the benefit of descendants and the poor, *Zanzibar Gazette*, November 5, 1917. While the spelling of the name Safor/Safer is slightly different, the details of the notice indicate that this was the same man who had two ex-slaves declare their property *wakf*.

students entered the local Quranic schools (called *chuo*, s., *vyuo*, pl.). In 1898, a missionary complained that he had difficulty procuring students for his school because "there are six mosques on the high road ... and probably others in the *mashamba* with a corresponding number of *Waalimu* [Quranic teachers]."[109] Such complaints from mission societies built for freed slave communities indicate that an increasing number of children of freed slaves instead chose to attend the local Islamic schools and gain *heshima* from their ability to recite verses of the Quran.[110] The perception remained within free societies that a slave was unlikely to "find pleasure in exalted pursuits" such as religious activities; thus, participating in religious activities allowed former slaves to show their "civility" and respectability while shedding their "slave" status.[111] Islamic knowledge in the twentieth century became a commodity that gave individuals *heshima* in ways unavailable to most ex-slaves in the nineteenth century.[112]

The Quranic schools were usually held on the *baraza* of the local teacher, or *mwalimu* (pl. *walimu*). The *mwalimu* was supposed to be someone educated in the Quran, although in many rural areas he was simply the most educated person in the village. Some *walimu* were very good and knew the Quran and could explain the meaning of the verses; however, many *walimu* were barely literate themselves, let alone able to teach children to understand the text. Regardless, in rural areas, many people believed that recitation of the holy words in Arabic was more important than comprehension.[113] Children memorized the first thirty *masura* of the Quran to become *hitimu*. Girls attended Quranic schools, and elite women were trained in their homes, but most girls stopped their Quranic education when they reached puberty and married, whereas boys could continue their studies.[114] Thus boys and men had an easier time

---

[109] UMCA, E2, Emily Key, "Notes from Pemba," January 18, 1898.

[110] Godfrey Dale says that almost every village had a mosque and *Quran* school; Reverend Godfrey Dale, *The Peoples of Zanzibar: Their Customs and Religious Beliefs* (London: Universities' Mission to Central Africa, 1920), pp. 11–12; William Ingrams also noted this in 1931. He lived on Pemba for two years as a magistrate; Ingrams, 1931, p. 433.

[111] Taylor, 1891, No. 449.

[112] Becker, pp. 202–4.

[113] See Bang, 2003; Allyson Purpura, "Knowledge and Agency: The Social Relations of Islamic Expertise in Zanzibar Town" (Ph.D. dissertation, City University of New York, 1997), pp. 188–9, 191–3.

[114] Halima Rashid, December 2004; Mattar Said Ahmed, November 2004; Farashuu Sleiman, December 2004; Iddi Ali Hamad, October 2004; McMahon, 2005, pp. 208–9; Roman Loimeier, *Between Social Skills and Marketable Skills: The Politics of Islamic Education in 20th Century Zanzibar* (Leiden: Brill, 2009), pp. 149–72; Mary Porter,

using Islam as a means of social mobility than women because they had more education and could become Quran teachers in the local mosques. The public nature of Quranic schools meant that neighbors knew which children attended classes and, consequently, which families had *heshima*. Also, during *maulidi* celebrations for the Prophet's birthday, children recited verses of the Quran in public presentations, which again helped them and their families build *heshima*. The reinvention of *maulidi* by ex-slaves in the twentieth century opened new avenues for publicly demonstrating Islamic piety. The largest *maulidi* were held during the month of the Prophet Mohammed's birth, but smaller *maulidi* were held throughout the year. During the nineteenth century, *maulidi* were staid affairs where only elite men recited verses about the Prophet.[115] However, by the early twentieth century, *maulidi* had become much larger events where entire families attended and participated at times.[116] For Pembans, *maulidi* were a family event.[117] Women also participated by singing during *maulidi*, although they were kept separated from the men performing recitations.[118] *Maulidi* were also a very public and popular space for women to show their religious beliefs because few women prayed in the mosques.[119]

Another form of education began in 1910 when the colonial government began operating schools on the island.[120] These schools were opened in response to a request by the Sultan because most people living on the islands refused to send their children to the Christian mission schools. In Pemba, most of the students in the first eight years of the government schools were all male Arabs and not former slaves, but the fees associated with the schools were removed in 1921, which opened the door for poorer male students to attend. Later in the 1920s, colonial schools for

"Resisting Uniformity at Mwana Kupona Girls' School: Cultural Productions in an Educational Setting," *Signs* 23, no. 3 (1998), pp. 619–43; Mohamed Kassim, "Colonial Resistance and the Local Transmission of Islamic Knowledge in the Benadir Coast in the Late 19th and Early 20th Centuries" (Ph.D. dissertation, York University, 2006), pp. 151–2.

[115] Middleton, 1992, p. 167.
[116] Ingrams, 1931, pp. 419–20.
[117] Halima Rashid, Pandani, December 2004.
[118] Ingrams, 1931, p. 420.
[119] Mzee Mohamed, Pemba, December 2004; Bi Asha, Pemba, December 2004; Halima Rashid, Pemba, December 2004; *maulidi* celebrations were the most popular activity of women interviewed in their sixties and seventies and also of their mother's generation.
[120] Loimeier, 2009, pp. 215–410; McMahon, 2005, pp. 199–238; Corrie Ruth Decker, "Investing in Ideas: Girls' Education in Colonial Zanzibar" (Ph.D. dissertation, University of California Berkeley, 2007), pp. 93–140.

girls opened up on the island. As one informant explained, "I saw Muslim children going to [government] school and I joined."[121] The government schools did teach the Quran, but for only a part of the day, which angered many parents.[122] The government schools had a bad reputation in general among most parents, especially because so few of the graduates actually got jobs with the government and students did not become *hitimu*.[123] Regardless of access to the colonial government schools, every Muslim parent strove to give his or her children an Islamic education, even if a minimal one, to show his or her Islamic piety and, as such, gain *heshima* for the family.

During the nineteenth century, Sufi *tarika*, especially the *Qadiriyya* but also the *Shadiliyya*, spread along the East African coast. Most of the scholars who brought these movements to the coast were either from the Comoros Islands, Brava in Somalia, or the Hadhramaut in Yemen. Elite patrician men were initially the adherents of Sufi sheikhs.[124] However, with the beginning of emancipation, former slaves flocked to the Sufi sheikhs as new disciples. In coastal communities this created tensions between elites and ex-slaves over who could be considered good Muslims. Numerous scholars have explored these tensions about status and Islamic knowledge and practice across the Swahili coast, but rarely has the gendered element to these tensions been discussed.[125] Maleness has been a central element in the discussion of the leadership of Sufi *tarika* in the historical literature. For example, Sufi *tarika* were generally referred to as "brotherhoods," explicitly gendering the organizations as male. Yet women were active participants in these associations. El-Zein consistently speaks of all Sufis as male because the leadership was primarily male.

---

[121] Juma bin Hamad, Pemba, November 2002.

[122] For examples of parents complaining on Pemba about the limited Quranic education in the government schools, see ZNA AB1/1, Report to Mr. Clarke, April 22, 1910; ZNA AB1/369, District Commissioner, Pemba, 1937.

[123] McMahon, 2005, pp. 199–238. However, children who learned arithmetic and writing in Swahili were valuable to families during the clove harvest, and parents kept them out of school to help during the harvest; Administrative Reports for the Year 1915, p. 25.

[124] B. G. Martin recorded that Shaykh Ali bin Adallah bin Nafi al-Mazrui went to Pemba in 1887 and began converting Arabs to the *Qadiriyya*, but this also entailed their conversion from Ibadhi to Sunni sects. Shaykh Ali's actions angered the Sultan of Zanzibar because the converts were Arab (and Ibadhi); if they had been ex-slaves, it is unlikely that the Sultan would have imprisoned Shaykh Ali; B. G. Martin, "Notes on Some Members of the Learned Classes of Zanzibar and East Africa in the Nineteenth Century," *African Historical Studies* 4, no. 3 (1971), pp. 525–45.

[125] The work of Felicitas Becker is one of the few to address the issue of gender in terms of status and Islam. Becker, 2008.

Yet El-Zein's footnotes show that it was the concubines of the elite men who financially supported the Sufi-run *maulidi*.[126] Many of the attendees of the *maulidi* on Pemba were women, reinforcing Felicitas Becker's argument that ex-slave women were often marginalized by their public work, but "women's visible participation in public performance [of the *tarika*] became a mark of religious commitment, hence of respectability rather than marginality."[127] Women joined the Sufi *tarika* as a means of accessing a community of practice and religious belief while demonstrating their *heshima* in the larger community.[128]

Participation in a Sufi *tarika* offered a route to ex-slaves, especially women, to gain Islamic *baraka* ("blessings") and *heshima* in their communities. Initially, Sufi practitioners needed little specialized knowledge beyond learning the *tarika* ("way") of the particular group. The way of each Sufi sect differed (and it could differ even between different sheikhs of one sect), but it was the prescribed practice of that group. Often a person needed to do little more than declare his or her commitment to learning the religious practices of the Sufi group to become considered an adherent. Participation among Sufis required little, if any, "book knowledge," and thus it was much easier for women and former slaves to become active members. Moreover, Sufi practices tended to be communal events where people chanted and in some cases danced together, which built on existing African practices found in female *msondo* ("initiation rituals") and *ngoma*.[129] Since most women did not pray in the mosques, they had few ways to publicly confirm their conversion to and practice of Islam. The introduction of new Sufi groups around the turn of the century opened new avenues for female participation in Islam. In northern Zanzibar, Bi Rahma was leading women's Sufi groups and education for girls by 1915, and women were leading *tarika* in Zanzibar

---

[126] Goldman, 1996, pp. 389–91. She notes that women regularly sponsored *maulidi* performances on Pemba in connection with wedding celebrations. While her fieldwork was conducted in the early 1990s, it corresponds with the comments from my informants who spoke of *maulidi* performances in the 1920s and 1930s.

[127] Becker, p. 196.

[128] As Helen Bradford noted in South Africa, assumptions of maleness in the historical record have shaped the way academics write about the past and the roles of women and men; Helen Bradford, "Women, Gender and Colonialism: Rethinking the History of the British Cape Colony and Its Frontier Zones, 1806–70," *Journal of African History* 37, no. 3 (1996), pp. 351–70.

[129] *Ngoma* is the word for "drum," but in the context of attending a *ngoma*, it means a dance of some kind; often these were competitive and festive occasions that were associated with pagan mainland practices. For further discussion of *ngoma*, see note 38 in this chapter.

Town and in rural southeastern Tanganyika by the 1930s.[130] According to Mohamed Kassim, women in Brava, a region from which many Sufi leaders in Zanzibar and Pemba came, were highly educated, and many were religious instructors.[131] This offers a very different perspective on Sufi *tarika* and their role along the Swahili coast than that given by numerous scholars.[132]

Tarika also offered ex-slaves who became economically powerful a means to translate their wealth into Islamic *baraka* by endowing mosques and other rituals.[133] The story of Shaykh Ramiya of Bagamoyo particularly illustrates how Sufi sects in East Africa became a path to *heshima* for former slaves. According to August Nimtz, Shaykh Ramiya was enslaved as a child to an elite Arab family. He was a house slave and, as such, was treated as a lesser member of the family. This gave him access to resources with which he had the means to build up a formidable business in the fish, copra, and coconut markets. As a wealthy adult, the Shaykh began his study of Islam, which took approximately ten years. He started his studies in the late nineteenth century before the end of slavery. During that time, he was made a *khalifa* ("leader") of the *Qadiriyya* Sufi in Bagamoyo.[134] Eventually, in 1916, the British colonial government appointed Shaykh Ramiya the *liwali* of the town. He was deeply respected in his community. He did not hide his origins nor his history as a slave. In fact, his ancestry combined with his commitment to Islamic studies convinced community

---

[130] Hanni Nuotio tells of Bi Rahma, a woman who started leading women's Sufi groups and who was educated around 1915 in northern Unguja. Bi Rahma's example hints at how women could become "leaders of women." Nuotio, "The Dance That Is Not Danced," in *The Global Worlds of the Swahili*, edited by Roman Loimeier and Rüdiger Seesemann (Berlin: Lit Vertag, 2006), p. 199. Also see Amina Ameir Issa, "The Legacy of *Qadiri* Scholars in Zanzibar," in *The Global Worlds of the Swahili* (Berlin: Lit Vertag, 2006), p. 353; Becker, p. 196; Purpura discusses several female Sufi leaders, one of whom, Bi Mwanasha, was born in the 1890s and opened a Quranic school by the 1930s in Zanzibar Town; Purpura, 1997, pp. 222–50.

[131] Kassim, 2006, pp. 245–70.

[132] Works such as that of Anne Bang, August Nimtz, and B. G. Martin, among others, have emphasized the male nature of Sufism. These authors have been focused on tracing the leadership of the *ulama*, as well as the *khalifa*, of the Sufi *tarika*, especially in the nineteenth century. Thus it is easy to see why women are left out of their scholarship. Bang, 2003; August H. Nimtz, *Islam and Politics in East Africa: The Sufi Order in Tanzania* (Minneapolis: University of Minnesota Press, 1980); B. G. Martin, *Muslim Brotherhoods in Nineteenth-Century Africa* (Cambridge University Press, 1976).

[133] See Mirza and Strobel, pp. 37–8; Glassman, 1995, pp. 79–114; Nimtz, 1980, pp. 118–34.

[134] See Purpura's work for a discussion of how individuals could translate "esoteric Islamic knowledge" into a commodity of value for accessing elite status; Purpura, p. 70.

members that he was particularly blessed and brought him even greater respect and honor in Bagamoyo.[135] Wealth was often associated with blessings from God, which is one reason why lower-status people who gradually became wealthy, such as Shaykh Ramiya, had such success in gaining *heshima* in their communities.[136] Yet Jonathan Glassman suggests that ex-slaves still had a hard time gaining acceptance from the social elite, especially the Ibadhi Arabs and the coastal *waungwana*, who looked down on Sufi practitioners.[137]

The earliest Sufi converts on Pemba were elite.[138] Because of the elite acceptance of Sufi practice, it is understandable that ex-slaves on Pemba would want to become Sufis as a means to attain *heshima*. Sufi sects expanded after the final emancipation in 1909 because a practice that had once been the domain of the elite was opened to everyone. By 1910, teachers in some of the Quranic schools were Sufis passing on their knowledge to their students, and enough people living in rural areas participated in Sufi groups that Craster was kept up at night with the sounds of *dhikiri* in 1912.[139] *Dhikiri* is "a Sufi ritual celebrating God by repeating the names of God ... and certain body movements" that helped Sufi adherents reach a meditative state and gain closeness with God.[140] Each of the Sufi sects had different *dhikiri* that they practiced; the most popular form among the *Qadiriyya* along the coast included a practice that had a distinctive "coughing" sound, which is the *dhikiri* that Craster heard. Both men and women participated in the *dhikiri* of the *Qadiriyya*, who met nightly outside the clove harvest season. Nimtz argues that the *dhikiri* was more important than the five pillars of Islam, and the simplicity of the *dhikiri* allowed more people to participate and to actively portray themselves as Muslim.[141]

Sufi *tarika* opened new doors to many newly freed slaves on Pemba and along the East African coast. The opportunity to learn more about Islam through their lessons from their sheikh made participation in Sufi *tarika* attractive to ex-slave men and women. Moreover, these communities of religious practice helped to form enduring networks that offered

---

[135] Nimtz, pp. 118–22.

[136] Pouwels, 1987, pp. 75–6.

[137] Glassman, 1995, p. 141; *waungwana* were the coastal elite in the pre-Omani era. See Pouwels, 1987, chaps. 6 through 10, for a detailed discussion of *waungwana* identity.

[138] Martin, 1971, pp. 525–45; Pouwels, 1987, p. 143.

[139] Nuotio, pp. 188–9; Craster, pp. 310–11.

[140] Kjersti Larsen, *Where Humans and Spirits Meet: The Politics of Rituals and Identified Spirits in Zanzibar* (New York: Berghahn Books, 2008), p. 36.

[141] Nimtz, p. 125.

support, education, respectability, and a sense of belonging to ex-slaves. The *tarika* were particularly important in the lives of women, which gives scholars a new perspective on how former slave women integrated into local communities beyond the discussion of marrying local men.

REPUTATION, CONTRACTS, AND THE COURTS

In the nineteenth century, the Mombasan poet Muyaka famously penned a series of poems, one of which included the warning, "Your home is in the water, hippo." In this poem, Muyaka reminded individuals that "you may walk on land Hippo, but your home is still in the water."[142] He added the explicit point that "he who borrows and pays back avoids a lot of trouble" because no matter what, a reputation for dishonesty would follow people, even when they walked on land away from where they borrowed the money. As noted in Chapter 1, reputation was a critical component of a person's *heshima*. While a person's *heshima* was a measure of his or her symbolic capital, the person's reputation was what allowed him or her to deploy that capital into a value.[143] As Taylor argues, honor was less a "motivational force for behavior" but rather should be seen as a "rhetorical strategy adopted ... to manage ... relationships with others in their communities."[144] Thus the symbolic capital of *heshima* was transformed into a reputation that either allowed individuals to capitalize through borrowing or kept them from accessing the credit systems of the community. By examining the ways that credit, trust, and contracts developed in Pemban communities, the symbolic capital of reputation and *heshima* appears as a value that individuals used to gain security in daily life.

The term *heshima* itself was remade during the emancipation period. *Heshima* was no longer based on perceptions of birth (freeborn versus slave-born) as Pembans asserted their rights to *heshima*. One significant means of both attaining and measuring *heshima* was through access to credit and building a reputation in the community as someone who repaid his or her debts. Because Pembans relied on the influx of cash

---

[142] Mohamed H. Abdulaziz, *Muyaka: 19th Century Swahili Popular Poetry* (Nairobi: Kenya Literature Bureau, 1979), p. 257.

[143] Pierre Bourdieu, "Structures, Habitus, Power: Basis for a Theory of Symbolic Power," in *Culture/Power/History: A Reader in Contemporary Social Theory*, edited by Nicholas B. Dirks, Geoff Eley, and Sherry B. Ortner (Princeton, NJ: Princeton University Press, 1994), pp. 166–78; Robinson, pp. 5–6.

[144] Taylor, 2003, p. 26.

during the two clove harvests to pay their debts, most of the year people lived on credit.[145] Moreover, the indebtedness of many of the landed elite on Pemba required that they also maintain their reputation of repaying loans to keep their *heshima*. One respected Arab advertised in the *Zanzibar Gazette* in 1911 that if anyone lent money to his nephew after the advertisement, he or she did so "at his [or her] own risk."[146] Clearly, the relatives of this profligate young man felt compelled to have this public order made so as to protect their reputation as a family who paid their debts. The Arab man who placed this advertisement was formerly a *kadhi*; thus his *heshima* would previously have been unquestioned, but by 1911 he could not afford for his family to have a reputation as people who did not pay their debts.

Ghislaine Lydon's work in the Sahara has done an exceptional job of illuminating the contracts of Muslim long-distance traders in the Sahara. Her work also shows the significance of trust and reputation in locally arranged contracts. She argues that as a starting point to making an agreement, it helped if both parties were recognized as Muslim.[147] Likewise, on Pemba people sealed contracts with an oath, and the people with whom they were contracting had to have confidence in the oath, something easier to accept if both were Muslim. As discussed in Chapter 3, oaths were made with the understanding of a common belief in Allah and, as such, the belief that an oath held the power to affect a person's afterlife. Thus, in order to make agreements, people in the community had to recognize the other person as a respectable Muslim. Individuals who fulfilled their part in an agreement such as paying back debt built their reputations as trustworthy and increased their *heshima*. However, a belief in Islam was not enough for one person to agree to lend or borrow money from another person. A person needed to have a good reputation. Again, turning to the work on long-distance trade illuminates the systems set up for building reputations of trust. Avner Greif offered a theory of a "reputation mechanism" that allowed for distant traders to work beyond familial networks based on reputations of trustworthiness.[148]

---

[145] Taylor, 2003, p. 12, argues that the lack of specie in peasant economies required that people live on credit. Pembans faced a similar situation.

[146] *Zanzibar Gazette*, July 11, 1911. The uncle advertising was formerly a *kadhi*, indicating his position in the community.

[147] Lydon, pp. 290–3. Ghislaine Lydon suggests that many Jews participated in the long-distance trade networks, which meant they had a higher standard for setting up a reputation as trustworthy.

[148] Avner Greif, "Reputation and Coalitions in Medieval Trade: Evidence on the Maghribi Traders," *Journal of Economic History* 49, no. 4 (December 1989), pp. 857–60.

The reputation mechanism allowed for individuals to trust nonkin in matters of contracts and economic agreements.

As Lydon shows, most contracts had written elements, but these were not accepted as evidence in Islamic courts. The British courts were distinctly uneven in how they handled written evidence, indicating that some magistrates had a better understanding of Islamic rules of evidence than others.[149] Nonetheless, Pembans knew that they needed witnesses for any economic agreement to be legitimate, as proved by the consistency with which they had contracts witnessed.[150] Another aspect of the difficulty with using written and oral evidence arose in Lydon's work and in the records from Pemba because most written contracts had oral elements, for example, the *bei kataa* discussed in Chapter 3, where moneylenders had to find ways to avoid the appearance of usury, so they would make written agreements to purchase property that appeared as an outright sale of the land. However, a further oral agreement was made with the property owner that the contract was a mortgage, and as long as payments were made, the property would be returned to the owner when the debt was paid. The oral elements of agreements made it likely that contracts would be disputed, which helps to explain why so many contract disputes ended up in the courts.[151]

Gender seemingly did not play a role in the making of economic agreements. Women on Pemba acted as both lenders and borrowers, similar to men. While far more male moneylenders existed and went to the courts to dispute debts, women remained as important arbiters of reputation and credit. When the brother of Hasina binti Nasibu went to a female moneylender to pawn his sister's land, the woman refused to lend him money. Moreover, she called him out as having an undesirable reputation and reminded him that he had been hauled into the court by his sister a decade previously for mortgaging her land without authorization.[152]

---

[149] The probate courts are an excellent example of the inconsistency found among magistrates, who often were only in their posts for a matter of months on Pemba. Some magistrates would accept written documents and "book debts," whereas others would look at the written evidence and then require the person to declare an oath in front of the *kadhi* before adding the debt to the probate records.

[150] Even in the case of Mzuri Kwao, discussed in Chapter 2, which was an illegal sale, but the contracting parties brought four witnesses.

[151] ZNA AM13/1 and ZNA AM14/1 contain hundreds of files of property contracts; Taylor found a similar phenomenon in early modern Spain, Taylor, 2003, p. 12.

[152] PNA AI1/19, HHSC, Civil Case No. 673 of 1919. The probate case of Binti Hemed bin Suleiman, an elite Arab woman, indicates that she was also a moneylender. At her death, nine unrelated men owed her debts ranging from 10 to 60 rupees for a total of 398 rupees. PNA AK1/86, Binti Hemed bin Suleiman, December 1910.

The female moneylender refused to tarnish her reputation by associating herself with Hasina's disreputable brother. As scholars throughout a variety of fields have shown, women in commercial endeavors relied on their reputations for honesty to buoy their honor in their communities.[153] Likewise, men and women in their everyday encounters used their reputations and *heshima* as a means to access credit.

Agreements or contracts of credit in Pemba were made both orally and in written form. They ranged from the detailed mortgages given by moneylenders to the everyday borrowing of a rupee or a few pice from neighbors. Three significant forms of credit on the island were borrowing from moneylenders; credit with shopkeepers, market people, friends, and family; and the unpaid dower portions when people married. Moneylenders were generally responsible for larger loans, especially those secured by property, although pawnbrokers also lent small sums based on items such as jewelry, clothing, and livestock.[154] Similarly to moneylenders, individual shopkeepers and market people extended credit to their communities in the seasons between clove harvests with the expectation of repayment at the end of the harvests. Dowers, locally called *mahari*, were rarely paid in full at marriage and created a credit between spouses, encouraging them to behave well toward one another for fear of economic consequences.

Records of debts to moneylenders are well represented in the historical record through court disputes and existing mortgage deeds. However, debts made orally are more difficult to trace.[155] Several sources give insight into small loans over time: probate records, British surveys of indebtedness, and oral interviews. After 1910, when the *sheha* reported the death of a person, if the person owned any property whatsoever, including jewelry and other movable property, his or her estate went into the probate

---

[153] For early modern Spain, see Taylor, 2003, p. 23; for early modern Britain, see Garthine Walker, "Expanding the Boundaries of Female Honour in Early Modern England," *Transactions of the Royal Historical Society*, Sixth Series, 6 (1996), pp. 235–45.

[154] Borrowing was common among people on Pemba. Interviews: Shaame Othman Ali, Pemba, November 2002; Mbarouk Seif Ali, Pemba, October 2002; Suleiman Hamad Suleiman, Pemba, October 2002; Mohamed Mbwana Mserembwe, Pemba, October 2002; Ali Rubea Makame, Pemba, October 2002; Absalla Omar Sharif, Pemba, October 2002.

[155] For mortgage deeds, see ZNA AM13/1. Hundreds of these deeds written in Ajami (Swahili in Arabic letters) remain in the archives of Zanzibar. For a discussion of these records, see McMahon, 2005, pp. 262–4; for the mainland, Becker notes that "villagers were attentive not only to what they owed or claimed from one another, but also to what they might be able to demand or might be asked for; not only to who had bewitched whom, but also who might bewitch whom." Thus she puts witchcraft on the same level as credit transactions; Becker, pp. 12–13.

court. All outstanding debts had to be paid before the inheritance could be settled. Debtors brought their claims to the probate court and had to prove their claims, most often by swearing an oath to the debt in front of the *kadhi.* Heirs had the right to contest debts but generally did not if the debtor swore an oath that the debt was contracted orally.[156] If a debt was a mortgage debt, it was recorded as such; likewise debts of *mahari* owed to widows. This makes it easy to identify these two forms of debt and, as such, credits and contracts. The less obvious debts were the ones mentioned in the records but not necessarily specified. In some cases, as discussed below, debts were specified and give insight into the systems of credit available and the oral nature of many agreements. However, the probate records only show the systems of credit used by people who owned property. A 1933 survey conducted by colonial officials indicated that the majority of Pembans used short-term loans as a means to carry them through the next harvest season.[157] This survey showed that 50 percent of all debt came from domestic expenses, such as purchasing food at shops on credit, illuminating the significant role of credit in daily interactions. Oral interviews conducted in 2002 also showed that by the 1940s and 1950s, at least 40 percent of Pembans used credit with shopkeepers, whereas 21 percent of people surveyed borrowed from relatives or others in their communities, indicating that use of credit was rampant.[158] All these sources point to the widespread use of unsecured credit on Pemba and thus demonstrate the role reputation played in maintaining this system.

The unsecured credit systems on Pemba worked in a myriad of ways and among many different people, men and women, poor and elite. Debts to shopkeepers were common in the probate records and indicate that people borrowed up to several months worth of food from the shops between harvests.[159] Many people held credits with shopkeepers and

---

[156] For an example of an orally contracted debt contested by a relative and then accepted after the debtor swore an oath, see PNA AK1/334, Musa Mchanja, March 1914.

[157] The survey results are incredibly skewed either because Pembans were more forthcoming than Ungujans or because Pembans had more problems with making ends meet. Either way, of the 1,261 responses that debt was incurred for domestic expenses, 1,239 came from Pemba. See Last and Bartlett.

[158] Interviews: Ali Khamis Faraj, Pemba, October 2002; Ali Hamad Omar, Pemba, October 2002; Mariam Mbarouk Khamis, Pemba, October 2002; Mayasa Hamad Kombo, Pemba, October 2002; Fatma Ali Hemed, Pemba, October 2002.

[159] See examples in PNA AK1/80, November 1910; PNA AK1/197, Kombo Usi, August 1912; PNA AK1/200, Abdalla bin Omar Swahili, July 1912; PNA AK1/206, August 1912; AK1/322, Haji bin Githenge, July 1913; PNA AK1/325, Omari bin Omari Swahili, January 1914; PNA AK1/332, Chousiku bin Abdalla, February 1914; PNA AK1/337,

would be given credit for food to be repaid after the clove harvest.[160] Yet shopkeepers were not the only ones who sold food on credit; even people with market stalls gave credit. In the 1920s, Mabruki bin Sadi received 12 rupees worth of meat from Hilal bin Seif on credit. Mabruki also received 19 rupees and 59 pice in food credit from Mohammed Hasim Sheriff.[161] Mabruki was an ex-slave; thus his ability to get credit shows how ex-slaves built reputations as trustworthy commerce partners. When a government-freed ex-slave named Ferezi died in 1912, he had a number of small debts brought to the court. Ferezi's case goes to show that slaves emancipated by the government were also able to get credit.[162] Orally contracted debts such as those held by Mabruki and Ferezi crossed lines of gender and class; men could owe women, and elites could owe ex-slaves, and vice versa.[163]

While it makes sense for creditors to go to the probate court to get repaid at the death of a debtor, it is important to note that debtors also went to the court when someone they owed money died. When Saleh bin Kombo died in 1926, four people came to the probate court to accept that they owed him money.[164] Each of the debtors who could not repay his or her debt immediately was then assigned to recompense a particular heir as part of the inheritance. The heirs accepted these debts as part of their inheritance, indicating that they trusted the debtors to pay off the loans either in cash or produce. Saleh left a wife, an adult daughter, and a minor son, all of whom would seemingly be vulnerable to others refusing to acknowledge the debts. Yet the debtors freely admitted their debts because if they did not, the wife and adult daughter could have either claimed the debts and forced the debtors to swear an oath or impugned

Said bin Abed bin Said, March 1914; PNA AK1/3097, Hamed bin Salim bin Abdulla el-Mazrui, March 1933, among others. These debts all ranged from 10 to 60 rupees.

[160] Both J. E. E. Craster and Arthur Hardinge mention that Indian shopkeepers controlled the dry good markets on Pemba. *Africa No. 7, Correspondence Respecting Slavery in the Zanzibar Dominions*, Hardinge's report (1896); Craster, 1913.

[161] PNA AK1/2614, Mabruki bin Ladi Manyema, October 1928.

[162] PNA AK1/198, Ferezi Hadim Sirkari, September 16, 1912.

[163] For examples, see PNA AK1/333, Mwana Kiamu binti Sholi, March 1914; PNA AK1/338, Rashid bin Geuar, February 1914; PNA AK1/1066, Khamisini Manyema, December 1919; PNA AK1/1639, Ali bin Abdalla el-Hinawi, 1923; PNA AK1/1987, Msengesi wadi Shoma Mnyaturu, January 1926; PNA AK1/1989, Yusuf bin Kombo Mswahili, January 1926; PNA AK1/3097, Hamed bin Salim bin Abdulla el-Mazrui, March 1933. Zuwalia hadim Kukas owed money for work done to her house by a *fundi* when she died; PNA AK1/54, Zuwalia hadim Kukas, June 1910.

[164] PNA AK1/2186, Saleh bin Kombo Swahili, October 1926; likewise, when Bakari Fakih Bakari died in 1910, his children made sure to acknowledge all his debts and make sure that they were paid; see PNA AK1/80.

the debtor's reputations in the community. The debts were frankly quite small; thus it was not worth losing a reputation over a few rupees.

People also borrowed and lent money and items to people connected to them through either kinship or other relationships. Binti Sudi was given 13 rupees' worth of hats by Abdulwadad bin Maalim Juma.[165] She intended to embroider the hats in the detailed designs popular on *kofia* and resell them at a profit. Her son, Khamis wadi Farhani, witnessed the debt for her, but it was her debt. When Khamis died, Abdulwadad asked that the estate of Khamis repay Binti Sudi's debt. She contested this request and stated that the debt was with her, not her son. Abdulwadad asked the probate court to honor his request because he felt that he could not ask Binti Sudi to repay the debt because she was his *ayah*, the woman who helped to raise him. This shows the complex systems of debt and credit. Binti Sudi was a slave of Abdulwadad's grandfather and imposed on him to give her credit so that she could purchase the hats. Binti Sudi's son, who was quite successful, secured the loan for her with Abdulwadad. Perhaps Abdulwadad knew that Binti Sudi would never pay back the loan, but because her son was so successful, Abdulwadad knew that Abdulwadad could get reimbursed if necessary – if necessary, because as a former slave of the family, Binti Sudi's request for the loan showed her expectation that her owner's family members should give her the means to subsist even after emancipation. Abdulwadad gave the loan with the expectation that it would not be repaid per se but that he could use that as a form of credit with Khamis, who was a substantial landowner.[166] Thus the credit to Binti Sudi was a way for Abdulwadad to build a reputation as a generous person, someone with *heshima* and as such worthy himself of credit from others.

Another means of credit was through *mahari* ("dower") paid to women at their marriages. Marriages along the Swahili coast were oral contracts that had explicit expectations for both men and women.[167] Men maintained their wives with clothing, shelter, and food, and women were expected to prepare food and take care of the household and any

---

[165] PNA AK1/1066, Khamisini Manyema, December 1919.

[166] Khamis left an estate valued at 2,000 rupees, which was a decent size for the time period on Pemba.

[167] This is not to say that Swahili marriages were loveless because they were not. Numerous ex-slaves described loving their spouses, and couples of all classes were known to seek help in getting married for love. See FIM TEMP MSS 419/1–7, Theodore Burtt, Notebook, 1899; Africa No. 6, *Correspondence Respecting the Abolition of the Legal Status of Slavery in Zanzibar and Pemba*, Inclosure 1, in No. 11, Reverend J. P. Farler to Sir L. Mathews, Pemba, June 17, 1897.

children.[168] This meant that women were in charge of the household budget and were responsible for purchasing food and, as such, having access to credit with shopkeepers and market people. If a man had a poor reputation as a provider, he would have a difficult time finding a marriage partner. Often the marriage contract was discussed in terms of men being able to provide and women being faithful, but that was not always the case.[169] Chastity was far less of an issue given that many people had at least two spouses in a lifetime.[170] For example, Songoro Makonde, an ex-slave living on the Friends *shamba*, had a wife who left him one day, taking everything in the house, including his clothes.[171] Because of the potential for economic loss in a marriage, it was an institution that emphasized a good reputation.

The *mahari* acted as a form of insurance for women, who were generally in a weaker position in marriage under Islamic law. Men gave dowers directly to their new wives rather than to the wives' families. When a couple married, a man paid anywhere from ten to several hundred rupees depending on the economic position of the man and the woman's family, as well as whether it was her first marriage. Usually a portion of the dower was given at the time of the marriage, with a portion left unpaid. At times of economic distress, the *mahari* was left completely unpaid before the marriage. As part of the marriage ceremony, the amount of the *mahari* was stated in front of multiple witnesses, including how much was given at the marriage and how much was left to pay. The unpaid portion of the *mahari* allowed women a measure of power in their relationships because they were not able to initiate divorce in Islamic law. However, women could offer their husbands a release from paying the final portion of the *mahari* in exchange for a divorce. Likewise, if a husband decided to divorce his wife, he had to pay her the rest of her *mahari*, which gave her something to live on during her *edda* ("period of waiting until she could remarry" – usually three months). Also, if a husband died, wives received the smallest share of the estate, but the unpaid portion of the *mahari* came out of the estate as a debt; thus it gave widows an additional part

---

[168] This was a customary interpretation, though, because legally women could not be made to take care of the house. However, women were legally bound to have sexual intercourse with their spouses; Hirsch, pp. 86–7.

[169] See especially the poetry of Muyaka in Abdulaziz, pp. 169, 175; Knappert, 1972, p. 25.

[170] Ingrams, 1931, p. 237; Gabrielle E. O'Malley, "Marriage and Morality: Negotiating Gender and Respect in Zanzibar Town" (Ph.D. dissertation, University of Washington, 2000), p. 62; Stockreiter, 2007, chap. 4; Mirza and Strobel, pp. 10–11; FIM TEMP MSS 419/1–7, Theodore Burtt, Notebook, 1899.

[171] FIM TEMP MSS 419/1–7, Theodore Burtt, Notebook, 1899.

of the estate.[172] In some cases this could be quite significant and allowed women to have choice about whether they wanted to remarry or remain unmarried. Dowers were a form of credit that almost everyone at one time or another participated in using. Marriage, credit, and debt agreements were all "social interactions" that allowed individuals to build or in some cases destroy their reputations and *heshima.*[173]

CONCLUSION

Heshima was about behaving in a manner that allowed the community to accord individuals respect. In general, this meant having enough wealth to offer feasts, build mosques, or participate in leisure activities instead of work. In the early period of the Protectorate, wealth was not the only indicator of *heshima,* but by the beginning of the twentieth century this had begun to change. *Heshima's* value within a community was also based on the desire of people to afford it to others. Prior to emancipation, *heshima* was primarily a function of the freeborn society – the servile classes could protect their reputations, but they lacked *heshima* ("honor") by definition; yet many still received *heshima* ("respectability") from their communities and their owners. With the emancipation order of 1897, many former slaves began asserting their rights as free people, one of the most important rights being that of access to *heshima.* To achieve this right, people first worked toward earning a reputation that was worthy of respect by showing their knowledge of Islamic codes of dress, behavior, and piety; through their honesty; and through their generosity to family and neighbors.

The credit arrangements of Pemban communities were complex and nuanced, yet all demonstrate the symbolic capital *heshima* held for individuals within society regardless of their social status. Reputation became the value of this symbolic capital, which, in turn, allowed people of all walks of life on Pemba to attain credit for their daily sustenance. Thus people's displays of piety could be important for them in their relationships with their neighbors but also with their creditors. The shifting

---

[172] For some examples of *mahari* payments in probate records, see PNA AK1/80, November 1910; PNA AK1/330, Shaibu bin Juma, February 25, 1914; PNA AK1/338, Rashid bin Geuar, February 1914; PNA AK1/1066, December 1919; PNA AK1/1993, November 1925, among many, many others.

[173] See Craig Muldrew's work for a discussion of "social transactions"; Craig Muldrew, *The Economy of Obligation: The Culture of Credit and Social Relations in Early Modern England* (New York: St. Martin's Press, 1998), pp. 63–8.

meaning of *heshima* demonstrates the ways in which elites and ex-slaves had to accommodate each other in their daily interactions because people at all levels of Pemban society were forced to use credit during the non-harvest seasons. The common practices of credit and debt across the spectrum on Pemba meant that everyone was vulnerable to attacks on their reputation, and everyone had to find ways to manage and isolate talk that could derail their ability to access credit. *Heshima*, then, no longer gave elites automatic prestige over ex-slaves because for everyone it was negotiable.

5

Changing Landscapes of Power

In 1897, in response to the British abolition order, Salim bin Ali el-Riami, a wealthy Arab landowner on Pemba, had his slaves raise the French tricolor flag out in front of his stone house.[1] El-Riami then made a public demonstration to his neighbors and the quickly collecting gawkers that he was France's honorary consul on Pemba and that the slavery Abolition Decree of 1897 did not apply to him. To emphasize his point, el-Riami shot off his guns in a salute to the French flag, the sounds of which brought even more onlookers. Quickly the story of el-Riami's defiance spread among Arabs and slaves alike until it reached the ears of the British Vice Consul. Officials were concerned about how to proceed. On the one hand, el-Riami was a powerful and influential Arab in the recently declared Protectorate of Zanzibar; on the other, he was engaging in a direct confrontation with the power of the British to impose unpopular laws. The head of the Protectorate government came from Zanzibar to meet with el-Riami, who eventually explained that he was afraid of losing *heshima* for his household because the abolition order left his boat, carrying his wives and harem, open to being searched by British sailors. While el-Riami's actions were meant to display his power – defying the colonial government and shooting off his guns – in reality, he meekly asked the First Minister to guarantee him that his family would not be open to inspection by infidels, which would cause him to lose the respect of his neighbors. El-Riami's request of the First Minster crystallized the shifting landscape of power on Pemba and along the Swahili coast as the expansion of British power and the end of slavery caused the demise of

[1] PRO FO 107/111, Jurisdiction in Pemba, 1897–1901.

157

elite honor along the coast and reordered the meaning of *heshima* from honor to respectability.

The landscapes of power on Pemba changed dramatically in a number of ways, both visible and invisible to colonial officials. Colonial officials focused on the ways in which the abolition order forced people of all levels of society into the court systems to settle disputes. No longer did elites back up their threats to lower-status people with the fear of enslavement or punishment for slaves. No longer could people legally take to the streets to settle disputes, as done in the past, because now British officials policed fighting and categorized it as assault or murder.[2] The colonial courts became a visible reminder of the changes to the power of local communities as the courts usurped the role of local elites to both police their communities and arbitrate the *heshima* of people. Yet this suggests that Pembans acquiesced to the demise of their power, which they most certainly did not. Even as colonial officials attempted to "civilize" Pemban society through policing and the courts, a precolonial form of power expanded on the island.

The use of *uchawi* ("witchcraft, occult, magic") expanded in lock step with the development of the new colonial courts. The practitioners of *uchawi*, called *wachawi*, were feared by people on Pemba, but they were not hunted because their knowledge and skill could also help people. *Wachawi* walked a fine line within Pemban society; people would not acknowledge that they were *wachawi* because they might then be accused of harming people. However, *wachawi* were not forced to go through ordeals to prove their innocence, as found in mainland societies. *Wachawi* were not hunted or punished by the communities; instead, they earned the grudging admiration and respect of the community. A person who was considered a powerful *mchawi* was offered *heshima* in the older understanding of the word – the person had honor because of his or her ability to control people through the fear of violence.

As discussed in Chapter 3, *uchawi* was not prosecuted in the courts because there were no laws against practicing *uchawi* in the Zanzibar Islands. In 1909, a witchcraft ordinance was promulgated in British East Africa on the mainland, and officials in Zanzibar considered adopting a similar ordinance. However, even though some officials supported the ordinance, it was ultimately not adopted. In general, officials on Zanzibar

---

[2] Craster mentions a fight between a group of Wanyamwezi and WaPemba laborers who kept their battle secret from the police in order to avoid incarceration; Craster, pp. 103–4.

thought the ordinance a good idea, but those on Pemba thought it was a waste of time. They argued that most of the *masheha* ("local officials") were implicated in the practice on the island and that none of the *askaris* ("police"), who were mostly from the mainland, would even patrol at night for fear of the *wachawi*.[3] Pemban officials argued that even if they wanted to prosecute *waganga* and *wachawi* for practicing magic, they would not be able to do so. A song collected in 1912 supports this concern. The song refers to a woman who killed her son in order to become *wachawi*, and she says, "I had no fear of the flag and law-courts of the English."[4] Officials suggested that if the British paid attention to *uchawi*, they would reify its power and importance to the Pemban population.

This chapter explores the varying landscapes of power on Pemba during the colonial period. The first half focuses on the ways in which officials sought to civilize Pembans by bringing disputes into the courts. It also demonstrates the very real power that colonialism had in shifting the relationships between slave owners and former slaves. Colonialism put everyone on a relatively equal playing field in terms of the courts; however, entrenched social relationships did not change so easily. The second half of the chapter examines in detail the role of *uchawi* on Pemba as a form of power used by elites to control others, as they had before the colonial period, and as a means for former slaves to move up the social hierarchy through skill as *wachawi*. The power of *uchawi* is twofold in that it both challenged colonial power through means "invisible" to officials and it also offered people of all levels of society the ability to achieve *heshima* as honor. While officials viewed themselves as policing the island and resolving disputes through the courts, Pembans viewed *wachawi* as a form of policing.

REORDERING *HESHIMA*

A classic example of the reordering of power and *heshima* comes in the story of Ali bin Abdallah el-Hinawi. Ali bin Abdallah was a powerful Omani Arab who owned the largest plantation in Pemba. In the early 1890s, he was appointed by the Sultan as his accredited agent on Pemba to deal with issues of probate and to make sure that duties owed to the Sultan were paid. However, this often meant that Ali would claim the

---

[3] ZNA AB31/20, District Officer, Paul Sheldon report, December 17, 1914; Assistant collector's report for Weti, January 14, 1910.

[4] Craster, p. 301.

land of people who died in the name of the Sultan but add it to his own property portfolio. Ali's plantation, Mgagadu, reputedly had over 5,000 clove trees, making it the largest single plantation on the island. His wealth was far above what any other person on Pemba could claim.[5] His birth as an Arab, his wealth in land and slaves, and his connections with the Sultan's family guaranteed him the highest *heshima*, even though he was generally disliked. Before the arrival of the British Vice Consul, Ali bin Abdallah clearly had great power and wealth and, with that power, fear and respect. The *liwali* refused to respond to complaints made by other Arabs against Ali because of his power. At one point around 1893, a group of Arabs of a less influential family unsuccessfully "took up arms against" him in a dispute.[6] Though Ali was clearly disliked, he seemed to have extraordinary power and the backing of the government. Ali's "friends and fellow men" included the Sultan; he was a member of a very elite and well-respected caste.

Ali's downfall came in 1895 with the arrival of the new British Vice Consul, who did not have any fear of or dealings with Ali bin Abdallah or his family. In May of 1895, several runaway slaves were caught and brought to the Vice Consul, who dutifully returned them to their owners, one of whom was Ali bin Abdallah. It was Ali's son Nasor who received the slaves and promised the Vice Consul that no punishment would be meted out to the three men, Songoro, Muftah, and Hailallah, who had been caught. When Nasor returned to the family plantation, his brother Abdallah, enraged by the slaves' behavior, punished the men by flogging them. Each of the three received 100 strokes. Songoro died from the flogging. The other two men were then laid on the ground next to two young clove trees. Irons were put on their ankles, with the trunk of the clove tree between their legs. The irons were put on hot to sear into the flesh of the men. When Ali returned to the plantation and found out what happened, he had Hailallah strangled but left Muftah attached to the clove tree. Muftah was left there for seven months and given only the juice of one coconut per day for sustenance. When Muftah was finally reported to the Vice Consul, Dr. O'Sullivan-Beare, the tree he was attached to had to be chopped down and Muftah had to be carried to the town of Chake

---

[5] When his estate of Mgagadu was probated in the 1930s, it was valued at 160,000 rupees. The wealthiest estates in the probate records I sampled were 15,000 rupees, less than 10 percent of the value of Ali's estate; PNA AI1/76, HBMCZ District Registry of the High Court, Civil Case No. 17 of 1934, Abdulla bin Ali el-Hinawi and Others vs. the Administrator General and Others.

[6] ZNA AC9/2, Vice Consul Pemba, December 22, 1895.

Chake because the irons could not be removed from his legs. The citizens of the town were horrified at what Ali and his sons had done to Muftah.[7] Two weeks later, a slave who had run away from another owner was found in a similar position. Though not her owner, Ali put her there to punish her for running away from her owner.

The "abhorrence" of the townspeople who offered "universal commiseration" with Muftah, combined with the growing resentment among fellow landowners about the family's ruthless interference in their affairs, ultimately harmed the reputation of Ali bin Abdallah and his sons. Yet Ali had perpetuated similar actions at earlier periods without condemnation. According to the Vice Consul's warning, "Ali bin Abdallah can command the services of over two thousand men, composed of his kinsmen and of his and of their slaves."[8] In the pre-Protectorate era, Ali's *heshima* was defined in part by his power to dominate others with his army of kinsmen and elite political support.[9] Ali's family had the power and influence to enforce its wishes and bully people into obeying. Fear was as much a factor as courtesy and piety in establishing honor and *heshima*.

The British government brought real changes in the way honor was negotiated when they began monitoring and intervening in the court system under the charge of the Arab *liwali*. As a colonial official reflected in 1920, "the days ... when men went armed, and a dispute was settled with a dagger thrust, is departed.... The law court has taken the place of the dagger."[10] On hearing the community's complaints, British officials promptly brought Ali bin Abdallah to court. While the *liwali* was unwilling to arrest any of Ali's family, the British had no such fears and felt fully justified in arresting, imprisoning, and banishing Ali from the islands. Ali never returned to Mgagadu. He served a seven-year prison term and was then exiled to Oman, where he resided until his death.[11] Though unintentional, British intervention on Pemba opened up the possibility for the community to formally rebuke powerful figures. No longer would people be forced to recognize one's *heshima*; now *heshima* would be acquired

---

[7] ZNA AC9/2, Vice Consul Pemba, December 20, 1895.

[8] ZNA AC9/2, Vice Consul Pemba, December 22, 1895.

[9] Cooper, 1977, p. 228. "For slave owners, such ties [and control of people] were part of *heshima*, part of the ideological foundations of their power and status."

[10] Frances Pearce, *Zanzibar: The Island Metropolis of Eastern Africa* (New York: T.F. Unwin, 1920), p. 219. Although this statement was not entirely true because fights periodically took place after the 1920s, see ZNA AB70/3 for examples.

[11] In 1934, Ali's heirs sued the administrators of his estate for not fairly apportioning the property; AI1/76 HBMCZ, Civil Case No. 17 of 1934. This suggests that Ali continued to live in Oman for several decades after he was banished from Zanzibar.

as much through one's ability to cultivate respect from neighbors and friends as through powerful associations and wealth.

The case of Ali bin Abdullah was an important turning point in showing that the Sultan and his followers no longer controlled the legal structures in Pemba. British intervention was the vehicle that allowed local communities to assert their perceptions of what *heshima* should mean from the elite to ex-slaves. The complaints about Ali indicate that most elite on Pemba found him troublesome, but he still represented the ideals of *heshima* – a powerful, well-born, wealthy Arab. These ideals would be reordered in the postemancipation era. In 1898, a year after emancipation, women working as *vibarua* ("day laborers") sang a song about Ali, "We used to cry for mercy, but for us there was no mercy; now he that had no mercy on us is shut up in the European's stone house in Zanzibar."[12] Slaves and ex-slaves publicly critiqued Ali's behavior and castigated him. Mercy would become an aspect of what ex-slaves would view as deserving of *heshima* among the elite, and they expected the British to hold individuals to their new interpretations of *heshima*. No longer could slave owners preserve their *heshima* from slaves and ex-slaves through a fear of punishment. The elite had to begin working for *heshima* through communal behavior.[13] Yet this indicates the weakened position of the elite, who now gained *heshima* as patrons and had to work to maintain their positions rather than simply be born to *heshima* and power.

FIGHTING FOR HONOR, DISPUTING FOR RESPECT

Dispute resolution on Pemba before the Protectorate government became involved with the courts was based on the power of the disputants to bring their case to a conclusion, whether that was through the courts or through physical retaliation. In many respects, honor helped to deter physical fights because an insult to a person's honor meant backing up that insult with force.[14] Disputants could take their case before the *kadhi* or the *liwali*, but even then they might not receive a resolution depending on the willingness of the *kadhi* or *liwali* to litigate the case.[15] The conflict of Ali bin Abdullah with his neighbors discussed earlier is a case in

---

[12] Newman, pp. 36–7.
[13] Glassman, 1995, pp. 139–43.
[14] Scott Taylor, "Credit, Debt, and Honor in Castile, 1600–1650," *Journal of Early Modern History* 7, nos. 1–2 (2003), pp 8–27.
[15] ZNA AC8/9, Letter from Friends Industrial Mission (Herbert Armitage), July 16, 1906; ZNA AC8/7, Vice Consul Pemba letter, February 9, 1904.

point.[16] Ali's Arab neighbors brought a dispute before the *liwali* because they did not want or could not engage Ali in a physical fight over Ali's propensity to encroach on their land and take their slaves. However, Ali was a well-connected man with links to the Sultan of Zanzibar, and the *liwali* refused to hear the case or make a decision. Ali was able to reinforce his *heshima* through his capacity to exert power over the legal system and his neighbors, who were too cowed by his ability to field an army of relatives and slaves in a fight. Ali bin Abdullah epitomized *heshima* as power in the nineteenth century, a model that many of the lower-status members of Pemban society would recognize as *heshima*.[17] As the British facilitated a transition in the meaning of *heshima*, many people still understood *heshima* to mean exerting physical force over others. Clashes over honor took a long time to be replaced by the courts as a system of dispute resolution, but by the 1910s a transition was occurring in which people of all levels of society brought disputes to the courts.[18]

In the twentieth century, those who fought over their disputes for *heshima* – mimicking the behavior of nineteenth-century elites – were often people of the lower classes, who were described in 1910 as "such fighting people."[19] One of the few areas where *heshima* still required physical interaction was over the respectability of wives, sisters, mothers, and daughters.[20] Slander of a person caused *fitna* or *fitina*, creating intrigue that potentially could turn into physical confrontations.[21] By the

[16] ZNA AC9/2, Letter from Consul Hardinge to Vice Consul O'Sullivan-Beare, June 29, 1895.

[17] FIM PZ(F)/3, Diary of the Boys' Home, April–June 1903, story of Zaidi and Cha Usiku, a brother and sister whose father was a slave. Their mistress put real fear into the children, and Cha Usiku feared leaving the woman, even though her father and brother lived with the Quakers.

[18] Disputes that did occur usually involved Manga Arabs, who were recent migrants and not acculturated to the British system. Records of large-scale street fights mostly occurred in Zanzibar Town starting after 1925, with an increase in migration from Arabia and the mainland.

[19] PRO FO 881/10268X, Annual reports for 1909 and 1910, Assistant collector of Weti report for 1910, p. 189; Africa No. 4, *Despatch from His Majesty's Agent and Consul-General at Zanzibar Furnishing a Report on the Administration, Finance, and General Condition of the Zanzibar Protectorate* (London: Harrison & Sons, 1909), p. 46. Fifty-seven people were convicted in Pemba of causing grievous bodily hurt, whereas only four people were convicted of this crime in Zanzibar; *Annual Report of the Judicial Department* (Zanzibar, 1923), Case No. 44 from Chake Chake; Hamis bin Ali was convicted of murder because he killed the *sheha* of Wawi over a property dispute.

[20] PRO FO 881/10268X, Annual reports for 1909 and 1910, p. 187.

[21] PRO FO 881/9334, Glossary of terms in reports; Steere defined *fitina* in 1882 as sowing discord, a disturbance, or a riot; Steere, pp. 39, 274; ZNA AB70/3, Disturbance created by Manga Arabs at Weti, Pemba; Sir William Murison and S. S. Abrahams, *Zanzibar*

1910s, physical conflicts were rare among the elite Arabs and generally only occurred when recently immigrated Manga Arabs attacked locally born Arabs.[22] However, the listing of assault cases in the annual reports for the Protectorate illustrate that among the lower classes, bodily assault was still a means of reflecting the "power" of the individual and attempts to gain *heshima* through the demonstration of physical power.

A dispute between two elite Arab factions from 1941 illustrates how gossip fueled disputes over reputation. Moreover, we see how the refusal to make a marital contract between two parties could create great discord because of the impugning of one party's *heshima* in the refusal. In July, Sheikh Issa bin Salim el-Mazrui went to the British District Commissioner complaining that he could not go home because Sheikh Ali bin Suleiman el-Hinawi was lying in wait with family members to attack Issa when he went to his house.[23] Apparently, Ali had proposed to marry the daughter of another Arab man but was turned down. Ali blamed Issa, claiming that Issa "had interfered and smirched his reputation in the eyes of the prospective father-in-law." This statement reiterates the vulnerability of reputation and respectability, even for elite Arabs. The colonial official seemed to be under the impression that Ali was a cantankerous old man and was constantly getting into disagreements with his neighbors so that no one wanted to have dealings with him if they could help it. Thus Ali's reputation was doubly questioned, by colonial officials and by other Arabs. Relatives brought the news to Issa that Ali was lying in wait for him, yet when police were sent to the village, none of Ali's family was found near Issa's home. Ali's public outburst of anger at Issa was exaggerated into a story of a battle about to ensue between the two families. Gossip among the men in the area undoubtedly blew the story out of proportion by the time it reached Issa, who was conducting business in northern Pemba at the time.

For Ali, though, his reputation was on the line. Because of the gossip, people expected him to physically defend his *heshima* by attacking Issa and his family. However, both the colonial officials and the disputants

---

Protectorate Law Reports Containing Cases Determined in the British Consular Court, and in His Britannic Majesty's Court and in the Supreme Court of His Highness the Sultan and in the Courts Subordinate Thereto, etc. 1868 to 1918 with Appendices Containing the Zanzibar Orders-in-Council from 1884 to 1916 (London: 1919); HBM Court, Zanzibar, Criminal Case No. 790 of 1910, Dayabhai Jivanlal Multani vs. Chaturbhooj Jagjivan, posted in the *Zanzibar Gazette*, January 3, 1911.

22 ZNA AB70/3, Disturbances created by Manga Arabs at Wete, 1928–1941.
23 ZNA AB70/3, Disturbances created by Manga Arabs at Wete, 1928–1941.

wanted to avoid physical conflict. Ali's family was not unfamiliar with physical conflict because they would get into a violent dispute with a group of Manga Arabs within weeks.[24] Nonetheless, in the dispute between Issa and Ali, both men, who had a localized understanding of *heshima*, wanted a respectable conclusion that allowed them to keep their reputations intact. This is particularly ironic because Ali bin Suleiman was related to Ali bin Abdallah, the man who intimidated his neighbors in the 1890s. Ali bin Abdallah had *heshima* – honor – regardless of his brutal reputation. However, for his descendants, *heshima* was no longer about power, but about respectability. Reputations were critical to maintaining respectability, a respectability that Ali bin Suleiman was having problems with, as seen in the refusal of his marriage proposal. The colonial state stepped into the dispute between Issa and Ali bin Suleiman, calling a *baraza* ("meeting") to resolve the dispute and allowing both men to "save face."

The shift in dispute resolution from one where individuals exerted their power through physicality to a move into the courts corresponds with the shift in the meaning of *heshima* as well. As people, especially elites, stopped "fighting in the streets" and thus reminding everyone in the vicinity of their power, their capacity to exert power over others declined. The thousands of slaves who sought their freedom papers between 1897 and 1909 indicate the loss of power of slave owners. The defiance shown by male children of their parent's slave owners is also telling of a shift in perceptions of power.[25] The meaning of reputation changed as well; reputation was no longer about physical strength and the number of family members, retainers, and slaves who could be brought to "resolve" a dispute. As *heshima* evolved into respectability rather than honor, so too did the ways disputes were resolved through the courts rather than physical violence. A person's ability to bring a case to court, an expensive endeavor in many cases, and their restraint in the face of conflict illustrated their respectability. Eventually, this shift filtered down to the lower classes, but it never fully took hold among the ex-slave and mainland communities on Pemba. Those of the lower classes who sought to enter into "society"

---

[24] Manga Arabs were recent migrants to the island; thus they had a different understanding of honor, one based on defending honor with violence.

[25] FIM PZ(F)/3, Diary of the Boys' Home, 1902–1906. Many of the boys taken in at the home were the children of slaves who had not received their freedom from their owners. The owners often sent the parents to the mission in order to bring the children back to the *shamba*. Nonetheless, these boys continued to move in a circuit between their parents and the missionaries.

on Pemba had to adapt and take on the new meanings of *heshima*, and that meant handling disputes through the courts.

"CIVILIZING" POWER

Colonial officials were pleased with their efforts to "civilize" Pemban society through the court systems. While fights still broke out on occasion, especially among recent migrants such as Manga Arabs, on Pemba, courts had become an accepted and well-used institution.[26] By 1910, people on Pemba were viewed as becoming more civilized, yet one major hurdle remained – the belief in witchcraft (*uchawi*). One medical official suggested that Pembans would lose interest in witchcraft and continue to become more civilized through "the influence of and association with Europeans."[27] When British East Africa (Kenya), the neighboring mainland colony of Zanzibar, passed a witchcraft ordinance in 1909, the Secretary of State asked officials on Zanzibar whether they thought Zanzibar needed an ordinance as well. This set off an ongoing debate among officials that would be revisited regularly into the 1920s – what to do about witchcraft. Pemba was known as a site of the occult, being described by several officials as "the very university of witchcraft for eastern Africa."[28] While officials knew of Pemba's reputation for occult practices and how these practices conflicted with the civilizing mission, they consistently chose not to respond to witchcraft because they saw it as nothing more than an atavistic healing practice and at worst "quackery." In no discussions committed to paper did colonial officials

---

[26] Violence continued to periodically plague Zanzibar Town until the moment of independence, either in strikes and riots against the government or in street fights among different ethnic groups, although it appears that a rise in street violence occurred in the post–World War I period. For strikes against the government, see the PRO FO367/25, Police strike, 1906; Anthony Clayton, "The General Strike in Zanzibar, 1948," *Journal of African History* 17, no. 4 (1976), pp. 417–34. For resistance against the government and other groups, see PRO CO 618/43/14, Rioting in Zanzibar, Mangas, and Shihiris, 1928; CO618/47/16, Disturbance at Central Prison, 1926; Zanzibar Protectorate, *Report on the Commission of Enquiry Concerning the Riot in Zanzibar on the 7th of February, 1936* (Zanzibar: Government Printer, 1936). For a discussion of the 1928 ground rent strike in Zanzibar Town, see Laura Fair, *Pastimes and Politics*, chap. 3. A common theme in many of these conflicts was the role played by "outsiders" – migrants from the mainland of either Africa or Arabia. Colonial officials were quick to distinguish between "their Zanzibaris" and "outsiders" in violent conflicts.

[27] ZNA AB31/20, Witchcraft in Pemba, Letter from Dr. MacDonald to Captain Barton, May 21, 1910.

[28] ZNA AB31/20, Witchcraft in Pemba; Ingrams, 1931, p. 6.

write of *uchawi* as a location of power struggles between the state and the indigenous population.

Colonial officials debated in 1910 whether they should institute a witchcraft ordinance to punish cases of witchcraft, as had been recently adopted in neighboring British East Africa (Kenya). Officials who wanted the ordinance argued that it would discipline and civilize the population of the islands, holding out the threat of punishment to those who fell back to their precolonial practices. Government officials had two interpretations of the purpose of witchcraft, healing and resolving disputes. They generally viewed the healing aspects of witchcraft such as charms and medicines as mostly harmless. However, it was the resolution of disputes through *uchawi* that officials were concerned about. Officials promulgated the idea that by moving disputes previously settled by witchcraft into the courts, the government would further civilize the population, just as it had with public fighting. An assistant collector of Pemba argued that "within the last two decades ... owing to the presence of Europeans in the country and a better system of administration of justice," witchcraft was declining.[29] He explicitly connected the waning use of witchcraft to changes in the courts.[30]

Other officials also suggested that their civilizing influence would cause the eventual disappearance of *uchawi* and its use on the islands. The High Commissioner of British East Africa went so far as to argue, "It appears to me that the only way to eliminate such practices is to so improve the intelligence and knowledge of the people as to make it possible to convince them of the impropriety and inutility of the ceremonies to which they now attach a superstitious importance. When such reaction sets in, its progress may be assisted by legislation, but the fact that such practices are forbidden by the law will not of itself be sufficient to effect their cessation."[31] Throughout the debate between 1910 and 1925, the language of the civilizing mission was used to discuss how officials could rid the islands of witchcraft. Witchcraft was viewed as one more remnant of antimodern, atavistic beliefs rather than considered as a form of indigenous power.

In the debates that ensued over whether to adopt a witchcraft ordinance, officials consistently decided against establishing an ordinance,

[29] ZNA AB31/20, Witchcraft in Pemba, Assistant collector Mkoani report, 1910.
[30] I would argue though that this particular official did not know the level of *uchawi* practiced on the island because he admitted himself that he had only recently arrived in Pemba when he wrote the report.
[31] ZNA AB31/20, Letter from High Commissioner BEA to resident of Zanzibar, 1915.

even when pressured by Universities Mission to Central Africa (UMCA) missionaries.[32] Why did Zanzibar remain the only African British possession to not have a witchcraft ordinance, even though officials saw the link between the civilizing mission and the eradication of belief in the efficacy of *uchawi*? Ostensibly, the records show with each permutation of the debate in 1910, 1915, 1917, 1921, and 1925 that while it was seen as an issue, it was not challenging state power. As opposed to cases found in mainland Africa, people on Pemba were not punished by their communities for practicing *uchawi*. Witch hunting was not practiced, and no witches were locally tried and killed by Pemban communities. This is a key distinction from other cases of witchcraft in Africa. Katherine Luongo argues that in Kenya the colonial state had to enforce a witchcraft ordinance not necessarily against witches but against those who punished witches because it was a direct challenge to colonial rights over who controlled state-sanctioned violence.[33] In the case of the Kamba of Kenya, local chiefs viewed themselves as having the right to punish wrongdoers in their communities. However, this meant that government officials had to respond because they saw witchcraft as a primitive superstition. Since the British did not believe in witches, they could not sanction a society that attempted to punish "innocent" people accused of being witches.[34] The focus in this scholarship is on the role of local communities to punish witches as a challenge to state power rather than seeing the practitioners of witchcraft as challenging state power.

However, contrary to the goals of colonial officials, their decision to ignore *uchawi* on Pemba in the early years of the Protectorate allowed

[32] The UMCA bishop to Zanzibar regularly wrote letters complaining to the government about witchcraft on both Pemba and Zanzibar. At one point he asked for the government to deport several Pemban converts because of their practices, which actually appear to be spirit possession not *uchawi*. The bishop also asked in 1915 for the government to exhume the body of one of the converts on Zanzibar in order to prove that the body had not been taken by *wachawi*.

[33] Katherine Luongo, *Witchcraft and Colonial Rule in Kenya, 1900–1955* (Cambridge: Cambridge University Press, 2011). See the Introduction for a discussion of state-sanctioned violence.

[34] This issue was found across the continent. For examples, see scholarship by Katherine Luongo in Kenya; Richard Waller, "Witchcraft and Colonial Law in Kenya," *Past and Present* 180, no. 1 (2003), pp. 24–275; Natasha Gray, "Witches, Oracles, and Colonial Law: Evolving anti-Witchcraft Practices in Ghana, 1927–1932," *International Journal of African Historical Studies* 34, no. 2 (2001), pp. 339–64; Alan Booth, "'European Courts Protest Women and Witches': Colonial Law Courts as Redistributors of Power in Swaziland 1920–1950," *Journal of Southern African Studies* 18, no. 2 (1992), pp. 253–76; T. C. McCaskie, "'Sakrobundi ne Aberewa': Sie Kwaku the Witch-finder in the Akan World," *Transactions of the Historical Society of Ghana* 8 (2004), pp. 82–135.

the practice to expand, not decline as some officials suggested. What officials did not understand was that *uchawi* was about power and the ability to control people through power. Pemba did not have the politics of chieftainship found in other places where colonial officials recognized witchcraft and "medicine murder" as a manifestation of power within the community, but *uchawi* played a similar role in politics and daily life on the island.[35] In the 1910s and 1920s, Zanzibari officials had not yet encountered the problem faced by officials in Basutoland in the 1950s, who bemoaned the resurgence of ritual murder as "the failure of our eighty years of administration to civilize the inhabitants and eradicate tendencies to savage practices of magic."[36] A consistent pattern in the discussion of witchcraft, even when it was explicitly acknowledged as an issue of power, was the language of the civilizing mission or its failure. In the early years of the Zanzibar Protectorate, though, colonial officials did not fathom *uchawi* as a source of power for people on Pemba, nor did they see it as a challenge to colonial power.

As officials tried to push local disputes into the courts and co-opt elite power through the state, *uchawi* expanded as an indigenous form of power and replaced the previous use and threat of violence as power (as implied in the older definition of *heshima*). *Uchawi*, though, unlike slave ownership and hereditary honor and power, was open to anyone who could fulfill the prerequisite of bringing a family member to be killed. This meant former slaves, Arab elite, WaPemba, and Indians living on the island could participate and access power through this means. Thus the British certainly transformed the visible landscapes of power through the new court systems but they also shaped the invisible landscape of power by ignoring its existence.

INVISIBLE LANDSCAPE OF POWER

At the same time that the courts created a space to shift the landscapes of physical and social power on the island *uchawi* expanded as an indigenous source of power, outside the control of the colonial state. *Uchawi*, as mentioned earlier, can be translated as witchcraft, sorcery, or magic

---

[35] For examples discussing the power dynamics associated with "ritual murder" elsewhere in Africa, see Rob Turrell, "Muti Ritual Murder in Natal: From Chiefs to Commoners (1900–1930)," *South African Historical Journal* 44 (2001), pp. 21–40; Roger Gocking, "A Chieftaincy Dispute and Ritual Murder in Elmina, Ghana, 1945–6," *Journal of African History* 41, no. 2 (2000), pp. 197–220.

[36] PRO DO35/4158, The Jones Report on Ritual Murder in Basutoland.

but it means all of those things and more. *Uchawi* represents the invisible world, a world of spirits and practitioners who could control forces of nature and use these to help or hurt other people. In other words, *wachawi* could control people through fear, as in the older meaning of *heshima*. The occult continued to represent power and the ability to control other people through fear. Consequently, practitioners of *uchawi* on Pemba continued to be treated with *heshima* in its nineteenth-century meaning of the word. Understanding the place of *uchawi* on Pemba offers glimpses into how multiple definitions of *heshima* came about; allowing older definitions of *heshima*, such as honor, to remain in Pemban society side-by-side with the newer meaning of respectability.

The world of *uchawi* on Pemba was central to peoples' lives. Every step on a path was fraught with the possibility of encountering *pepo* ("spirits") and *uchawi*. Perhaps a charm to bring harm was left for one person, but another person accidently trod over it; well, then they were harmed. People on Pemba constantly encountered the occult in their lives, and any history written about Pemba that does not address *uchawi* is missing a significant aspect of peoples' daily experience. Understanding the details of *uchawi* on Pemba is critical for imagining what life was like for someone on the island but also for seeing how such a person viewed power. Power had visible manifestations, such as in the courts, but it also had invisible manifestations that had as much, if not more, relevance to individuals' daily life. Pembans did not often take cases to the courts, but they experienced the invisible world of the occult every day. Thus a history of the shifting landscapes of power must include an in-depth discussion of the occult on Pemba.

The use and belief in the occult are familiar topics in African studies, although more commonly discussed by anthropologists than historians. Steven Feierman has suggested that this is so because in the historical record "events" are connected with the occult – such as the magical water used during the Maji Maji resistance.[37] Yet, before and after the event, magic disappears from the record, becoming "invisible" to historians and, as such, forgotten or overlooked.[38] Felicitas Becker's informants told her that a number of witchcraft cleansers never made it into colonial documents, demonstrating that people who were not connected to specific

---

[37] Steven Feierman, "Healing as Social Criticism in the Time of Colonial Conquest," *African Studies* 54, no. 1 (1995), pp. 73–88.

[38] The inability of historians "to see" the significance of the occult in everyday life corresponds with Pembans' beliefs that *uchawi* and *wachawi* were "invisible" to those without "eyes."

events often were left out of the historical record.[39] Yet in many societies the occult was and still is significant in the daily lives of communities and individuals. Harry West's work in Mozambique has shown the way the invisible realm intrudes into the visible to exert social, moral, and political pressure on people.[40] Likewise, Nathalie Arnold argues that on Pemba, anyone with authority was viewed as being an *mchawi* (a "practitioner of the occult").[41] Many scholars who examine the occult suggest that this is a means of accessing power and control in societies that is open to and used by people at every level of society.

According to Peter Geschiere, in Cameroon, fear of witchcraft was a leveling device that forced the elite to share any wealth they had gained with their kin in the village. This suggests a way that slaves could use witchcraft as a means to force elites and former owners to honor their role as patrons.[42] Geschiere argues that sharing by the elite was based on their fear of accusations of witchcraft. However, Jan Vansina found that "accusations of witchcraft included both ends of the social scale: the hapless and the successful."[43] Felicitas Becker and others have pointed out that concerns about witchcraft (and accusations of practicing it) often said more about anxieties among community – and at times family – members.[44] Thus the witchcraft accusation discussed at the beginning of Chapter 3 framed concerns the brother had about his dependency on his sister and uncle with whom he lived. Vulnerability is a fundamental aspect of discussions of witchcraft across the continent; since people felt defenseless, they looked at theirs family members and neighbors as sources of both aid and potential malice.

Several scholars have linked witchcraft and witch-finding ordeals to the trade in slaves in the Atlantic world.[45] Much as was found in the mainland

[39] Becker, pp. 166–7. Witchcraft cleansers "cleaned" communities of witchcraft practices in order to bring "normalcy."

[40] Harry West, *Kupilikula: Governance and the Invisible Realm in Mozambique* (Chicago: University of Chicago Press, 2005), pp. 40–7.

[41] Arnold, pp. 247–8.

[42] Peter Geschiere, "Kinship, Witchcraft and the Moral Economy of Ethnicity: Contrasts from Southern and Western Cameroun," in *Ethnicity in Africa: Roots, Meanings and Implications*, edited by Louise de la Gorgendière et al. (Edinburgh: Centre of African Studies, University of Edinburgh, 1996), p. 177.

[43] Jan Vansina, *Paths in the Rainforests: Toward a History of Political Tradition in Equatorial Africa* (Madison: University of Wisconsin Press, 1990), p. 97.

[44] Becker, p. 164. For further discussion, see also Jean and John Comaroff, *Modernity and Its Malcontents: Ritual and Power in Postcolonial Africa* (Chicago: University of Chicago Press, 1993).

[45] Ralph Austen, "The Moral Economy of Witchcraft: An Essay in Comparative History," in *Modernity and its Malcontents: Ritual and Power in Postcolonial Africa*, edited by

of East Africa, people in West Africa accused of being witches were sold into slavery. This argument ties witches and the practice of witchcraft to the enslavement of African people and the slave trade. According to Rosalind Shaw, in mainland societies, witchcraft accusations often benefited the powerful and destroyed the lives of the weak – because the powerful were accusing the weak of being witches.[46] Often, when powerful people were accused of being witches, they had methods of escaping enslavement, but vulnerable members of the community, people without connections, were forced into the Atlantic slave trade. Shaw notes the role of witch finders or witch hunters continued into the modern era, but the punishments of those accused changed over time in response to elimination of the Atlantic slave trade. The role of the witch hunter is one discussed often in the scholarship on witchcraft in Africa. Numerous anthropological studies have argued that witchcraft and witch hunters are key elements in African responses to modernity.[47] Witchcraft explains the deep disjuncture in modern African communities, and witch hunters are used to help alleviate these problems by finding the causes, that is, the people guilty of causing them.

European travelers in East Africa made extensive reference to the practice of *uchawi* among mainland ethnic groups during the nineteenth and twentieth centuries.[48] The treatment of *wachawi* on the mainland varied. The *Desturi za Waswahili* ("Customs of the Swahili"), written down in Bagamoyo during the 1890s, described a number of "ordeals" that tested whether a person had participated in occult practices. The ordeals often included the accused drinking a poison or placing his or her tongue on a red-hot metal object such as a hatchet.[49] If the tongue did not blister or the person survived the poison ordeal, then he or she was considered innocent, and the accuser had to go through an ordeal to see if he or she had made the accusation in good faith. Although this suggests

Jean Comaroff and John Comaroff. (Chicago: University of Chicago Press, 1993); Rosalind Shaw, *Memories of the Slave Trade: Ritual and the Historical Imagination in Sierra Leone* (Chicago: University of Chicago Press, 2002), pp. 201–224.

[46] Shaw, pp. 201–24.

[47] Comaroff and Comaroff, 1993; Henrietta L. Moore and Todd Sanders, eds., *Magical Interpretations, Material Realities: Modernity, Witchcraft, and the Occult in Postcolonial Africa* (London: Routledge, 2001); Peter Geschiere, *The Modernity of Witchcraft: Politics and the Occult in Postcolonial Africa* (Charlotteville: University of Virginia Press, 1995); James Howard Smith, *Bewitching Development: Witchcraft and the Reinvention of Development in Neoliberal Kenya* (Chicago: University of Chicago Press, 2008).

[48] See Burton (1860) for one example of a travelers' description; Bakari, 1981 pp. 182–5.

[49] For descriptions of the ordeals, see Bakari, 1981, pp. 182–5; Burton, 1860, p. 347; these were known as *mwavi* trials. See also Becker, pp. 163–7.

that witchcraft was something to be feared or punished, mainlanders did show admiration for *wachawi* because they had power through fear.[50] On Pemba, people accused of being *wachawi* were rarely, if ever, made to go through an ordeal to prove their innocence, as found on the mainland.[51] However, Pemba was not alone in a general wariness of witch hunting as found in other parts of the continent.[52] In another part of the Swahili coast, the Comoros Islands, Michael Lambek found that *wachawi* were not hunted because, as one informant in the 1970s explained, "the villages would then be virtually empty; practically everyone was engaged in sorcery (meaning by this not just the practitioners but their clients).... [A]n additional reason that sorcerers were not asked to leave was that their knowledge is also indispensable to the community for its positive effects."[53] This point about the value of an *mchawi*'s knowledge is important to reiterate, especially given the belief that *wachawi* could use the occult for both good and bad. It is entirely possible that some of the slaves living on Pemba had watched their loved ones "hunted" in the interior and killed after going through a witch-finding ordeal, which would have made them less inclined to accuse others.[54]

Sources regarding *uchawi* on Pemba prior to the colonial period are scarce. Historically, slaves from various parts of the world used witchcraft as a form of agency through psychological escape and as a method for controlling their owners and/or their situations; thus it is likely that slaves on Pemba practiced witchcraft before the arrival of the British.[55]

---

[50] Abdullah M. Mzee, "Some Experiences of Witchcraft," *Tanganyikan Notes and Records* 57 (September 1961), p. 149.

[51] I have found two vague references to accused *wachawi* going through an ordeal of some sort, although they were not killed. See ZNA AB31/20, Collector of Pemba, January 24, 1910; District Officer Paul Sheldon, December 17, 1914. However, I have several examples of people accused of practicing *uchawi* trying to resist the accusation, but when they went to the colonial officials for help, they never mentioned being forced to go through an ordeal.

[52] See Allen Isaacman and Derek Peterson, "Making the Chikunda: Military Slavery and Ethnicity in Southern Africa 1750–1900," *International Journal of African Historical Studies* 36, no. 2 (2003), pp. 257–81.

[53] Michael Lambek, *Knowledge and Practice in Mayotte: Local Discourses of Islam, Sorcery, and Spirit Possession* (Toronto: University of Toronto Press, 1993), p. 238.

[54] Burton, 1860, p. 352, notes that people accused of *uchawi* on the mainland were killed, and their families were either killed or enslaved. It is entirely possible that some of these slaves ended up living on Pemba.

[55] See John W. Blassingame, *The Slave Community: Plantation Life in the Antebellum South* (New York: Oxford University Press, 1972); Walter Rucker, "Conjure, Magic and Power: The Influence of Afro-Atlantic Religious Practices on Slave Resistance and Rebellion," *Journal of Black Studies* 32, no. 1 (2001), pp. 84–103. Both Rucker and Blassingame

It is impossible to know if *uchawi* became more prevalent with the demise of slavery on Pemba or not. References to witchcraft practices in preemancipation travelers' accounts of Pemba are few, although one official was told in 1910 that in *zamani sana* ("olden times") Pemba had been famous for its wizards.[56] Another official in 1910 argued that the WaPemba used *uchawi* as a means to isolate their communities from the Arabs and slaves. This would certainly give another reason why the WaPemba were not alienated from their land by Arabs as fully as the WaHadimu on Unguja. Regardless of when and among whom *uchawi* started on the island, by the turn of the century it was integral throughout Pemban society.

Many colonial officials and academics have written about *uchawi* in the Zanzibar Islands over the years, but definitions as to what constitutes *uchawi* have varied greatly. Often in the colonial records any *ngoma* was classified as *uchawi*, whether it was an *uchawi* feast, spirit possession, *maulidi*, Sufi *dhikiri*, competitive dance group, initiation, or even a wedding. If it involved a dance, then it was invariably viewed by Europeans as witchcraft.[57] Even within scholarly articles, though, the descriptions

suggest a pseudoreligious connection with the occult in America, which is very different from that found on Pemba. Also see Kris Lane, "Taming the Owner: Brujería, Slavery, and the Encomienda in Barbacoas at the Turn of the Eighteenth Century," *Ethnohistory* 45, no. 3 (Summer 1998), pp. 477–507, for a discussion of indigenous occult practices being used as resistance by Native Americans who were being treated like slaves in colonial Columbia.

[56] ZNA AB31/20, Collector of Pemba, January 24. 1910. Ingrams was able to purchase several books on *uchawi*, one of which was estimated by British Museum officials to have been written sometime between 1800 and 1830, but Ingrams does not clarify where in the islands the book was from; Ingrams, 1931, p. 477. Precolonial references include the first description of *uchawi* by a European, which appeared in W. W. A. Fitzgerald's 1897 publication of his trip in 1892, five years before the emancipation of all slaves but two years after the declaration of the Zanzibar Protectorate and after twenty years of a British blockade of the coastal slave trade. Earlier visitors to the island did not mention the practice of *uchawi*. For example, John Studdy Leigh, an avid observer of local customs in the 1840s, spent almost a week on Pemba but never mentioned the practice. James S. Kirkman, "The Zanzibar Diary of John Studdy Leigh, Part I", *International Journal of African Historical Studies* 13, no. 2 (1980), pp. 281–312. One of the most notable nineteenth-century accounts of Pemba came from Richard Burton, who disliked the island intensely, describing it as a "great green grave" and speaking of the WaPemba as lower than slaves. While his 1860 book on Central Africa offered an extensive description of *uchawi* on the mainland, he made no mention of it on Pemba in his 1872 book on the Zanzibar Islands. Given his fascination with the subject, it seems odd that Burton did not report on occult practices on Pemba if they were widely practiced in the late 1860s when he was there. Burton, 1860, 1872.

[57] For examples, see ZNA AB31/20, Assistant collector reports from Mkoani and Wete, 1910; Craster, pp. 196, 307–8. Harold Ingrams was one of the few colonial officials

of *uchawi* exhibit confusion because the different forms are particularly nuanced. Nathalie Arnold, an anthropologist who spent two years on Pemba studying *uchawi*, gives the clearest description of *uchawi* as practiced on Pemba, and it is her work that I reference for the details of *uchawi*. According to Arnold, there are seven levels of *uchawi* corresponding to the seven doors of the house in *Giningi'i*, which is the "invisible city" of the *wachawi* on Pemba. Arnold argues that in order to progress through the seven levels, one must master the skills within each door. However, in many respects the seven levels are divided into two broader categories, those with true knowledge and skills of *uchawi* and those without. It is only at the fifth level that practitioners become *wachawi*; in the first four levels true knowledge of *uchawi* is not necessary. I focus here on the last three levels of *uchawi* because these are the skills that gave a person power and *heshima*.

Mganga (pl. *waganga*) was the general term used for anyone who used specialized occult knowledge to help others. Leaders of spirit possession groups were called *waganga*, as were people who were practicing a form of *uchawi* (which is technically separate from spirit possession).[58] The term *mganga* was often used to describe an indigenous healer. Although Europeans often translated it as "witchdoctor," its use generally referenced healing practices as opposed to the sorcerer's black magic. Arnold, who classifies *waganga* as the fifth level of *uchawi*, distinguishes the *mganga*'s practice as "publicly consultative" magic.[59] The *mganga* acted as a "medicine" person – treating people for their illnesses, love problems, help with winning court cases, and other minor problems.[60] *Waganga* worked to protect their community by offering charms to protect babies, matadors during bullfights, and people with other kinds of weakness in their lives.[61] *Waganga* also acted as diviners, foreseeing who had stolen

---

who really tried to understand the distinctions between *ngoma* and various forms of *uchawi*. Certainly not all British officials and missionaries remained clueless about the differences, but the historical documents show an incredible amount of blending. For an especially good example, see ZNA AB31/20, Letter from Bishop Frank of the UMCA, December 12, 1914.

[58] *Waganga*, in both forms of practice, also were often called *fundi*, which means people who fix things. See examples in Giles, 1989; ZNA AB31/20, Mkoani Collectorate report, 1910.

[59] Arnold, pp. 116–23.

[60] Lyne, 1905, p. 237. Robert Lyne states that a person going into a court case would ask for "a prescription from an *mchawi* to enable him to plead his cause with advantage."

[61] "A specially aggressive bull may become the object of witchcraft; for, in the hope of bewitching him and protecting the men who will fight him, the women in the stockade will sometimes put in the earth where he will be thrown before the fight the roots

property from owners, who had caused misfortune to occur to someone through *uchawi*, and other activities.[62] In general, *waganga* were viewed by locals as an aide to the community and were given their "due respect."[63] Many *waganga* along the Swahili coast mixed aspects of Islam with other practices. For instance, they might write a verse of the Quran on a piece of paper to make a protective amulet or write a verse on a plate with ink and then wash it off the plate into a cup and have an individual drink the water and ink.[64] *Waganga* could produce harm to individuals as well as benefits.[65]

The sixth level of *uchawi* was one that generally existed outside colonial records and showed the most agency of Pembans because it implied a level of skill that was invisible to the colonial state. This form, called *uwanga* by Arnold, was characterized by a complete knowledge and skill in all things *uchawi*.[66] In general, a person who was an *mwanga* (pl. *wanga*) was one who had mastered skills both in *uchawi* and Islamic knowledge. Many religious leaders on Pemba were presumed to be *wanga*. The skills of the *wanga* were so great that they could fly and control the weather. There is a certain whimsy to the acts of the *wanga*, and Pembans delighted in telling stories of how the *wanga* defeated the colonial state.[67] Some of the famous stories Arnold collected included *wanga* who made villages invisible to labor recruiters during World Wars I and II. A famous *mwanga*, Mzee Barazanji, would hold off the rain if a *maulidi* was happening in his compound. This story in particular illuminates the links between Islamic knowledge and occult power on Pemba. These were viewed as compatible by Pembans, of all levels of society, and the person who could wield both had the respect of the community. Moreover, the *uwanga* was used in ways that directly challenged state power, even if the colonial state did not see it.

---

of certain trees or a written charm. Alternatively, a matador who feels a bit apprehensive may conceal the magic object round his waist." *A Guide to Zanzibar* (Zanzibar: Government Printer, 1949), p. 95.

[62] Robert Lyne tells of the time he successfully used an *mganga* to detect which of his servants was a thief; Lyne, 1905, pp. 225–6; Ingrams, 1931, pp. 455–65.

[63] F. R. Hodgson, "Medicine Man's Kit," *Central Africa* 21, no. 250 (October 1903), pp. 194–6.

[64] For examples, see Bakari, pp. 61–2; Craster, pp. 236, 324–5.

[65] As Arnold notes, it is not knowledge that makes a person do bad things; it is their personal disposition; Arnold, p. 124.

[66] Wilfred Whiteley recorded a poem in the 1950s about needing the skills of a *mwanga*; Whiteley, 1958, p. 46, n. 24.

[67] Arnold, pp. 125–36.

The last form of *uchawi* was an *mchawi ya kobwe*, a person who practices *uchawi wa kobwe*. To become a *mchawi*, a person joined the "guild
of witchcraft," which required a person to offer up one of his or her relatives as a blood sacrifice. This relative would be "killed" through a variety
of different means, but it usually did not happen right away. People who
had many relatives die were often assumed to be *wachawi*, regardless
of whether their relatives died from diseases, accidents, or old age. On
Pemba, the *wachawi* would meet at night in "the invisible city" (*Giningi'i*),
where they would feast on food and the flesh of their sacrificial victims.[68]
The practices of the *wachawi ya kobwe* horrified Europeans living on
Pemba, but no one could ever prove that the cannibalism described in the
practices was real or not. The *wachawi* would meet at night for feasts,
where they would "eat" the victim brought to the feast, dance, and have
intercourse.[69] *Wachawi* had the ability to turn themselves into animals,
especially dogs, and to fly. They could appear to be asleep at home in bed
but really have flown hundreds or thousands of miles away and return by
morning. Many Europeans living on Pemba reported hearing "packs of
dogs" barking in the night, which all local people knew were the *wachawi*
during their feasts.[70] Much like the *mganga*, a *mchawi* could be either
good, in that he or she would help to protect someone from another
mchawi who was trying to kill him or her, or bad, in that the *mchawi*
might be the one committing the murder.

When a person was marked to die, a *mchawi* could try to save the
victim by bargaining with the other *wachawi* and paying to save the person. However, this did not always work because powerful *wachawi* could
demand the sacrifice. The victims of sacrifice were most often the favorite child of the *mchawi* making the sacrifice. The *wachawi* demanded
that initiates give up their most beloved relative, which illustrates the

---

[68] The "eating" of the dead was of particular interest and horror to the Europeans
who reported it, as all of them did. See Fitzgerald, 1897, pp. 243–4; Ingrams, 1931,
pp. 465–77.

[69] Arnold's informants explained one of the main benefits of becoming an *mchawi* was that a
person could have sex with anyone he or she wanted, including incestuous intercourse.

[70] A famous story from the 1930s, called "The Dogs of Pemba," told the story of a colonial official who "went native" by living with a Pemban woman whose father was a
famous *mchawi*. When the colonial official rejected the Pemban woman in favor of a
European woman, the Pemban woman's father slowly turned the colonial official into
a dog. Margery Lawrence, "The Dogs of Pemba," in *The Terraces of Night: Being the
Further Chronicles of the Club of the Round Table* (London: Hurst & Blackett, 1932).
Several Europeans tried to become *wachawi* (without offering up a relative), including
Harold Ingrams. See his 1931 and 1942 books; see also ZNA AB31/20, Report, January
14, 1910.

contradiction of *uchawi* – it could bring power, but it was also very destructive of the familial fabric. At times, a *mchawi* could "save" a beloved relative by making him or her into a zombie. These zombies were the servants of the *wachawi* during their feasts. The *wachawi* often chose people who were talented musicians and cooks to become their zombie servants. According to Arnold, enemies were not killed by the *wachawi ya kobwe*. The assistant collector of Wete argued in 1910, however, that "when *mchawi* wish to do away with an enemy, he is supposed to use an invisible bludgeon with which he strikes him."[71] It may be that the collector could not imagine a person killing someone he or she loved and assumed that all deaths were of enemies, but this points to the possibility that deaths could be for reasons other than initiation into the guild.

UCHAWI ON PEMBA

In the 1990s, Helle Goldman, an anthropologist studying identity on Pemba, was told by a neighbor explaining *uchawi* that "there are only two kinds of people to fear: relatives and everyone else."[72] This joke expresses not only the prevalence of *uchawi* but also its dominance in people's lives – they always had to worry about *uchawi*. Almost a century earlier, the life histories of ex-slaves written down by Friends missionaries echo the encompassing aspects of *uchawi* for people, where stepping on the wrong spot in the road could cause misfortune and being the beloved relative of an *mchawi* certainly carried the risk of being killed. The joke told to Goldman illustrates the enduring power of *uchawi* to control the behavior of people. *Wachawi* had the power to control others, and they were the only people on Pemba during the colonial period who seemingly had this ability to control others, besides, of course, for colonial officials. During the slaveholding era, slave owners had control over people and, as such, the respect and fear – the *heshima* – attendant on that position on Pemba. With the demise of slavery, the power to truly control people was limited. Wealthy patrons could try to control their clients, but there was always a give-and-take element of the relationship that implied an actual lack of power on the part of patrons. However, *wachawi* did not have to offer patronage to gain the respect and fear of their neighbors and relatives. *Wachawi* had *heshima* in the older meaning of the word.

---

[71] ZNA AB31/20, Assistant collector of Weti, January 31, 1910.
[72] Goldman, p. 355.

This significant turnabout gave potentially anyone the possibility to gain power through *uchawi*, not just the wealthy or well born.

The Friends missionary, Herbert Armitage, expressed his frustration in 1904 about two students in the boys' school who kept wetting their beds at night. After months of trying everything known to him to stop the problem, he finally allowed the other pupils in the school to give the boys *dawa* ("medicine"). Armitage expressed his opinion of the proceedings as "the *dawa* consisted of putting them [the two boys] on a sack and beating tin cans and singing and in other ways making them look foolish."[73] To the missionary, this was just a "foolish" exercise, but to the boys, it had real meaning. While the boys were certainly not experienced practitioners or *waganga*, they were trying to replicate a procedure they had obviously witnessed or heard about within their own families. Many children's games are about preparation for life, playacting what it means to be an adult. Likewise, in 1905, Armitage chastised two boys on the mission for "playing *pepo*."[74] One of the boys was throwing stones at the other with the explanation that he was pretending to be a *pepo* ("spirit"). These children were replicating their cultural understandings of the pantheon of occult practices and the integral place they had in Pemban life. Spirits and witches abounded on Pemba, and they could have a positive impact, such as providing *dawa* for a problem, or they could be implicated in misfortunes, such as being hit by stones.

Participants in *uchawi* represented the full spectrum of Pemban society. As one missionary on the island charged, "[P]ractically everyone, Indian, Arab, free-born Mpemba or slave-born Swahili, was infected with the taint of witchcraft."[75] In 1912, J. E. E. Craster convinced his servants, much against their will, to take him to the caretaker of *Giningi'i*. When he saw the house of the caretaker, he remembered previously seeing "an Arab woman and two or three Arab boys about the house." Yet, when he inquired of the caretaker, whom he described as being surprisingly fair in complexion, "lighter in colour than that of any Arab in the island, … he said he was a Pemba man, and the negro boy who had answered

---

73 FIM PZ(F)/3, Diary of Boys' Home, October 12, 1904.
74 FIM PZ(F)/3, Diary of Boys' Home, September 29, 1905. *Pepo* are spirits, so the boys were playacting at spirit possession.
75 Eleanor Voules, *Witchcraft* (London: Central Africa House Press, 1951), p. 28; in the poems collected by Wilfred Whitely in the 1950s on Pemba, a number of "witches" were named; some were Arab, and others were clearly ex-slaves; Whiteley, pp. 40–6; see also comment from an official on Pemba that everyone, including Indians, used *uchawi*; ZNA AB31/20, Letter, January 31, 1910.

FIGURE 5.1. Magician writing a charm. (Reprinted from J. E. E. Craster, *Pemba: The Spice Island of Zanzibar.* London: T.F. Unwin, 1913.)

our summons was his son." In order to counteract the potential harm caused by meeting the caretaker of *Giningi'i,* Craster and his servants then went to a *mganga* to get a charm (Figure 5.1). The *mganga* was a Kharusi Arab, who told Craster that the Kharusi were "famous magicians throughout Arabia."[76] Meanwhile, UMCA missionaries described many participants in witchcraft as ex-slaves of mainland origin, as clearly indicated by the play from the children of slaves on the Friends mission. J. E. E. Craster noted, "The natives of Pemba have a great reputation as magicians throughout East Africa, and I found that, whereas the mainlanders and natives of Zanzibar regard the devils as their enemies, the Wa-Pemba look on them as friendly and helpful to themselves, though

[76] Craster, 1913, pp. 320–5, for all the quotations.

evilly disposed to all other human beings. In fact, the Wa-pemba regard themselves as a chosen people in the world of demons."[77] Arabs, enslaved Africans, WaPemba – these descriptions of the practitioners of *uchawi* point to the intermixture on Pemba of African and Arab practices found at all levels of society.

Thus far it appears that making an accusation of *uchawi* against a person was rare or at least not openly discussed. Yet talk and rumors of *uchawi* were rampant and certainly could cause a person harm.[78] Dr. O'Sullivan-Beare told a missionary in 1897 that an old woman came to him to prove to her son that she was not a *mchawi*, as accused by her neighbors.[79] On the one hand, this suggests that women were vulnerable to accusations of witchcraft. However, some women used such accusations to gain power through fear. Bi Kirembo was a particularly famous female *mchawi* who lived in the late nineteenth and early twentieth centuries.[80] She was highly respected, and no one crossed her for fear of what she might do to them. Descriptions of Bi Kirembo and her clothing of choice, the *kaniki*, indicate her status as someone who was enslaved at some point in her life.[81] And yet she became so powerful on Pemba that an Anglican bishop denounced her to the Sultan in an attempt to curb her power.[82] Thus even a woman identified by others as formerly enslaved could find power through the use of *uchawi*. A story recounted by J. E. E. Craster reinforces the notion that *wachawi* hoped to earn social capital through their practices. In 1912, Craster asked his employee, Yabu, if he

[77] Craster, 1913, p. 313.

[78] See ZNA AB31/20, Letter from Bishop Frank Weston, December 12, 1914. Bishop Weston listed six couples and several men who were accused by his converts of practicing *uchawi* on Pemba. Bishop Frank asked that these people be exiled from the island based on the talk of his converts. However, it appears from his description that these were practitioners of spirit possession, not *uchawi*.

[79] UMCA, E2, Emily Key, "Notes from Pemba," January 18, 1898; Key writes, "Dr. O'Sullivan told me some interesting stories of his contests with witchcraft, his medical skill having enabled him to expose many of the lies of the native doctors (who extort much money from cases they are quite unable to cure), and to work what seemed something like miracles to the natives – with the curious result that he (as being the chief of the magicians!) was called upon by an old woman to testify to her son that she was not a witch, as her neighbours declared, and his judgment was to be final! He had challenged one of the head native doctors undertaking to work all the wonders of which he professed to be capable and to exceed his powers in all ways."

[80] See reference in Whiteley, p. 41.

[81] See Arnold, p. 172, for a description of Bi Kirembo; for a discussion of clothing as a status indicator in Zanzibar, see Fair, 1998, pp. 64–109.

[82] Muhammed Abdurahman, "Anthropological Notes from the Zanzibar Protectorate," *Tanganyika Notes and Records* 8 (1939), p. 78.

was from the mainland. Yabu replied that he was from Pemba originally but ran away to the mainland as a young teenager because he feared his mother was going to kill him. Yabu explained that his mother had "killed" all but one of his brothers and that Yabu's neighbors warned him that he was next. When Craster asked why Yabu's mother would kill her children, Yabu replied, "[S]he hoped to obtain good health and much power over spirits and devils, and so to make herself rich and respected by her neighbours."[83] However, Craster also recorded a song that implies that women did not always find respect through *uchawi*. In the song, which was "supposed to be sung by a woman who has sacrificed her son" for the *wachawi*, the woman complains to the *wachawi* that she "thought you would have given me much more honour." She proceeds to complain that having children is no easy task, and it was a major sacrifice on her part to give up her child.[84] These two stories indicate the conflicting nature of *uchawi* on Pemba, where people saw it as a means toward wealth and respect, although clearly not for everyone. In daily life, *uchawi* was a source of heartbreak for many because it usually resulted in illness and, at worst, death for loved ones.[85]

As seen with Bi Kirembo, being *mchawi* could give people *heshima* in their communities, but this was a nineteenth-century form of *heshima*, which implied the ability to control people. Nathalie Arnold noted, "[B]eing *mchawi*, especially in the past, was primarily a means of acquiring pubic honor and respect."[86] *Heshima* was gained through both fear and respect for the individual's power. *Wachawi* had access to regular feasts and money because people paid them to spare their relatives. Thus they usually had a certain amount of wealth, which gave them respectability in their communities, in addition to the fear they inculcated in their neighbors. Former slaves who were practitioners could tap into the power of *uchawi* to recreate themselves as respected, powerful members of their communities, but risk remained in the fact that if they were not powerful *wachawi*, the rumor made them vulnerable to condemnation and ostracism from their community. Vulnerability was a double-edged sword: it allowed the path for increased power, but it left the individual open to rumor that could affect his or her reputation and, thus, his or her *heshima*.

---

[83] Craster, pp. 296–7.
[84] Craster, pp. 299–301.
[85] FIM TEMP MSS 419/1–7, Theodore Burtt, Notebook, 1899.
[86] Arnold, p. 91.

Colonial officials on Zanzibar took a jocular attitude toward *uchawi*, as seen in the Swahili examination for government officials. In the 1925 version of the exam, one sentence to translate stated, "Then I told him that when we came back, if one of those things was missing, I would kill him and his people by witchcraft." Clearly, officials thought it was appropriate to threaten indigenous employees with *uchawi*, and yet this sentence emphasizes colonial inability to fully comprehend the power *uchawi* held locally. Likewise, a case from a mainland court in 1938 tells of a powerful *mchawi* taken to court. In the court, the British judge asked the *mchawi* if he had power over the actions of the judge. The *mchawi* responded that "no he didn't over the judge but he did over everyone else in the packed courtroom." The courtroom was immediately cleared as the audience scattered for fear of what the *mchawi* would do to them.[87] The recounting of these links with *uchawi* and the law tickled colonial officials, emphasizing their unwillingness to take it seriously as a potential source of power or a threat to their own.

Although colonial officials on Pemba were loath to police *uchawi*, missionaries on the island consistently called for its abolition and control. Between 1910 and 1938, both Anglican and Quaker missionaries complained to colonial officials about the practice of *uchawi*, but no one was arrested for the practice.[88] It seems that the push for an ordinance after 1914 came from the UMCA bishop of Zanzibar rather than any official interest, which explains why it was quashed in the council discussions. Nonetheless, the seriousness with which missionaries took *uchawi* and *pepo* shows how prevalent the practices were on the island and the threat that they constituted to making and keeping Christian converts. The missionaries, unlike colonial officials, had a clear understanding of the power of *uchawi*.

REINTERPRETING THE ARCHIVES

Uchawi was a powerful force in the everyday lived experience of people in early-twentieth-century Pemba. Anthropologists have amply shown this to be true in modern experiences along the Swahili coast, yet historians also need to bring a local perspective to the stories found in archival

[87] C. P. Lyons, "A Witch-Doctor at Work," *Tanganyika Notes and Records* 1 (1936), p. 98.
[88] FIM P2/F, Committee of Missionaries, 1933–, February 21, 1935; the Friends reported a case of a convert practicing witchcraft "to the authorities." Several Anglican complaints are found in ZNA AB31/20, Witchcraft in Pemba, 1910–1917.

documents. This section reinterprets one small-scale "event" to suggest the everyday nature of how *uchawi* affected people's lives. From the haunted spots and roadside shrines that had to be propitiated with a handful of grass as people walked past to the regular lament of mothers over their children killed by *uchawi*, a picture emerges of a society encompassed by a constant fear and acceptance of the occult, what Adam Ashworth described as "living in a world with witches."[89] The stories recorded in the colonial archives seemingly offer a straightforward picture of what happened at the moment of emancipation, but some examples – from extraordinary events to everyday practices – suggest the prevalence of belief in *uchawi*.

On Pemba, the story of Binti Mabrooki, recorded by Vice Consul O'Sullivan-Beare in February 1898, would appear to simply illustrate the role *heshima* played in gaining acceptance locally and with court officials.[90] According to Vice Consul records, in August of 1897, Salim bin Abdullah, a man from the northern part of Pemba, was visiting Chake Chake when he saw a woman named Binti Mabrooki, whom he claimed was his slave. Salim tried to convince Binti Mabrooki to return with him, but she refused. As it happened, another man named Tendeja saw them on the street and remembered witnessing the sale of Binti Mabrooki some seven or eight years earlier. The three of them went to the British port authority, Mr. Edib, who completely misunderstood what was being said to him. He understood Binti Mabrooki to claim that Tendeja was trying to sell her to Salim; thus Mr. Edib immediately sent them all to the *liwali* because slave dealing was illegal by this time.

Once Salim and Tendeja were able to testify in front of the Swahili-speaking *liwali*, it became clear that Binti Mabrooki had indeed been sold to Salim, but she claimed that she had been illegally seized by the Tumbatu man who sold her to Salim.[91] Arguing that she had run away from her original Tumbatu owner, a different man from the one who sold her to Salim, she asserted that the sale to Salim was invalid. The *liwali* asked for the help of Dr. O'Sullivan-Beare to find the two Tumbatu men to corroborate her story. While the case was being investigated, the Vice Consul employed Binti Mabrooki on a construction job. During this time, Dr. O'Sullivan-Beare decided that Binti Mabrooki was

[89] Adam Ashforth, *Witchcraft, Violence, and Democracy in South Africa* (Chicago: University of Chicago Press, 2005).
[90] ZNA AC5/3, Vice Consul Pemba, Letter, July 5, 1899.
[91] Tumbatu is the third largest island of the Zanzibar Isles. A large population of WaTumbatu (people from Tumbatu) live in the southern part of Pemba Island.

not a trustworthy person. He could not find the two Tumbatu men, and at one point he impugned her *heshima* by stating, "She herself told me that she was living with her 'husband,' but doubtless that was her euphemistic manner of describing what would seem to have been entirely a temporary alliance. So much then for the first part of Binti Mabrooki's story."[92] Seemingly, Dr. O'Sullivan-Beare came to realize what others had suggested, that Binti Mabrooki did not have *heshima* and, as such, was open to condemnation from British officials and the man Tendeja. This was the official interpretation of Binti Mabrooki's story.

In 1899, Mr. Edib filed a complaint against his supervisors for forcing him to quit his job on Pemba. In his complaint, he gave more details about Binti Mabrooki that offer another way of looking at her story. Binti Mabrooki's story highlights the problems related to issues of respect, but it is also a cautionary tale of what happened to slaves who did not respect their owners and tried to gain their emancipation through British officials. Binti Mabrooki told her story to numerous officials and their servants during her stay in Chake Chake. She changed her story over the year or so that she interacted with colonial officials. Initially, the story tells of Binti Mabrooki's former owner seeing her on the street in 1897 and trying to convince her to return with him to his *shamba*. She refused and requested help from the British officials. Her initial request for help came around the time of the Emancipation Decree of 1897 that required owners to free their slaves if the slaves asked for their freedom. But her story does not stop there.

After Binti Mabrooki's appeal to the British, she disappeared for a number of months before returning in 1898 to Chake Chake. When she returned, she told Mr. Edib that she had been taken by Tendeja and her former owner to an unspecified location where she was held by them and beaten. However, Dr. O'Sullivan-Beare remarked that she had no marks on her body and showed no signs of being beaten. According to her, after she was beaten, she escaped back to town. Binti Mabrooki soon fell ill with fever and died a week later. While the story seems a mystery, it makes far more sense when viewed through the lens of *uchawi*. When the *wachawi* "took" a victim, the person would be taken at night (presumably under hypnosis) to a feast with a number of other *wachawi* present. The person was then "beaten" and returned to her home. The next day, the person would show no marks on her body, but she would begin to feel very unwell and sore all over. The person would then die within a few

---

[92] ZNA AC5/3, Vice Consul Pemba, Letter, July 5, 1899.

days or weeks after the "beating." Binti Mabrooki's story of being taken to an undisclosed location and beaten, followed by her death soon after, may have been recognized by people on Pemba as a case of *uchawi*.[93]

The case of Binti Mabrooki had gained notoriety in the community of Chake Chake in 1898 because of O'Sullivan-Beare's public appeals for information concerning the two Tumbatu men. Many of the British residents of Chake Chake at the time of her initial appeal in 1897 were also involved. They made inquiries with all the local officials of the Sultan, including the *liwali* of the district and the *masheha* of the neighboring villages. Government employees learned the story of Binti Mabrooki, the slave who refused to return to her owner even though he did not ill-treat her (at least according to him). Moreover, not only did she show a lack of respect toward her former owner, but she also questioned the legality of his purchase of her, directly impugning his *heshima*. Binti Mabrooki's case may have been viewed by the local elite as a test and a warning to other slaves. Embedded in this story of a slave killed by the *wachawi* for refusing to return to her owner was an important lesson. Even when Binti Mabrooki tried to get help from the British officials, she was still killed. In fact, she died under the very noses of the British in a house owned by the Vice Consul. This was a very powerful message to other slaves that they should not resist their owners and that not even the British could protect former slaves from their owners' retaliation through *uchawi*.

As this story demonstrates, reinterpreting the archive can be a difficult process. However, in many daily stories, *uchawi* is directly implicated in the events. These, too, must be reinterpreted in the framework of power and vulnerability. Craster's story of the policeman who was paralyzed by his encounter with an Arab over a donkey makes clear that the policeman saw the interaction as the practice of *uchawi*.[94] The policeman, who was of a mainland ethnic group, accosted an Arab who was being cruel to his donkey. The policeman told the Arab that if he saw the donkey being mistreated again he would report the Arab to a colonial official. The next day the Arab was again mistreating his animal, but when the *askari* ("policeman") responded to him, the Arab appeared to put a spell on the man, and the *askari* soon had a seizure and ended up in the hospital.

---

[93] Binti Mabrooki's story sounds like a case of a killing by *wachawi ya kobwe*. However, as Nathalie Arnold points out, since she was not a "beloved" of her owner, it was unlikely a *kikoa* killing. However, Arnold suggested that perhaps Binti Mabrooki was turned into a "zombie servant" to work for the *wachawi ya kobwe*. What better revenge by her owner than to make her serve for eternity? Arnold, Personal communication, January 2011.

[94] Craster, p. 334.

As Craster stated, "[T]he man himself [the policeman] had no doubt but that they [the seizures] were due to witchcraft." Yet this interaction is far more symbolic of resistance by elites to changing power dynamics on the island. Craster was on Pemba three years after the final Emancipation Degree, when Arabs could no longer hold power over another person, regardless of whether the person accepted a position of servitude. The policeman not only represented the ex-slave trying to tell an elite man what to do, but he also was representative of the new colonial power that had changed the balance of power. The Arab man who cast his spell was using *uchawi* to symbolically reinscribe his power on the body of the policeman. Through *uchawi*, some elite could still physically control those they perceived to be "lesser" than themselves.

The gendered element of the reinvention of power through *uchawi* becomes even clearer in several charms discussed by Harold Ingrams.[95] One of the charms, the *azima* charm, had once been used to recover run-away slaves. By the 1920s, it had been transformed into a love charm, specifically to make a woman fall in love with a man. Women were directly paralleled with slaves in the new interpretation of *uchawi*. No longer were slaves the most vulnerable people, after emancipation, women were clearly viewed as the most vulnerable actors in the community. In case any women thought of trying to exert power against men, another common charm was to keep a divorced wife from remarrying. By divorcing a woman and then keeping her from being able to remarry, her ex-husband made her doubly vulnerable; she could not receive maintenance from a new husband or potentially have children who would be able to support her in her old age. An ex-husband had no rights over his ex-wife or her body; thus this charm was a punitive effort on his part to punish her, much like ex-slaveholders no longer had rights over the bodies of their slaves but used *uchawi* to exert an "invisible" power over others.

Uchawi, which was discussed in the colonial archives and certainly among officials, was to the colonial state a concrete system. At night, they heard "ceremonies" and Pembans "barking like dogs," which they simply called *ngoma*, not distinguishing between the *ngoma* of *uchawi* and any other form of *ngoma*. They saw "killings" as caused by poison. In 1917, they even exhumed a body to physically prove to people in the islands (and undoubtedly to themselves) that the "body" was still in the ground and had not been "eaten" at a ceremony of witches.[96] To the state, then,

---

[95] Ingrams, 1931, p. 458.
[96] ZNA AB31/20, Witchcraft in Pemba.

uchawi was a visible, material system that it could understand, and as long as it was not visibly seen as challenging the power of the colonial state, it was left alone. Steven Feierman, on the other hand, offers up the examples of colonizers persecuting "mediums" in Tanganyika through witchcraft ordinances in order to show how the colonial state responded to those they viewed as challenging their power.[97] But *uchawi* on Pemba was viewed by the state as an atavistic relic, but a seemingly toothless one, not worth trying to prosecute or control. However, even though *uchawi* was not a religious practice per se, in several ways it directly confronted the control of mission Christianity. This helps to explain why periodically the missionaries would request the government to monitor and punish the practice of *uchawi* but that Zanzibari officials declined to bother. Moreover, this explains how *uchawi* came to be viewed as a matter of "religion" rather than one of power.

Feierman suggests in his thoughtful essay on the "invisibility" of Nyabingi mediumship in the Great Lakes Region that topics such as public healing are often eclipsed in the academic historical narrative because they are missing from the colonial archives. He argues that "the particular domains of African life which the conquerors saw as irrational are precisely the ones most difficult for historians to interpret. The European sources hang like a veil between the historians and the African actors of that period.... actions within the domain of public healing would appear irrational in terms of the logic of academic historical narratives."[98] He finds that often public healing is put in the context of religion and thus can be discussed in terms of symbolic practice rather than as a form of power that directly challenged both precolonial and colonial forms of power. Colonial government sources on Pemba most certainly described *uchawi* as "irrational," but interestingly, missionaries did not. The UMCA missionaries very much understood *uchawi* as a source of challenge to them, yet this again was interpreted in the framework of religion rather than power.

However, the dominance of Islamic belief in Pemban life, regardless of social status, indicates the hegemony of Islamic religion on the island. Colonial officials would often suggest that Pembans were not "good

[97] Steven Feierman argues that the witchcraft ordinances in colonial Tanganyika were about controlling the power of "mediums," who were viewed as anticolonial agitators, and had little to do with trying to control *uchawi*; Steven Feierman, "Colonizers, Scholars, and the Creation of Invisible Histories," in *Beyond the Cultural Turn: New Directions in the Study of Society and Culture*, edited by Victoria E. Bonnell and Lynn Hunt (Berkeley: University of California Press, 1999), p. 201.

[98] Feierman, 1999, p. 186.

Muslims" because of their "pagan" practices such as *uchawi*. However, people on Pemba did not see a problem between *uchawi* and Islam because *uchawi* was not a religious practice. European narratives of witchcraft, spirit possession, and similar practices generally frame these in terms of religion or even health and healing, but rarely are they truly treated as a form of administrative, coercive, or bureaucratic power in historical sources. Ralph Austen states that "the conception of witchcraft as an ambiguous attribute of power within Africa is often presented in ahistorical terms," suggesting that the use of witchcraft to negotiate power relations in continental societies has been "timeless."[99] For decades, anthropologists have considered witchcraft as indicative of power relations within societies, and it is noticeable that the first academic work to really consider the position of *uchawi* on Pemba was done by an anthropologist, not a historian.[100] Yet, with all the anthropological focus on witchcraft as related to power and all the many documentary sources that discuss *uchawi* on Pemba specifically, historians of the Zanzibar Islands have consistently ignored the role *uchawi* has played in brokering power relations in society.

Steven Feierman's call for historians to pull back the veil of European sources reinforces the significance of reconsidering the emancipatory period in Pemban history, where seemingly the emancipation of slaves went "so smoothly." Did elite slave owners so easily give up their power? Did the majority of slaves willingly stay with their owners? Did the colonial state impose new forms of "rationalized" labor to bring plantations into line with a capitalist society and thus Westernize and civilize notions of power on Pemba? What happened to the localized forms of power during the early colonial period? *Uchawi* is not seen as contesting colonial power in the documents, but does that mean it did not? Does this suggest that the low numbers of slaves seeking emancipation actually represent the power of the invisible world exerting itself on the visible? When J. E. E. Craster stated in 1912 that the WaPemba viewed themselves "as the chosen people among devils," was he really illuminating an invisible power structure on the island that explains how the population, from enslaved to elite, viewed and localized power? Was the story of Binti Mabrooki a lesson on how the invisible world could affect the visible? In many respects these questions are unanswerable because the colonial records do not explicitly discuss *uchawi* as anything other than a tangible set of practices akin to religious beliefs or simply silly superstitions.

---

[99] Austen, p. 92.
[100] Arnold, 2003.

For people on Pemba, though, the invisible world, the world of *uchawi*, was one of power, wealth, and escape from the control of the colonial state.[101] In the twentieth century, the world of *uchawi* came to represent a state in and of itself. There was an entire bureaucracy for the *wachawi* on the island, which kept both *wachawi* and everyone else in line. Each region on the island had its own council, which met in particular spots and controlled the *wachawi* of its region. It had a high council, which had the final say and control over all subordinate councils. To hold power in the visible world – the colonial world – a person likewise had to either hold power in the invisible world or at least pay homage to those in control of the invisible world.[102] The landscapes of power had indeed changed, but not in the ways colonial officials expected.

The most difficult question is exploring whether emancipation affected the invisible world. Because sources do not discuss how *uchawi* represented power in the precolonial era, we are again left with the "timeless" aspect of *uchawi*, a timelessness that implies no change. What we do know from the anthropological work done by Harold Ingrams in the 1920s and Nathalie Arnold in the 1990s is that *uchawi* came to represent to people on Pemba a form of resistance to the colonial state. Both collected stories about *wachawi* protecting their villages from the efforts of colonial officials to conscript soldiers and porters during World Wars I and II.[103] Likewise, Wilfred Whitely collected poems in the 1950s that indicated resistance by local *wachawi* councils when the government attempted to appropriate the land used by them for their meetings.[104] While political power in the visible world may have been controlled by the colonial state, regardless of their social status, people on Pemba could move freely within the social hierarchy of the invisible world.

CONCLUSION

The landscapes of power on Pemba before the colonial period emphasized power through strength of numbers. A person who could call on

---

[101] Harry West likewise refers to the "invisible world" of the Muedan of Mozambique. This is a world that exists side-by-side with the visible realm, yet the invisible world exerts incredible power on the visible world in a way that is rarely reversed; see West, pp. 40–7.

[102] Arnold, pp. 253–4.

[103] Ingrams, 1931, p. 472; Pembans trying to stop the requests of the colonial government for porters in World War I; Arnold, pp. 168–245.

[104] Whiteley, pp. 40–6; two poems deal with this topic, "Mwembe Jivuli" and "Mkadi wa Ngenge."

many dependents, relatives, and slaves in a conflict had *heshima*. Even if the person was disliked locally, such as Ali bin Abdullah, he or she had power and honor through his or her control over people. However, when the colonial state entered Pemba, it dramatically redrew the landscapes of power. Slaves and other lower-status individuals were able to go to the courts in an effort to get their side of a dispute heard and enforced. This change presented a tremendous opportunity to the nonelites because they no longer had to have the power of force to settle disputes. Changing means of dispute resolution meant that *heshima* was no longer calculated by lineage or physical and political power. Colonial officials still recognized certain prerogatives of elites, such as allowing Salim bin Ali el-Riami to avoid his boat being searched, but acts defined as criminal by British law were punished regardless of status. This reordering of *heshima* affected elites more than former slaves in many ways because it brought them to the same level in the courts as everyone else.

Yet former slave owners did not hand over power so readily to the colonial state. The story of Binti Mabrooki and the lesson it held for the enslaved population reminded everyone on the island that another, less visible landscape of power remained on the island. *Uchawi* was definitely practiced by a variety of people on Pemba, and use of it could allow marginalized people respect and membership in the postemancipation community. *Uchawi* gave individuals access to *heshima*, but the level of *heshima* differed radically between individuals. For some former slaves, such as Bi Kirembo, great wealth and power were attainable, but for the vast majority, *uchawi* offered less tangible rewards. Negative consequences could be found with *uchawi* as well. For example, the woman in the song who killed her child to join the *wachawi* discovered that her child had been more valuable to her than the *heshima* she received from the *wachawi*.

Rereading the archives for hints of *uchawi* is an act of imagination because few European observers acknowledged the role of witchcraft in colonial documents. Dr. O'Sullivan-Beare scrupulously avoided mentioning *uchawi* in a single dispatch to the Consul's office in Zanzibar, although he would regale missionaries with stories of challenging powerful *wachawi* on the island. He was very aware of its presence on the island and in people's lives, but he was unwilling to give it a place in formal reports. Europeans were fascinated by *uchawi* and tried to learn its secrets. Anglican bishops led several exorcisms in order to banish its power over their converts, and Friends missionaries would patiently recount when someone living on their mission stations said a death was caused by *uchawi*. Given its pervasive existence on the islands, British readings of events and stories in the archives appear lacking. Recreating the way locals would interpret such events is an important method of examining everyday meanings and manifestations of power in the transformative period after abolition.

6

Mitigating Vulnerability through Kinship

Enslavement was a moment of severe rupture in the lives of the people taken from the interior regions of East Africa and transported to work in homes and plantations along the Swahili coast. Life histories of slaves on Pemba, written down by Friends missionaries, poignantly testify to the ruptures when individuals were torn from their children, parents, spouses, and other family members. The story of Mwajuma Mama Saburi, a woman who was captured during an attack on her village and who never saw her husband or child again and had no idea what happened to them, is testimony to the very real heartbreak that enslaved people faced. But many enslaved people also struggled to regain and recreate the networks of friends and family they had lost through enslavement. Mwajuma herself remarried on Pemba, and when her husband died, she remarried again. Mwajuma's efforts to constantly remain linked to others through marriage or friendship illustrates the very real need slaves and ex-slaves had to maintain kinship ties in order to mitigate the economic and social vulnerabilities associated with their lower-status positions in Pemba.

Kinship was critical to making life livable for people on Pemba, whether of freeborn or slave descent. Orlando Patterson famously claimed that enslavement was equal to "social death."[1] According to Patterson's definition, slaves had no social network, which was what allowed them to be enslaved, yet all the slaves in the records from Pemba show that they continually worked to build social links with each other and even with their owners and, as such, had a "social life" regardless of their status as

---

[1] Patterson, 1982.

slaves. As discussed in Chapter 1, ex-slaves chose with whom they would share their lives, triumphs, vulnerabilities, and wealth. In the scholarship, the term "fictive kin" is often used, but that betrays a Western fixation with "blood" and marriage as the only means of kinship – if there were not blood or marital ties, then the relationships were defined as "fictive." For ex-slaves, there was nothing fictive about these relationships that bound people together. The wills of ex-slaves show these ties most clearly, although their life histories also indicate the ways in which ex-slaves relied on the kin they chose, their networked kin.[2]

Scholars have continued to discuss the importance of kinship for former slaves in creating their identities postemancipation.[3] As Dylan Penningroth noted in Ghana, "[B]oth slaves and owners used shifting strategies, but they shared the language of kinship and descent."[4] Yet linkages between former owners and slaves were not the only links that former slaves maintained. Many slaves on Pemba left their owners in pairs or groups, relying on one another for support in finding new or better employers.[5] As Vincent Brown found among Jamaican slaves who "drew fictive kin and intimate friends into familial relationships that extended through time," unrelated emancipated slaves on Pemba created kinship ties with each other.[6] Pamela Scully argued, "[T]o be free was to be imbricated in dependencies and obligations to a variety of people, and especially to one's family and fictive kin."[7] Kinship, and the various ways in which it was created, was crucial to the survival of ex-slaves as they sought to adapt to "freedom."

The ties that bound former slaves to their former owners were similar to the ties linking former slaves to each other. Many of these individuals used these ties to create kinship links. The stories of former slaves who sought help from the Friends missionaries on Pemba indicate the ways in which slaves tried to build family networks while enslaved and after

---

[2] I would prefer to describe these relationships as kin rather than qualifying with terms such as "fictive" or "networked" because that is how people defined one another. However, the term "kin" alone lacks precision, and to avoid confusion, I use "networked" rather than "fictive kinship." I find it deeply problematic that only relationships created by enslaved people are defined as "fictive," rhetorically revictimizing enslaved populations.

[3] McDougall, 1998, pp. 285–315; Dylan Penningroth, "The Claims of Slaves and Ex-Slaves to Family and Property: A Transatlantic Comparison," *American Historical Review* 112, no. 4 (2007), pp. 1039–69.

[4] Penningroth, p. 1051.

[5] FIM PZ(F)/3, Register of slaves, Banani, 1897–1909.

[6] Brown, p. 118.

[7] Scully, p. 26

emancipation. For instance, Feruzi "married a fellow slave for love," and they had a child. However, the child died soon after the blood brother of Feruzi's wife fled with her in an attempt to return to their natal home.[8] In the twenty-five brief life histories of former slaves written down by Friends missionaries between 1898 and 1923, the frailty of life is apparent. Most of the children born to slaves died before reaching adulthood, and most of the slaves were widowed at least once if not multiple times, as seen with Mwajuma. As if to show their contempt for the fragility of life, slaves continued to marry, give birth, and fight to build families with one another.

Former slaves had a variety of outlets for building new networks, including with their former owners or other former slaves. As Frederick Cooper argued, many former slaves initially remained squatting on the land of former slave owners, although not necessarily *their* former owners.[9] Some slaves who were trusted and born into their owner's household (*wazalia*) were treated as lesser members of the family, even inheriting land at times from their former owners.[10] These former slaves identified themselves as the *hadim* of their owners and took on the clan names (*nisba*) of their owners. The slaves of the elite, wealthy, and well-respected individuals attained *heshima* through this connection.[11] Many of these slaves remained connected to the families, even leaving property to their owners in their wills. For some, slave-owner relationships broke down at the moment of emancipation, but by the 1930s, far more of these ties were broken as former owners and slaves found the patron-client relationship constrictive and unproductive.[12]

The historical work of Vincent Brown suggests death rituals as a site to examine the relationships created among enslaved people. The burial practices, inheritance patterns, and methods of remembrance all shed light on the ways in which the enslaved forged links with one another, the families of their owners, and members of the free community. Ex-slaves on Pemba exhibited anxiety about their funerals and the ways

[8] FIM TEMP MSS 419/1–7, Theodore Burtt, Notebook, 1899.

[9] Cooper, 1980, pp. 72–83.

[10] Mirza and Strobel discuss a *mzalia* who inherited from his mistress p. 30; Mtoro Bakari said that when some owners emancipated their slaves, the owners adopted the slaves as their children or brothers; Bakari, 1981, p. 176; FIM TEMP MSS 419/1–7, Theodore Burtt, Notebook, 1899, Fundi Kamna.

[11] Cooper, 1980, p. 76.

[12] Lyne mentions that on Pemba, ties were more often broken than not because slaves refused to work after emancipation, regardless of whether they had been freed; Lyne, 1905, pp. 184–6.

they wanted their estates distributed. As discussed in Chapter 4, their wills indicate that not all slaves or ex-slaves were buried in an acceptable manner, meaning that they were buried with the proper treatment of the body, Islamic prayers, and a celebratory feast.[13] Brown argues that "in the course of their mortuary obligations, the enslaved also defined familial belonging. Preparations for burial reinforced the significance of kinship and friendship."[14] Therefore, by examining the practices of burial, we can see how people situated their familial networks. The probate court records, although showing only a small part of the community, illuminate the varying familial networks on Pemba among former slaves and in the wider community.

Several important forms of kinship show up in the records: blood, marriage, and networked kinship bonds. Blood kinship was most commonly found among parents and their children, although cooperation among ex-slave siblings is also evident in the records. However, when applying for freedom, most people were accompanied by friends, spouses, and younger children rather than their adult siblings.[15] Yet we know siblings kept track of one another even in enslavement.[16] As mentioned earlier, one brother fled slavery before emancipation and retrieved his sister before leaving the island. They had been enslaved on the mainland together but sold to different owners on Pemba. The brother hoped that they could return to their mainland family. The sister left her enslaved husband and child behind, illustrating the difficult choices enslaved people faced concerning their familial ties and the preeminence preenslavement blood ties had over enslavement ties. Other preenslavement blood relatives show up in the records after emancipation as people sought to find their relatives whether by chance or on purpose.[17]

Fictive kinship has been discussed extensively in terms of enslavement, both in Africa and in the Americas. In many places and cases, slaves and ex-slaves built kinship networks based on the commonalities of their enslavement experience and fondness for one another, what I prefer to

---

[13] Ingrams, 1931, pp. 201–3; 239–43.

[14] Brown, p. 73.

[15] FIM PZ(F)/3, Register of slaves, Banani, 1897–1909.

[16] FIM TEMP MSS 419/1–7, Theodore Burtt, Notebook, 1899, provides examples of siblings who remained in touch – including stories of Sanura Mama Sudi and Feruzi Manyema; ZNA AC9/2, Letter to Vice Consul, December 4, 1903, tells of a brother seeking to return to the mainland with his sister.

[17] FIM TEMP MSS 419/1–7, Theodore Burtt, Notebook, 1899; Bahati Mnasura was recognized by a first cousin walking down the street; ZNA AC8/5, Farler to Cave, November 12, 1903.

call "networked kinship." The strongest networked bonds were those of adoption. On the government and missionary plantations for freed slaves, orphaned children were assigned to families to be raised.[18] In the case of the Friends mission, as the father of a child lay dying, he made his neighbors swear an oath to raise his child.[19] His neighbors committed to this task and took his child into their home. These forms of adoption happened frequently because life was precarious for many slaves and even ex-slaves whose health was compromised during enslavement. At times, networked kinship bonds were strained by the choices made at emancipation. For example, Khamisini Manyema had been raised by Binti Sudi when his birth mother died, but in the late 1890s he sought government emancipation while Binti Sudi remained with her owner. Khamisini's adoptive mother remained a slave by her choice. This suggests a certain amount of strain between the two. When Khamisini died, Binti Sudi made a claim on the estate. Khamisini's daughter, Basira, refused in the probate court to acknowledge Binti Sudi as the mother of Khamisini. Basira stated that her father had been an orphan; thus Binti Sudi could not be his mother. The relationship was unlocked by Khamisini's wife, Riziki, who testified to the court that Binti Sudi was indeed her husband's "mother." While Basira was of a postemancipation generation that did not honor or know of the bounds of enslavement, Riziki knew and understood the relationship. The money Binti Sudi received was minimal; it was more a matter of recognition of their relationship. Binti Sudi's efforts to raise Khamisini during slavery were honored by Riziki's recognition of her as Khamisini's "mother."

The British probate officials would only let blood relatives inherit. Thus, for people enslaved together, they had to claim blood kinship. Similar to the case of Binti Sudi, at the death of ex-slaves, "blood" relatives appeared out of the ether. Binti Sudi is the only woman in the probate records I have found who claimed blood ties when they were really networked; all other cases of this sort have involved men as the petitioners. This explains why the granddaughter did not know her "grandmother" as a blood relative. The men who claimed kinship to the deceased were often slaves of the same owner and of the same ethnic group, indicating that they had a relationship with the deceased at one time or another. But

---

[18] *Report by Vice Consul O'Sullivan on the Island of Pemba, 1899*; O'Sullivan-Beare states, "[A] warm feeling of affection seems to have arisen between the foster parents and their adopted children."

[19] FIM PZ(F)/3, Meeting minute book for 1898–1902, December 15, 1902.

these relationships seemingly did not survive emancipation because the wives and children, as well as their local *masheha*, questioned the relationship of the men to the deceased. In several instances discussed later, the slave owners came to testify on behalf of the "brother," indicating that perhaps the owners were attempting to gain the property of their former slaves and implicitly trying to exert their control over their former slaves, even in death.

FRIENDSHIP AND NETWORKED KIN

As discussed in previous chapters, a number of different forms of organization existed on the island, such as the Sufi *tarika,* *pepo* spirit possession groups, and practitioners of *uchawi*, along with various *ngoma* ("dance") groups. These groups, which are all forms of communities of practice, expanded in the postemancipation era on the islands and the mainland as a means for free and enslaved people to both network with one another and negotiate the difficulties they encountered in life. These communities offered individuals a network of other people with similar concerns, beliefs, or interests. These communities of practice offered women, especially, networks of support that they previously would have sought within their owner's plantation community. It is important to note that these communities offered psychological support as well as the potential economic and social support of a typical network.

Work of other scholars along the Swahili coast reinforces the social and economic role of communities of practice in building support networks and friendships among men and women. In the nineteenth century, the members of *pepo* groups, called *wari*, created a "society of mutual assistance" among themselves in Zanzibar.[20] By the twentieth century, the initiates of these groups on Pemba had begun using terms of kinship to show their connections to one another.[21] The work of Margaret Strobel and Laura Fair demonstrates how women of the Swahili coast used *ngoma* groups to facilitate links across social and ethnic lines.[22] Women on Pemba remembered the participation of their female relatives in Sufi *maulidi, msondo* initiation for girls, and weddings as times of great communal support.[23] Laura Fair explains that initiation after emancipation

---

[20] Alpers, 1983, p. 695.
[21] Linda Giles, "Spirit Possession on the Swahili Coast: Peripheral Cults or Primary Texts?" (Ph.D. dissertation, University of Texas at Austin, 1989), p. 122, n. 2, p. 127.
[22] Fair, 2001, p. 63; Strobel, 1979, chaps. 6 through 8.
[23] Interviews: Farashuu Suleiman, Pemba, December 2004; Halima Rashid, Pemba, December 2004.

was a critical process for women who participated across social and ethnic lines.[24] "The bonds formed between initiates and between the young women and their instructors lasted a lifetime. Through *unyago* [initiation ceremonies on Unguja] women created intimate gender-based social networks whose strength women drew upon throughout their lives for personal, economic, and political empowerment."[25] But women were not the only ones who participated and found friendships at dances and through initiation. Iddi Ali Hamad recollected that men young and old would dance for two or three nights during times of celebration.[26] Mzee Mohamed also belonged to a group of nineteen young men who performed stick fighting dances (*kirumbizi*) together and in competitions with other communities.[27] Boys living in the Friends boys' home would leave together to be initiated among their families and then return to the school.[28] The recollections of these men and women speak to the importance of friendships created through participation in communities of practice as a means of social belonging and even having a network of economic support. Laura Fair emphasized the role of *ngoma* groups in breaking down social and ethnic barriers in urban areas between free-born and ex-slave women in the postemancipation period. Court cases indicate that people of varied ethnicities had daily interactions on Pemba, and it may well be that these interactions came out of involvement in *ngoma* and other communities of practice.

The bonds of friendship often began in childhood, even for those who were born into slavery. At the Friends boys' school, the daily diary records the many exploits of boyhood friends, much to the chagrin of the missionaries.[29] The boys would go out carousing together, spending the night with other friends who lived in town or their own families who lived nearby. The boys rarely went off from the school alone, although they were often dragged back by the missionaries one at a time.[30] The boys in the school played and fought with one another, but they regularly

---

[24] Fair, 2000, p. 147.

[25] Fair, 2000, p. 152.

[26] Iddi Ali Hamad, Pemba, October 2004.

[27] Mzee Mohamed, Pemba, December 2004. Boys were also initiated together, helping to create similar bonds as found among girls. See FIM PZ(F)/3, Diary of boys home 1902–1906, March 14, 1904.

[28] FIM PZ(F)/3, Diary of boys home 1902–1906.

[29] FIM PZ(F)/3, Diary of boys home 1902–1906. Almost every day had a notation about a boy wandering off and then coming back; for examples, see November 28, 1905; March 14, 1904; August 14, 1903; February 14, 1904; February 1, 1905.

[30] FIM PZ(F)/3, Diary of boys home 1902–1906; for examples, see November 10, 1902; June 4, 1903.

helped and shared with each other as well. Girls who went through *msondo* and boys who went through circumcision together had a bond like blood ties because they formed a group, much like the age-grade systems found among mainland communities.[31] These friendships were especially important in the liminal years for those born on the island after 1890 but whose parents were enslaved. Legally, these children were born free, but they were often treated as slaves by their parents' owners.[32]

Friendship was important throughout the life process of enslaved people. It gave them networks of support, whether based on common interests, ownership, or ethnicity. Children relied on these lines of support at the mission when they would run away from the mission. Their friends would come and tell them what the punishment was going to be from the missionaries.[33] As people aged and had fewer options of where to go, they would rely on friends for help. When squatters aged and could no longer take care of land to the satisfaction of landowners and they were without relatives, owners forced them to move. Friendships helped them find a place to go. Sanura went to the Friends mission because Mama Taki, an old friend invited her to move onto her plot of land.[34] The example from a capital murder case in 1910 helps to illuminate the linkages and ways friends helped each other out.[35] This case involved the murder of a man named Majaliwa wadi Uledi. In the case we learn that Majaliwa regularly lived with his friend Saburi and his wife in their house because he did not have housing of his own. When the accused murderer's wife, Halima, heard rumors that revenge would be sought against her husband and household, she immediately fled to her friend Asikiyai's house. Not only did the friends of Majaliwa make threats in support of their deceased friend and try to avenge him, but Halima also sought support, protection, and assistance from her friend. Friends were witnesses to contracts and in courts. They also supported each other in fights and helped each other in the day-to-day details of life, even when they became too infirm

---

[31] Fair, 2000; Farashuu Suleiman, December 2004; Halima Rashid, December 2004.

[32] For examples of this treatment, see FIM PZ(F)/3, Diary of boys home 1902–1906, September 22, 1902; December 10, 1902; April 8, 1903; July 30, 1903; August 1, 1903; September 2, 1905.

[33] In general, the boys would run away to visit friends or family or go to *ngoma* that they were forbidden to attend by the missionaries. The boys generally returned to the mission a few days later to face their punishment.

[34] FIM TEMP MSS 419/1–7, Theodore Burtt, Notebook, 1899, Sanura.

[35] "In the Supreme court of the H.H. the Sultan, Criminal Appeal No. 1 of 1910" *Zanzibar Gazette*, June 14, 1910.

to support themselves.[36] Friendships were a survival strategy to mitigate the vulnerability of life, but they also made life more enjoyable.

For people originally from the mainland, especially those who were brought over as slaves, aging was very difficult without a family network.[37] Friendships were critical to survival; thus, when men and women arrived in Pemba as slaves, they began building links to others among their owners' other slaves and among those in the surrounding area. These links were obvious when slaves sought emancipation from the government and left together. In the case of Mfalme Shame's four slaves, Jena Heri, Fikirini, Mrashi, and Mauwa, they all left together.[38] The three men and one woman decided that their owner was "too hard" and decided to get their emancipation and find another *shamba* on which to work. One of the men and the woman were married, but the other men were friends with the couple. Likewise, Fatahi wadi Juma heard about the abolition order and left his owner with three other slaves to seek their emancipation through the government.[39]

In many cases, though, friendship was more than a survival strategy; it represented individuals' choices of who they defined as their "family." In 1941, a seventy-year-old Yao woman named Binti Hamis died.[40] She had a few possessions, which included some clothes and a mud hut, but had no heirs to inherit her limited property. Her age, ethnicity, and possessions indicate she had once been enslaved. But it was her funeral that demarcated her relationships in the community. Another woman, Amina binti Saad, paid for Binti Hamis' funeral, ensuring that she was properly celebrated and buried. The actions of Amina illustrate Vincent Brown's findings in

---

[36] FIM PZ(F)/3, Meeting minute book 1898–1902, April 16, 1898. The interpreter for the Friends, Alexander Masudi, got in a fight with his wife and was helped by his friend Hamisi. Both men ended up with jail sentences for their assault on the wife; FIM PZ(F)/3, Diary of boys home 1902–1906, October 7, 1902.

[37] Mzee Mohamed, December 2004; Farashuu Suleiman, December 2004. When the Friends went to get permission for a boy named Mbwewe to attend the mission school, they found that his father was frail and could not walk. The father, named Mabruki, was "dependent for all his needs upon his fellow slaves"; FIM PZ(F)/3, Diary of boys home 1902–1906, October 7, 1902. Mabruki died just seven months after moving to the Friends mission on April 8, 1904.

[38] ZNA AC8/5, Vice Consul, Pemba, Letters.

[39] FIM TEMP MSS 419/1–7, Theodore Burtt, Notebook, 1899, Fatahi wadi Juma. Fatahi travelled with Songoro, Marazuhu, and Ndamuyema to the mission. Given that his story was written down twenty years after he was emancipated, this suggests that he remained friends with the three men. The Friends slave register showed that many people left their owners together; FIM PZ(F)/3, Register of slaves, Banani, 1897–1909.

[40] PNA AK1/4197, April 1941.

Jamaica that "death rites provide an opportunity for people to enact social values, to express their vision of what it is that binds their community together."[41] He argues that by examining how a person is buried and by whom indicates their position in the community and their networks of kinship and friendship. While Binti Hamis died without blood kin, she still had a network of friends, such as Amina, who honored her in death and made sure that she had a proper burial and feast. Slaves and ex-slaves on Pemba built relationships with one another in an effort to support each other in life and death. In some cases people framed their relationships in terms of kinship; even though they were not related by blood, they were kin through their choice and networks with one another.

Friendships are one of the hardest relationships to tease out of the records about enslaved people, and yet they were a crucial element of everyday life. Binti Hamis and Amina had a friendship of support in which they cared for one another. These two women were not the only people on Pemba to care for each other in this manner. When Juma bin Khamis died in 1928, he was buried by a friend.[42] When a man claimed to be Juma's brother, the *sheha* of the area doubted the claim because Juma was buried by a friend and not the purported "brother," and the closest kin to the deceased were responsible for handling the funeral and paying the funeral expenses. Hashima binti Baraka left a substantial portion of her small estate to two different women who were unrelated to her.[43] Hashima shared her good fortune with her two close friends, Biubwa binti Swedi and Hidaya binti Chande, when she died. How Hashima became friends with Biubwa and Hidaya is not explained in the probate record, although their names indicate their slave pasts. These three women were obviously close friends, and Hashima made sure that her friends would benefit at her death. Friendships among slaves were at times based on kinship networks, but people could also be close friends without trying to claim common descent. Networked kin were important for more than simple survival; they made life better. In a society that valued people above all else, friendships were critical at all stages in life.

FAMILY TIES AMONG EX-SLAVES

The way in which estates were settled by the Islamic, and later British, courts give insight into which relatives were privileged by the state and,

---

[41] Brown, p. 61.
[42] PNA AK1/2165, November 1926.
[43] PNA AK1/3310, August 1934.

at times, individuals. Just as some networked kin were written into wills by ex-slaves, blood and marital ties were also important means of building kinship links that could mitigate vulnerability. Blood and marital ties were the two forms of kinship most recognized by both British and Islamic laws. While British law often prioritized martial ties by making the spouse the main beneficiary at the death of the other spouse, Islamic law gave precedence to blood relatives such as siblings, children, and even male paternal relatives, who could receive the majority of an estate to the detriment of a spouse. The difference in how the legal systems dealt with kinship helps to illuminate the debates that occurred in the probate records among relatives who wanted their position to be prioritized over other kin. Seemingly, blood ties would be the strongest bonds between people, yet many enslaved people and ex-slaves did not have the luxury of knowing their blood kin. Ex-slaves clearly cherished the children they had and attempted to protect them from the experience of being slaves. These blood ties between parents and children, as well as among siblings, were often stronger than any other forms of kinship.[44] Children were especially important for ex-slaves, who sought to alleviate their vulnerability through parenthood.

The creation of families during enslavement was not always done by choice. At times, owners assigned female slaves to their male slaves as "wives."[45] Most women spoke of these marriages in a matter-of-fact manner, indicating that they may not have had much choice in marriage in their previous lives.[46] However, both men and women recognized the choices that emancipation offered them about marriage partners. After emancipation, they could now get divorced if they wished and often did, much to the dismay of Christian missionaries on the island.[47] Fatahi wadi Juma fell in love with a woman named Hanzorani, whom he met after emancipation, but Hanzorani was already married, so they remained friends.[48] Fatahi lived with a woman named Andihalo during those years, but he never married her. When Hanzorani was widowed, Fatahi quickly proposed marriage. Hanzorani and Fatahi remained together until her death, very much in love. He married and divorced four women in quick

---

[44] For examples of blood relatives working together to cut out spouses, see PNA AK1/4209, November 1941; PNA AK1/2184, Abdulrahman bin Idarus el-Maalawi, October 1926.

[45] FIM TEMP MSS 419/1–7, Theodore Burtt, Notebook, 1899, Mama Juma; Cooper, 1977, pp. 223–4.

[46] FIM TEMP MSS 419/1–7, Theodore Burtt, Notebook, 1899.

[47] FIM TEMP MSS 419, Private letters of Theodore Burtt, November 24, 1909.

[48] FIM TEMP MSS 419/1–7, Theodore Burtt, Notebook, 1899.

succession after Hanzorani's death, illustrating both the fragility of marriage among ex-slaves and the desire to avoid living alone.

The story of Fatahi indicates the free will ex-slaves showed in their marital partners, but his constant remarriages show a man trying to replicate
the patriarchal ideal of the male head of household. The evidence suggests that while men may have tried to control women, after emancipation,
ex-slave women had considerable agency in their relationships with men.[49]
Given the higher ratio of female ex-slaves to men, it would seem that men
should have had an easy time of finding suitable marriage partners and
that women would be in a weak position vis-à-vis the marriage market.
Nonetheless, men and women both remembered men aggressively intervening in marriages and luring married women to leave their husbands.
Ndaniyenu, an ex-slave woman living at the Friends mission, recalled that
she "was persuaded by another man ... to leave her husband." Likewise,
Feruzi's wife Mtahawi, whom he "married for love," had his "home broken" by Songoro Mnyasa, another ex-slave who convinced Mtahawi to
leave her husband.[50] In 1910, a man was brought up on murder charges,
with the motive being jealousy over a woman.[51] The murdered man,
Majaliwa, reputedly was having an affair with a woman named Tausi, who
the murderer Nasibu wanted to marry. Tausi declared that she had not
had a relationship with Majaliwa but that she was afraid of Nasibu, who
had beaten her and tried to make her marry him. Tausi's refusal to marry
Nasibu, even when afraid of him, indicates the difficulty men had in controlling women in the postemancipation era. Ex-slave men had a difficult
time imitating the forms of patriarchy they had seen among slave owners.

The patterns of marriage and divorce made family structures among
ex-slaves as complicated as those found among freeborn Pembans.[52]
For example, when Ulaiti binti Musa, an ex-slave, died in 1925, she had
four daughters with three different fathers.[53] Other ex-slave families

---

[49] Marcia Wright discusses how even during the colonial era, men on the mainland sought
to control women and their labor; Wright, 1993, pp. 129–30.

[50] FIM TEMP MSS 419/1–7, Theodore Burtt, Notebook, 1899, Ndaniyenu, Feruzi and
Songoro Makonde.

[51] *Zanzibar Gazette*, June 14, 1910.

[52] For examples of complex family structures among freeborn, see PNA AK1/4219, Fadhil
bin Khamis Ngazija, September 1942; PNA AK1/4210, Juma bin Khamis Shirazi,
October 1941; PNA AK1/4220, Mussa bin Muhamed, October 1940; PNA AK1/4574,
Kombo bin Mussa bin Faki Shirazi, January 1944; PNA AK1/4579, Suleiman bin Salim
bin Mohamed el-Bimani, February 1944; PNA AK1/5026, Amani bin Hamadi bin Amani
Shirazi, September 1946.

[53] PNA AK1/2188, Ulaiti binti Musa Swahili, November 1926.

were equally complex. Mwanaache binti Haji had two sets of children with two husbands. Mwanakiamu binti Shali had three brothers and one sister, yet none of them were full siblings.[54] Her parents had both remarried at later points in their lives and had other families. In some families, blood and marriage ties merged, such as when Maushamba binti Hasidi's nephew married her granddaughter.[55] Marriage and divorce were as common among ex-slaves as they were among the freeborn population.[56] The very high numbers of remarriages among ex-slaves, as many as eight marriages in a person's lifetime, indicates that marriage was a key to survival and mitigating the weakness of being without social and familial networks, yet it was a fragile and unreliable relationship in many cases.

One of the most valuable aspects of marriage for individuals was the possibility of having children. For enslaved and emancipated people (as well as freeborn), children were highly prized. Colonial officials and missionaries complained about enslaved women using abortion to avoid motherhood, and this may have been the case, but it is unlikely given the emphasis placed on having children in East African societies.[57] In an example that truly questions the choice to have abortions, out of ninety-six families who sought their freedom in 1898 via the Friends mission, forty-six included multiple generations of a family. Most of the families had only one child, and from the life histories recorded by the Friends, it is clear that a number of these children did not live to adulthood. Mama Juma is an example of an enslaved woman who fought to keep the child born to her during her enslavement. She had a husband and an infant before she was enslaved, never to see them again. Her new owner on Pemba married her to a slave husband, and within a year she gave birth to a boy she named Juma. At emancipation, her owner offered to free Juma and raise him within the owner's family. Mama Juma refused her owner's request; she wanted to keep her only child with her, so she fled with him to the Friends mission. Sadly, a year later Juma died, leaving his mother childless and bereft. Even without a living child, she insisted on keeping her name as "Mama Juma," signifying to others that she had

---

[54] PNA AK1/4207, Mwanaache binti Haji, September 1941; PNA AK1/333, March 1914.

[55] PNA AK1/323, Manashamba binti Hadidi Swahili, January 1914.

[56] Ingrams, 1931, p. 237; O'Malley, p. 62; Stockreiter, chap. 4; Mirza and Strobel, pp. 10–11; FIM TEMP MSS 419/1–7, Theodore Burtt, Notebook, 1899.

[57] *Report by Vice Consul O'Sullivan on the Island of Pemba, 1899*. Also note that officials never gave proof for this theory, only their opinion. Father Bale told O'Sullivan-Beare that he believed jealous wives sterilized concubines; ZNA AC8/5, February 28, 1903.

been a mother. Life was precarious, and most enslaved parents worked very hard to protect their children.

Debates over who controlled slave children were common in postemancipation societies. Martin Klein found that owners in West Africa fought to keep assimilated enslaved children in order to continue to benefit from their labor.[58] In both East and West Africa, enslaved children were especially vulnerable. Often slave children would come to the Friends schools and ask to live on the mission, where they received free clothes and food. On a number of occasions slave owners would send for the children because owners perceived them to be disobedient slaves. The Friends missionaries would only hand the children over to their parents, not the owners. Many slaves who remained with their owners would resist the wishes of their owners and let their children stay with the Friends.[59] These slaves thought that the regular meals and education their children received were worth the displeasure of their owners. For so many of the enslaved parents, having children allowed them to replace the families they lost when they were enslaved, and they clearly wanted their children to have a better, more stable life than their own. It is the actions of these parents that undercut the argument that people remained enslaved out of loyalty to their owners or a feeling of kinship with their owners because if that were truly the case, they would not have encouraged their children to defy their owners, especially by going to Christian missionaries. These enslaved parents accommodated their owners' demands for their labor, but they did not acquiesce to the desire for their children's labor.

During slavery and after emancipation, the bonds of blood held many siblings together. Brothers and sisters helped each other out, especially after the deaths of their parents. In 1919, Ali bin Juma died, leaving his pregnant wife one small piece of land and a lot of debt to a moneylender.[60] Her brother swiftly sold the land before it was reported to the probate court. When the probate court tried to collect on the debt to the moneylender, there was nothing left of the estate. The widow's brother weighed the choices facing his sister and decided to sell the land in an effort to assist her, regardless of the loss of respect and credit they might

---

[58] Klein, 1998, pp. 207–8.
[59] FIM TEMP MSS 419, Private letters of Theodore Burtt, November 17, 1908; FIM PZ(F)/3, Diary of boys home 1902–1906; see entries for the following dates December 10, 1902; August 26, 1903; April 15, 1903; February 1, 1905; September 2, 1905; March 14, 1904; August 21, 1903; October 7, 1902; April 8, 1903; July 7, 1903; November 28, 1905; May 16, 1906; and August 24, 1903.
[60] PNA AK1/1074, Ali bin Juma Swahili, December 12, 1919.

encounter for not paying the debt to the moneylender.[61] Brothers and sisters also took care of each other when marriage partners would not. When Hasina binti Nasibu's brother contracted leprosy, his wife kicked him out of the house.[62] Hasina took him into her home and cared for him until his death, even though his wife lived nearby. Hasina and her brother had a difficult relationship because he regularly swindled and took advantage of her. Yet she also illustrates the fidelity of blood kinship among ex-slaves who tried their best to support each other.

Some ex-slave siblings were very close, whereas others lost touch. Slavery created a paradox that blood relatives were highly valued but rarely known, yet could suddenly appear because of the process of enslavement. The appearance of relatives after many years apart often created a quandary as to how they should be treated by the networked and marital kin of individuals. Preenslavement relatives did on occasion meet up again after many years apart. One woman who lived at the Friends plantation, Banani, was walking down the street in Chake Chake and heard a voice that she recognized as a cousin from the mainland. It was indeed her cousin, and the two remained in contact for the rest of their lives.[63] However, the probate records show a number of "relatives," most often men, who claimed to be blood relatives of the deceased. Generally these men showed up after the deceased had been buried, claiming a share in the estate. Whether these relatives were blood or networked kin, they tried to impose themselves into the familial structure, against the wishes of the spouses. In some cases, it is clear the men were claiming kinship based on their common enslavement to one owner. In other cases, people claimed to be preenslavement relatives, fusing the two worlds of the enslaved. Yet not all of these new kin were welcomed, especially by female heirs, and with good reason.

For the audacious, claiming kinship to another person after his or her death was not terribly difficult. In two cases, the men claiming kinship simply had to swear an oath before the *kadhi* that they were indeed related to the deceased. As discussed in Chapter 3, swearing an oath was a solemn business, and most people took it very seriously. However, examples exist of people who lied under oath. Moreover, for most people

---

[61] Moneylenders were generally unpopular among the landowning classes. Thus it may be that within their community people were sympathetic to the pregnant widow about the debt.

[62] PNA AI1/19, HHSC, Civil Case No. 673 of 1919; another sister who paid off the debt of her brother can be found in ZNA AP26/160.

[63] FIM TEMP MSS 419/1–7, Theodore Burtt, Notebook, 1899, Mnasura.

claiming kinship, they may have felt fully in their right to claim kinship based on networked ties of enslavement. Thus, when Chuma bin Ali claimed to be a paternal relative of Ame bin Dadi, both of whom were ex-slaves, Chuma may have truly believed that the "paternal" tie of kinship came from a common owner in their fathers' pasts.[64] As an *assaba* ("male paternal relative") to Ame's estate, Chuma stood to inherit half the estate – almost 1,000 rupees. Fatuma, Ame's daughter, fought long and hard to have Chuma's claim removed and was successful at proving that Chuma was not a blood relative of Ame. The female kin of Subeti bin Jaya were not so lucky.[65] When Subeti's "brother," Khamis wadi Jaya, appeared out of nowhere, his wives stated that they did not know Subeti to have a brother. However, the *kadhi* accepted the proof and oath of Khamis that he was Subeti's brother. Khamis then turned and testified to the court that one of the widows had been divorced by his brother, and he thought it highly unlikely that his brother had ever married the other woman. All of a sudden the two widows went from being the only heirs to being removed from inheriting altogether. Khamis was unsuccessful in disinheriting the women completely, but this case shows how tenuous marital ties were versus the perceived value of blood ties in the probate courts.

The case of Subeti's widows versus Khamis illustrates the fragile position of female kin, who by Islamic law received half the portion of male heirs. Another case shows how families would negotiate with these imposed blood kin who appeared at the death of relatives. The negotiations between the newly appeared "nephew" of Mzee bin Bora and the maternal grandfather of Mzee's only granddaughter indicate the potential fear of marital relatives about losing inheritance.[66] In 1938, when Mzee died and the nephew appeared, Mzee's wife's family was not sure if the man was really related. As a member of Mzee's family noted, "[T]he deceased came from the mainland many years back," indicating that he lost family when enslaved, and perhaps those family still existed. The nephew claimed that his father and Mzee were full brothers on the mainland before Mzee was captured into slavery. Mzee's family decided to split the inheritance in half between the nephew and granddaughter, recognizing both the pre- and postenslavement families of Mzee and pointing to the significance of blood kinship, among other forms.

[64] PNA AK1/2187, Chuma bin Khamis Swahili, August 1926.
[65] PNA AK1/2777, Subeti bin Juya Mdigo, July 1930.
[66] PNA AK1/3690, Mzee bin Bora, March 1938.

Blood kinship was one of the strongest bonds among ex-slaves on Pemba, and yet for many people it was the least common link they had to others. For enslaved people brought to Pemba to work, stripped of their kinship ties on the mainland, it meant starting from scratch to build a new family, which was not an easy endeavor. Men and women who received their freedom wanted to start families and build blood ties. Mama Juma's insistence on being called by her son's name decades after his death highlights the importance of blood ties to ex-slaves. Marital ties allowed men to replicate their understanding of patriarchy and hopefully become the founder of a lineage. For women, though, marital ties were much looser, and women were far more likely to leave their husbands, showing their agency in the face of "too much patriarchy."

CONCUBINES

Claims of kinship for slaves and ex-slaves were about mitigating their vulnerability, but likewise so was rejecting forms of "kinship" if such relationships could lead to increasing vulnerability over time. Concubinage in the colonial records was classified as a form of kinship that placed slave concubines, called *masuria* (s. *suria*), as members of their owners' families. Yet concubinage was a double-edged sword in that it had the potential to leave female slaves *more* vulnerable than wives, who could be divorced. Becoming a concubine on Pemba was a move for many enslaved women that offered them stability and a much easier life than that as a field slave, yet women did reject this life choice, especially on Pemba. The refusal to become a concubine on the part of some enslaved women illuminates the vulnerability inherent in the colonial understanding of "kinship" found on the islands.

As British officials began wrestling with how and when to end slavery in Zanzibar, they particularly struggled with the role of concubines. Their struggle and their eventual justification for exempting concubines from the Abolition Decree of 1897 played out in their annual reports on slavery from 1895 to 1902. Customarily, in late-nineteenth-century Zanzibar, a concubine who bore a child to her owner could not be sold and was typically freed on death of her owner. In addition, her child was treated as a legitimate heir to the slave owner, implying a form of kinship for these women. But in a colonial report from 1895 it was noted that concubines who had not borne children could be compelled to labor in the fields for their owners and that fathers were not required by law to recognize the children of concubines – even if there was no question about the paternity.[67] Buried within this report was the fear that concubines of lower- and middle-class men, who generally did all the housework, would leave their homes and become prostitutes.[68] Colonial officials feared that ending concubinage would create an "immoral" population of women who would become prostitutes because, in reality, officials viewed concubines as sexualized beings rather than in terms of kin relations, as they later claimed. By 1897, however, British officials declared that "a concubine has a very important legal status, second only to that of a wife. She has a house and servants assigned to her, she is handsomely clothed and receives many presents of jewellery, and her children take rank immediately after the children of the legal wife.... A concubine as soon as she has become a mother is free."[69] Within two years, British officials had upgraded their description of the life of *masuria*. No longer did lower- and middle-class *masuria* exist, only upper-class concubines, whose life of ease was one of envy among free and slave women. These claims were reiterated in the reports of the following years on slavery, constantly justifying to British citizens in the metropole why concubines were exempted from the abolition order.[70] The British argued that if the position of *masuria* was abolished, illegitimacy would become rampant, and the kinship structures of coastal society would be severely broken.[71]

When writing about concubines, colonial officials explained that the only reason a woman refused to become a *masuria* was that she did not want to be confined to a harem.[72] The idea that the position of *masuria* was vulnerable within a household no longer entered the British dialogue after 1895. As far as colonial officials were concerned, *masuria* were

---

[67] Africa No. 6, *Correspondence Respecting Slavery in Zanzibar* (1895), p. 29.

[68] Africa No. 6, *Correspondence Respecting Slavery in Zanzibar* (1895), p. 41.

[69] Africa No. 6, *Correspondence Respecting the Abolition of the Legal Status of Slavery in Zanzibar and Pemba* (1898), p. 57; this description of *masuria* as "elite" and not living in lower- or middle-class households is generally replicated in Prestholdt, p. 121; Glassman, 1995, p. 90; Romero, 1997, pp. 123–4.

[70] Africa No. 7, *Correspondence Respecting Slavery in the Zanzibar Dominions* (1896); Africa No. 6, *Correspondence Respecting the Abolition of the Legal Status of Slavery in Zanzibar and Pemba* (1898).

[71] Africa No. 6, *Correspondence Respecting the Abolition of the Legal Status of Slavery in Zanzibar and Pemba* (1898), p. 61; Fair states that after 1909, children born to concubines were considered illegitimate by the colonial state because "concubine" was no longer a legal category; see Fair, 2001, p. 217, wherein Romero argues that men in Lamu continued to take concubines into the 1950s; Romero, 1997, p. 141.

[72] Africa No. 6, *Correspondence Respecting the Abolition of the Legal Status of Slavery in Zanzibar and Pemba* (1898); letter from Vice Consul O'Sullivan, February 16, 1898; Africa No. 4, *Correspondence Respecting Slavery and the Slave Trade in East Africa and the Islands of Zanzibar and Pemba* (1901); Farler's report for 1899.

members of the family and had full rights within the family and a choice about their decision to accept the status of a *masuria*.[73] They pointed to the role *masuria* had played in the social hierarchy of Zanzibari Sultans; Sultan Barghash had been the son of a *suria*. In an 1896 cable from the Sultan to the Foreign Office, he discussed *masuria* as "practically wives" and begged the British government not to break up the "families" of slave owners.[74] The position of *masuria* was presented by the colonial state as one of luxury and support, free from the vulnerabilities of enslavement, and the reality for many *masuria* was likely one of relative comfort and ease. Nonetheless, some *masuria* obviously felt vulnerable because they complained to colonial officials. These officials viewed the complaints of *masuria* as "domestic issues" that were frivolous, such as an owner taking on a new concubine.[75] However, for an older *suria*, a new *suria* in the household meant very real competition for resources and the potential that an "older" *suria* would lose her position, especially if she did not have children. The lives of *masuria* were constantly vulnerable to the whims of their owners.

But what was the relationship between *masuria* and their owners like? Patricia Romero explains that in Lamu, the relationships between owners and *masuria* was one of "love."[76] Likewise, Katrin Bromber notes that she had doubted the "romantic image painted in Velten's *Desturi za Wasuaheli*" of the relationship between *masuria* and their owners, but that "the respected status of many of these women has now been confirmed by numerous interviews."[77] Thus some women gained real value and fulfillment from their positions as *masuria*. No matter what, though, *masuria* were still enslaved. As Lovejoy and Hogendorn point out, in northern Nigeria, a place where concubines had a similar social position as those found along the Swahili coast, the majority of women who sought their emancipation were concubines.[78] Concubinage had its benefits, but

---

[73] Cooper, 1980, p. 195; "refusal [to become a concubine] was unlikely."

[74] Africa No. 7, *Correspondence Respecting Slavery in the Zanzibar Dominions*, No. 1, Sir L. Mathews to Mr. A. Hardinge, Zanzibar November 14, 1896.

[75] Africa No. 6, *Correspondence Respecting Slavery in Zanzibar* (1895), p. 32; Africa No. 6, *Correspondence Respecting the Abolition of the Legal Status of Slavery in Zanzibar and Pemba*, No. 29, Sir A. Hardinge to the Marquess of Salisbury, April 23, 1898; Africa No. 4, Correspondence *Respecting Slavery and the Slave Trade in East Africa and the Islands of Zanzibar and Pemba* (1901); Farler's report for 1899.

[76] Romero, 1997, pp. 123–4.

[77] Bromber, 2007, p. 120.

[78] Paul Lovejoy and Jan Hogendorn, *Slow Death for Slavery: The Course of Abolition in Northern Nigeria, 1897–1936* (Cambridge: Cambridge University Press, 1993), p. 117 – quoting Lord Lugard.

it also left women vulnerable, as illustrated by this Zanzibari song lyric, "*Suria*, you slave! *Suria*, you slave! Don't think you can make yourself comfortable on your owner's mattress. *Suria*, you slave!"[79] *Masuria* may have lived within the family but their position as kin was tenuous.[80] On Pemba *masuria* were presented "as women without a sense of shame, conveyers of bad luck, people who would not know what to do with their freedom."[81] The Friends missionaries also noted that colonial officials regularly portrayed *masuria* as "fallen women."[82] In a society where reputation was so important, the risk to a slave woman's respectability by becoming a *suria* may have outweighed the perceived benefits of concubinage, especially for those women with an already established kinship network.

The linkage of kinship between *masuria* and their owners was only confirmed if children borne of the relationship survived into adulthood.[83] Many children did not live past the age of five, so in reality the position of *masuria* was fragile in a household.[84] Additionally, many women resisted this form of "kinship" as exploitative and unwelcome. Being a *suria* offered little stability to a woman, who could be demoted from the position unless she had living children with her owner – and he recognized the children.[85] One missionary even suggested that *masuria* risked being sterilized by their owners' wives, which left them in a doubly vulnerable position, as slaves and infertile women.[86] It is difficult on Pemba to get a clear picture of how women felt about concubinage because few women came forward to complain and those who did were viewed as an aberration. Ideally, concubines were confined to the harem; thus they were not able to easily go into town and complain to officials about their treatment. However, on Pemba, some, if not many, concubines on the

---

[79] Cited in Bromber, 2007, p. 121; this citation comes from the papers of Reverend Taylor held at SOAS; also cited by Glassman, 1995, p. 91.

[80] Lovejoy and Hogendorn do note that older concubines without children were often treated as members of the family, but they argue that it was still an individual process; Lovejoy and Hogendorn, p. 116.

[81] Bromber, 2007, p. 121. Citing a poem collected by Willard Whiteley on Pemba in the 1950s.

[82] FIM TEMP MSS 419, Private letters of Theodore Burtt, July 24, 1908.

[83] See Deutsch, 2006, p. 69; Strobel, 1979, p. 50.

[84] Deutsch describes the position of *masuria* as family members as "ambivalent"; Deutsch 2006, p. 78.

[85] Africa No. 6, *Correspondence Respecting Slavery in Zanzibar* (1895). In this report, the Vice Consul notes that owners did not have to recognize children born to their *masuria* as legitimate heirs.

[86] ZNA AC8/5, Vice Consul Pemba, Letters, February 28, 1903.

island were not kept confined but rather continued to work in the house and fields for their owners, which may explain why some Pemban concubines refused to remain with their owners and were able to leave.[87]

In 1895, when he first arrived on the island, Dr. O'Sullivan-Beare estimated that about 2,000 women on Pemba were concubines.[88] But he was careful to state that this was a guess and that he really had no way of knowing for certain how many women were concubines. He noted that a few elite men were reputed to have fifty concubines each, but that was a rare situation. In the 1890s, concubines had little leverage if they had problems with their owners. One *suria* went to the Vice Consul to complain that her owner did not give her enough *heshima*, which she translated to mean a separate house and good cloth. When she went to the Vice Consul, she indicated that her complaint was not responded to by either the *liwali* or the *kadhi*. Why they did not respond to her is unclear; perhaps they found her complaint frivolous or ignored it because she was viewed as a slave. Either way shows a dismissiveness toward and lack of power for concubines in Pemban society. Moreover, the woman's complaints about lack of *heshima* reflected the very real concern she had that her owner was not treating her as a concubine but rather as a female slave he could use sexually. She was trying to use her position as a concubine, along with British interpretations of what privileges that entailed, to force her owner to give her resources, such as a house and cloth, in order to help her lessen the vulnerability of being a slave woman without resources.

Enslaved women on the Swahili coast did not uniformly desire to become *masuria*. Cases of runaway or unhappy *masuria* contradict the image portrayed in Romero of *masuria* who "loved" their owners.[89] Women who faced concubinage had a number of reasons for refusing to accept the position of concubine, which included the desire to control their own sexuality as much as they could and refusal to accept their enslavement, among other reasons. British officials regularly explained any woman's opposition to the position of becoming a *suria* as her

---

[87] Msichoke claimed that she had been doing regular field and house work and thus was not being treated as a concubine. The forms of work that women did in the household became the measuring stick for the Slavery Commissioner on whether the women were concubines or not. See *Africa No. 6, Correspondence Respecting Slavery and the Slave Trade in East Africa and the Islands of Zanzibar and Pemba* (1902), for discussion.

[88] *Report by Vice Consul O'Sullivan on the Island of Pemba, 1896–1897.*

[89] For discussion of runaway *masuria*, see Strobel, 1979, p. 51; Fair also talked about *masuria* who were known for being unhappy; Fair, 2001, p. 101.

objection to living in *purdah*.[90] After 1897, when concubines could apply for their freedom based on cruelty, a number of women on Pemba (but far fewer on Zanzibar) applied for their freedom, reiterating the point that enslavement on Pemba was different from that on Zanzibar.[91] According to the 1897 Abolition Decree, "A concubine not having borne children may be redeemed with the sanction of the Court." However, the reality was that the court was unwilling to free concubines unless they could prove cruelty. One woman on the Friends mission who had been a concubine lied to the Slavery Commissioner, claiming that she had not been a concubine, and was successful in her case.[92] Several other women refused to be made concubines and took measures to avoid it.[93] The case of Msichoke is one of the best documented of a woman refusing to be made a concubine (Figure 6.1).

In 1902, Msichoke went to the Friends mission in order to enlist the aid of the missionaries in attaining her freedom. Msichoke had run away from her owner around 1900 and had survived by picking up day work for other people on the island, but she wanted to become free. She went to the Slavery Commissioner to get her freedom from her owner, but at the court, her owner claimed her as a concubine, and as such, she was not eligible for freedom. Msichoke was then handed over to her owner, who took her home and strung her up in a room of his house, using rope to hang her by her hands from the ceiling. According to Msichoke, he then beat her with his fists rather than a whip because a whip would

---

[90] Africa No. 6, *Correspondence Respecting Slavery and the Slave Trade in East Africa and the Islands of Zanzibar and Pemba* (1902), No. 5, Mr. Cave to the Marquess of Lansdowne, Zanzibar, October 2, 1902.

[91] Africa No. 6, *Correspondence Respecting the Abolition of the Legal Status of Slavery in Zanzibar and Pemba* (1898), No. 29, Sir A. Hardinge to the Marquess of Salisbury, April 23, 1898; Africa No. 4, *Correspondence Respecting Slavery and the Slave Trade in East Africa and the Islands of Zanzibar and Pemba* (1901); Farler's report for 1899 notes that forty-two *masuria* applied for their freedom and twenty-eight received it.

[92] FIM TEMP MSS 419/1–7, Theodore Burtt, Notebook, 1899; Sanura was a concubine in the 1890s and lied to Farler about her status in order to get her freedom.

[93] For examples, see FIM TEMP MSS 419/1–7, Theodore Burtt, Notebook, 1899; Mame Taki refused to become a concubine, so her owner sold her; Africa No. 6, *Correspondence Respecting the Abolition of the Legal Status of Slavery in Zanzibar and Pemba* (1898), for the case of Hamida, who refused to become the concubine of her owner's brother. Also, Msichoke, 1902; Africa No. 6, *Correspondence Respecting Slavery and the Slave Trade in East Africa and the Islands of Zanzibar and Pemba* (1902), pp. 18–27; FIM TEMP MSS 419, Private letters of Theodore Burtt, January 30, 1909; Burtt states that they had four concubines of Rashid bin Salim on the mission in addition to several other former concubines; Machengewe and Nganima, cases from the *Zanzibar Gazette*, 1908–1909.

MSICHOKE.

FIGURE 6.1. Msichoke. [Reprinted from *The Friend* (British), October 3, 1902.] Courtesy Friends House Library.

leave permanent marks. Eventually, the owner's wife let Msichoke down. Afterwards, Msichoke dug her way out of the room through the floor of the house and ran away again. She went to the court to protest that she was not a concubine and had never been treated as a concubine, but she was shouted down in the court by other owners who were attending the court. It was then that she went to the Friends missionaries, who called on the Vice Consul to hear the case. In the court, the Slavery Commissioner told Msichoke's owner that he could get a good compensation for her, but the owner refused. He insisted that Msichoke was his concubine and that he wanted to keep her, even though she had continued to run away from him. At one point in the testimony, the owner stated that he wanted to keep Msichoke because he "loved her" – a statement that made Msichoke spit at him, "What is the profit of your love?"[94]

[94] "The Story of Msichoke," *The Friend* (British), October 3, 1902, p. 646.

Msichoke's refusal to be made a concubine and her owner's refusal to give her freedom raises issues about the relationships between slaves and owners, *heshima*, and kinship. For most concubines, their position allowed them to link up to a kinship network through their owner. However, clearly some women rejected this link. Msichoke still lived with people she described as her parents, although they appear to have adopted her, indicating that her parents were slaves of her owner as well.[95] Msichoke had networked kinship links; therefore, she did not need the link that most concubines accepted as the main benefit of the relationship with their owners. The complaints of Msichoke and her persistent defiance of her enslavement echoed the petition Mzuri Kwao made to O'Sullivan-Beare just seven years previously. Enslaved women knew that their positions were vulnerable and that they needed to find a position of stability. Msichoke did not view concubinage as offering her a viable existence because she already had a network of support. Moreover, if she received her freedom, which was a possibility because of the abolition order, she would be able to attain a higher level of *heshima* than that of a *suria*.[96]

Msichoke was right that her position in the household would be weak. If she did not bear living children who survived to adulthood, she could be cast aside.[97] The stories of Tufaa and Bahati binti Serenge tell of concubines whose children died young and thus who were discarded by their owners as concubines. Both women were married off to other slaves and eventually pushed off the land of their owners.[98] Tufaa was lucky enough to end up on the Friends mission and be taken care of within the refuge of the mission for sick, lame, or elderly ex-slaves. Bahati was not so lucky. In 1930, she was still squatting on the land of her ex-owner when her slave husband died. Her story is a distressing

---

[95] Africa No. 6, *Correspondence Respecting Slavery and the Slave Trade in East Africa and the Islands of Zanzibar and Pemba* (1902), Inclosure No. 3, Mr. Armitage to Consul Cave, August 20, 1902, p. 18; in this letter, Cave states that these were not Msichoke's "blood" parents; Africa No. 6, *Correspondence Respecting the Abolition of the Legal Status of Slavery in Zanzibar and Pemba* (1898), No. 21, Sir A. Hardinge to the Marquess of Salisbury, Zanzibar, January 3, 1898.

[96] FIM TEMP MSS 419, Private letters of Theodore Burtt, July 24, 1908. In describing a former *suria*, he states, "[H]er great desire seems to be to be lawfully married to a respectable native and to settle down as his wife."

[97] Strobel, 1979, p. 50.

[98] FIM TEMP MSS 419/1–7, Theodore Burtt, Notebook, 1899, Tufaa; PNA AI1/44 HHSCZ, Civil Appeal No. 15 of 1934; Mirza and Strobel, p. 32; in the story of Kaje, her father's first concubine had the same thing happen to her.

one because she clearly still believed that having borne a child for her owner, regardless that the child had died, gave her the right to claim kinship of him. Her ex-owner, Abdulla bin Amur el-Miskiri, tired of dealing with Bahati by 1930, decided to sell the land he had let her squat on for decades.

Bahati's bewilderment and then anger were palpable in the court records. Abdulla was effective at evicting her from his land because she had no legal claim on him – she had no living child to prove their past relationship and, because of the 1909 emancipation order, she had long been "free." Bahati also had a hard time bringing her case to court because she had no money, having asked her "guardian" and former owner, Abdulla, to hold her money for her, which he now refused to return. Moreover, as an old slave woman with no children or other relatives, she had no one but migrant laborers to testify for her in court. Her problems in court indicated the vulnerable position that Bahati found herself in – she was a woman without a guardian and without a network. Her trustee was the one who sold the property out from under her, so the one person she classified as a "relative" was not someone who would help her.[99] At one point in the records, Bahati told Abdulla that he needed to give her either the land or her money because "there is no slavery now-a-days." She clearly resented his efforts to control her, showing that she kept up the front of kinship ties not out of loyalty to Abdulla but out of desperation and need. The case of Bahati illustrates the weak position of concubines within the community if they did not belong in the household of a wealthy man or did not have living children with their owner. Moreover, her experience confirms that many slaves remained in the location of their enslavement because they had few options.

While concubines certainly carried a differential position to other slaves, they were still in the end slaves who could be disposed of by their owners. Moreover, as women, in many respects their positions were even more vulnerable than that of free or enslaved women because of the emphasis on control. The loss of control over slaves that came with the initial emancipation order exacerbated the position of concubines who were exempted from the decree and, as such, the last domain of male power and prestige, making the position of concubine untenable for

---

[99] The migrant workers attested that she called Abdulla bin Amur a "relative," which was a common practice among former slaves who often took the ethnic appellation of their former owner.

women who had a choice.[100] A key thread running through the actions of
Msichoke and other women who refused to be concubines was that they
had a support network of other people who helped them rebuff efforts to
make them *masuria*.

CLAIMING AND DENYING KINSHIP

Most scholarship on slavery in Africa that explores the ongoing relationships between owners and slaves after manumission discusses the use of
claimed kinship with slave-owning families by slaves in order to gain
benefits and prestige.[101] This certainly happened in Pemba, but the general system of kinship claims between former slaves and their owners was
far more complex in this rural location. One of the points that becomes
clear from a variety of records, including civil court and probate cases,
missionary records, and consular documents, is that it behooved owners
to claim kinship to slaves, especially in the post-1909 period as much
as claims of kinship benefited ex-slaves. While slaves generally received
prestige and invitations to feasts by maintaining ties, former owners had
the potential to get property out of their ex-slaves.[102] Even more than the
value of the property claimed, though, was the value of *heshima* gained
by the former owner because of his or her success at exerting control over
ex-slaves who defied their owners by asking for their emancipation from
the government. When an owner successfully claimed kinship, even after
the death of the ex-slave, the owner publicly received acknowledgment
of what the ex-slave had tried to deny – the owner's right of control over
slaves. This section explores the ways in which former owners and slaves
made claims of kinship on one another and shows that when ex-owners
claimed kinship, it was often predatory rather than as an exhibition of
patronage and prestige or to control labor, as often seen elsewhere.[103] In
many cases, although certainly not all, slaves who maintained links of
kinship with their owners did so simply out of economic necessity rather
than loyalty. The slaves from the most elite families, who derived benefits

---

[100] Strobel argues that owning concubines was "a means of displaying wealth in a society
     with few other forms of investment"; Strobel, 1979, p. 49
[101] Miers and Kopytoff argued that female slaves attached to families for a long time were
     viewed as kin; Miers and Kopytoff, pp. 73–74. Also see Strobel, 1979, pp. 137–47, for
     similar arguments; Klein, 1998, pp. 239–41.
[102] Romero argues that it was "mutual dependency … that kept slaves and owner tightly
     bound" after emancipation; Romero, 1997, p. 129.
[103] Klein, 1998, p. 240.

from this relationship through a boost in their social status, maintained their relationships as a form of kinship, yet for the vast majority of slaves on Pemba, these were not typical ties of kinship.

The scholarship on slavery in urban locations of the Swahili coast indicates that often slave owners and their house slaves developed strong bonds of affection for one another, so much so that former slaves would assist their former owners for years after slavery had been abolished.[104] As Frederick Cooper noted, around the time of abolition in the Zanzibar Islands, 6,000 slaves were voluntarily manumitted by their owners under Islamic law, indicating their close relationships. Additionally, a total of almost 12,000 slaves were emancipated by the government. However, the breakdown of where these emancipations occurred is telling about the difference in relationships between slaves and owners on Pemba and Unguja Islands. In Unguja, 5,280 slaves were voluntarily manumitted, whereas 5,141 slaves were emancipated by the government. Yet, in Pemba, only 740 slaves were voluntarily manumitted, but almost 6,700 sought their emancipation from the Slavery Commissioner.[105] The disparity in voluntary manumission is very telling. Most slaves on Pemba were not the favored slaves of their owners, and they were not treated as family members. And yet the majority of slaves still did not seek their emancipation on Pemba. Cooper points to the story of Mshangama from 1904 to explain this phenomenon. Mshangama was a slave who lost all his land and animals to his owner when he asked for his freedom from the government.[106] Mshangama's case set a precedent that stated that owners could claim any property of their slaves at emancipation, a precedent that remained on the books until the final abolition order of 1909. Cases exist in the records that show violent reactions from owners when their slaves sought emancipation, which could certainly be a deterrent, yet violence alone would not keep slaves on their owners' land.[107] Thus slaves may have feared their owners or the loss of their property to their owners if they sought emancipation. Nonetheless, something else kept many slaves bound to their owners. As Cooper argues, it may be that many were

---

[104] Craster, pp. 80, 146, 341; Romero, 1997, pp. 119, 122–4; Mirza and Strobel, pp. 31–9.

[105] Cooper, 1980, pp. 73–4.

[106] Cooper, 1980, pp. 75–6; ZNA AC8/7, January 19, 1904; FIM PZ(F)/3, Diary of boys home 1902–1906, May 16, 1906. A boy was placed with the Friends by his "guardians" because his father had died while enslaved. Although his father had owned property, the boy, Ramathani, did not receive it because the owner laid claim to the property.

[107] FIM PZ(F)/3, Meeting minute book, 1898–1902, August 1898. A slave was attacked and badly wounded by his owner when he returned to his *shamba* after gaining his emancipation.

bound simply by economics. Nonetheless, an idiom of kinship resounds through the records, showing that slaves and owners still placed their relationships with one another in a framework of kinship, although this may have been an emphasis created by the colonial state that wanted to show slavery as a paternalistic and benign system. However, as Igor Kopytoff noted, kinship could have very real implications of submitting to the authority and obligations of the larger clan and patriarch rather than the nurturing nuclear family.[108] In many respects, the exploitation of former slaves by ex-owners was done through a lens of kinship. Even when former slaves tried to break ties of kinship with their owners, the owners used the language of kinship to claim ties between them. The claims of kinship between owners and ex-slaves was a two-way street that both used at various times to their benefit.

The relationships between owners and slaves changed over the period of government emancipation. Initially, many slaves remained with their owners because their other options were limited in terms of access to land to grow food, but that does not mean that these slaves were completely loyal to their owners. As discussed earlier, a growing number of slaves allowed their children to attend mission schools, much to the chagrin and anger of their owners. This shows that slaves truly had hope for a different future for their children, one in which being enslaved was something of the past. Yet it is also in the children where we see the difference in how they responded to enslavement. Many children treated enslavement as something flexible; they could go back to their owners or they could leave at any time.[109] This flexibility allowed them to pick and choose the elements of the slave system that worked for them. Owners certainly tried to regulate the ability of slave children to wander away, but this was limited by the intervention of missionaries and parents. Likewise, the colonial government tried to control adult slaves from wandering between landowners, yet the government was equally unsuccessful.[110]

The case of Ali bin Sababu's will illuminates the intricate connections between slaves and owners and the difficulties they all encountered in negotiating a postemancipation reality.[111] The relationships that come out of Ali's will represent the ideals of house slavery in the nineteenth-century

---

[108] Igor Kopytoff, "The Cultural Context of African Abolition," in *The End of Slavery in Africa*, edited by Suzanne Miers and Richard Roberts, p. 491.

[109] Legally these children were born free because of the 1890 decree, but most did not realize this and would seek their emancipation via the missionaries.

[110] Cooper, 1980, chap. 2.

[111] PNA AI1/34, Civil Case No. 986 of 1928.

Swahili coast and show that this form did exist on Pemba. The genealogy connected to Ali's will is complex, indicating the complicated familial arrangements in Zanzibari communities. It is necessary to look at the generation before Ali to understand the dynamics after his death. Ali's father, Sababu, had at some point been a slave to an elite Arab family, but he was manumitted around the 1870s. Sababu was an *mzalia* – a person born into slavery on the coast – an important distinction made in Swahili coast families.[112] Because he was born to the house, he was raised within the household, trained in a profession, and given his freedom as a young adult, whereupon he became a *hadim* of the el-Mauli family. Sababu's sister, Amina, also received her freedom before the turn of the century.[113] The case files do not mention whether Sababu owned slaves after his freedom, but Amina purchased slaves, indicating that she was financially able to do so. The links to their owner's family gave Sababu and Amina caché in Pemban society, so much so that Sababu's granddaughter had no qualms about admitting her slave heritage in 1928 because with it she was able to claim links to the el-Mauli family, a powerful Arab clan on the island. Thus the links to a powerful family remained beneficial to some ex-slaves well into the twentieth century. However, these ties were traced back over sixty years of freedom and held a very different meaning than for those who had only recently received their emancipation between 1897 and 1909 and who had been field slaves. Most former slaves on Pemba were not linked to powerful families and raised within the household. The case in point comes from the generation after Sababu and Amina and their own slaves, who were not owned by a powerful Arab clan but by ex-slaves.

In the 1880s, Amina's female slave, Bahati, asked permission to marry another slave named Kheri. Amina, who viewed enslavement through her own experience, where the slave owner acted as a patri/matriarch to the "family" of slaves, allowed Bahati to marry, and encouraged the couple to settle nearby. Amina asked her brother Sababu to allow the married couple to live on his land, which he gladly did because it meant that he could call on Kheri's labor on occasion, even though he was a slave of

---

[112] I make this assumption because Sababu knew his blood sister and continued to live near her until his death. I have not found examples of cases where blood siblings were enslaved together and then able to remain together. I have found a case of blood siblings who found each other after their emancipation, but they returned to the mainland together and did not stay within Swahili society.

[113] In this case, many of the people were not named, so I give them place marker names for ease of reading. Thus Sababu's sister was never named in the case file, and I use Amina to represent her.

someone else. When Sababu died, his property went to his only child, Ali, who continued to allow Kheri, Bahati, and their children to reside on the property. Ali treated Kheri's three sons as family servants, with all the privileges and obligations attendant to their position, replicating the form of enslavement in which Sababu and Amina had been raised. Sometime between 1897 and the end of slavery in 1909, Bahati, Kheri, and their children were freed.

Regardless of status, the relationship between Ali and Kheri was certainly close, and as Kheri's sons became adults, they built houses on Ali's property and made a permanent home for themselves there. As a lawyer later argued in court, Kheri's sons "were just like [Ali's] slaves who were born there among his children; and therefore they were not interfered with as regards their stay in this *shamba* [land]." Ali continued the tradition of patronage of slaves and ex-slaves found among the el-Mauli, who had raised his own father and aunt. According to a number of witnesses, Ali made an agreement with two of Kheri's sons, Hamadi and Juma, that if they planted trees on Ali's land where they lived, then Ali would divide the land between them and himself. This process, called *nusu-bin-nusu* ("half and half"), allowed landowners access to free labor in exchange for turning unprofitable land into property with value. It was a means for Ali to offer patronage toward Hamadi and Juma while still putting them in a servile position to himself. This agreement was made around 1906 or 1907, at which point most slaves were treated as free individuals on the islands, so Ali may have had difficulty paying for labor to develop his land. By agreeing to have Hamadi and Juma plant clove trees, Ali was able to expand his clove crops and profits with little economic output. The relationship between Ali, Kheri, and the sons Hamadi and Juma was one of benign patronage that had economic benefits for the former slaves. Yet, as shown later, in the generation of Ali's daughter and Kheri's sons, the notion of nineteenth-century benign patronage broke down.

However, the ties of kinship or patronage as claimed by slaves in the nineteenth century to their owners was often less connected than the experiences of Sababu and Amina or even Fundi Kamna, who was mentioned in Chapter 2. The case of Kichipele Mrashi indicates a bond of kinship between a former slave and a slave owner, but it was not with her own owner that she formed this bond. Mrashi died on October 10, 1910, leaving an estate that included four pieces of land and two houses.[114] One piece of land included forty-six clove and twenty-six coconut

---

[114] PNA AK1/76, October 1910.

trees, providing her a small income during her lifetime. She also owned three pieces of "bush" land, which usually meant it had a sandy soil and was mostly used for planting cassava, a food commonly eaten among ex-slaves on the island. Her ownership of two houses meant that she generated additional income through rent. Mrashi was not a wealthy woman, but she was a person of some means at her death. Moreover, she had been a landowner for a long time because the records show that she gave her husband, Fundi Idi, a piece of land in 1892. Much like Sababu and Amina, Mrashi's experience of slavery allowed her to consider purchasing her own slave. But also demonstrating the ideal of benign ownership (an ideal much ballyhooed by colonial officials), Mrashi gave a piece of land to her own slave, Mapili, in 1906 at the time she manumitted her. Clearly, Mrashi used land to solidify the relationships between herself and those who were important to her.

Mrashi did not leave money to her former owner; instead, in her 1906 will Mrashi left several bequests to the relatives of her husband's owner. She left a small sum to Maua binti Nasor bin Khalef, the sister of Idi's owner, and designated Maua's father, Nasor bin Khalef, to be an executor for the will. Neither Maua nor Nasor would have been eligible under colonial probate rules to inherit from Mrashi because they were neither blood nor marital relatives to her. Thus Mrashi used her will to bind them to her and Idi as networked members of their family. It also suggests that while former slaves may have claimed kinship to their former owners, they were just as likely to build ties to other powerful people in their communities.

These examples show ex-slaves who experienced a form of enslavement that had positive connotations for them, so much so that they went on to purchase slaves for themselves, who they also manumitted in a fashion similar to their own manumission. However, the records also show that many slaves stayed with their owners for a variety of reasons other than loyalty to a benign patriarch or social prestige. Two-thirds of the children who sought their freedom and attended mission schools had family members who remained enslaved, pointing to the different moments of emancipation within one family, even within a generation. For example, Mbwewe, a slave boy, came to the Friends mission school with his father. Mbwewe's father, named Mabruki, was too old and frail to work anymore. Both the father and son received their freedom through the government, yet Mbwewe's little sister, Cha Usiku, remained enslaved to her mistress. Mabruki only left his owner because she no longer provided for him. Mabruki was reliant on Mbwewe, an eight-year-old boy, and the other slaves on the property for food and shelter.[115] Cha Usiku, who was only six or seven years old, had few options and feared leaving her owner. Mbwewe ended up as a boarder at the Friends boys' school, and Mabruki moved into the refuge for the infirm and disabled run by the Friends, so Cha Usiku could not remain with either of them. Another of the students at the school, Mnubi, sought his freedom, but his mother and three siblings all remained with their owner, of whom they "were in awe."[116] These examples involve slaves who had young children to care for or were young children themselves and who had limited economic possibilities, which influenced their decision to remain enslaved.

Examining the life histories of slaves who ended up living at the Friends mission, it is clear that many slaves remained with owners who they felt were "good" because they both had nowhere else to go and feared trying to leave. Mamba, who hated being a slave, learned the hard way what could happen to a slave without a place to go when he fled a "good" owner. He was quickly captured, reenslaved, and sold to an owner who regularly beat him.[117] His experience was one that many slaves feared. Freedom did not necessarily mean being free from fear and economic insecurity, which was a reason why people may have remained with an owner who, at the very least, was seen as offering some level of security because freedom for many meant increased vulnerability. Once emancipation became a legal possibility for slaves, if their owner sold them (illegally) or they were inherited by the owner's children and they did not like the new owners, they left.[118] Many of the slaves interviewed by the Friends missionaries did not leave their owners until 1904 to 1912, well after most of those who sought government emancipation. This shows that social and economic security was a significant reason slaves remained with owners, and as soon as that security disappeared, slaves sought emancipation. Moreover, slave parents' "longing" for their children to receive a Western education indicates their vision of a nonenslaved future for their children.[119]

Following emancipation, slave owners who were angry about the loss of their slaves, power, and honor, which were all attendant with the loss of patronage, sought new ways to exert their control over former slaves.

---

[115] FIM PZ(F)/3, Diary of boys home 1902–1906.

[116] FIM PZ(F)/3, Diary of boys home 1902–1906, July 30, 1903, August 1, 1903.

[117] FIM TEMP MSS 419/1–7, Theodore Burtt, Notebook, 1899, Mamba.

[118] FIM TEMP MSS 419/1–7, Theodore Burtt, Notebook, 1899; see Mamba, Mlinao, Salama, Mama Chogo, Mama Taki, Bahati, Binti Farahani, and Tafarani for examples.

[119] FIM PZ(F)/3, Diary of boys home 1902–1906, March 2, 1903.

Violence against individual people was certainly one means, as well as stripping slaves of property as they received emancipation and forcing slaves into a position of economic insecurity as they moved into freedom. However, another significant means that developed well into the 1920s and is not treated in much of the scholarly literature on slavery involved owners claiming kinship to their former slaves. Kinship could be claimed in a variety of ways. The first was based on the relationship of *wala* discussed in Chapter 4, which allowed owners to claim the remains of a former slaves' estates.[120] However, in some cases *wala* was used to keep a slave from devolving property onto his or her heirs. In other parts of the Swahili coast, Islamic judges still upheld *wala* into the 1920s, allowing an owner to inherit all his or her former slaves' land.[121] The judges argued that the slaves were not freed by their owners but by decree of the government; therefore, according to Islamic law, they were still slaves and must follow the legal precedents that technically any property "owned" by a slave belonged to the owner. This remained a problem for slaves after their emancipation on Pemba as well.[122] Yet British officials after 1909 were keen to keep ex-owners from usurping the property of their ex-slaves. In 1928, Kombo bin Khamis claimed to be the brother of Juma bin Khamis, who had recently died.[123] Juma had gained his emancipation many years before from his owner, Rashid bin Nasur el-Kharusi. Rashid came to the court to testify on behalf of Kombo, whom he described as his slave – nineteen years after the full emancipation order – and said that the two were brothers. It is very possible that Rashid was trying to get access to Juma's estate because he had no heirs to contest the claims of Kombo.[124]

---

[120] Bakhtiar, 1996, p. 289; Anderson, 1970, p. 378, for Zanzibar-specific cases.

[121] Anderson, 1970, p. 118; see also the case of Raschid bin Abdulla and another vs. Administrator General, originally heard in 1924 in the Kathi court at Chake Chake, appeal heard January 28, 1925, found in *Law Reports Containing Cases Determined by the High Court for Zanzibar and on Appeal Therefrom by the Court of Appeal for Eastern Africa and by the Privy Council*, Vol. III, 1923–1927, compiled by Sir T. S. Tomlinson and G. K. Knight-Bruce (London: Waterlow and Sons Limited, 1928), p. 32; see Strobel, 1979, p. 51, n. 30, for examples of slave owners who tried to claim the property of their ex-slaves into the 1920s. She cites cases dated 1912 and 1942; Cooper 1977, p. 236.

[122] ZNA AC8/7, January 19, 1904. Another tactic of kinship found in Mombasa by Strobel was of owners and kadhi refusing to marry ex-slaves who had been freed by the government rather than their owners; Strobel, 1979, pp. 52–3.

[123] PNA AK1/2165, November 1926.

[124] Real resentment, especially among Arabs, existed against the probate court, which taxed the estates of all deceased and interfered with the distribution of inheritances.

Likewise, when Baraka Mnyasa died in May 1910, he left three plots of land with a total of 163 clove and 20 coconut trees plus a house. In witness testimony from the probate court, we learn that Baraka had three stores and "a good many things in the house," including 350 pounds of rice.[125] The same witness said that he saw the executors of Baraka's will unearth nearly 450 rupees near Baraka's house after his death. Baraka had a wife, to whom he had bequeathed fifty clove trees in his will, but otherwise he had no other blood or marital heirs. A few days after his death, a man named Uledi bin Mnyasa came to the probate court claiming to be Baraka's brother. If he was indeed Baraka's brother, he would inherit all but the portion of trees Baraka designated for his wife. No direct testimony from the wife exists in the probate record, but she did hire a *wakil* to argue in the court that Baraka and Uledi were not brothers. The probate judge must have scared Uledi because he later stated that he and Baraka were not blood brothers but rather "brothers" in that they had the same slave owner.[126] Uledi tried using the linkage of enslavement and a common ethnicity (Nyasa) to claim kinship, but the English judge was unwilling to accept anything but blood relatives. Nonetheless, if Baraka's wife had accepted Uledi's claim, the judge would not have questioned it.[127]

But Uledi was not claiming the estate for himself, as he explained to the court; he had been offered money to make the claim. His former owner, Sudi bin Farazi el-Barhawi, testified to the court that Uledi and Baraka were "brothers," implicating him in the plot to get Baraka's estate.[128] The case of Baraka shows a real difference in the relationships that some ex-slaves had with their former owners, as well as those people they had been enslaved with. Contrary to the case of Kichipele Mrashi, where an ex-owner received property left to him by an ex-slave, the story of Baraka shows that many ex-slaves remained in the location of their enslavement but broke off ties with their owners.

Technically, neither of the two former owners claimed their slaves as kin. Neither said before a British judge, "I claim *wala*, and therefore

---

[125] PNA AK1/46, May 1910.

[126] Uledi pleaded to the court that "I am ignorant and beg your pardon."

[127] PNA AK1/1066, December 3, 1919. In this case, a woman claimed to be the mother of the deceased, which the daughter of the deceased contested, but the wife of the deceased did not contest. It was clear that the mother had adopted the deceased and raised him, which the wife recognized as a valid relationship.

[128] Baraka's lack of a relationship with his former owner indicates that he was manumitted by the state.

I should receive the remnants of the estate." But they also knew that the British would only accept blood ties or marriage partners as acceptable heirs to any estate. By presenting their other slaves as "brothers" to the deceased ex-slaves, they were trying to circumvent the legal question of blood ties required by the British probate judges. Moreover, if the two male slaves were "brothers" through their enslavement, it made a "father" of their owner, thus creating the claim of kinship by the owner. The genealogy of slavery allowed these owners a measure of public recognition of their "rights" to control their "slaves," even if the slaves had been emancipated by the government.

The will of Hashima binti Baraka, written in 1924, well after the British emancipation order, suggests a link between a former slave and owner, yet it is framed in terms of a financial transaction rather than as a claim for kinship.[129] According to the executor of her will (a man who was also an ex-slave), Hashima "directed in her Will that 20 clove trees in Shamba Mgeni-Maji be given to her owner Said bin Suleiman bin Abdulla El-Marhubi for the debt owed by her."[130] Clearly, Hashima had been able to go to Said bin Suleiman to borrow money from him, indicating that she continued to have a relationship with him. Hashima maintained her relationship with her former owner as an economic necessity rather than from affection. She used the framework of patronage to ask Said to lend her money and made an agreement that she would pay him back out of her estate. As discussed earlier in the section on networked kin, Hashima's will shows far more linkage to other ex-slaves than to her former owner, indicating that the ties between former slaves and owners in the twentieth century was shaped more by the position the ex-slave held in the owner's household before emancipation, the distance in time from emancipation, and the general benevolence of the former owner. Even one such as Said bin Suleiman, a powerful Arab who lent his former slave money, would not expect her to make claims of kinship with him if she was a field slave.[131] Even more so than Hashima, the case of Bahati binti Serenge, discussed in the section on concubines, illustrates the deterioration between owners and ex-slaves by 1930.[132] While she still needed to maintain economic ties to the man, she clearly had little

---

[129] PNA AK1/3310, August 1934.
[130] PNA AK1/3310, August 1934.
[131] Hashima's ethnicity, Mgindo, was a mainland ethnicity. This means that she was most likely either not born on the island or born to field slaves on the island who were not treated as *wazalia*.
[132] PNA AI1/44, HHSCZ, Civil Appeal No. 15 of 1934.

love left for someone with whom she once had a child. For her owner, the value of patronage connected to slavery had long lost its worth to him, and he gladly ended his responsibilities to his former slave by selling the land she lived on.

But it was not always the owner who broke off ties of kinship and patronage with their slaves. In some cases, it behooved slaves to break the ties. Coming back to the story of Ali bin Sababu that started this section, the response of Kheri's sons to Ali's daughter illuminates the ways and reasons that ex-slaves had for breaking their ties to former owners.[133] Within a year or two of making the verbal agreement to let Kheri's sons, Hamadi and Juma, clear and plant trees on Ali's land in exchange for half the land and trees, Ali died. When he died, Hamadi and Juma reported Ali's possessions to the probate court and continued to care for Ali's properties for the benefit of Ali's heirs, which included bringing the heirs food on a regular basis. All the heirs were women. Ali's mother was still alive, along with his four wives and an infant daughter, Fatuma. The number of Ali's wives indicates that he was either wealthy or unable to reproduce when he died. Very few men on Pemba had more than one or two wives. Given that Ali had only one infant daughter when he died, it is likely that his other wives had had difficulty with infertility or infant mortality, which were both common at the time. Nonetheless, these women were all placed in a vulnerable position because his daughter received the bulk of the estate. After a few years, the probate office took over the care of Ali's estate from Hamadi and Juma. It is not clear from the record if Hamadi and Juma made this request or if someone else did on behalf of Fatuma.

In 1928, Fatuma initiated a lawsuit against Hamadi and Juma claiming that they were living on her land and that she wanted possession of the land. Initially in the court case brought by Fatuma through her step-father, she identified Hamadi as "like an executor he was the man who was looking after the properties." However, Hamadi tried to side-step his previous relationship with Ali and Ali's family. Hamadi used a two-prong approach to the court case arguing that "we [he and Juma] did not keep the property for the plaintiff [Fatuma]" meaning that he did not act as an executor and that "this Ali bin Sababu had no right in the shamba whatever." Hamadi explained that first one man had been assigned executor, then another, and eventually it was taken over by the Administrator General. This shows that Hamadi had an intimate knowledge of who

---

[133] PNA AI1/34, Civil Case No. 986 of 1928.

was acting on behalf of Fatuma. Hamadi understood that if he could be proved as an executor, then he could be held responsible for a wide range of complaints from Fatuma. When Fatuma pleaded her case in court she testified that "since I reached the age of puberty I do not know how many things I have lost." Thus she was trying to expand her claim not only to the land itself but also to anything in her father's house. She did not know the name of her father's other wives, who could have claimed items twenty years previously. Hamadi knew that he could try to evade Fatuma's accusation that he had stolen from her father's estate, but the larger point of whether Ali had an interest in the land was going to be a difficult point to prove. This was so because Ali had been buried in a family cemetery on the land, proving that it had once belonged to him. In the end, the judge decided to side with Hamadi and Juma because they had lived on the land for approximately forty years. In previous generations, the two families were able to find mutual benefits in their relationships even after emancipation, but the ties that once bound the families of owners and slaves had begun to break down. Fatuma did not treat Hamadi and Juma with a patriarchal patronage, as her father had; thus the relationship held little value for them. Even though Fatuma continued to maintain her claim to ties with the el-Mauli family that had held her grandfather as a slave, it was because this relationship still offered a benefit of potential prestige. By the late 1920s and 1930s, few former slaves continued to seek a relationship with their former owners because most of the newer generations in the owners' families did not value these relationships, as seen when Fatuma sued Hamadi and Juma.

CONCLUSION

This chapter discusses three elements of kinship on Pemba among ex-slaves – the ways ex-slaves defined and created family ties, the ways in which the colonial state tried to define kinship, and the process by which former owners and slaves negotiated their bonds with one another. Throughout the process of family creation during enslavement and after emancipation, slaves, owners, and the colonial state all sought to define these relationships. Yet no single definition of kinship existed on Pemba, where people created relationships with one another based on linkages borne from social groups, economic necessity, and friendship, among other reasons. If anything, this chapter demonstrates the wide variety of relationships and the difficulty of making singular arguments about the kinship ties of ex-slaves in the postemancipation era.

Changes certainly occurred over time in terms of kinship among ex-slaves. The discussion of concubines, who the government was so adamant were "family," demonstrates the ability of women to resist concubinage, even against the colonial Abolition Decree. But it was the actions of missionaries and in some cases colonial officials that helped these women to reject their position as "little wives" to their owners. Perhaps female slaves could have resisted their position before the British colonial period, but the increasing efforts of women to resist concubinage indicate that this was a new phenomenon and a welcome one for some women. The ability of ex-slaves to write wills, recognizing their networked families, also was a significant change in how ex-slaves defined their kin. While they had developed similar relationships before emancipation, once freed, they had the right to legally solidify their friendships as kinships.

In the end, the ties of "kinship" as they were between owners and ex-slaves were so variable on Pemba that no one pattern explains every case. With the change to a free workforce, the value of the relationships between these groups shifted because owners no longer exerted direct control over their slaves and ex-slaves. The benefit of *heshima* derived from this control diminished in the postemancipation era. Yet the individuals in the preceding examples did continue to claim ties to each other in one form or another. During the expansion of a cash-based economy in the 1910s through 1930s, where access to property allowed a person respectability, the value of slavery-based kinship ties changed. If links between families offered the ability to gain economically or socially from each other, then the ties were maintained or claimed. However, if either side of the relationship lost value, it was repudiated by the side with the most to lose.

Conclusion

Understanding how the process of emancipation affected the lives of individuals on Pemba, especially ex-slaves, was the purpose of this book. Examining the life stories of ex-slaves and the many people they encountered in the processes of enslavement and emancipation demonstrates that in the late nineteenth century Pemba was a central transit spot along the Swahili coast connecting both the mainland of Africa and the wider Indian Ocean worlds. Slaves and elite alike may have viewed Pemba as a rural outpost; nonetheless, it still had been in regular communication via *dhows* with other parts of the Swahili coast. However, colonization of the islands by the British government and emancipation of slaves reversed this trend so that as Pembans entered the twentieth century, they saw their island become more cut off from the wider Indian Ocean world. No longer did *dhows* go from Zanzibar to Pemba to Mombasa and onward into the Indian Ocean because Pemba was no longer a depot for slaves. The demise of slavery effectively began the isolation of Pemba. Thus emancipation was a singularly important moment in the history of the island. However, many other elements came out of emancipation than simply isolation of the island.

The scholarship on resistance against colonizers and elite by marginalized populations is standard fare in African historical studies. Resistance did occur across the continent, but at the root of conflict with colonizing agents was an effort to lessen the vulnerabilities of day-to-day life. Little moments of resistance occurred every day, but these efforts demonstrate the desire of people across the East African coast to improve their lives and achieve access, even if only temporarily, to a modicum of power otherwise missing in their lives. When the British government colonized

Zanzibar, it changed the landscapes of power on the islands, especially on Pemba. Rather than using these changes to resist, slaves on Pemba found ways to accommodate the changes in their everyday lives. Slaves were able to use colonial officials and missionaries as sources to alleviate the vulnerabilities they faced. Women in particular found allies within the colonial and missionary communities. Yet women on Pemba did not become "feminists" in any sense of the word, but they did begin to resist the societal assumptions about what they should and could do with their lives. Thus woven throughout this book are the themes of changing positions for women and shifting power dynamics across the spectrum of Pemban society. People on Pemba did not wholly resist or acculturate to colonial changes; different groups accommodated changes in a variety of ways over time.

RESISTANCE OR VULNERABILITY AMONG WOMEN

Marcia Wright noted in her book on women and slavery in Central Africa that the sources she used emphasized the vulnerability of women. Ned Alpers, too, commented on the way the sources describing the lives of female slaves in the nineteenth century suggested that women were far more vulnerable than men both to enslavement and to control within patriarchal communities.[1] As Wright so succinctly described, "To be born a woman and to be dislodged from a conventional social setting in the late nineteenth century was to be exposed to the raw fact of negotiability."[2] Were slave women on Pemba also more vulnerable to the "raw fact of negotiability"? The life histories of slaves recorded by Friends missionaries suggest that male children were as likely as female children to be enslaved. However, adult women were kidnapped at levels that men simply were not. This begs the question, Were women more vulnerable than men? Or was the factor of vulnerability an issue of poverty in lands, family, and power? The stories from Pemba examined for this study show that both gender and poverty played into the problems men and women faced in terms of control. However, women were more likely to lack land, family, and power within their communities than men and consequently enter more often in the records as vulnerable communities. It was not necessarily their biology that made women more vulnerable, but the gendered positions within patriarchal societies that left women in a weaker

[1] Alpers, 1983, pp. 186–9.
[2] Wright, 1993, p. 43.

situation at the moments of famine and slave raiding, two of the most prevalent reasons for enslavement in East Africa.[3]

Legally, men were supposed to act as guardians for their female relatives, who were jural majors but were forced by maintaining respectability to use male interlocutors in the courts. Nonetheless, male relatives were more often a burden than a help to women on Pemba. Collectively owned land between siblings or wider families often was mortgaged to the benefit of male members of the family. Women often learned about the mortgages when the land was sold out from under them, and they were unceremoniously put off of it by the purchasing moneylender. At other times, male relatives used their position as representative of their female relatives to usurp ownership of property that belonged solely to their female relatives. The courts became an important site where women contested male relatives' efforts to take ownership of their property. While on occasion women were unable to win because they were in *purdah*, most women were very successful after 1910 in publicly chastising their brothers and other male relatives for taking their land.

The majority of ex-slaves on Pemba were women; thus they made up a sizable percentage of the population of Pemba island. Women certainly could marry into elite and freeborn households more easily than ex-slave men could. Nonetheless, it seems that many did not do so. All the ex-slave women living at the Friends mission were married to ex-slave men; moreover, even in the probate records most women who were ex-slaves were either widowed or married to ex-slave men, regardless of whether the women were still connected to elite families through patronage or not. Perhaps ex-slave women who married into freeborn families seamlessly blended into those families, but several cases suggest otherwise. Ex-slave women without living children who married freeborn men had little chance of receiving any inheritance from their husbands if other heirs could claim the property.

The role of concubinage is one accepted and even privileged in Islamic societies, yet women on Pemba began to resist this position in the late nineteenth and early twentieth centuries. Even before the emancipation order was issued, female slaves sought the help of the courts to avoid being made concubines. However, after the emancipation order, a flood of women claimed as concubines by their owners went to the Slavery Commissioner to gain their freedom. When they found the Slavery

---

[3] Wright, 1993, p. 2; see chapters in Henri Médard and Shane Doyle, eds., *Slavery in the Great Lakes Region of East Africa* (Athens: Ohio University Press, 2007).

Commissioner obdurate about their release, because concubines were exempted from the 1897 Abolition Decree, they allied themselves with the Friends missionaries in an effort to have choice about their position. Not all concubines joined this group, but at least 3 percent of the concubines on the island sought their freedom from what they considered an onerous position.[4] Concubines could not seek their freedom nor divorce their owners as wives could; thus the women who fought their status as concubines demonstrated that not all women accepted such a powerless position in their households or communities.

Women were also in a weaker position as they moved past the age of child bearing. While, as I noted in Chapter 6, women were clearly sought as marriage partners by men, once they could no longer bear children, their value as spouses declined. Men tended to marry women younger than themselves; therefore, men were more likely to remain married until their deaths, whereas women were not. Twice as many women as men in the probate records died without a living spouse. This indicates that ex-slave women may have been sought as marriage partners and could easily leave their husbands for another man, yet once they reached their late forties, the number of viable male partners dwindled. This also emphasized the vulnerability of women as they aged over men.

Yet, even with the weaker position of women in the patriarchal practices on Pemba, women of all statuses on the island began to assert their newfound access to the courts to take care of themselves rather than relying on male family members who were supposed to care for them. Women brought their male relatives to court in defense of their property, even when in previous years they had not done so. Women sought to create alliances with colonial officials and missionaries in an effort to escape the pervasive economic, social, and cultural control exerted by male relatives. Even young women such as Mzuri Kwao fought against positions they deemed unacceptable. Hashima binti Baraka's legacy to her female friends suggests that women did look out for one another and forged links that allowed them to alleviate the vulnerability associated with their gender and status. Thus the sources do tell tales of female vulnerability, but they also show women's incredible resourcefulness in their confrontations with patriarchy on the island. In this way, the opening up

---

[4] It is impossible to know exactly how many concubines were on the island. At one point, O'Sullivan-Beare hazarded the guess that 2,000 concubines resided on the island, but he acknowledged that it could be far fewer because he had no idea because concubines were generally secluded. At least sixty concubines sought their freedom, which is where I come up with 3 percent, but the percentage actually could be far higher.

of the courts was a huge help to women on Pemba and represents one of the shifts in the landscape of power on the island during the postemancipation era.

SHIFTING LANDSCAPES OF POWER

In many respects, the bulk of this book focuses on the changing power dynamics on the island – between men and women, between owners and slaves, between the colonial state and residents of Pemba, and between the visible and invisible worlds. Yet these shifts in the landscapes of power were not immediate, nor did they happen in obvious ways. Even emancipation did not bring abrupt changes to the island. The shifts in power occurred in more subtle ways through language, oral communication, ownership of land, participation in courts, practice of *uchawi*, and the little resistances of everyday life. Reputation in its many permutations was important in the ways in which power shifted. Large-scale shifts in reputation affected the relationships individuals had with one another. Thus the understanding that elites could no longer back up their threats with physical violence altered the ways in which other people responded to their power and reputations. Likewise, new means of creating reputations allowed ex-slaves the ability to access credit and change their status in their community.

Ustaarabu, or "Arabness," as a hegemonic ideal of civility and "civilization" continued to expand on Pemba, offering Arab elites cultural power in society. However, their political, social, and economic power as slave owners was gone. Some people continued to offer fealty to the families of their parents' (or even grandparents') owners. However, this was a cultural practice that was no longer supported through fear or the ability to control others. As in Martin Klein's study of French West Africa, many descendants of slaves continued to maintain links with the descendants of their owners' families – but only for the ability to call on these "owners" for help in difficult times.[5] These relationships had a very real economic element to the descendants of slaves, but they were framed through the prism of their cultural interactions rather than being an explicitly economic practice. The hegemony of *ustaarabu* in the Zanzibar Islands encouraged scholars to consider Arab elites as maintaining a strong cultural and social power over lower-status populations.[6] Nonetheless,

[5] Klein, 1998, pp. 239–41.
[6] Goldman, *passim*.

much as Laura Fair argues about ex-slaves in Zanzibar Town, ex-slaves on Pemba had their own ways of interpreting what was "civilized" and adapting the accoutrements of elite power to their own status needs.

Language changes on Pemba articulated the shifting power dynamics. For example, the shifting meaning of *heshima* from "honor" derived from the control of people to a "respectability" based on the reputation of individuals provides the most obvious demonstration of change in power relations on the island. When scholars of the islands have studied emancipation, they have looked at how many slaves sought their freedom and what that meant for the control of labor; works such as Frederick Cooper's books on labor along the Swahili coast suggest that the elite remained in power because slaves simply became squatters, a position lacking control over their lives.[7] Yet the shifting discourses of *heshima* and reputation are key indicators of the multifaceted changes that occurred on the island after emancipation. Ex-slaves may have been squatters, but elites no longer had full control over slaves or ex-slaves. The elite had to go to great lengths to keep the goodwill of their clients, a vulnerable position for the elite, reiterating the transition in the definition of *heshima*.

Heshima was not the only word that changed on the island, though. The different terminology for "slave" and "ex-slave" also indicates the difficulty Pembans and Zanzibaris had in creating new paradigms that incorporated the variety of societal positions on the island. Regardless of whether a person was a *hadim* who maintained a relationship with his or her owner or a *mateka* who was emancipated by the government in the end, both were legally free and had the same rights in the courts – to purchase land and to work for whom they wanted. *Hadim* may have had an easier time after emancipation than those treated as *mateka*, and just as slaves differentiated socially among themselves, ex-slaves also made distinctions. Yet, as both missionaries and government officials noted, by the early twentieth century, little distinction economically could be made between the two groups. Association with elite members of Pemban society did not necessarily mean wealth or power. *Mateka*, nonetheless, made efforts to conform to Pemban cultural practices through their adherence to Islamic practices, educating their children in *vyuo*, and dressing as proper Muslims. Both sides of the enslavement process ended up conforming to one another during the emancipation era, illustrating the changing landscapes of power at all levels of the social spectrum.

---

[7] Welliver; Cooper, 1977, 1980.

Despite the dramatic new emancipation laws, the inconsistency of their implementation in the courts made their impact difficult to discern. The British could compel the Islamic judges to hear the cases of slaves and women, but only the cases of which they were familiar. In the early years of the changes in the court systems, a roundabout method developed wherein slaves, ex-slaves, or women who took their complaints to the courts could be refused a hearing but then appeal to colonial officials or missionaries, at which point the British interlocutors could intercede on their behalf. However, no consistent policy existed on the books. As the British began consolidating their control over the courts, they still fell back from creating equalizing policies. The 1904 example of Mshangama, the slave who lost all his property when he sought emancipation from the government, set a policy for five years that continued to give slave owners considerable control over their slaves. The example of Mshangama, as well as the concubines discussed in Chapter 6, illustrates both the ways in which British officials exerted their power in their relationships with Islamic judges and the inconsistency of transformations in the colonial courts before 1910.

By 1910, the policies of the courts had been consolidated, and British magistrates took greater control over them. Women and men and slaves, ex-slaves, and owners all could bring cases to court without fear of rejection, although there was no guarantee of the outcome of the case. Again, even with the efforts by the colonial state to control the *makadhi* by giving magistrates more control and eventually abolishing the *liwali* position (in 1924), colonial officials could not predict the outcomes. Harold Ingrams' recollections of his first day as a magistrate, given in Chapter 3, demonstrate the inconsistency of the British courts. However, contrary to the wishes of colonial officials, the *kadhi* courts became an ideal location for women and ex-slaves to take their disputes with the elite. The *makadhi* resisted efforts by colonial officials to change the *sheria* rules of evidence, thus maintaining the preeminence of orality in the courts. By accepting British changes, such as giving women and slaves equal weight as witnesses, while rejecting others, such as the prohibition against using oaths as evidence, *makadhi* shifted power within society through the venue of the colonial courts.

The refusal by *makadhi* to end the use of oaths and the new opportunities afforded to ex-slaves and women in the courts made the *kadhi* courts into arbiters of reputation in the community. While community gossip continued to be an important site to contest reputations, the courts became an institutionalized route to respectability or social ruin.

Reputation increasingly offered individuals, regardless of social status, an important means of accessing credit and social support in the island communities. The orality of the *kadhi* courts merged with the expectations of local communities that a person staked his or her reputation on his or her statements. Declarations of "*Utaapa!*" ("upon your oath!") were only as good as the reputations of the speakers. The court was a central site at which a person's word and reputation were publicly confirmed or denied. This shifted power away from the elite as mediators of reputation into the wider community. As such, the *kadhi* courts became a location where ex-slaves challenged elite power.

WITCHCRAFT, POWER, AND SLAVERY

As discussed in Chapter 5, the scholarly focus on linking modernity to witchcraft and witch hunters in African societies does not explain how Pembans responded to *uchawi* and colonialism in the twentieth century. Contrary to the experience of West African societies, Pemba was not a site of slave export, except for the people kidnapped off the island by passing *dhow* captains. Typical of locations that were destinations for enslaved people from Africa, witch hunting was not a phenomenon viewed as necessary or desirable on Pemba. Since Pembans did not use witch hunters, after emancipation, elites could not use the threat of witch hunting to discipline ex-slaves and lower-status members of society. Thus accusations of practicing *uchawi* on Pemba were not a means for elites to regulate lower-status populations, although it was still a means of control because *wachawi* wielded considerable power on Pemba. Nonetheless, the ability to become *wachawi* was open to people across the social spectrum and offered new opportunities to a variety of people regardless of status or gender.

The invisible world of *uchawi* may have been a level playing ground for people living on Pemba, but it was still a site of resistance. Over the colonial period, *uchawi* transformed from witchcraft that could discipline individuals into one that Pembans viewed as disciplining the colonial state. As Pembans of all levels of society lost power to colonial officials and systems, the invisible world of *uchawi* expanded. By changing the landscapes of power on Pemba, the colonial state inadvertently drew together elites and poor, who found a common antagonist in colonial policies. It is this common inability to fully realize local authority within the colonial context that would bring all classes of people on Pemba together in an effort to change the landscape of power from one focused on the colonial state to one centered on local social and cultural beliefs and understandings of hierarchy. For this effort, Pembans looked to the invisible world of *uchawi*, a world that colonial officials could not see and most certainly did not fully understand, even when they tried.

WHY PEMBA?

In the end, court and missionary records cannot illuminate all aspects of the history of Pemba during the early twentieth century. Silences in the records leave obvious gaps in the story of emancipation. Nonetheless, existing records point to the fundamental shifts in the structures and meanings of power on the island. Colonialism had a significant impact on the lives of individuals on Pemba, yet it was what those individuals did with the colonial changes that shifted the manifestations of power on the island. The 1897 Abolition Decree could have been completely ignored by slaves and elites, and in many cases, it was disregarded. However, thousands of slaves took the opportunity to change their lives through emancipation, and as they did, it had a dramatic effect on the ways people related to one another on the island. Ex-slaves were not the only people on the island whose lives changed or who responded to the new colonial shifts in power. Rather than a decisive story about local elites collaborating with colonial officials, the history of Pemba finds accommodation and collaboration occurring across levels of society through precolonial Islamic beliefs and practices such as *uchawi*. The ongoing cooperation of social, economic, and cultural groups across the island helped to facilitate new identities beyond slave and elite, moving people into a localized identity of "Pemban-ness."

Bibliography

Primary Sources

Interviews

Absalla Omar Sharif, Pemba, October 29, 2002.
Ali Hamad Omar, Shengejuu, Pemba, October 30, 2002.
Ali Khamis Faraj, Shengejuu, Pemba, October 30, 2002.
Ali Rubea Makame, Pemba, October 29, 2002.
Bi Asha, Wete, Pemba, December 18, 2004.
Bishara Rashid Bakar, Shengejuu, Pemba, October 30, 2002.
Farashuu Suleiman, Tundauwa, Pemba, December 21, 2004.
Fatma Ali Hemed, Chasasa, Pemba, October 31, 2002.
Halima Rashid, Pandani, Pemba, December 11, 2004.
Iddi Ali Hamad, Junguni, Pemba, October 17, 2004.
Jamila Said Ali, Wete, Pemba, November 2, 2002.
Juma bin Hamad Tumbe, Pemba, November 2, 2002.
Mariam Mbarouk Khamis, Bopwe, Pemba, October 31, 2002.
Mattar Said Ahmed, Pemba, November 10, 2004.
Mayasa Hamad Kombo, Bopwe, Pemba, October 31, 2002.
Mbarouk Seif Ali, Pemba, October 28, 2002.
Mohamed Mbwana Mserembwe, Pemba, October 29, 2002.
Muhammed Khamisi, Mtambile, Pemba, November 10, 2004.
Mzee Mohamed, Mtambile, Pemba, December 24, 2004.
Mzee Suliman, Konde, Pemba, October 29, 2002.
Shaame Othman Ali, Pemba, November 3, 2002.
Suleiman Hamad Suleiman, Pemba, October 29, 2002.

House of Commons, Parliamentary Papers

No. 101 (1885), *Correspondence with British Representatives and Agents Abroad, and Reports from Naval Officers and the Treasury Relative to the Slave Trade.*

Africa No. 1 (1889), *Further Correspondence Respecting Germany and Zanzibar*.
Africa No. 6 (1895), *Correspondence Respecting Slavery in Zanzibar*.
Africa No. 7 (1896), *Correspondence Respecting Slavery in the Zanzibar Dominions*.
Africa No. 6 (1898), *Correspondence Respecting the Abolition of the Legal Status of Slavery in Zanzibar and Pemba*.
Africa No. 4 (1901), *Correspondence Respecting Slavery and the Slave Trade in East Africa and the Islands of Zanzibar and Pemba*.
Africa No. 6 (1902), *Correspondence Respecting Slavery and the Slave Trade in East Africa and the Islands of Zanzibar and Pemba*.
Africa No. 14 (1904), *Correspondence Respecting Slavery in the Islands of Zanzibar and Pemba*.
Africa No. 4 (1909), *Despatch from His Majesty's Agent and Consul-General at Zanzibar Furnishing a Report on the Administration, Finance, and General Condition of the Zanzibar Protectorate*.

Newspapers

The London Times, UK.
The Daily Mail, UK.
The Anti-Slavery Report, UK.
The Zanzibar Gazette, Zanzibar.

Friends House Library, London (FIM)

Friends Industrial Mission, Annual Report for 1912.
Friends Industrial Mission, Annual Report for 1913.
Friends Industrial Mission, Annual Report for 1914.
Friends Industrial Mission, PZ(F)/3, Register of slaves, Banani, 1897–1909.
Friends Industrial Mission, PZ(F)/3, Diary of boys home, 1902–1906.
Friends Industrial Mission, PZ(F)/3, Meeting minute book for 1898–1902.
Friends Industrial Mission, PZ(F)/3, Meeting minute book for 1903–1915.
Friends Industrial Mission, PZ(F)/3, Committee of missionaries, 1916–1932.
Friends Industrial Mission, P2/F/, Committee of missionaries, 1933–.
TEMP MSS 419/1–7, Theodore Burtt, Notebook, 1899.
TEMP MSS 419, Private letters of Theodore Burtt, 1908–1909.
"Abolition of Slavery in Zanzibar," *The Friend* (British), September 1, 1890.
"The Story of Msichoke," *The Friend* (British), October 3, 1902, pp. 644–6.
"Visit of Sir Arthur Hardinge," *The Friend* (British), April 27, 1900, p. 253.
"Letter from Armitage Detailing Further Developments in Case of Msichoke," *The Friend* (British), November 7, 1902, p. 738.
"The Story of Msichoke," *The Friend* (British), November 14, 1902, p. 747.
"Pemba," *The Friend* (British), September 5, 1902, pp. 578–88.

National Archives (Formerly the Public Records Office), London (PRO)

CO618/43/14, Rioting in Zanzibar, 1928.
CO618/47/16, Disturbance at central prison, 1926.

CO618/52/9, Deportation of H. Lister from USA to UK.

CO691/126/10, Death penalty, murder and witchcraft, 1932.

CO847/13/11, Laws relating to witchcraft, 1938.

DO35/4158, The Jones Report on ritual murder in Basutoland, 1953.

FO2/188, Despatches to and from the Consul General Zanzibar, 1898.

FO2/284, Despatches to and from the Consul General Zanzibar, 1900.

FO84/1417, Euan-Smith to Foreign Office, July 31, 1875.

FO107/108, Mr. R. G. Edib's charges against the Zanzibar Slavery Administration, 1899.

FO107/111, Jurisdiction in Pemba, 1897–1901.

FO367/25, Police strike, 1906.

FO881/9209, Distress in Pemba, 1906.

FO881/9334, Glossary of terms in reports.

FO881/10268X, Annual report for Zanzibar, 1909 and 1910.

Rhodes House, Oxford (UMCA)

Universities Mission to Central Africa, A1 (XIV), No. 54, "The Two Thieves of Pemba," by Leslie Matolo, a translation from Swahili, n.d.

Universities Mission to Central Africa, A1 (XIV), No. 51, Herbert Armitage to Rev. Duncan Travers, Pemba, March 16, 1903.

Universities Mission to Central Africa, A1 (XIII), No. 214, Hines to Travers, Pemba, May 19, 1904.

Universities Mission to Central Africa, A1 (XIII), No. 216, Hines to Travers, Pemba, May 30, 1904.

Universities Mission to Central Africa, A1 (XIII), No. 252, Hines to Travers, Wete, February 23, 1905.

Universities Mission to Central Africa, E2 Emily Key, "Notes from Pemba," January 18, 1898.

Zanzibar National Archives, Tanzania (ZNA)

AA12/4, Confidential Report on Indian Slave Holdings in Pemba, 1875.

AB1/1, Report to Mr. Clarke, April 22, 1910.

AB1/369, District Commissioner, Pemba, 1937.

AB31/20, Witchcraft in Pemba, 1910–1917.

AB70/3, Disturbances Created by Manga Arabs at Wete, 1928–1941.

AC2/24, Vice Consul Pemba, Letters.

AC5/1, Vice Consul Pemba, Letters.

AC5/2, Vice Consul Pemba, Letters.

AC5/3, Vice Consul Pemba, Letters.

AC5/4, Vice Consul Pemba, Letters.

AC5/5, Vice Consul Pemba, Letters.

AC7/26, Vice Consul Pemba, Court Register.

AC8/5, Vice Consul Pemba, Letters.

AC8/7, Vice Consul Pemba, Letters.

AC8/8, Vice Consul Pemba, Letters.

AC8/9, Vice Consul Pemba, Letters.

AC9/2, Vice Consul Pemba, Letters.

AM13/1, General Deeds from Pemba, 1893–1929 (in Arabic).

AM14/1, General Deeds from Pemba, 1893–1929 (in Arabic).

AP26/160, Clove Growers Association Receivership File for Salima binti Khamis bin Isa Miskery.

AP29/5–8, Bonus Scheme Registers, Chake Chake Districts.

BA34/2, Report of Native Census, 1924.

Pemba Branch of Zanzibar National Archives (PNA)

AI1/2, His Highness's Court for Zanzibar and Pemba (hereafter HHCZP), Appeal Case No. 11 of 1918, Khalid bin Marenge Shirazi vs. Mohamed bin Juma el Rassadi.

AI1/4, HHCZP, Appeal Case No. 2 of 1920, Juma bin Ahmed Swahili vs. Mwana Kombo binti Said Nabahani.

AI1/5, HHCZP, Appeal Case No. 4 of 1920, Fatuma binti Dadi vs. Seif bin Hassan.

AI1/6, HHCZP, Appeal Case No. 5 of 1920, Idi bin Haji vs. Ahamed bin Khalfan.

AI1/7, HHCZP, Appeal Case No. 5 of 1920, Mame Saifu, Mwana Asha, and Salima binti Ahmed bin Juma el-Swahili vs. Ismail bin Fakih and Mvitanga Swahili.

AI1/12, HHCZP, Appeal Case No. 10 of 1920, Kombo bin Makurizo of Chanjani vs. Hilal bin Amur.

AI1/14, HHCZP, Appeal Case No. 13 of 1920, Mwajuma binti Abud of Mkanjuni vs. Khamis bin Nadhar.

AI1/19, HHSC, Civil Case District Court at Weti, No. 673 of 1919, Hasina binti Nasibu vs. Abed bin Said el Mayyahi of Jambaji.

AI1/20, HBM District Registry of High Court for Pemba, Civil Case No.16 of 1926, Abdulhussein Mussaji vs. Mohamed bin Muhijaji bin Mzee el-Bajuni.

AI1/21, High Court for Zanzibar, Civil Case No. 189 of 1920, Khamis bin Hathar Freed Slave of Ebrahim bin Msondo vs. Labuda bin Suroor Freed Slave of Bani Riany, Juma binti Abood (Ex-Wife of Labuda), Makame bin Labuda, Mwana Mkoo binti Labuda.

AI1/34, HBMCZ FCS Court, Chake Chake Civil Case No. 986 of 1928, Fatuma binti Ali bin Sababu vs. Hamadi Kheri and Juma Kheri.

AI1/44, HHSCZ, Civil Appeal No. 15 of 1934, Bahati binti Serenge vs. Mohamed bin Musa bin Burhan Shirazi.

AI1/58, HHSCZ, in the Court of Kathi Sheikh Abdulrahim bin Mahmoud, Mkoani, Civil Case No. 8 of 1933, Sanda binti Ali bin Salim by Her Attorney Mohammed bin Issa bin Salim el-Menthri vs. Suleiman bin Abdalla el-Mazuri and Rashid bin Abdulla el-Mazrui.

AI1/76, HBMCZ, District Registry of the High Court, Civil Case No. 17 of 1934, Abdulla bin Ali el-Hinawi and Others vs. the Administrator General and Other.

AI1/77, HHSCZ, in the court of Kathi Sheikh Said bin Nasor, Civil Case No. 189 of 1934, Asha binti Seif bin Hamed el-Ismailia, Represented by Ahmed bin Kheri (*Wakil*) vs. Abdulla bin Salim el-Ismaili.

AI1/78, HHCZ, the District Registry of the High Court, Appeal No. 10 of 1934, Mariam binti Khamis bin Bakari el-Mafazi vs. Hamadi bin Shame

AI1/89, HHSCZ, in the Resident Magistrates Court, Chake Chake, Civil Case No. 135 of 1952, Salim bin Ahmed bin Juma al-Mazrui vs. Muhenne bin Ahmed bin Juma Mazrui.

AI1/90, HHCZ, the Resident Magistrate's Court Pemba, Civil Case No. 136 of 1952, Athman bin Bakari vs. Salim bin Rashid el-Husni.

No accession number: Kadhi's Court, Wete, Civil Case No. 253 of 1945, Hamida binti Athman vs. Abdulla bin Omar and Athman bin Omar.

No accession number: Kadhi's Court, Chake Chake, Civil Case No. 263 of 1945, Said bin Suleiman Bajuni vs. Omar bin Juma Swahili.

No accession number: HHCZ, the District Registry of High Court Pemba, Appeal No. 6 of 1946, Jokha binti Abdulla el-Maskria vs. Mbaruk bin Abeid el-Mahrusi.

AK1/46, Probate record of Baraka Mnyasa, May 1910.

AK1/50, Probate record of Zubeda binti Yakuti, May 26, 1910.

AK1/52, Probate record of Bakari bin Faki, May 21, 1910.

AK1/54, Probate record of Zuwalia hadim Kukas, June 1910.

AK1/55, Probate record of Ali bin Mohamed Bashmak, June 5, 1909.

AK1/57, Probate record of Hadia binti Uledi, July 5, 1910.

AK1/58, Probate record of Mabruk Wadi Sunizani, July 1910.

AK1/61, Probate record of Khamis Alawi Mpemba, July 24, 1910.

AK1/63, Probate record of Said bin Hamed bin Ali Lemki, August 21, 1909.

AK1/68, Probate record of Mohamed bin Abdullah Mendiri, August 1910.

AK1/71, Probate record of Mohamed Hemed Sawafi, May 1910.

AK1/76, Probate record of Kichipele Mrashi, October 1910.

AK1/77, Probate record of Fundi Feruzi bin Mkelef, October 1910.

AK1/80, Probate record of Bakari Fakih Bakari, November 14, 1910.

AK1/86, Probate record of Binti Hemed bin Suleiman, December 20, 1910.

AK1/197, Probate record of Kombo Usi, August 24, 1912.

AK1/198, Probate record of Ferezi hadim Sirkari, September 16, 1912.

AK1/200, Probate record of Abdalla bin Omar Swahili, July 8, 1912.

AK1/206, Probate record of Fundi Haji bin Sharbo, August 25, 1912.

AK1/321, Probate record of Hamadi wadi Nasibu, June 11, 1913.

AK1/322, Probate record of Haji bin Githenge, July 1913.

AK1/323, Probate record of Manashamba binti Hadidi Swahili, January 1914.

AK1/325, Probate record of Omari bin Omari Swahili, January 1914.

AK1/330, Probate record of Shaibu bin Juma, February 25, 1914.

AK1/332, Probate record of Chousiku bin Abdalla, February 1914.

AK1/333, Probate record of Mwana Kiamu binti Sholi, March 1914.

AK1/334, Probate record of Musa Mchanja, March 1914.

AK1/337, Probate record of Said bin Abed bin Said, March 1914.

AK1/338, Probate record of Rashid bin Geuar, February 1914.

AK1/565, Probate record of Kingwaba wadi Salmini, June 3, 1917.
AK1/1066, Probate record of Khamisini Manyema, December 1919.
AK1/1074, Probate record of Ali bin Juma Swahili, December 1919.
AK1/1639, Probate record of Ali bin Abdalla el-Hinawi, 1923.
AK1/1643, Probate record of Rehandi bin Amani, December 10, 1925.
AK1/1987, Probate record of Msengesi wadi Shoma Mnyaturu, January 1926.
AK1/1989, Probate record of Yusuf bin Kombo Mswahili, January 1926.
AK1/1993, Probate record of Waziri bin Khamis el-Murimi, November 1925.
AK1/2165, Probate record of Juma Khamis Mgindo, November 1926.
AK1/2184, Probate record of Abdulrahman bin Idarus el-Maalawi, October 1926.
AK1/2186, Probate record of Saleh bin Kombo Swahili, October 1926.
AK1/2187, Probate record of Chuma bin Khamis Swahili, August 1926.
AK1/2188, Probate record of Ulaiti binti Musa Swahili, November 1926.
AK1/2614, Probate record of Mabruki bin Ladi Manyema, October 1928.
AK1/2773, Probate record of Alley bin Usi Mtumbatu, June 1928.
AK1/2777, Probate record of Subeti bin Juya Mdigo, July 1930.
AK1/3097, Probate record of Hamed bin Salim bin Abdulla el-Mazrui, March 1933.
AK1/3310, Probate record of Hashima binti Baraka Mgindo, August 1934.
AK1/3315, Probate record of Bahati binti Muya Manyema, November 1935.
AK1/3683, Probate record of Tofilli wadi Zaid, June 1938.
AK1/3690, Probate record of Mzee bin Bora, March 1938.
AK1/4195, Probate record of Mmanga binti Khamis el-Husunia, 1945.
AK1/4197, Probate record of Muweza binti Khamis Mhiyao, April 1941.
AK1/4207, Probate record of Mwanaache binti Haji, September 1941.
AK1/4209, Probate record of Deluu binti Simba Mhiyao, November 1941.
AK1/4210, Probate record of Juma bin Khamis Shirazi, October 1941.
AK1/4219, Probate record of Fadhil bin Khamis Ngazija, September 1942.
AK1/4220, Probate record of Mussa bin Muhamed, October 1940.
AK1/4574, Probate record of Kombo bin Mussa bin Faki Shirazi, January 1944.
AK1/4579, Probate record of Suleiman bin Salim bin Mohamed el-Bimani, February 1944.
AK1/5026, Probate record of Amani bin Hamadi bin Amani Shirazi, September 1946.
AK1/5029, Probate record of Hamad bin Musa bin Hamadi el-Bahasani, September 1947.

Published Reports

Annual Report of the Judicial Department (Zanzibar: Zanzibar Protectorate, 1911–1925).
A Guide to Zanzibar (Zanzibar: Government Printer, 1949).
A Note on Agricultural Indebtedness in the Zanzibar Protectorate, 1936.
Report by Vice Consul O'Sullivan on the Island of Pemba, 1896–97 (London: Harrison and Sons, 1898).

Report by Vice Consul O'Sullivan on the Island of Pemba, 1898 (London: Harrison and Sons, 1899).

Report by Vice Consul O'Sullivan on the Island of Pemba, 1899 (London: Harrison and Sons, 1900).

Wilson, F. B. *Report of the Commission Appointed to Investigate Rural Education in the Zanzibar Protectorate.* Zanzibar: Government Printer, 1939.

Zanzibar Protectorate. *Administrative Reports for the Year 1915.* Zanzibar: Government Printer, 1916.

Administrative Reports for the Year 1918. Zanzibar: Government Printer, 1919.

Administrative Reports for the Year 1919. Zanzibar: Government Printer, 1920.

Administrative Reports for the Year 1921. Zanzibar: Government Printer, 1922.

Report on the Commission of Enquiry Concerning the Riot in Zanzibar on the 7th of February, 1936. Zanzibar: Government Printer, 1936.

Secondary Sources and Published Primary Sources

Abdulaziz, Mohamed H. *Muyaka: 19th Century Swahili Popular Poetry.* Nairobi: Kenya Literature Bureau, 1979.

Abdurahman, Muhammed. "Anthropological Notes from the Zanzibar Protectorate," *Tanganyika Notes and Records* 8 (1939), 59–84.

Abu-Lughod, Lila. *Veiled Sentiments: Honor and Poetry in a Bedouin Society.* Berkeley: University of California Press, 1986.

Agmon, Iris. *Family and Court: Legal Culture and Modernity in Late Ottoman Palestine.* Syracuse, NY: Syracuse University Press, 2006.

Akehurst, F. R. P. "Good Name, Reputation, and Notoriety in French Customary Law," in *Fama: The Politics of Talk and Reputation in Medieval Europe*, edited by Thelma Fenster and Daniel Lord Smail, pp. 75–94. Ithaca, NY: Cornell University Press, 2003.

Aley, Juma. *Zanzibar in the Context.* New Delhi: Lancers Books, 1988.

Allen, Julia. "Slavery, Colonialism and the Pursuit of Community Life: Anglican Mission Education in Zanzibar and Northern Rhodesia 1864–1940," *History of Education* 37, no. 2 (March 2008), 207–26.

Allen, Richard B. "The Mascarene Slave-Trade and Labour Migration in the Indian Ocean During the Eighteenth and Nineteenth Centuries," in *The Structure of Slavery in Indian Ocean, Africa and Asia*, edited by Gwyn Campbell, pp. 33–50. London: Routledge, 2004.

Alpers, Edward. *Ivory and Slaves in East Central Africa: Changing Pattern of International Trade in East Central Africa to the Later Nineteenth Century.* Berkeley: University of California Press, 1975.

"Story of Swema," in *Women and Slavery in Africa*, edited by Claire Robertson and Martin Klein, pp. 185–99. Madison: University of Wisconsin Press, 1983.

Anderson, Benedict. *Imagined Communities: Reflections on the Origin and Spread of Nationalism*, revised edition. London: Verso, 1991.

Anderson, J. N. D. *Islamic Law in Africa.* London: Cass, 1970.

Arnold, Nathalie. "Wazee Wakijua Mambo! Elders Used to Know Things!: Occult Powers and Revolutionary History in Pemba, Zanzibar." Ph.D. dissertation, Indiana University, 2003.

Ashforth, Adam. *Witchcraft, Violence, and Democracy in South Africa*. Chicago: University of Chicago Press, 2005.

Askew, Kelly. "Female Circles and Male Lines: Gender Dynamics along the Swahili Coast," *Africa Today* 46, nos. 3–4 (1999), 67–102.

Austen, Ralph. "The Moral Economy of Witchcraft: An Essay in Comparative History," in *Modernity and Its Malcontents: Ritual and Power in Postcolonial Africa*, edited by Jean Comaroff and John Comaroff, pp. 89–110. Chicago: University of Chicago Press, 1993.

Bakari, Mtoro bin Mwinyi. *The Customs of the Swahili People: The Desturi za Waswahili of Mtoro bin Mwinyi Bakari and Other Swahili Persons*, edited and translated by J. W. T. Allen. Berkeley: University of California Press, 1981.

Bakhtiar, Laleh. *Encyclopedia of Islamic Law: A Compendium of the Major Schools*. Chicago: ABC International Group, 1996.

Bang, Anne K. *Sufis and Scholars of the Sea: Family Networks in East Africa, 1860–1925*. London: RoutledgeCurzon, 2003.

"Cosmopolitanism Colonised? Three Cases from Zanzibar, 1890–1920," in *Struggling with History: Islam and Cosmopolitanism in the Western Indian Ocean*, edited by Edward Simpson and Kai Kresse, pp. 167–88. New York: Columbia University Press, 2008.

Baron, Beth. *Egypt as a Woman: Nationalism, Gender, and Politics*. Berkeley: University of California Press, 2005.

Beachey, R. W. *The Slave Trade of Eastern Africa*. London: Rex Collings, 1976.

Becker, Felicitas. *Becoming Muslim in Mainland Tanzania, 1890–2000*. Oxford: Oxford University Press for the British Academy, 2008.

Beech, Mervyn W. H. *Aids to the Study of Ki-Swahili: Four Studies Compiled and Annotated*. London: K. Paul, Trench, Trubner, 1918.

Behrend, Heike, and Ute Luig, eds. *Spirit Possession: Modernity and Power in Africa*. Oxford, James Currey, 1999.

Bellville, Alfred. "Journey to the Universities' Mission Station of Magila, on the Borders of the Usambara Country," *Proceedings of the Royal Geographical Society of London* 20, no. 1 (1878), 74–8.

Bennett, Norman. *A History of the Arab State of Zanzibar*. London: Methuen, 1978.

Berry, Sara. *No Condition Is Permanent: The Social Dynamics of Agrarian Change in Sub-Saharan Africa*. Madison: University of Wisconsin Press, 1993.

Blassingame, John W. *The Slave Community: Plantation Life in the Antebellum South*. New York: Oxford University Press, 1972.

Booth, Alan. "'European Courts Protest Women and Witches': Colonial Law Courts as Redistributors of Power in Swaziland 1920–1950," *Journal of Southern African Studies* 18, no. 2 (1992), 253–76.

Bourdieu, Pierre. "Structures, Habitus, Power: Basis for a Theory of Symbolic Power," in *Culture/Power/History: A Reader in Contemporary Social Theory*, edited by Nicholas B. Dirks, Geoff Eley, and Sherry B. Ortner, pp. 155–99. Princeton, NJ: Princeton University Press, 1994.

Bowles, B. D. "The Struggle for Independence, 1946–1963," in *Zanzibar Under Colonial Rule*, edited by Abdul Sheriff and Ed Ferguson, pp. 79–106. Athens: Ohio University Press, 1991.

Bowman, Jeffrey. "Infamy and Proof in Medieval Spain," in *Fama: The Politics of Talk and Reputation in Medieval Europe*, edited by Thelma Fenster and Daniel Lord Smail, pp. 95–117. Ithaca, NY: Cornell University Press, 2003.

Bradford, Helen. "Women, Gender and Colonialism: Rethinking the History of the British Cape Colony and Its Frontier Zones, 1806–70," *Journal of African History* 37, no. 3 (1996), 351–70.

Bravman, Bill. *Making Ethnic Ways: Communities and Their Transformations in Taita, Kenya, 1800–1950*. Portsmouth, NH: Heinemann, 1998.

Bromber, Katrin. "Mjakazi, Mpambe, Mjoli, Suria: Female Slaves in Swahili Sources," in *Women and Slavery: Africa, the Indian Ocean World, and the Medieval North Atlantic*, Vol. I, edited by Gwyn Campbell, Suzanne Miers, and Joseph C. Miller, pp. 111–28. Athens: Ohio University Press, 2007.

Brooks, George. "A Nhara of the Guinea-Bissau Region: Mae Aurelia Correia," in *Women and Slavery in Africa*, edited by Clarie C. Robertson and Martin A. Klein, pp. 295–319. Madison: University of Wisconsin Press, 1983.

Brown, Vincent. *The Reaper's Garden: Death and Power in the World of Atlantic Slavery*. Cambridge, MA: Harvard University Press, 2008.

Burgess, Gary. "Youth and the Revolution: Mobility and Discipline in Zanzibar, 1950–1980." Ph.D. dissertation, Indiana University, 2002.

Burgess, Thomas. *Race, Revolution, and the Struggle for Human Rights in Zanzibar*. Athens: Ohio University Press, 2010.

Burton, Sir Richard Francis. *The Lake Regions of Central Africa: A Picture of Exploration*. New York: Harper & Bros., 1860.

Zanzibar: City, Island, and Coast. New York: Tinsley Brothers, 1872.

Campbell, Gwyn. "Slavery and Other Forms of Unfree Labour in the Indian Ocean World," in *The Structure of Slavery in Indian Ocean, Africa and Asia*, edited by Gwyn Campbell, pp. vii–xxxii. London: Routledge, 2004.

Carretta, Vincent. *Equiano, the African: Biography of a Self-Made Man*. Atlanta: University of Georgia Press, 2005.

"Response to Paul Lovejoy's 'Autobiography and Memory: Gustavus Vassa, Alias Olaudah Equiano, the African,'" *Slavery and Abolition* 28, no. 1 (2007), 115–19.

Caviness, Madeline H., & Charles G. Nelson. "Silent Witnesses, Absent Women, and the Law Courts in Medieval Germany," in *Fama: The Politics of Talk and Reputation in Medieval Europe*, edited by Thelma Fenster and Daniel Lord Smail, pp. 47–72. Ithaca, NY: Cornell University Press, 2003.

Chambers, Sarah. *From Subjects to Citizens: Honor, Gender, and Politics in Arequipa, Peru, 1780–1854*. University Park: Pennsylvania State University Press, 1999.

Clayton, Anthony. "The General Strike in Zanzibar, 1948," *Journal of African History* 17, no. 4 (1976), 417–34.

The Zanzibar Revolution and Its Aftermath. Hamden, CT: Archon Books, 1981.

Colomb, Captain. *Slave-Catching in the Indian Ocean: A Record of Naval Experiences*. New York: Longmans, Green and Co., 1873.

Colson, Elizabeth. "Possible Repercussions of the Right to Make Wills upon the Plateau Tonga of Northern Rhodesia," *Journal of African Administration* 2, no. 1 (1950), 24–35.

Comaroff, Jean and John. *Modernity and Its Malcontents*. Chicago: University of Chicago Press, 1993.

Cooper, Barbara. *Marriage in Maradi: Gender and Culture in a Hausa Society in Niger, 1900–1989*. Portsmouth, NH: Heinemann, 1997.

Cooper, Frederick. *Plantation Slavery on the East Coast of Africa*. New Haven, CT: Yale University Press, 1977.

From Slaves to Squatters: Plantation Labor and Agriculture in Zanzibar and Coastal Kenya, 1890–1925. New Haven, CT: Yale University Press, 1980.

Cooper, Frederick, Thomas C. Holt, & Rebecca Scott. *Beyond Slavery: Explorations of Race, Labor, and Citizenship in Postemancipation Societies*. Chapel Hill: University of North Carolina Press, 2000.

Coquery-Vidrovitch, Catherine. *The History of African Cities South of the Sahara: From the Origins to Colonization*. Princeton, NJ: Princeton University Press, 2005.

Craster, John Evelyn Edmund. *Pemba: The Spice Island of Zanzibar*. London: T.F. Unwin, 1913.

Dabhoiwala, Faramerz. "The Construction of Honour, Reputation and Status in Late Seventeenth and Early Eighteen Century England," *Royal Historical Society Transactions* 6, no. 6 (1996), 201–13.

Dale, Rev. Godfrey. *The Peoples of Zanzibar: Their Customs and Religious Beliefs*. New York: Negro Universities Press, 1969; first published 1920 by Universities Mission to Central Africa.

Decker, Corrie Ruth. "Investing in Ideas: Girls' Education in Colonial Zanzibar." Ph.D. dissertation, University of California Berkeley, 2007.

Deutsch, Jan Georg. *Emancipation without Abolition in German East Africa c.1884–1914*. Athens: Ohio University Press, 2006.

"Notes on the Rise of Slavery and Social Change in Unyamwezi," in *Slavery in the Great Lakes Region of East Africa*, edited by Henri Médard and Shane Doyle. Athens: Ohio University Press, 2007.

Dooling, Wayne. *Slavery, Emancipation and Colonial Rule in South Africa*. Athens: Ohio University Press, 2007.

Dore, Elizabeth. *Myths of Modernity: Peonage and Patriarchy in Nicaragua*. Durham, NC: Duke University Press, 2006.

Fair, Laura. "Kickin' It: Leisure, Politics, and Football in Colonial Zanzibar, 1900s–1950s," *Africa* 67, no. 2 (1997), 224–51.

"Dressing Up: Clothing, Class and Gender in Post-Abolition Zanzibar," *Journal of African History* 39, no. 1 (1998), 63–94.

"Identity, Difference, and Dance: Female Initiation in Zanzibar, 1890 to 1930," in *Mashindano!: Competitive Music Performance in East Africa*, edited by Frank Gunderson and Gregory Barz, pp. 143–65. Dar es Salaam: Mkuki Na Nyota Publishers, 2000.

Pastimes and Politics: Culture, Community, and Identity in Post-Abolition Urban Zanzibar, 1890–1945. Athens: Ohio University Press, 2001.

Fallers, Lloyd. *Law Without Precedent: Legal Ideas in Action in the Courts of Colonial Busoga*. Chicago: University of Chicago Press, 1969.

Farrant, Leda. *Tippu Tip and the East African Slave Trade*. New York: St. Martin's Press, 1975.

Feierman, Steven. "Healing as Social Criticism in the Time of Colonial Conquest," *African Studies Review* 54, no. 1 (1995), 73–88.

"Colonizers, Scholars, and the Creation of Invisible Histories," in *Beyond the Cultural Turn: New Directions in the Study of Society and Culture*, edited by Victoria E. Bonnell and Lynn Hunt, pp. 182–216. Berkeley: University of California Press, 1999.

Fenster, Thelma, & Daniel Lord Smail. *Fama: The Politics of Talk and Reputation in Medieval Europe*. Ithaca, NY: Cornell University Press, 2003.

Fitzgerald, William Walter Augustine. *Travels in the Coastlands of British East Africa and the Islands of Zanzibar and Pemba: Their Agricultural Resources and General Characteristics*. London: Chapman & Hall, 1898.

Foucault, Michel. *Discipline and Punish: The Births of the Prison*, translated by Alan Sheridan. New York: Vintage Books, 1979.

Franken, Marjorie Ann. "Anyone Can Dance: A Survey and Analysis of Swahili Ngoma, Past and Present." Ph.D. dissertation, University of California Riverside, 1986.

Freamon, Bernard. "Islamic Law and Trafficking in Women and Children in the Indian Ocean World," in *Trafficking in Slavery's Wake: Law and the Experience of Women and Children in Africa*, edited by Benjamin Lawrance and Richard L. Roberts, pp. 121–41. Athens: Ohio University Press, 2012.

"Geography and Travels," *American Naturalist* 12, no. 11 (1877), 763.

Geschiere, Peter. *The Modernity of Witchcraft: Politics and the Occult in Postcolonial Africa*. Charlottesville: University of Virginia Press, 1995.

"Kinship, Witchcraft and the Moral Economy of Ethnicity: Contrasts from Southern and Western Cameroun," in *Ethnicity in Africa: Roots, Meanings and Implications*, edited by Louise de la Gorgendière et al. Edinburgh: Centre of African Studies, University of Edinburgh, 1996.

Getz, Trevor. *Slavery and Reform in West Africa: Toward Emancipation in Nineteenth-Century Senegal and the Gold Coast*. Athens: Ohio University Press, 2004.

Giles, Linda L. "Possession Cults on the Swahili Coast: A Re-Examination of Theories of Marginality," *Africa: Journal of the International African Institute* 57, no. 2 (1987), 234–58.

"Spirit Possession on the Swahili Coast: Peripheral Cults or Primary Texts?" Ph.D. dissertation, University of Texas at Austin, 1989.

Glassman, Jonathon. *Feasts and Riot: Revelry, Rebellion, and Popular Consciousness on the Swahili Coast, 1856–1888*. Portsmouth, NH: Heinemann, 1995.

"Slower Than a Massacre: The Multiple Sources of Racial Thought in Colonial Africa," *American Historical Review* 109, no. 3 (2004), 720–54.

"Sorting Out the Tribes: The Creation of Racial Identities in Colonial Zanzibar's Newspaper Wars," *Journal of African History* 41, no. 3 (2005), 395–428.

War of Words, War of Stones. Bloomington: Indiana University Press, 2011.

Gluckman, Max. "Gossip and Scandal," *Current Anthropology* 4, no. 3 (June 1963), 307–16.

Gocking, Roger. "A Chieftaincy Dispute and Ritual Murder in Elmina, Ghana, 1945–6," *Journal of African History* 41, no. 2 (2000), 197–220.

Goldman, Helle. "A Comparative Study of Swahili in Two Rural Communities in Pemba, Zanzibar, Tanzania." Ph.D. dissertation, New York University, 1996.

Gowing, Laura. "Women, Status and the Popular Culture of Dishonour," *Transactions of the Royal Historical Society*, Sixth Series, 6 (1996).

Graham, Sandra Lauderdale. "Honor Among Slaves," in *The Faces of Honor: Sex, Shame, and Violence in Colonial Latin America*, edited by Lyman L. Johnson and Sonya Lipsett-Rivera. Albuquerque: University of New Mexico Press, 1998.

Grandmaison, Colette Le Cour. "Rich Cousins, Poor Cousins: Hidden Stratification Among the Omani Arabs in Eastern Africa," *Africa* 59, no. 2 (1989), 176–83.

Gray, John. *History of Zanzibar: From the Middle Ages to 1856.* Oxford: Oxford University Press, 1962.

Gray, Natasha. "Witches, Oracles, and Colonial Law: Evolving Anti-Witchcraft Practices in Ghana, 1927–1932," *International Journal of African Historical Studies* 34, no. 2 (2001), 339–64.

Greif, Avner. "Reputation and Coalitions in Medieval Trade: Evidence on the Maghribi Traders," *Journal of Economic History* 49, no. 4 (Dec 1989), 857–82.

Gross, Ariela. "Litigating Whiteness: Trials of Racial Determination in the Nineteenth-Century South," *Yale Law Journal* 108 (1998), 109–88.

Hallaq, Wael B. *Shari'a: Theory, Practice, Transformations.* Cambridge: Cambridge University Press, 2009.

Hanretta, Sean. *Islam and Social Change in French West Africa: History of an Emancipatory Community.* Cambridge: Cambridge University Press, 2009.

Hirsch, Susan. *Pronouncing and Persevering: Gender and the Discourse of Disputing in an African Islamic Court.* Chicago: University of Chicago Press, 1998.

Hodgson, F. R. "Medicine Man's Kit," *Central Africa* 21, no. 250 (October 1903), 194–6.

Hollingsworth, L. W. *Zanzibar Under the Foreign Office 1890–1913.* London: Macmillan, 1953.

Iliffe, John. *Honour in African History.* New York: Cambridge University Press, 2004.

Ingrams, William Harold. *Zanzibar: Its History and Its People.* London: H.F. & G. Witherby, 1931.

Arabia and the Isles, 3rd ed. London: John Murray, 1942.

Issa, Amina Ameir. "The Legacy of *Qadiri* Scholars in Zanzibar," in *The Global Worlds of the Swahili*, edited by Roman Loimeier and Rüdiger Seesemann. Berlin: Lit Vertag, 2006.

Isaacman, Allen, and Derek Peterson. "Making the Chikunda: Military Slavery and Ethnicity in Southern Africa 1750–1900," *International Journal of African Historical Studies* 36, no. 2 (2003), 257–81.

Johnson, Frederick. *A Standard Swahili-English Dictionary.* Nairobi: Oxford University Press, 1939.

Kassim, Mohamed. "Colonial Resistance and the Local Transmission of Islamic Knowledge in the Benadir Coast in the Late 19th and early 20th centuries." Ph.D. dissertation, York University, 2006.

Kingdon, Hugh. *The Conflict of Laws in Zanzibar.* Zanzibar: Government Printer, 1940.

Kirkman, James S. "The Zanzibar Diary of John Studdy Leigh," Part I, *International Journal of African Historical Studies* 13, no. 2 (1980), 281–312.

Kirkham, Vincent H. *Zanzibar Protectorate: Memorandum on the Functions of a Department of Agriculture with Special Reference to Zanzibar.* Zanzibar: Government Printer, 1931.

Klein, Martin. *Slavery and Colonial Rule in French West Africa.* Cambridge: Cambridge University Press, 1998.

"The Concept of Honour and the Persistence of Servility in the Western Soudan," *Cahiers D'Estudes Africaines* 45, nos. 3–4 (2005), 179–80.

"Review of *Honour in African History* by John Iliffe," H-Net; available at: http:/www.h-net.org; posted July 12, 2006.

Knappert, Jan. *An Anthology of Swahili Love Poetry.* Berkeley: University of California Press, 1972.

"Pemba." *Annales Aequatoria* 13 (1992), 39–52.

Kollmann, Nancy Shields. *By Honor Bound: State and Society in Early Modern Russia.* Ithaca, NY: Cornell University Press, 1999.

Kopytoff, Igor. "The Cultural Context of African Abolition," in *The End of Slavery in Africa*, edited by Suzanne Miers and Richard Roberts, pp. 485–506. Madison: University of Wisconsin Press, 1988.

Krapf, Johann Ludwig. *A Dictionary of the Suahili Language.* London: Trubner and Co., 1882.

Lambek, Michael. *Knowledge and Practice in Mayotte: Local Discourses of Islam, Sorcery, and Spirit Possession.* Toronto, Canada: University of Toronto Press, 1993.

Lane, Kris. "Taming the Master: Brujería, Slavery, and the Encomienda in Barbacoas at the Turn of the Eighteenth Century," *Ethnohistory* 45, no. 3 (Summer 1998), 477–507.

Larsen, Kjersti. *Where Humans and Spirits Meet: The Politics of Rituals and Identified Spirits in Zanzibar.* New York: Berghahn Books, 2008.

Last, J. S., & C. A. Bartlett, *Report on the Indebtedness of the Agricultural Classes, 1933.* Zanzibar: Government Printer, 1934.

Lawrence, Margery. "The Dogs of Pemba," originally published in *The Terraces of Night: Being the Further Chronicles of the Club of the Round Table.* London: Hurst & Blackett, 1932.

Lodhi, Abdulaziz Y. *The Institution of Slavery in Zanzibar and Pemba.* Uppsala: Scandinavian Institute of African Studies, 1973.

Lofchie, Michael. *Zanzibar: Background to Revolution.* Princeton, NJ: Princeton University Press, 1965.

Loimeier, Roman. *Between Social Skills and Marketable Skills: The Politics of Islamic Education in 20th Century Zanzibar.* Leiden: Brill, 2009.

Lovejoy, Paul E. "Concubinage and the Status of Women slaves in Early Colonial Nigeria," *Journal of African History* 29, no. 1 (1988), 245–66.

Transformations in Slavery, 2nd ed. Cambridge: Cambridge University Press, 2000.

"Muslim Freedmen in the Atlantic World: Images of Manumission and Self-Redemption," in *Slavery on the Frontiers of Islam*, edited by Paul E. Lovejoy. Princeton, NJ: Markus Wiener Publishers, 2004.

"Autobiography and Memory: Gustavus Vassa, alias Olaudah Equiano, the Africa," *Slavery & Abolition* 27, no. 3 (2006), 317–47.

"Issues of Motivation – Vassa/Equiano and Carretta's Critique of the Evidence," *Slavery & Abolition* 28, no. 1 (2007), 121–5.

Lovejoy, Paul E., & Jan S. Hogendorn. *Slow Death for Slavery: The Course of Abolition in Northern Nigeria, 1897–1936*. Cambridge: Cambridge University Press, 1993.

Luongo, Katherine. *Witchcraft and Colonial Rule in Kenya, 1900–1955*. Cambridge: Cambridge University Press, 2011.

Lydon, Ghislaine. *On Trans-Saharan Trails: Islamic Law, Trade Networks, and Cross-Cultural Exchange in Nineteenth-Century Western Africa*. Cambridge: Cambridge University Press, 2009.

Lyne, Robert N. *Zanzibar in Contemporary Times: A Short History of the Southern East in the Nineteenth Century*. London: Hurst and Slackett, 1905.

Lyons, C. P. "A Witch-Doctor at Work," *Tanganyika Notes and Records* 1 (1936), 97–8.

Madan, Arthur Cornwallis. *English-Swahili Dictionary*, 2nd ed. Oxford: Clarendon Press, 1902.

Mann, Kristin. *Slavery and the Birth of an African City: Lagos, 1760–1900*. Bloomington: Indiana University Press, 2007.

Mann, Kristin, & Richard L. Roberts. *Law in Colonial Africa*. Portsmouth, NH: Heinemann, 1991.

Manning, Patrick. *Slavery and African Life: Occidental, Oriental, and African Slave Trades*. Cambridge: Cambridge University Press, 1990.

Mapuri, Omar. *Zanzibar, The 1964 Revolution: Achievements and Prospects*. Dar es Salaam: TEMA Publishers, 1996.

Martin, B. G. "Notes on Some Members of the Learned Classes of Zanzibar and East Africa in the Nineteenth Century," *African Historical Studies* 4, no. 3 (1971), 525–45.

Muslim Brotherhoods in Nineteenth-Century Africa. Cambridge: Cambridge University Press, 1976.

Martin, Esmond Bradley. *Zanzibar: Tradition and Revolution*. London: Hamilton, 1978.

Martin, Phyllis. *Leisure and Society in Colonial Brazzaville*. Cambridge: Cambridge University Press, 1995.

McCaskie, T. C. "'Sakrobundi ne Aberewa': Sie Kwaku the Witch-Finder in the Akan World," *Transactions of the Historical Society of Ghana* 8 (2004), 82–135.

McDougall, E. Ann. "A Sense of Self: The Life of Fatma Barka," *Canadian Journal of African Studies* 32, no. 2 (1998), 285–315.

McMahon, Elisabeth. "Becoming Pemban: Identity, Social Welfare and Community During the Protectorate Period." PhD dissertation, Indiana University, 2005.

"'A Solitary Tree Builds Not': *Heshima*, Community and Shifting Identity in Post-emancipation Pemba Island," *International Journal of African Historical Studies* 39, no. 2 (August 2006), 197–219.

"Trafficking and Re-enslavement: Social Vulnerability of Women and Children in Nineteenth Century East Africa," in *Trafficking in Slavery's Wake: Law and the Experience of Women and Children in Africa*, edited by Benjamin Lawrance and Richard Roberts. Athens: Ohio University Press, 2012.

Médard, Henri, & Shane Doyle, eds. *Slavery in the Great Lakes Region of East Africa*. Athens: Ohio University Press, 2007.

Middleton, John. *The World of the Swahili*. New Haven, CT: Yale University Press, 1992.

Miers, Suzanne. "Slavery to Freedom in Sub-Saharan Africa: Expectations and Reality," in *After Slavery*, edited by Howard Temperley, pp. 237–64. London: Frank Cass, 2000.

Miers, Suzanne, & Igor Kopytoff, eds., "African 'Slavery' as an Institution of Marginality," in *Slavery in Africa: Historical and Anthropological Perspectives*, pp. 3–88. Madison: University of Wisconsin Press, 1977.

Miller, William Ian. *Humiliation and Other Essays on Honor, Social Discomfort, and Violence*. Ithaca, NY: Cornell University Press, 1993.

Mirza, Sarah, & Margaret Strobel, eds. *Three Swahili Women: Life Histories from Mombasa, Kenya*. Bloomington: Indiana University Press, 1989.

Mitchell, Timothy. *Colonising Egypt*. Berkeley: University of California Press, 1991.

Moore, Henrietta L., & Todd Sanders, eds. *Magical Interpretations, Material Realities: Modernity, Witchcraft, and the Occult in Postcolonial Africa*. London: Routledge, 2001.

Morton, Fred. *Children of Ham: Freed Slaves and Fugitive Slaves on the Kenya Coast, 1873 to 1907*. Boulder, CO: Westview Press, 1990.

Muldrew, Craig. *The Economy of Obligation: The Culture of Credit and Social Relations in Early Modern England*. New York: St. Martin's Press, 1998.

Murison, Sir William, & S. S. Abrahams. *Zanzibar Protectorate Law Reports Containing Cases Determined in the British Consular Court, and in His Britannic Majesty's Court and in the Supreme Court of His Highness the Sultan and in the Courts Subordinate Thereto, etc., 1868 to 1918, with Appendices Containing the Zanzibar Orders-in-Council from 1884 to 1916*. London: Waterlow and Sons, 1919.

Mzee, Abdullah M. "Some Experiences of Witchcraft" *Tanganyikan Notes and Records* 57 (September 1961).

Newbury, M. Catherine. "Colonialism, Ethnicity, and Rural Political Protest: Rwanda and Zanzibar in Comparative Perspective," *Comparative Politics* 15, no. 3 (1983), 253–80.

Newman, Henry Stanley. *Banani: The Transition from Slavery to Freedom in Zanzibar and Pemba*. London: Headley Brothers, 1898; reprint Negro Universities Press, 1969.

Nimtz, August H. *Islam and Politics in East Africa: The Sufi Order in Tanzania*. Minneapolis: University of Minnesota Press, 1980.

Nuotio, Hanni. "The Dance That Is Not Danced, the Song That Is Not Sung: Zanzibari Women in the *Maulidi* Ritual," in *The Global Worlds of the Swahili*, edited by Roman Loimeier and Rüdiger Seesemann. Berlin: Lit Vertag, 2006.

Nwulia, Moses D. E. *Britain and Slavery in East Africa*. Washington, DC: Three Continents Press, 1975.

"The Role of Missionaries in the Emancipation of Slaves in Zanzibar," *Journal of Negro History* 60, no. 2 (1975), 268–87.

Ogot, Bethwell, & J. A. Kieran, eds. *Zamani: A Survey of East African History*. Nairobi: East African Publishing House, 1968.

O'Malley, Gabrielle E. "Marriage and Morality: Negotiating Gender and Respect in Zanzibar Town." Ph.D. dissertation, University of Washington, 2000.

Patterson, Orlando. *Slavery and Social Death*. Cambridge, MA: Harvard University Press, 1982.

Pearce, Frances. *Zanzibar: The Island Metropolis of Eastern Africa*. New York: T.F. Unwin, 1920.

Penningroth, Dylan. "The Claims of Slaves and Ex-Slaves to Family and Property: A Transatlantic Comparison," *American Historical Review* 112, no. 4 (2007), 1039–69.

Peterson, Derek. "Morality Plays: Marriage, Church Courts, and Colonial Agency in Central Tanganyika, ca. 1876–1928," *American Historical Review* 111, no. 4 (2006), 983–1010.

Petterson, Donald. *Revolution in Zanzibar: An American's Cold War Tale*. Boulder, CO: Westview, 2002.

Porter, Mary A. "Resisting Uniformity at Mwana Kupona Girls' School: Cultural Productions in an Educational Setting," *Signs* 23, no. 3 (1998), 619–43.

Pouwels, Randall Lee. *Horn and Crescent: Cultural Change and Traditional Islam on the East African Coast, 800–1900*. Cambridge: Cambridge University Press, 1987.

"Eastern Africa and the Indian Ocean to 1800: Reviewing Relations in Historical Perspective," *International Journal of African Historical Studies* 35, nos. 2–3 (2002), 385–425.

Prestholdt, Jeremy. *Domesticating the World: African Consumerism and the Genealogies of Globalization*. Berkeley: University of California Press, 2008.

Purpura, Allyson. "Knowledge and Agency: The Social Relations of Islamic Expertise in Zanzibar Town." Ph.D. dissertation, City University of New York, 1997.

Ranger, Terrence O. *Dance and Society in Eastern Africa, 1890–1970: The Beni Ngoma*. Berkeley: University of California Press, 1975.

Roberts, Richard L. *Litigants and Households: African Disputes and Colonial Courts in the French Soudan, 1895–1912*. Portsmouth, NH: Heinemann, 2005.

"Women, Household Instability, and the End of Slavery in Banamba and Gumbu, French Soudan, 1905–1912," in *Women and Slavery: Africa, the Indian Ocean World, and the Medieval North Atlantic*, edited by Gwyn Campbell, Suzanne Miers, and Joseph C. Miller, pp. 281–305. Athens: Ohio University Press, 2007.

Roberts, Richard, & Martin Klein. "The Banamba Slave Exodus of 1905 and the Decline of Slavery in the Western Sudan," *Journal of African History* 21, no. 3 (1980), 375–94.

Robinson, David. *Paths of Accommodation: Muslim Societies and French Colonial Authorities in Senegal and Mauritania, 1880–1920*. Athens: Ohio University Press, 2000.

Rockel, Stephen J. *Carriers of Culture: Labor on the Road in Nineteenth-Century East Africa*. Portsmouth, NH: Heinemann, 2006.

Rolingher, Louise. "Constructing Islam and Swahili Identity: Historiography and Theory," *MIT Electronic Journal of Middle East Studies*, Special Issue: *Islam and Arabs in East Africa: A Fusion of Identities, Networks and Encounters* (Fall 2005), 9–20.

Romero, Patricia. "'Where Have All the Slaves Gone?' Emancipation and Post-Emancipation in Lamu, Kenya," *Journal of African History* 27, no. 3 (1986), 497–512.

Lamu: History, Society, and Family in an East African Port City. Princeton, NJ: Markus Wiener, 1997.

Ross, Robert. *Status and Respectability in the Cape Colony 1750–1870*. Cambridge: Cambridge University Press, 1999.

Rucker, Walter. "Conjure, Magic and Power: The Influence of Afro-Atlantic Religious Practices on Slave Resistance and Rebellion," *Journal of Black Studies* 32, no. 1 (2001), 84–103.

Sarr, Dominique, & Richard Roberts. "The Jurisdiction of Muslim Tribunals in Colonial Senegal, 1857–1932," in *Law in Colonial Africa*, edited by Kristin Mann and Richard Roberts. Portsmouth, NH: Heinemann, 1991.

Schacht, Joseph. "Notes on Islam in East Africa," *Studia Islamica* 23 (1965), 91–136.

Scully, Pamela. *Liberating the Family? Gender and British Slave Emancipation in the Rural Western Cape, South Africa, 1823–1853*. Portsmouth, NH: Heinemann, 1997.

Shaw, Rosalind. *Memories of the Slave Trade: Ritual and the Historical Imagination in Sierra Leone*. Chicago: University of Chicago Press, 2002.

Sheriff, Abdul. *Slaves, Spices and Ivory in Zanzibar: Integration of an East African Commercial Empire into the World Economy, 1770–1873*. London: James Currey, 1987.

"The Slave Trade and Its Fallout in the Persian Gulf," in *Abolition and Its Aftermath in Indian Ocean Africa and Asia*, edited by Gwyn Campbell. New York: Routledge, 2005.

Sheriff, Abdul, & Ed Ferguson. *Zanzibar Under Colonial Rule*. Athens: Ohio University Press, 1991.

Silving, Helen. "The Oath: I," *Yale Law Journal* 68, no. 7 (1959), 1329–90.

Skene, Ralph. "Arab and Swahili Dances and Ceremonies," *Journal of the Royal Anthropological Institute of Great Britain and Ireland* 17 (December 1917), 413–34.

Smith, James Howard. *Bewitching Development: Witchcraft and the Reinvention of Development in Neoliberal Kenya*. Chicago: University of Chicago Press, 2008.

Smith, James Patterson. "Empire and Social Reform: British Liberals and the 'Civilizing Mission' in the Sugar Colonies, 1868–1874," *Albion: A Quarterly Journal Concerned with British Studies* 27, no. 2 (1995), 270–1.

Steere, Edward. *A Handbook of the Swahili Language as Spoken at Zanzibar.* Society for Promoting Christian Knowledge, 1884.

Stewart, Frank Henderson. *Honor.* Chicago: University of Chicago Press, 1994.

Stiles, Erin. "A Kadhi and His Court: Marriage, Divorce, and Zanzibar's Islamic Legal Tradition." Ph.D. dissertation, Washington University, 2002.

Stockreiter, Elke. "Tying and Untying the Knot: Kadhi's Courts and the Negotiation of Social Status in Zanzibar Town, 1900–1963." Ph.D. dissertation, SOAS, University of London, 2007.

Strayer, Robert W. *The Making of Mission Communities in East Africa: Anglicans and Africans in Colonial Kenya, 1875–1935.* London: Heinemann, 1978.

Strobel, Margaret. *Muslim Women in Mombasa.* New Haven, CT: Yale University Press, 1979.

Sullivan, George Lydiard. *Dhow Chasing in Zanzibar Waters and on the Eastern Coast of Africa: Narrative of Five Years' Experiences in the Suppression of the Slave Trade.* London: Dawsons of Pall Mall, 1873.

Swartz, Marc J. "Shame, Culture, and Status Among the Swahili of Mombasa," *Ethos* 16, no. 1 (March 1988), 14–27.

Taylor, Rev. W. E. *African Aphorisms; or, Saws from Swahili-Land.* London: Society for Promoting Christian Knowledge, 1891.

Taylor, Scott. "Credit, Debt, and Honor in Castile, 1600–1650," *Journal of Early Modern History* 7, nos. 1–2 (2003), 8–27.

Tomlinson, Sir T. S., & G. K. Knight-Bruce. *Law Reports Containing Cases Determined by the High Court for Zanzibar and on Appeal Therefrom by the Court of Appeal for Eastern Africa and by the Privy Council,* Vol. III, 1923–1927. London: Waterlow and Sons, 1928.

Tuck, Michael. "Women's Experiences of Enslavement and Slavery in Late Nineteenth- and Early Twentieth-Century Uganda," in *Slavery in the Great Lakes Region of East Africa,* edited by Henri Médard and Shane Doyle, pp. 174–88. Athens: Ohio University Press, 2007.

Turrell, Rob. "Muti Ritual Murder in Natal: From Chiefs to Commoners (1900–1930)," *South African Historical Journal* 44 (2001), 21–40.

Twinam, Ann. *Public Lives, Private Secrets: Gender, Honor, Sexuality, and Illegitimacy in Colonial Spanish America.* Palo Alto, CA: Stanford University Press, 1999.

Vansina, Jan. *Paths in the Rainforests: Toward a History of Political Tradition in Equatorial Africa.* Madison: University of Wisconsin Press, 1990.

Vaughan, J. H. *The Dual Jurisdiction in Zanzibar.* Zanzibar: Government Printer, 1935.

Vaughan, Megan. *Creating the Creole Island: Slavery in Eighteenth-Century Mauritius.* Durham, NC: Duke University Press, 2005.

Vianello, Alessandra, & Mohamed M. Kassim, eds. *Servants of the Shari'a: The Civil Register of the Qadis' Court of Brava, 1893–1900.* Leiden: Brill, 2006.

Voules, Eleanor. *Witchcraft.* London: Central Africa House Press, 1951.

Walker, Garthine. "Expanding the Boundaries of Female Honour in Early Modern England," *Transactions of the Royal Historical Society,* Sixth Series, 6 (1996), 235–45.

Walker, Tamara. "He Outfitted His Family in Notable Decency': Slavery, Honour and Dress in Eighteenth-Century Lima, Peru," *Slavery and Abolition* 30, no. 2 (September 2009), 383–403.

Waller, Richard. "Witchcraft and Colonial Law in Kenya," *Past and Present* 180, no. 1 (2003), 24–275.

Welliver, Timothy. "The Clove Factor in Colonial Zanzibar 1890–1950." Ph.D. dissertation, Northwestern University, 1990.

West, Harry. *Kupilikula: Governance and the Invisible Realm in Mozambique.* The University of Chicago Press, 2005.

White, Luise. *Speaking with Vampires.* Berkeley: University of California Press, 2000.

Whiteley, Wilfred Howell. *The Dialects and Verse of Pemba.* Kampala, Uganda: East African Swahili Committee, 1958.

Wickham, Chris. "*Fama* and the Law in Twelfth-Century Tuscany," in *Fama: The Politics of Talk and Reputation in Medieval Europe*, edited by Thelma Fenster and Daniel Lord Smail, pp. 15–26. Ithaca, NY: Cornell University Press, 2003.

Willis, Justin. *Mombasa, the Swahili and the Making of the Mijikenda.* Oxford: Oxford University Press, 1993.

Wright, Marcia. "Justice, Women, and the Social Order in Abercorn, Northeastern Rhodesia, 1897–1903," in *African Women and the Law*, edited by Margaret Jean Hay. Boston University, African Studies Center, 1982.

    Strategies of Slaves and Women: Life-Stories from East/Central Africa. New York: L. Barber Press, 1993.

el Zein, Abdul Hamid M. *The Sacred Meadows: A Structural Analysis of Religious Symbolism in an East African Town.* Evanston, IL: Northwestern University Press, 1974.

Index

BOOKS IN THIS SERIES